THE
AMERICAN CHALLENGE

---------- ❧ ----------

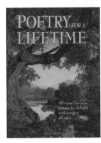 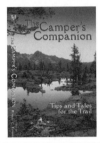 
About the Author

Robert C. Etheredge is the founder of MiraVista Press and editor of *The Camper's Companion*, *The Camper's Digital Companion*, and *The Military Companion*. An Eagle Scout and former U.S. Navy officer, he has also written a number of software programs, including two software tools, *myWriterTools* and *myWordCount*, for writers, editors, and proofreaders.

THE
AMERICAN CHALLENGE

PRESERVING THE GREATNESS OF
AMERICA IN THE 21ST CENTURY

What Every American Should
Know About Their Country

Freedom is a fragile thing and is never more than one generation away from extinction. It is not ours by inheritance; it must be fought for and defended constantly by each generation, for it comes only once to a people. Those who have known freedom and then lost it have never known it again.

—RONALD REAGAN

BY

ROBERT C. ETHEREDGE

MIRAVISTA PRESS

THE AMERICAN CHALLENGE
© Copyright 2011 by MiraVista Press

ISBN 978-0-96-658044-0

Library of Congress Catalog Card Number: 2011912666

MiraVista Press
P.O. Box 961
Orinda, CA 94563
925-253-9472
Email: challenge@miravista.com
Web: http://www.miravista.com

Printed in the United States of America.

Declaration of Independence
(on the cover)

by John Trumbull

1. George Wythe, Virginia
2. William Whipple, New Hampshire
3. Josiah Bartlett, New Hampshire
4. Benjamin Harrison, Virginia
5. Thomas Lynch, South Carolina
6. Richard Henry Lee, Virginia
7. Samuel Adams, Massachusetts
8. * George Clinton, New York
9. William Paca, Maryland
10. Samuel Chase, Maryland
11. Lewis Morris, New York
12. William Floyd, New York
13. Arthur Middleton, South Carolina
14. Thomas Heyward, Jr., S. Carolina
15. Charles Carroll, Maryland
16. George Walton, Georgia
17. Robert Morris, Pennsylvania
18. * Thomas Willing, Pennsylvania
19. Benjamin Rush, Pennsylvania
20. Elbridge Gerry, Massachusetts
21. Robert Treat Paine, Massachusetts
22. Abraham Clark, New Jersey
23. Stephen Hopkins, Rhode Island
24. William Ellery, Rhode Island
25. George Clymer, Pennsylvania
26. William Hooper, North Carolina
27. Joseph Hewes, North Carolina
28. James Willson, Pennsylvania
29. Francis Hopkinson, New Jersey
30. John Adams, Massachusetts
31. Roger Sherman, Connecticut
32. * Robert R. Livingston, New York
33. Thomas Jefferson, Virginia
34. Benjamin Franklin, Pennsylvania
35. Richard Stockton, New Jersey
36. Francis Lewis, New York
37. John Witherspoon, New Jersey
38. Samuel Huntington, Connecticut
39. William Williams, Connecticut
40. Oliver Wolcott, Connecticut
41. John Hancock, Massachusetts
42. * Charles Thomson, Pennsylvania
43. George Read, Delaware
44. * John Dickinson, Pennsylvania
45. Edward Rutledge, South Carolina
46. Thomas McKean, Delaware
47. Philip Livingston, New York

❧

There were 56 signers of the Declaration of Independence. The painting
portrays only 47. The 5 men whose names are starred were not signers.
The portraits of the following 14 signers do not appear in the painting.

Matthew Thornton, New Hampshire
John Hart, New Jersey
John Morton, Pennsylvania
James Smith, Pennsylvania
Thomas Nelson, Jr., Virginia
Francis Lightfoot Lee, Virginia
Carter Braxton, Virginia

John Penn, North Carolina
George Taylor, Pennsylvania
George Ross, Pennsylvania
Caesar Rodney, Delaware
Thomas Stone, Maryland
Button Gwinnett, Georgia
Lyman Hall, Georgia

This book is dedicated to my father, Samuel N. Etheredge, who has inspired me my entire life. He was a member of that greatest generation who went to war during World War II to keep this country and the world safe and free. He loved his country and taught me to love it as well. He passed away this year at the age of 97 on the same day that I finished this book. During his last days in the hospital, he could be heard singing old songs and reciting poems memorized as a child, including many of those found in the back of this book.

I am sure he would have been proud to be a part of any effort to help Americans learn more about their country and keep the American dream alive.

TABLE OF CONTENTS

INTRODUCTION

Chapter 6
WHAT IS AMERICA?

Chapter 7
AMERICAN HEROES

Chapter 8
SPEECHES

Chapter 9
POEMS AND SONGS

Chapter 10
U.S. Citizenship Test

Chapter 11
Conclusion

Index

Introduction

————————— ❦ —————————

THIS BOOK HAS MANY INSPIRATIONS. I was involved with the Boy Scouts as my son advanced from Tenderfoot to Eagle Scout, and I marvelled at what those boys learned about their country and their flag during their time as Scouts. I started comparing the experience of many children today to what I experienced as a child many years ago, and realized that something was missing today in our country—that innate love of country and knowledge of its history that I think existed when I was growing up just isn't as common now.

I chanced to pick up a book designed to help non-citizens prepare for the U.S. Citizenship Test. After looking over the questions, I realized that a majority of native-born Americans probably couldn't answer the questions themselves. They haven't learned or remembered the basic American history and civics needed to allow them to properly fulfill their obligations as citizens.

It is easy to forget the sacrifices, hardships, and accomplishments of the generations of Americans that have gone before. The world is a far better place because of the existence of the United States of America and the world continues to need a strong and free America. But the world is rapidly shrinking with daily advances in technology and communication, and those changes threaten the very traits that make this country great. To maintain that greatness, we need to know what made it special in the first place. That became my goal—to help every American learn about their country, to make sure they possess at least the minimum knowledge that a naturalized citizen possesses, and to ensure that they, too, could pass the U.S. Citizenship Test.

Then, I happened to read Ronald Reagan's 1989 farewell address to the nation. He ended his speech with a challenge to every

American that sums up the reasons behind this book. He was talking about the 1990s, but his speech applies just as much today.

> An informed patriotism is what we want. And are we doing a good enough job teaching our children what America is and what she represents in the long history of the world? Those of us who are over 35 or so years of age grew up in a different America. We were taught, very directly, what it means to be an American. And we absorbed, almost in the air, a love of country and an appreciation of its institutions. If you didn't get these things from your family, you got them from the neighborhood, from the father down the street who fought in Korea or the family who lost someone at Anzio. Or you could get a sense of patriotism from school. And if all else failed you could get a sense of patriotism from the popular culture. The movies celebrated democratic values and implicitly reinforced the idea that America was special. TV was like that, too, through the mid-sixties.

> But now, we're about to enter the nineties, and some things have changed. Younger parents aren't sure that an unambivalent appreciation of America is the right thing to teach modern children. And as for those who create the popular culture, well-grounded patriotism is no longer the style. Our spirit is back, but we haven't reinstitutionalized it. We've got to do a better job of getting across that America is freedom—freedom of speech, freedom of religion, freedom of enterprise. And freedom is special and rare. It's fragile; it needs protection.

> So, we've got to teach history based not on what's in fashion but what's important—why the Pilgrims came here, who Jimmy Doolittle was, and what those 30 seconds over Tokyo meant...If we forget what we did, we won't know who we are....

So I put together this book. I added a concise timeline of American history, copies of our important documents, details on how our government works, information about our national flag and our military, maps depicting our country's growth, lots of Americana, and what I feel are the most important American speeches made since our founding. The book contains things you should know, interesting things you may not know, and everything you need to know to pass the citizenship test.

The U.S. Citizenship Test questions are in the back of this book. You might want to see just how well you know your country—it is depending on you.

Chapter 1

HISTORY OF AMERICA

❧

A MERICA HAS ALWAYS BEEN A SPECIAL PLACE. She is filled with an industrious people who have always pushed the limits—whether the limits of the western frontier, or the limits of imagination. But she cannot claim that hard work or innovation alone created her dominant position in the world, or that any other nation can achieve the same success if they just try hard enough. From her creation, America has benefited from a set of conditions that the world has never seen before, nor will it ever see again. It was the classic case of being in the right place at the right time.

AMERICA'S SPECIAL ATTRIBUTES

The unique characteristics of the North American continent, along with the political and philosophical climate of the 1700s, helped shape the country that was destined to become the greatest the world had ever seen. It was the perfect recipe.

Geography: America had a unique geography. Its coasts ran north and south which, in a day when ships could only calculate latitude and not longitude, was invaluable for discovery, colonization, and commerce. Its eastern shore was washed by a Gulf Stream that moderated its climate while transporting ships to and from its shores. The eastern coastal areas that were the first to be settled were hospitable, and supplied the required shelter, food, and water. The settlers were not immediately faced with imposing mountain ranges, impassable jungles, or searing deserts (though some of these would come later). It had plenty of coastlines, protected harbors, and deep rivers to allow for transportation, commerce, fishing, and projecting their future naval seapower. It did have mountains and deserts, but with plenty of flat prairies, farmland, and forests in between. And it stretched all the way to a western coast on a new-found ocean, providing the magnetic allure that would pull the country westward until it achieved its manifest destiny.

Climate: It was blessed with a *Goldilocks* climate—not too hot and not too cold. Crops could be grown everywhere in the summer, and ports were not ice-bound in the winter. The land was not lashed with seasonal monsoons, nor parched by searing temperatures. It almost always received enough rain to grow crops.

Natural resources: Abundant game kept early settlers alive until they could get crops established, and the plentiful forests provided wood for building and fuel. Later generations would use the fertile Great Plains and California Central Valley to feed the world. There was abundant fresh water, both above and below the ground. The earth yielded valuable minerals, chemicals, coal, and petroleum. Ironically, the gold that early explorers came here seeking was not found until 1848 in California, when it provided the impetus for the final push of settlement across the country.

A fresh start: Other than the Native American tribes, the continent was a clean slate upon which a new country could be written. There was no history of conquests and re-conquests, feudal lords, or countrysides ravaged by war. There had never been kings, emperors, dictators, coup d'états, or centuries of religious or ethnic hatred. The founders could start from scratch and do it right.

Political and philosophical environment: The world had emerged from the Dark Ages and was experiencing the bloom of the Renaissance. The printing press allowed the wisdom of the Age of Enlightenment and the French philosophers to spread throughout the world, and news to quickly travel throughout the colonies. The founders of this country were the products of that enlightenment. America would have been very different if it had been born in a different era, and not in this Age of Reason.

Incomparable leaders: The country was blessed with a collection of remarkable leaders during its critical early years. These were brave, thoughtful men who were unafraid to take the risks of starting a new country, but educated enough to understand how best to design the required framework of government. The founders understood human nature, power, and the nature of governments. They knew they could not create a "perfect" nation. Instead, they wrote a Constitution to form a "more perfect" Union. They knew that a government could never *guarantee* prosperity or happiness—

it could only help protect those unalienable rights that every person possessed. The world has never seen a more remarkable and talented group of leaders in one place and at one time.

An educated electorate: The colonials had descended from a country that honored reason, fairness, and the rule of law. They were well-read and involved in the political situation. They were careful, deliberate, and understood the consequences of their actions.

A frontier: The ever-expanding western frontier lasted almost 300 years, continually challenging Americans to confront and overcome obstacles and adversity. It shaped the American character.

But these factors alone didn't guarantee America's greatness. Other countries arose on the same continent as America, or at the same time in history, but they all fell short of her greatness. There is just something special about this country. That's what is meant by the term "American Exceptionalism."

The painting of a continent

Imagine it is 1492 and you are watching America evolve from a point in space above the country. The North American continent is a vast, almost empty canvas, waiting to be painted with the brush of American civilization. Upon it, in just a few short centuries, will emerge the most powerful nation the world has ever seen.

From your vantage point in space, you see the early settlers leave their native countries in small ships to brave the unknown to make a new home. They came for religious or political freedom, to escape persecution, and for economic opportunities. Two small settlements at Plymouth and Jamestown slowly grow, and settlers begin to flow over the canvas. They grow crops, build towns, create industries, and soon form a new government unlike any in the world. They act on their dreams and build railroads that span the continent, and fight each other in a Civil War that ends the evil of slavery.

Watch them build a school system, hold town meetings, and peacefully elect a new government every four years. The western frontier expands across the deserts, giving rise to the iconic cowboy and the Gold Rush miner. Wooden sailing ships change to steamships, and then to great ironclad vessels. A giant Statue of Liberty appears in their main harbor to welcome the immigrants that continue to arrive, attracted to the limitless opportunities in this new land. Dirt roads give way to an enormous network of paved roads, while horse carts are replaced by automobiles and airplanes.

You'll see the nighttime darkness suddenly brightened by millions of electric lights. You see their ships, their planes, and their men stream forth around the world to defeat evil and tyranny, then return home, leaving the world a safer and better place. Radio and TV signals beam into space. Towering skyscrapers sprout from their cities. Spaceships are soon leaping into the heavens, circling the Earth, landing on the moon, and transiting the solar system. A web of electronic communication branches out to envelop the world. The citizens do whatever it takes to succeed—they invent; they innovate; they discover; and they work tirelessly.

AMERICAN HISTORY TIMELINE

The important events of American history have been placed on a timeline to help you understand their importance in the context of what was happening at the time. It does not list every event, nor go into much detail. This timeline lists acts of exploration, wars, inventions, presidential elections, contributions to our culture, and changes to our government. Every American should understand the relationship and context of these events to fully understand our country. Ignoring our history only leads to repeating the mistakes of yesterday.

The timeline also includes details about each presidential election which is helpful in understanding the mood and direction of the country every four years. The elections emphasize how divided the nation can be, but still elect a government and move forward. Our peaceful transition of power is a hallmark of our democratic system. Usually, only candidates receiving at least one electoral vote are listed, since almost all elections include a number of candidates from smaller parties. The timeline also lists the election year, not the year the president takes office, except in cases of death or resignation. You can watch the size of the country grow by watching the votes received by the winner grow from 38,000 to 69 million. You can also watch the country grow from 13 colonies toward its *manifest destiny*, which was the commonly held belief that America was destined to grow until it stretched from "sea to shining sea."

❧ TIMELINE OF AMERICAN HISTORY

1000 — **Vikings land in North America**
Leif Ericson lands in Newfoundland, leading to centuries of sporadic Viking visits.

1100 — **Anasazi Indians thrive in southwest North America**
Supported by agriculture, they build roads and massive cliff dwellings that will endure for 1000 years.

1492 — **Christopher Columbus "discovers" America**
He lands on San Salvador Island in the Bahamas, but thinks it is in the "East Indies" and calls the natives "Indians."

1497 — **English explorer John Cabot reaches North America**
The first European since the Vikings lands in North America at what is now Newfoundland, Canada.

1 5 0 0

1507 — **The new continent is named *America***
World maps now label the new continent "America" after the Italian explorer Amerigo Vespucci.

1513 — **The Spanish discover Florida**
The explorer Juan Ponce de Leon discovers Florida in search of treasure and the fabled Fountain of Youth.

1524 — **The Italians discover New York Harbor**
The Italian explorer Giovanni da Verrazano is the first European to see New York Harbor.

1565 — **Spain creates the first permanent settlement in America**
St. Augustine, Florida becomes the first permanent European settlement in North America.

1579 — **The English discover San Francisco Bay**
Sir Francis Drake supposedly lands at Drakes Bay, north of San Francisco, and claims the area for England.

1590 — **The English "Lost Colony" fails at Roanoke**
The settlement in North Carolina is found deserted with only the word "Croatoan" carved on a tree. The settlement had seen the birth of the New World's first English child, Virginia Dare.

1 6 0 0

1607 — **First permanent English settlement—Jamestown, Virginia**
Godspeed, Discovery, and *Susan Constant* bring 144 settlers to the James River. Captain John Smith helps 38 settlers survive the first winter and befriends Pocahontas. The winter of 1609 reduces the number of settlers from over 200 to only 60. They discover a new cash crop, tobacco, which saves the colony by giving it a lucrative crop to trade.

1619

Virginia hosts a colonial government

The Jamestown House of Burgesses is the first representative meeting in America. It will move to Williamsburg in 1699. The first slaves in the new world are brought by Dutch traders, and a large number of single women arrive.

1620

Mayflower brings Pilgrims to Plymouth Rock

Separatist Pilgrims fleeing religious persecution in England arrive at Plymouth, Massachusetts. The settlers sign the *Mayflower Compact* establishing local government and majority rule. Half the settlers die during the first year, but Indians help them plant crops, and together they celebrate the first Thanksgiving. Their descendants will include eight U.S. Presidents and millions of Americans.

1622

Indian Massacre of 1622 in Virginia

The Powhatan Indians launch surprise attacks on English settlers near Jamestown, killing 347 men, women, and children. This is one-quarter of the population of Jamestown.

1624

Dutch West India Company founds New Amsterdam

They settle Manhattan and build a fortress wall at the future site of Wall Street. Two years later, they formally buy Manhattan from the Indians for $24 in goods, taking advantage of the Indians' general lack of the concept of "ownership."

1629

Religious differences reach the New World

The 1629 grant of the Massachusetts Bay Colony charter leads to tens of thousands of new settlers in the Northeast. The 1600s will see many other religious settlements and events. Catholic colonists settle Maryland in 1632 and pass laws calling for freedom of religion. In 1636, Quakers under Roger Williams found Rhode Island based on religious freedom. William Penn will found Quaker Pennsylvania in 1682. His "Great Law" states that man cannot be deprived of life, liberty, or property, except by fair trial. The strict Puritan life leads to the Salem Witch Trials which put 19 people to death.

Roots of American democracy

New England town meetings are some of America's first democratic institutions. Every church member has a vote.

1636

Massachusetts founds Harvard

The first institute of higher learning in America educates leaders and ministers. It is named for John Harvard who donates his library and half of his estate.

1645 Minutemen selected from local militia
Towns in Massachusetts select portions of their militias to be "Minutemen" who will be ready to fight on a moment's notice. They will be crucial in skirmishes against the British in the next century.

1660 Britain passes the Navigation Acts
Colonists must import and export goods only on ships built in Britain with crews that are at least 75% British.

1664 New Amsterdam becomes New York City
British warships capture New Amsterdam without a fight and rename it New York in honor of the Duke of York.

1675 *King Phillip's War* destroys New England settlements
The Indian chief known as King Phillip leads tribes in bloody battles against New England towns, leading to a huge loss of life and property. In proportion to the population, this will be the costliest war in the country's history. The settlers win only when they combine forces to form a united front. The war is caused by the Indian loss of life due to European disease, and their loss of property due to confiscation by settlers.

1676 *Bacon's Rebellion* in Virginia
Nathaniel Bacon leads a thousand Virginians against Governor Berkeley, angry over his friendly treatment of Indians. The mob attacks and burns Jamestown.

1689 *King William's War*
Indians, backed by the French, attack English settlements. The English capture Port Royal in Nova Scotia. The Treaty of Ryswick in 1697 ends the conflict and restores the borders that existed before the war.

Triangle Trade benefits everyone (except the slaves)
The Triangle Trade involves Britain, Africa, the Caribbean, and the American colonies. It will be a cornerstone of the economy for 100 years, with over half a million slaves brought from Africa. It generally consists of:

- **Britain**: supplies finished goods and a market for American products;

- **Africa**: provides slaves;

- **Caribbean Islands**: buy slaves, and provide sugar cane and molasses;

- **Colonies**: buy slaves, sugar, and molasses to make rum. Sell rum, tobacco, and other goods to England.

1693 ⊢ **College of William and Mary founded**
The second oldest college in America opens in Williamsburg, Virginia. It will educate Thomas Jefferson, James Monroe, and sixteen signers of the Declaration.

1 7 0 0

1701 ⊢ *Queen Anne's War*
The English capture St. Augustine, destroy Spanish towns, and wipe out the Apalachee Indians. French and Indian allies then massacre English settlers. The war ends with the Treaty of Utrecht which gives England control of Newfoundland, Acadia, and Hudson Bay.

Europe continues to fight its wars in America
The British and French use North America as a battleground for their conflicts, each side employing native Indians as needed. This leads to long-lasting resentment against the Indians from the English settlers.

1703 ⊢ **First American *Mardi Gras* in Mobile, Alabama**
New Orleans will start their celebration in a few decades.

1711 ⊢ **Fighting in the Carolinas**
The Tuscarora Indians attack after settlers take their land. Hundreds are killed on both sides. South Carolina provides military help, wiping out the entire tribe.

1718 ⊢ **French found New Orleans**
Jean-Baptiste Le Moyne de Bienville picks the site on important trade routes and calls it *Nouvelle-Orléans*.

1733 ⊢ **Former convicts settle Georgia**
James Oglethorpe imports former British prisoners, many who were in jail for non-payment of debts. He outlaws slavery, but slaves are eventually brought in to help with farming.

1737 ⊢ **St. Patrick's Day makes its debut in Boston**
The religious holiday honors the patron saint of Ireland.

1744 ⊢ *King George's War*
Another European war is fought in the Americas. The British capture the French fortress of Louisbourg in Nova Scotia. The war ends with the 1748 Treaty of Aix-la-Chapelle.

1754 — **"Join or Die" becomes a rallying cry**
Benjamin Franklin prints the first political cartoon in America which becomes an icon for the revolution.

French and Indian War
Friction between British forts in the Ohio Valley and French settlements leads to war. The British and colonials fight against the French and their Indian allies. George Washington commands a British Army that is defeated at Fort Necessity, losing half his troops. British General Braddock is repulsed at Fort Duquesne the next year, but the British gain control of the territory by taking Quebec in 1759. The Treaty of 1763 gives control of Canada back to the British along with everything east of the Mississippi. Spain cedes control of Florida to England.

Prelude to war
A century of continual conflicts in America sets the scene for the upcoming Revolution. Great Britain has doubled their national debt and needs help paying it, so King George keeps levying new taxes on the colonies. France has lost a large portion of their American holdings and wants revenge. With new land opening up in the West, the settlers turn more in that direction, away from England.

1763 — **Proclamation of 1763**
To placate the Indians and keep the settlers stuck on the coast, the British forbid settlement west of a boundary set by the King. This thwarts the colonial desire to move westward, and inflames their animosity towards the Indians.

1764 — **Sugar Act of 1764**
Along with the earlier Molasses Act of 1733, this act tries to raise revenue and assist British growers in the Caribbean by taxing sugar and molasses coming into the Colonies.

Currency Act
This British act restricts colonists from issuing their own currency and using it for payment of debts.

1765 — **Stamp Act**
Requires special stamps on all documents. This leads to the cry of "no taxation without representation."

Quartering Act of 1765
Forces colonists to house and feed British soldiers.

Sons of Liberty **founded in Boston**
The group is formed to oppose Britain, and quickly spreads to the other colonies.

1766 — **Declaratory Act**
Relenting to colonial protests, this repeals the Stamp Act, but reasserts the British right to tax the colonies.

1767 **Townshend Acts**
These impose more taxes, punish non-compliance with the Quartering Act, and reinforce the right of Britain to tax and pass laws governing the colonies.

Mason-Dixon Line survey finished
Charles Mason and Jeremiah Dixon finish their survey of the border between Pennsylvania, Maryland, Delaware, and West Virginia. The line will separate the *North* from the *South*.

1769 **First Mission built in San Diego, California**
Father Junipero Serra builds the first mission in what will become a chain of missions along California's El Camino Real.

1770 **Boston Massacre—March 5**
Friction between British troops stationed in Boston and angry colonists leads to an altercation resulting in the death of 5 civilians. As a result, Britain repeals the Townshend Acts, **except for the tax on tea.** John Adams subsequently represents the British soldiers at their trial to ensure fairness, and gets them acquitted. The first man killed in the Revolution is the former slave, Crispus Attucks, shown in this picture. News of the massacre quickly spreads to all of the other colonies.

1773 **Boston Tea Party—December 16**

With the tax on tea still in place, the colonies turn away tea-carrying ships at Philadelphia and New York, but not at Boston. Sam Adams and Paul Revere, along with colonists disguised as Indians, board ships in Boston Harbor and dump 342 chests of tea into the harbor, worth about $1 million today.

1774 **Intolerable Acts**
In reaction to the destruction of tea, Britain passes a series of five laws that lead directly to the formation of the Continental Congress in America. These new laws:

- Close Boston Harbor until the destroyed tea is paid for.
- Allow Britain to appoint members of the Massachusetts Legislature.
- Allow Britain to move trials from America to other locations, including England.
- Enlarge the boundaries of Canada to include land previously belonging to the colonies.

1774 — **First Continental Congress meets in Philadelphia**

Formed to protect the rights of the colonies against an increasingly oppressive England, it issues a list of grievances to the Crown, along with an ultimatum. The complaints include taxation without representation, onerous laws, quartering of troops, and loss of the right to self govern. All the members risk being charged with treason and beheaded. Patrick Henry states, "I am not a Virginian, but an American."

(Now—let's see what happens when a government imposes too many taxes and laws on its people...)

1775 — ***The Shot Heard 'Round the World*** **- Lexington and Concord**

Britain orders the arrest of dissidents John Hancock and John Adams, and the confiscation of arms and ammunition. Paul Revere rides to alert the colonists of the danger. On April 19, fifty Minutemen meet 700 British soldiers at Lexington where eight colonials are killed. The British proceed to Concord to seize arms, and are attacked again by 500 militiamen. More than 250 British soldiers are killed or wounded, compared to only 90 colonials. A number of black Minutemen participated. The British retreat to Boston where they are surrounded by over 15,000 colonial militiamen. They will remain there until forced out the next year.

THE AMERICAN REVOLUTION HAS BEGUN

Fort Ticonderoga attacked—May 10

In the first victory for the colonies, the Green Mountain Boys, under the command of Ethan Allen and Benedict Arnold, successfully attack this vital Lake Champlain fort.

Continental Army formed on June 14

The Continental Congress authorizes the army and appoints George Washington as Commander. The present-day U.S. Army honors this day as their birthday.

Battle of Bunker Hill, Boston—June 17

General Gage leads 3,000 British troops attacking colonials on Breed's Hill (it wasn't really Bunker Hill). The colonials are instructed *"Don't fire until you see the whites of their eyes"* and kill or wound almost half of the British force, one of their highest losses of the Revolution.

December failure at Quebec

Forces under General Montgomery and Colonel Benedict Arnold attack Quebec but are defeated with heavy losses, ending the colonial attempt to make Canada an ally.

1776

Thomas Paine writes *Common Sense*

This 50-page pamphlet lays out the case for separation from England. Paine feels strongly that the colonists have to fight for more than just a cessation of unfair taxes.

Colonel Knox helps end the siege at Boston

The British are still surrounded in Boston when Colonel Henry Knox hatches a plan to help end the siege. On his own initiative, he travels to Fort Ticonderoga and hauls back 60 cannon. Under cover of darkness, Washington secretly hauls them to the top of Dorchester Heights. The next morning, the British awake to see their position compromised, and shortly thereafter leave Boston.

The Declaration of Independence—July 4th

Thomas Jefferson finishes the document, but southern states remove his condemnation of slavery. The founders sign the document at Independence Hall in Philadelphia—a treasonable act punishable by death. British troops have already landed in New York, less than 100 miles away. There is no time for further debate or refinements—the formation of a new country is too important. America announces her separation from England...now she must fight to guarantee it.

British force Washington out of New York

General Howe moves his troops from Boston to New York and trap Washington's army on Long Island. Only a miracle allows Washington to successfully evacuate his entire force under cover of night and a fortuitous fog. He almost loses his army again on Manhattan, and again at Fort Washington where 3,000 colonial soldiers surrender.

Submarine *Turtle* attacks British warships

David Bushnell invents a small submarine that attempts to place explosives on the hulls of British warships in New York Harbor. None of the attacks are successful.

Washington retreats across the Delaware River

Washington's meager force of 19,000 is reduced to less than 4000, with enlistments due to expire for half of those men.

British hang Nathan Hale as a spy in New York City

His last words are, "I only regret that I have but one life to lose for my country."

1776—
Washington rows across the Delaware

Early December 26, Washington rows his troops across the river to attack the Hessian troops in Trenton, catching them by complete surprise. He captures or kills 1,000 soldiers with only 6 American casualties. The victory is a huge morale booster for America.

1777—
Victory at Princeton
Washington follows up his victory at Trenton with a successful surprise attack on the British at Princeton.

Another defeat for the British at Saratoga
British General Burgoyne retakes Fort Ticonderoga, but is forced out and defeated at the battle of Saratoga. However, Washington suffers defeats at Brandywine and Germantown, and retreats to Valley Forge, Pennsylvania for the winter. The British occupy Philadelphia in November.

Articles of Confederation adopted on November 15
Approved by the Second Continental Congress, they must be ratified by the states which will not happen until 1781. They will be used to guide the government until then.

Winter at Valley Forge
Washington and his troops spend a dismal winter in Pennsylvania, lacking proper food, clothing, and shelter. It is the low point of the Revolution with 2,500 of his 11,000 troops dying from exposure or disease.

1778—
France joins the fight
Benjamin Franklin and the Marquis de Lafayette convince the French King to fight the British in America. French help will be instrumental in the final American victory.

1779—
British capture Georgia and South Carolina
The "Swamp Fox" Francis Marion harasses enemy troops in South Carolina, eventually forcing the British northward to Virginia where Cornwallis will meet his final defeat.

John Paul Jones wins an American victory at sea

In command of the *Bonhomme Richard* fighting the British frigate *Serapis*, he issues his famous line, "I have not yet begun to fight" before defeating the enemy ship.

1780—
Surrender of Charleston is worst American defeat of war
On May 12, Major General Lincoln surrenders his entire army of 10,000 to the British in loyalist-leaning South Carolina. Lincoln gets his revenge the next year when he accepts the British surrender at Yorktown.

1780 Pivotal battle of Kings Mountain, South Carolina

A band of patriot mountain men wipe out a loyalist army led by the British Major Ferguson. The colonial soldiers then head back into the mountains to their homes.

1781 Battle of Cowpens a colonial success

Daniel Morgan ambushes a superior British force under Lt. Col. Tarleton, killing or capturing almost all of his men. Tarleton is known as "The Butcher" after he killed colonial troops that had surrendered at the Battle of Waxhaws. He escapes capture.

LT. COL. TARLETON

Cornwallis surrenders at Yorktown

Cornwallis is trapped in Virginia with the York River and French fleet to his back, and the Colonial Army to his front. The British surrender on October 19 to the combined American and French forces as their band plays "The World Turned Upside Down."

1783 Washington stops the Newburgh Conspiracy in New York

At Newburgh, Continental Army officers demand their back pay and benefits, and threaten to disband and leave the country without an army. Washington denounces their actions, but meets them and urges calm. When he reads a letter outlining the country's financial problems, he finds he needs his glasses, and states that he is sorry but that he has grown old in the service of his country. His men, not even knowing he needs glasses, are deeply moved realizing the sacrifices Washington himself has made for his country. He finishes the letter and leaves, and his men unanimously agree to accept the government's terms. The nation is saved.

Revolution officially ends with the Treaty of Paris

After fighting continues for two more years, the English Parliament decides that it has had enough, and sues for peace. America finally wins her independence.

1784 Articles of Confederation prove unworkable

The articles were passed in 1777 and ratified in 1781, but there are still major deficiencies, including:

• No president, no navy or army, and no courts to interpret laws. States can make their own money.

• States have one vote each and most power is left to the states, under a mostly ineffective federal government.

• The government cannot levy taxes or regulate commerce.

1786 — Shays' Rebellion tests the Confederation

Daniel Shays leads an armed rebellion in Massachusetts, primarily fueled by debts and government taxes. The rebellion underscores the problems with the Confederation's lack of an effective central government, and helps bring attention to the need for a new constitution. Thomas Jefferson writes to a friend and says, "The tree of liberty must be refreshed from time to time with the blood of patriots and tyrants."

1787 — Northwest Ordinance establishes the path to statehood

Passed under the Articles of Confederation, this act establishes guidelines for new states and prohibits slavery in the Northwest territories. The procedures are:

- First, a territory is appointed a governor and judges.
- When the adult male population reaches 5,000, they can vote for their own legislature.
- When the population reaches 60,000, they can write their own constitution and apply for statehood.
- Slavery is outlawed in the territory and freedom of religion is guaranteed.

Constitutional Convention meets in Philadelphia

George Washington heads the convention convened to fix the problems of the Articles of Confederation. However, an entirely new form of government is proposed by Virginia's Edmund Randolph and James Madison. This leads to months of heated debate until the final Constitution is agreed on in September. Highlights of the final debate and agreement include:

- The Virginia plan relies on a strong central government and limited state sovereignty.
- The Great Compromise gives each state two Senators and a House representation proportional to state population.
- The new government contains an executive branch, judicial branch, and a bicameral legislative branch.
- A slavery compromise allows slavery importation until 1808, lets southern owners reclaim runaway slaves, and counts slaves as only 3/5 of a person to prevent southern states from acquiring too many seats in the House.
- The president will be elected by electors, not directly by the citizens.
- States are prohibited from issuing their own currency.
- A national bank and currency is approved.
- The civilian president is made Commander-in-Chief over the armed forces.
- Federal and state governments get the ability to tax.

1788 ┤ **Constitution finally ratified**

Once approved, the Constitution must be ratified by at least nine states to take effect. There are still concerns about granting a central government too much power. Alexander Hamilton, John Jay, and James Madison write *The Federalist Papers* to make the case for a strong central government. Virginia agrees to ratify the Constitution only after being promised a Bill of Rights to protect individual and state rights. New Hampshire is the 9th state to ratify, and the Constitution takes effect on March 4, 1789.

★**1789**★   GEORGE WASHINGTON   **1**

CANDIDATE	PARTY	ELECTORAL VOTE	POPULAR VOTE
George Washington	*(no party)*	69	38,818
John Adams	*(no party)*	34	
Various	*(no party)*	35	

The Constitution gives each elector two votes. The candidate who receives the most votes becomes president; the runner-up becomes vice president. All 69 electors vote for Washington—he remains the only unanimous choice in our history. Adams receives the second largest number and becomes vice president. Washington takes the oath of office on April 30, 1789 in New York City.

1789 ┤ **"The Father of Our Country" sets the tone**

The government temporarily moves to New York City before a move to Philadelphia a year later. Washington sets the tone for the entire government since the Constitution does not specify every detail of government. He names Cabinet members, establishes a precedent for dealing with Congress, and sticks to his belief that a president should serve only two terms, a tradition upheld until 1940.

1790 ┤ **U.S. Coast Guard established as part of Treasury Department**

1791 ┤ **Bill of Rights added to Constitution**

The Constitution works by "enumerated powers" meaning it can exercise only those powers specifically granted to it by the Constitution. The Constitution is finally ratified only because the writers promise to add more protection for state and individual rights. These protections are added in the first 10 amendments to the Constitution, known as the Bill of Rights. These are penned by James Madison, modeled after Jefferson's Statute for Religious Freedom in Virginia, and are the cornerstone of what the Constitution guarantees every U.S. citizen.

1791

BILL OF RIGHTS

★ **1ˢᵀ AMENDMENT** ★

Congress will not establish or prohibit any religion. Freedom of speech and press; right to assemble and petition the government.

★ **2ᴺᴰ AMENDMENT** ★

Right to keep and bear arms.

★ **3ᴿᴰ AMENDMENT** ★

Bars the government from housing soldiers in citizen homes.

★ **4ᵀᴴ AMENDMENT** ★

Prohibits unreasonable searches and seizures. Establishes requirements for search warrants based on probable cause.

★ **5ᵀᴴ AMENDMENT** ★

Establishes rules for grand jury indictment and eminent domain, establishes right to due process, prohibits double jeopardy and self-incrimination.

★ **6ᵀᴴ AMENDMENT** ★

Establishes the right to a fair and speedy trial by jury, the right to be confronted by one's accuser and notified of the accusations, the right to obtain witnesses, and the right to legal counsel.

★ **7ᵀᴴ AMENDMENT** ★

Establishes the right to a jury trial for certain civil cases.

★ **8ᵀᴴ AMENDMENT** ★

Prohibits excessive fines and bail; prohibits cruel and unusual punishment.

★ **9ᵀᴴ AMENDMENT** ★

Asserts rights of citizens to retain unenumerated rights.

★ **10ᵀᴴ AMENDMENT** ★

Limits the powers of the federal government to those stipulated in the Constitution.

1792

New York Stock Exchange starts

The stock exchange informally starts under a tree on what is now Wall Street when 24 brokers sign the *Buttonwood Agreement*. The Exchange is formalized in 1825.

1792— **U.S. Post Office Department is created**

★**1792**★ GEORGE WASHINGTON RE-ELECTED

CANDIDATE	PARTY	ELECTORAL VOTE	POPULAR VOTE
George Washington	*Federalist*	132	13,332
John Adams	*Federalist*	77	
George Clinton	*Anti-federalist*	50	

A record low turnout unanimously picks Washington, but attempts are made to make Clinton the vice president. Political parties are already involved in the elections.

1793— **French Revolution**
King Louis XVI is executed and France declares war on Britain, Spain, and the Netherlands. The U.S. issues a Proclamation of Neutrality, being too weak to get involved.

Eli Whitney invents the cotton gin
The gin is a machine that quickly separates cotton fiber from the seeds. The South becomes dependent on cotton...and cotton is dependent on slavery.

1794— **Britain seizes neutral shipping trading with France**
U.S. approves construction of more Navy ships, realizing a strong Navy is critical to their survival.

1795—

★ **11**ᵀᴴ **AMENDMENT** ★

Grants states immunity from lawsuits from out-of-state citizens, or from foreigners not living inside the state.

★**1796**★ JOHN ADAMS 2

CANDIDATE	PARTY	ELECTORAL VOTE	POPULAR VOTE
John Adams	*Federalist*	71	35,726
Thomas Jefferson	*Dem-Rep*	68	31,115
Thomas Pinckney	*Federalist*	59	
Aaron Burr	*Dem-Rep*	30	

This is the first contested presidential election, and the only one to pick a vice president from an opposing party. Adams wins the vote for president, but his running mate, Pinckney, receives fewer votes than Jefferson, so Jefferson becomes the vice president, even though he is running for president.

1798 France attempts to extort money from the U.S.

The discovery of the *XYZ* affair leads to a mini-war with France at the height of their Revolution. X, Y, and Z are aliases for three French agents who try to extort money from the U.S. in return for continuing peace negotiations.

U.S. Marine Corps and U.S. Navy officially established

Alien and Sedition Acts

These unpopular acts give the government power over determining citizenship, and lead to the arrest of foreigners and even civil dissenters. They are strongly opposed, though the Alien Enemies Act stays in effect and is used to justify the internment of Japanese citizens in World War II.

1 8 0 0

1800 Government moves to Washington, D.C.

The new capital, designed by French architect Pierre L'Enfant, is finished and the government moves in. Originally named Federal City, it is created with no representation in Congress, but with 3 electors in the Electoral College. John Adams is first to occupy the White House (shown).

★1800★ THOMAS JEFFERSON **3**

CANDIDATE	PARTY	ELECTORAL VOTE	POPULAR VOTE
Thomas Jefferson	Dem-Rep	73	41,330
Aaron Burr	Dem-Rep	73	
John Adams	Federalist	65	25,952
Charles Pinckney	Federalist	64	

The 1800 election is extremely contentious. Thomas Jefferson, with Aaron Burr as his vice president, runs against John Adams, with Charles Pinckney as his vice president. Electors vote for any two candidates, resulting in a tie between Jefferson and his own running mate Burr, each with 73 electoral votes. Adams finishes third with 65 votes. The Constitution stipulates that ties are decided by the House of Representatives, which must now decide between Jefferson and Burr. The Federalists control the lame-duck Congress and support Burr. Alexander Hamilton detests Burr and works to get Jefferson elected. The House deadlocks for 35 ballots until finally picking Jefferson. As stipulated, Burr becomes his vice president, and is ignored by Jefferson during his administration. Burr kills Hamilton in a duel, though he is not prosecuted. The main outcome of this discord is the passage of the 12th amendment which changes how electors elect the president.

1800

Congress establishes Library of Congress
The British burn the library in 1814, after which Thomas Jefferson sells Congress his 6,000-book collection which becomes the core of the new library. Today, the library contains more than 140 million items, adding 10,000 new items a day.

1803

Marbury v. Madison establishes principle of "judicial review"
Historic Supreme Court case is the first time a court has ever invalidated a law because it is unconstitutional.

Jefferson buys Louisiana Territory
France sells 828,800 square miles for $15 million to help pay off war debts, doubling the area of the U.S.

U.S. battles the Barbary Pirates in Tripoli
The USS *Philadelphia* is captured when she runs aground, and the captain and crew are taken hostage.

1804

Lewis and Clark Expedition heads West
Meriwether Lewis and William Clark lead an expedition of 30 people from Illinois to chart a route to the Pacific. They will return, after a successful trip, in September of 1806.

U.S. Marines launch a daring raid in Tripoli
Lt. Decatur leads Marines in Tripoli harbor to burn the captured frigate USS *Philadelphia*.

Aaron Burr kills Alexander Hamilton in a duel

Vice President Aaron Burr mortally wounds Alexander Hamilton in a duel. Hamilton, who lost his son in a duel, purposely fires in the air. Burr, however, aims and shoots Hamilton in the stomach. He dies the next day.

★ 12ᵀᴴ AMENDMENT ★
Outlines the procedure to elect the president using the electoral college. Candidates will run for either president or vice president, and electors vote for each position separately.

★1804★ THOMAS JEFFERSON RE-ELECTED

CANDIDATE	PARTY	ELECTORAL VOTE	POPULAR VOTE
Thomas Jefferson George Clinton	*Dem-Rep*	162	104,110
Charles Pinckney Rufus King	*Federalist*	14	38,919

The Twelfth Amendment establishes new rules for elections requiring electors to specify their choices for president and vice president. Jefferson selects Clinton to replace Burr as his vice president. Jefferson's popularity has improved with his Louisiana Purchase. His 45% popular vote victory margin will remain the highest in any contested election.

1806 **Webster publishes first American dictionary**

Noah Webster publishes the first edition of what would later become the *American Dictionary of the English Language.* It standardizes spelling in America, changing many British spellings to shorter American versions, such as *program* instead of *programme*, and *flavor* instead of *flavour*. He also includes technical and scientific terms. He will spend the next 20 years improving the dictionary.

1807 **Congress prohibits import of slaves**

Jefferson signs law at earliest date allowed by Article 1 of the Constitution. It takes effect on January 1, 1808.

Robert Fulton builds steamboat

The first commercial steamboat in America, the *Clermont,* makes a 150-mile trip in New York, averaging 5 miles-per-hour.

★1808★   JAMES MADISON   4

CANDIDATE	PARTY	ELECTORAL VOTE	POPULAR VOTE
James Madison George Clinton	*Dem-Rep*	122	124,732
Charles Pinckney Rufus King	*Federalist*	47	62,431
George Clinton James Monroe	*Dem-Rep*	6	4,848

George Clinton runs as Madison's running mate, but is also a candidate for president, receiving six electoral votes from electors dissatisfied with Madison. Clinton becomes vice president when Madison wins. It is one of only two times in our history when a sitting vice president continues to serve under a new president.

1809 **Non-Intercourse Act of 1809**

This act, and the earlier Embargo Act of 1807, prohibits trade with France and Great Britain, but results in great harm to the U.S. economy.

1811 **Chief Tecumseh organizes Indian rebellion**

The Indians continue to fight the relentless westward U.S. expansion. Future president William Henry Harrison defeats the Indians at Tippecanoe, Indiana.

1811

New Madrid earthquakes

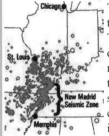

The first in a series of huge earthquakes hits the Mississippi River town of New Madrid. The quakes continue into 1812, causing damage across an enormous area. They remain the strongest earthquakes to ever hit the eastern U.S. The threat of another massive earthquake will continue into the 21ˢᵗ century. This map shows earthquake activity in the area from 1974 to 2010.

1812

War of 1812 with Great Britain

Britain has been interfering with American shipping for years. They also support the Spanish who claim a large part of the American Southwest. And, of course, Britain is at war again with France. The U.S. declares war even though she is not prepared, having only a 12,000 man army, and a Navy of 14 ships, compared to a British Navy of 1,000 ships.

USS *Constitution* defeats HMS *Guerriere*

Cannonballs bounce off her thick oak sides earning her the name *Old Ironsides*.

★1812★ JAMES MADISON RE-ELECTED

CANDIDATE	PARTY	ELECTORAL VOTE	POPULAR VOTE
James Madison Elbridge Gerry	Dem-Rep	128	140,431
DeWitt Clinton Jared Ingersoll	Federalist	89	132,781

The 1812 election takes place shortly after war is declared on Great Britain. DeWitt Clinton is the nephew of the former vice president who had died before the election. He actually changes his campaign in each region, trying to appear anti-war in the North, while pro-war in the South and West. The Federalists oppose the war, but Madison declares war in the summer before the election.

1813

Don't give up the ship!

The HMS *Shannon* captures the USS *Chesapeake* whose captain, James Lawrence, lies mortally wounded. His last words are "Don't give up the

up the ship!" Admiral Perry also issues memorable words as he defeats the British fleet on Lake Erie, sending the message "We have met the enemy and they are ours." This drawing depicts Perry transferring his command to the *Niagara*.

1814 — The British burn Washington

British troops capture Washington D.C. and set fire to the White House and Capitol. The arrival of a rare hurricane forces them to leave the Capitol and helps douse the fires.

Francis Scott Key writes *The Star Spangled Banner*

Imprisoned on a British ship watching the battle for Ft. McHenry in Baltimore, Key pens the words to our anthem. This is a picture of the actual flag that flew over the fort.

The Treaty of Ghent ends the war

The British sign the treaty in Belgium on December 24, 1814, ending all hostilities.

1815 — Andrew Jackson wins the Battle of New Orleans

His ragtag army soundly beats the British at the Battle of New Orleans. He has no idea that a peace treaty had been signed two weeks earlier. Jackson's outnumbered troops lose 13 fighters, but inflict 2,000 casualties on the British.

★1816★   JAMES MONROE   5

CANDIDATE	PARTY	ELECTORAL VOTE	POPULAR VOTE
James Monroe Daniel Tompkins	Dem-Rep	183	76,592
Rufus King John Howard	Federalist	34	34,740

Four Federalist candidates for vice president receive electoral votes, but Monroe easily wins the election. The Democratic-Republican party receives credit for a successful end to the War of 1812, while the Federalists have been opposing the war. Madison has also implemented economic steps that were favored by Federalists.

1817 — First public gas street light in U.S. in Baltimore

1819 — Jefferson founds University of Virginia

Thomas Jefferson designs and builds the famous university in sight of his classic home, *Monticello,* in Charlottesville, Virginia.

Florida, California, and Oregon territories added to country

Spain cedes Florida to the U.S., and a treaty with Russia gives us California and Oregon, but Russia keeps Alaska.

1820 ⊣ Missouri Compromise—Maine and Missouri admitted

Maine is admitted as a free state to balance the new slave state of Missouri, and slavery is prohibited in new territories north of 36°30', except for Missouri.

★1820★ JAMES MONROE RE-ELECTED

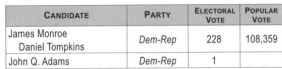

CANDIDATE	PARTY	ELECTORAL VOTE	POPULAR VOTE
James Monroe Daniel Tompkins	Dem-Rep	228	108,359
John Q. Adams	Dem-Rep	1	

Monroe is the only candidate to essentially run unopposed, other than George Washington. There are issues around the Panic of 1819 and the recently passed Missouri Compromise, but Monroe easily wins. Only a vote for John Quincy Adams from a New Hampshire elector prevents the election from being unanimous. Missouri's vote is contested with opponents saying she is not officially a state yet. Monroe would have 231 electoral votes if Missouri is counted.

Whaleship *Essex* sunk by a whale

The Nantucket whaler is in the Pacific Ocean harpooning whales, when a large whale appears and rams the ship. The whale then retreats several hundred yards away, turns around, and then speeds directly toward the ship. She rams the bow, causing the ship to almost immediately sink. The crew board their three small whaleboats, but most die before being rescued. This incident later inspires Herman Melville to write *Moby Dick*.

1823 ⊣ Monroe Doctrine protects the western hemisphere

Monroe's policy states that the U.S. will not interfere with Europe, European colonies, or in European wars. In return, the U.S. makes it clear that it will not tolerate any interference in the western hemisphere by any European power.

★1824★   JOHN Q. ADAMS   6

CANDIDATE	PARTY	ELECTORAL VOTE	POPULAR VOTE
John Q. Adams John Calhoun	Dem-Rep	84	113,122
Andrew Jackson John Calhoun	Dem-Rep	99	151,271
William Crawford Nathaniel Macon	Dem-Rep	41	40,856
Henry Clay Nathan Sanford	Dem-Rep	37	47,531

The Federalist party has collapsed, and the Democratic-Republican party runs four candidates. It will soon split into the Democratic, Republican, and Whig parties. Adams is the son of the 2nd President, and Jackson is the hero of the Battle of New Orleans. No candidate receives a majority votes, so the House of Representatives has to decide the election. Only the top 3 candidates are considered, which is interesting since the 4th candidate is Henry Clay, the Speaker of the House, who detests Jackson. Adams is picked, even though Jackson has more electoral and popular votes. Calhoun becomes vice president after easily getting the most votes for vice president.

1825— **Erie Canal opens in New York**

This ushers in the building of hundreds of canals to facilitate transportation and commerce. Hundreds of workers die, mainly of disease, building the 363-mile canal. Travel time from Buffalo to Albany is shortened from 3 weeks to 1 week.

1826— **Thomas Jefferson and John Adams die on July 4**

These two signers of the Declaration and ex-presidents both die on July 4, 1826—50 years to the day after signing the Declaration. John Adams' last words are "Thomas Jefferson still survives." He doesn't know Jefferson has died hours before.

★1828★   ANDREW JACKSON   7

CANDIDATE	PARTY	ELECTORAL VOTE	POPULAR VOTE
Andrew Jackson John Calhoun	Democratic	178	642,553
John Q. Adams Richard Rush	Natl. Republican	83	500,897

Jackson uses broad public support and backing of Vice President Calhoun, to win an easy electoral victory. The campaign is marked by a number of personal attacks, including one concerning Jackson's wife. Jackson, meanwhile, accuses Adams and Clay of a corrupt bargain in the previous election that gave Adams the victory. Jackson's wife dies weeks after the election, leading to Jackson blaming Adams for her death.

1830

Indian Removal Act

The government moves eastern Indian tribes to western lands, usually against their wishes. The government often makes treaties with one small part of a tribe, and then applies that to the entire tribe.

Railroads open up the country

The Baltimore and Ohio is the first public U.S. railroad.

1831

Slave rebellion in Virginia

Nat Turner leads a violent slave rebellion in Virginia but is caught and hung. Virginia passes tougher slavery laws in response. William Lloyd Garrison publishes *The Liberator* which pushes for an end to slavery.

1832 ★ Andrew Jackson re-elected

Candidate	Party	Electoral Vote	Popular Vote
Andrew Jackson Martin van Buren	Democratic	219	701,780
Henry Clay John Sergeant	Natl. Republican	49	484,205
John Floyd Henry Lee	Nullifier	11	picked by legislature
William Wirt Amos Ellmaker	Anti-Masonic	7	100,715

The process of nominating candidates for each party changes to using national party conventions. The Anti-Masonic Party holds the first national nominating convention in our history. His opponents portray Jackson as a tyrant trampling the Constitution, but he easily wins another term.

1834

Cyrus McCormick invents the grain reaper

The mechanical grain reaper revolutionizes agriculture. There is a competing design from Obed Hussey, and McCormick incorporates some of Hussey's innovations in 1850 to produce a truly effective machine.

1835

Indian *Trail of Tears*

The government forcibly relocates tens of thousands of Native Americans to the Indian Territory

(Oklahoma). Thousands die on the march. The Choctaw had been moved in 1831, the Cherokee will be moved in 1838, and most tribes are relocated by 1855.

1836
Texas Revolution and the Alamo

Mexico gained her independence from Spain in 1821, but American settlers had poured into Texas and now outnumber the Mexicans 10 to 1. Texas finally declares independence from Mexico. In response, Mexican President Santa Anna and 2,400 troops march north and surround 189 Texans at the Alamo. After a week-long battle, they capture the fort and kill every defender, including Davy Crockett and Jim Bowie. The Mexicans suffer more than 600 casualties. Three weeks later, Colonel Fannin surrenders his 300-man force of Texans to Mexican General Urrea at Goliad, Texas. Under orders from Santa Anna, Urrea executes all the Texans and burns their bodies, though some escape to tell the story.

On April 21, Sam Houston defeats the Mexican Army at the Battle of San Jacinto in a fight that lasts only 15 minutes, amidst shouts of "Remember the Alamo!" and "Remember Goliad!" The fight kills 630 Mexicans and the rest are taken prisoner. The captured Santa Anna grants Texas its independence in exchange for his life. Texas wants to become a state but, since that will upset the balance of free and slave states, statehood is put off until 1845.

Colt revolver patented

Samuel Colt's new revolver mechanism makes his handgun an instant legend.

★1836★   MARTIN VAN BUREN   8

CANDIDATE	PARTY	ELECTORAL VOTE	POPULAR VOTE
Martin Van Buren Richard Johnson	Democratic	170	764,176
William H. Harrison Francis Granger	Whig	73	550,816
Hugh White John Tyler	Whig	26	146,107

This is the last election until 1988 that results in an incumbent vice president becoming president. The Whigs run several candidates in different areas of the country hoping to force a stalemated election that the House of Representatives will then decide. This ploy is unsuccessful and the Democrat Van Buren wins. The vice presidential race is decided by the Senate for the only time in history when Richard Johnson initially comes up one vote short. Two other Whig candidates, Daniel Webster and Willie Mangum, also receive electoral votes, .

1838| **Mormons driven from Missouri**
Governor Boggs issues an executive order to use military force to drive the Mormons from Missouri.

★1840★ WILLIAM HENRY HARRISON 9

CANDIDATE	PARTY	ELECTORAL VOTE	POPULAR VOTE
William Henry Harrison John Tyler	*Whig*	234	1,275,390
Martin Van Buren Richard Johnson	*Democratic*	60	1,128,854

The Panic of 1837 hurt Van Buren's popularity. The Whig Party unifies behind the war hero Harrison, and campaign with the popular slogan, "Tippecanoe and Tyler, too" referring to Harrison's victory at the Battle of Tippecanoe in 1811. James Polk receives one electoral vote resulting in an election with four former or future presidents receiving votes—Polk, Harrison, Tyler, and Van Buren. The Whigs make two big mistakes: their presidential pick, Harrison, is too old and will soon die; and their vice-presidential pick, Tyler, does not agree with their platform, which will soon be a problem when he becomes president.

★1841★ JOHN TYLER 10

President Harrison delivers an almost two-hour inaugural address in freezing rain and snow, and dies one month later from pneumonia, resulting in Vice President Tyler becoming president. He is the first vice president to become president this way. However, the path of succession is not clear, and many in Congress treat Tyler as only a temporary president. The exact succession procedure will not be codified until the 25th amendment, but Tyler sets the example used until then. However, Tyler's policies align more with the Democratic-Republican Party than the Whigs. Most of his cabinet resigns. Days before leaving office in 1845, he succeeds in formalizing the annexation of Texas.

First emigrant train to California
John Bidwell leads a wagon train on a 5-month trip to California, unleashing a continual flood of pioneers westward. Their large *Conestoga* wagons were also called *Prairie schooners*.

1844| **Samuel Morse starts telegraph service**
The line opens between Baltimore and the Washington, D.C. Samuel Morse sends the words, "What hath God wrought" from the Supreme Court chamber in the U.S. Capitol building.

1844 — **Angry mob kills Mormon leader Joseph Smith**

Besides being a religious leader, Smith is a mayor and presidential candidate. He is in a Carthage, Illinois jail on charges of destroying the facilities of a newspaper that had exposed his polygamist views. An angry mob storms the jail (shown above), shooting and killing Joseph and his brother, Hyrum.

★1844★   JAMES POLK   11

CANDIDATE	PARTY	ELECTORAL VOTE	POPULAR VOTE
James Polk George Dallas	Democratic	170	1,339,494
Henry Clay Theodore Frelinghuysen	Whig	105	1,300,004

Tyler had been kicked out of the Whig Party and finally decides not to run. Clay opposes the annexation of Texas, while Polk supports it and more territorial expansion, including Oregon. The popular vote is very close, and this election sees perhaps the first role of a third party as a "spoiler." The anti-slavery Liberty Party receives more than enough votes in New York to keep Clay from winning that state, which he loses by only 5,100 votes. If Clay had New York's 36 electoral votes instead of Polk, he would have won the election.

1845 — **U.S. annexes Texas**

This happens six days before Polk takes office, giving Tyler a significant accomplishment for his time in office.

U.S. Naval Academy opens in Annapolis, Maryland.

1846 — **Baseball starts**

The first official baseball game is held with the New York Nine defeating the New York Knickerbockers, 23-1.

Oregon Territory is acquired from England

The U.S. now spreads from sea to sea, achieving its Manifest Destiny. Oregon will become a state in 1859.

Mormons move to Salt Lake City, Utah

Forced westward mainly by anger against their practice of polygamy, Brigham Young leads his followers to Salt Lake City. Their solitude is permanently broken two years later when gold is discovered in California. By 1861, they will have constructed 300 irrigation canals and made thousands of miles of desert bloom.

1846

Donner Party meets disaster

A party of 87 settlers, led by George Donner, leaves Wyoming for California using a new route called the "Hastings Cutoff." The route is a disaster and they arrive in the Sierra Nevadas perilously late in the year. They are one day too late and are turned back by snowstorms. Stuck for the winter, half the party dies. Some even resort to cannibalism to stay alive.

Texas annexation touches off the Mexican-American War

The annexation of Texas touches of a 2-year war with Mexico. The U.S. invades the area of New Mexico, California and parts of northern Mexico. The U.S. Marines capture Mexico City in 1847 to end the war and add the phrase "the halls of Montezuma" to the Marines' Hymn. The Treaty of Guadalupe Hidalgo in 1848 gives the territory of California, Nevada, Utah, New Mexico, and Arizona to the U.S., and sets the Rio Grande as the new border. In return, Mexico receives $15 million in payment. Many Americans worry that the treaty will add more slave states to the union.

1848

California Gold Rush

James Marshall discovers gold at Sutter's Mill in California, forever changing the state and the country. Thousands of miners cross the country or sail around Cape Horn to find their fortune. Few make money, but grocers and shop owners prosper. The California population booms to almost 400,000 by the start of the Civil War.

Seneca Falls Convention in New York

A major meeting of supporters of women's rights, this is the first shot in the battle for women's suffrage that will end with the passage of the 19th amendment in 1919. The convention produces a *Declaration of Sentiments*, that declares, "We hold these truths to be self-evident: that all men and women are created equal..."

★1848★	ZACHARY TAYLOR			12

CANDIDATE	PARTY	ELECTORAL VOTE	POPULAR VOTE
Zachary Taylor Millard Fillmore	*Whig*	163	1,361,393
Lewis Cass William Butler	*Democratic*	127	1,223,460
Martin Van Buren Charles Adams	*Free Soil*	0	291,501

Polk accomplished many of his goals, but is in bad health and decides not to run for re-election. He dies four months after leaving office. Polk had ended the Mexican-American War, and the Whigs pick a popular hero from that war, Zachary Taylor. This election is the first presidential election held on the same day in every state. Taylor wins with less than 50% of the popular vote due to the showing of the Free Soil Party.

1850— **Underground Railroad**

The escaped slave Harriet Tubman uses the Underground Railroad to help escaped slaves. This network of people and safe houses was started by the Quakers in the 1790s, and will save 60,000 slaves during its lifetime.

★1850★	MILLARD FILLMORE	13

President Taylor dies from an illness less than halfway through his term and Vice President Fillmore takes over. He will be the last Whig to hold the high office.

Compromise of 1850

California is admitted as a free state; Utah and New Mexico's slave status will be decided by their voters; and the slave trade is outlawed in Washington, D.C. The compromise also contains the Fugitive Slave Act which requires all runaway slaves be arrested and returned to their masters.

1851— ***America's Cup* competition starts**

The U.S. sailboat *America* wins a yacht race in England, starting an international competition for the trophy now known as the *America's Cup.*

1852 ┤ ***Uncle Tom's Cabin* is published**

Harriet Beecher Stowe writes the famous anti-slavery book that helps ignite anti-slavery sentiment.

★1852★   FRANKLIN PIERCE   14

CANDIDATE	PARTY	ELECTORAL VOTE	POPULAR VOTE
Franklin Pierce William King	Democratic	254	1,607,510
Winfield Scott William Graham	Whig	42	1,386,942

The Whigs nominates Mexican-American War hero General Scott instead of the incumbent Fillmore. The Democrats have a unknown candidate in Pierce, whose obscurity the Whigs try to use in their campaigning. Other parties also run candidates, including the Free Soil, Union, and Southern Rights parties.

1854 ┤ **Gadsden Treaty**

A treaty with Mexico gives U.S. territory in Arizona and New Mexico in return for $10 million. The U.S. hopes to build a railroad through the territory. It is the last major acquisition of land by the U.S.

Kansas-Nebraska Act

The government creates the territories of Kansas and Nebraska, allows those territories to determine their own slavery laws, and repeals the Missouri Compromise.

Republican Party founded as an anti-slavery party

The new party opposes slavery and believes in the modernization of the America, free land for farmers, modern banking, and industry. They believe that free labor is superior to slave labor. John Fremont is their first candidate in 1856.

★1856★   JAMES BUCHANAN   15

CANDIDATE	PARTY	ELECTORAL VOTE	POPULAR VOTE
James Buchanan John Breckinridge	Democratic	174	1,836,072
John Fremont William Dayton	Republican	114	1,342,345
Millard Fillmore Andrew Donelson	Know-Nothing	8	873,053

The incumbent Pierce loses the nomination to Buchanan, the UK Ambassador. The new Republican party selects California Senator and Governor John Fremont. He campaigns against the Kansas-Nebraska Act and expansion of slavery, while Buchanan warns that Fremont's actions will lead to civil war. The *Know-Nothing Party* ignores slavery and runs on an anti-immigration platform. Fremont receives almost no votes from any slave state.

1857 **Supreme Court *Dred Scott* decision**

The slave Dred Scott has lived with his owner in free states and believes himself free. The Supreme Court rules that slaves and their descendents are not protected by the Constitution and thus cannot be citizens. It also rules that Congress cannot prohibit slavery in territories, and that slaves cannot be taken away from their legal owners. The decision comes to be known as one of the worst Supreme Court decisions in history.

First passenger elevator

Elisha Otis installs the world's first passenger elevator in a 5-story building in New York City. (The original elevator is still in working condition in the building.)

1859 **Silver Comstock Lode in Nevada**

A huge silver discovery is made under Virginia City, Nevada, sparking another mad rush similar to the Gold Rush of the decade before. Huge fortunes are made and much of the wealth flows to San Francisco. The mines last into the 1870s.

John Brown's Revolt at Harper's Ferry

The white, radical abolitionist John Brown and his followers seize a federal armory at Harper's Ferry, Virginia, intending to arm slaves and start an insurrection. He is captured, tried for treason by Virginia, and executed. His abolitionist activities, capture, and subsequent execution are important events leading to the Civil War, and he is a hero to many in the North. An abolitionist song about Brown, *John Brown's Body*, is the basis for the stirring song *The Battle Hymn of the Republic,* written by Julia Ward Howe.

1860 **Pony Express**

William Russell starts a service to deliver mail from Missouri to Sacramento in 10 days, using 500 horses ridden by 80 riders, 40 in each direction. The service goes bankrupt in two years due to the invention of the telegraph.

Candidate	Party	Electoral Vote	Popular Vote
Abraham Lincoln Hannibal Hamlin	Republican	180	1,865,908
Stephen Douglas Herschel Johnson	Democratic	12	1,380,201
John Breckinridge Joseph Lane	Southern Democratic	72	848,019
John Bell Edward Everett	Constitutional Union	39	590,901

The 1860 election is dominated by the impending civil war. The issues of slavery and states' rights divide the Democratic Party into a Northern and Southern faction. Douglas is the first presidential candidate to campaign in person throughout the country. Remnants of the Whig and Know-Nothing parties form the Constitutional Union Party. The country is split right down regional lines—Lincoln does not receive a single electoral vote from a southern state. He is not even on the ballot in ten southern states. Within a month of his election, southern states start seceding from the Union.

South Carolina secedes from the Union on December 20
Lincoln receives no electoral votes from any Southern state, and South Carolina wastes no time in leaving the nation.

1861 **Civil War engulfs the nation**

The war pits the North, a commercial and industrial region that has outlawed slavery and relies on immigrants, against the South, which relies on farming, cotton, and slaves. However, the South has many great military leaders, including their new top general, the Virginian Robert E. Lee. Foreign countries rely on Northern exports and markets, but use the South mainly as a source of cotton. The South also views the slavery issue as a state's right issue.

Photography documents the Civil War
It is the first war to be documented by the new technology of photography, used by photographers like Mathew Brady.

Telegraph connects the coasts
A transcontinental telegraph wire is connected allowing telegrams to be sent from coast to coast. The Western Union Telegraph Company runs one line eastward from Carson City, and another line westward from Omaha, Nebraska. Stringing three to eight miles of wire a day, the lines meet in Salt Lake City.

1861 ┤ **The fighting begins at Fort Sumter**

The rest of the South secedes: Mississippi, Florida, Alabama, Arkansas, Louisiana, Georgia, Texas, Virginia, North Carolina, and Tennessee—most before Lincoln's inauguration. They form the the Confederate States of America (CSA) with Jefferson Davis as president, and Richmond, Virginia their capital. Eleven Southern states with a population of 9 million (including 3 million slaves) confront 23 Northern states with a population of 22 million. The Union troops wear blue uniforms, while the South wears gray. The American Civil War (War Between the States) starts with the Confederate attack on Fort Sumter, South Carolina on April 12, 1861. Major Anderson surrenders the fort after 4,000 rounds have been fired...but no one is killed.

First Battle of Bull Run (First Battle of Manassas)

The first major engagement takes place near Washington. "Stonewall" Jackson leads the rebels to defeat the overconfident Northern troops. Sightseers from Washington, anticipating an easy northern victory, clog the roads while fleeing back to Washington.

1862 ┤ **Ironclads *Monitor* and *Virginia***

The South's new ironclad *Virginia* (built from the burned hull of the USS *Merrimack*) destroys Union ships in Chesapeake Bay with impunity, killing 240 sailors. The just-finished Northern ironclad, *Monitor*, steams into battle the next day and fights the *Virginia* to a stalemate. The era of ironclad ships has arrived.

Battle of Shiloh, Tennessee

A Union army under Ulysses Grant meets the Confederates in Tennessee in a bloody battle that kills 3,600 soldiers.

Homestead Act of 1862

The government encourages settlement of the West by offering 160 acres of public land in return for living on the land for 5 years and improving it.

Indian attacks continue

The Santee Sioux kill hundreds of Minnesota settlers but surrender the next year. Thirty-eight Indians are convicted and hung by the government. The Indian attacks in the West continue throughout the Civil War.

1862

Battle of Antietam, Maryland

The first major clash on Northern soil results in the bloodiest one-day battle in American history with 23,000 casualties.

First *Medal of Honor* presented

America's first *Medal of Honor* is given to Private Jacob Parrott for his bravery in commandeering the Confederate railroad engine *General* in Georgia.

1863

Emancipation Proclamation takes effect on January 1

Lincoln frees all slaves in the outlaw confederate states and areas still in rebellion. It does not address slavery anywhere else...this has to wait until the 13th amendment is passed.

New York City Draft Riots

A week of violent rioting breaks out in New York City in what will be the worst civil insurrection in our history. Anywhere from 120 to 2,000 people are killed, and 11 blacks are lynched. President Lincoln has just issued the Emancipation Proclamation, and many worry about the loss of jobs due to freed slaves fleeing northward. The government issues a new draft law, making all males between 20 and 35, and unmarried men between 35 and 45, subject to military conscription. The men are entered into a national lottery, but can pay the government $300 to be exempt, or can hire a substitute. Blacks are exempt from the lottery, since they are not considered citizens. The rioters are initially angry at the unfair draft law which targets the poorer working class, but the riots soon turn racial, and many blacks are killed. Lincoln sends in federal troops to restore order.

Battle of Gettysburg

General Robert E. Lee meets the Union troops in July at a sleepy town in Pennsylvania in what is to be the high-water mark for the Confederacy in the war. The bloody 3-day battle results in casualties of 25,000 on each side. On the last day of battle on July 3, General Pickett leads a suicidal charge up Cemetery Ridge resulting in thousands of casualties. General Lee retreats to Virginia, and only the lack of pursuit by the Northern General George Meade keeps Lee's army from being completely destroyed.

1863
Mississippi River controlled by North
Grant defeats the rebels at Vicksburg, giving the North control of the river, and splitting the South in two.

Gettysburg Address
President Lincoln delivers one of the most memorable speeches in our history at the dedication of the Gettysburg cemetery. His two-minute speech follows Edward Everett's two-hour talk which truly will be little noted nor long remembered.

1864
Lincoln appoints U.S. Grant leader of the Northern Army
Grant proceeds to use brute force to wear down and defeat the South. The Battle of the Wilderness results in 18,000 Union casualties, and the Spotsylvania Courthouse Battle kills or wounds another 18,000 troops.

CSS *Hunley* sinks the USS *Housatonic*

The Confederate submarine *Hunley* attacks and sinks the Union ship in Charleston harbor, but is lost with her crew of eight and never found again until 1995. This is the first time in history a submarine sinks a enemy ship.

First burial in Arlington Cemetery
Considering General Lee a traitor, the Union converts his estate outside the capital to a military cemetery. (Today, it holds 300,000 graves, including one for President John Kennedy, and the Tomb of the Unknown Soldier.)

Battle of Mobile Bay

Admiral Farragut leads Union ships against the Confederate fort at Mobile Bay, Alabama. The water is heavily mined (mines were then called torpedoes) and one of his ships strikes a mine, sinking with heavy loss of life. The attack falters, but Farragut seizes the initiative and commands, "Damn the torpedoes! Full speed ahead!" The Union ships proceed to win the battle.

Sherman's "March to the Sea"

The Union General William T. Sherman marches through Georgia all the way to the ocean, destroying everything in his path and burning Atlanta. His memory will forever be reviled by true Southerners.

★1864★ Abraham Lincoln re-elected

Candidate	Party	Electoral Vote	Popular Vote
Abraham Lincoln Andrew Johnson	National Union	212	2,218,388
George McClellan George Pendleton	Democratic	21	1,812,807

The Republican party is divided over slavery, and War Democrats join with some Republicans to form the National Union Party which nominates Lincoln. The Democrats are also divided, and run General McClellan as a "peace candidate" pushing for a negotiated peace. The Republicans run John Fremont until he withdraws, fearing that his entry will help McClellan. Confederate victories make the election outcome uncertain, but the victory in Atlanta in September turns sentiment towards Lincoln and final victory against the South. Lincoln wins the election with strong support from the military, who are allowed to vote from the field for the first time. His slogan is "Don't change horses in the middle of a stream."

1865

The Civil War ends at Appomattox Courthouse, April 9

General Grant finally captures the Confederate capital of Richmond. General Lee surrenders the Army of Northern Virginia at Appomattox Courthouse, Virginia. Grant chooses not to humiliate the losers since they are now his countrymen again. He allows Lee's men to keep their horses and sidearms, and return home freely. The bloody struggle ends. More than 500,000 lives have been lost. Southern states will have to accept the 13th amendment ending slavery as a condition to being re-admitted to the Union. By the end of the war, more than ten percent of the Union soldiers are black.

President Lincoln assassinated

On April 14, John Wilkes Booth, an actor and southern sympathizer, shoots Lincoln in the head at Ford Theater. The shooting is part of simultaneous plans to kill the Vice President and Secretary of State. President Lincoln dies, and Secretary Seward is seriously injured. Booth escapes to Virginia after being treated by Dr. Samuel Mudd for a broken leg. He is surrounded a few days later by troops and killed. Lincoln's loss is a severe blow to the reconstruction of the South, and has enormous, negative long-term consequences. Dr. Mudd is imprisoned for four years for his actions.

1865 ANDREW JOHNSON 17

After Lincoln's assassination, Vice President Johnson becomes president. He will preside over Reconstruction for the next four years. He had been a Southern Senator before the war and his pro-South policies will anger Republicans.

Steamboat *Sultana* blows up

The steamboat returning Union veterans from the South blows up on the Mississippi River in the worst U.S. maritime disaster, killing 1,700.

★ 13ᵀᴴ AMENDMENT ★

Abolishes slavery and involuntary servitude except as punishment for a criminal conviction.

1866

Transatlantic cable is completed

Cyrus W. Field, after a number of failed attempts, finally lays a 2000-mile transatlantic cable using the world's largest steamship, the *Great Eastern*. Europe and America are finally connected by telegraph.

Reconstruction of the South begins

President Johnson is sympathetic to the South. His rush to welcome southern states back into the Union, and his vetoes of civil rights bills (he vetoes the *Civil Rights Act of 1866*), make him unpopular. The reconstruction of the South is extremely difficult since the former slaves were the backbone of the economy.

1867

Seward's Folly—the purchase of Alaska

Secretary of State Seward (who narrowly escaped assassination when Lincoln was shot) purchases Alaska from the Russians for only $7.2 million. He is publicly ridiculed for the purchase. Pictured is the original check given to the Russians for the purchase.

1868

Impeachment of President Andrew Johnson

Johnson is unpopular even before he replaces some cabinet members illegally, thus violating the Tenure of Office Act. He is impeached, becoming the first sitting U.S. President to be impeached. He is acquitted by a margin of one vote.

Confederates are pardoned

President Johnson grants an unconditional pardon to former Confederate soldiers.

1868

★ 14ᵀᴴ AMENDMENT ★

Ensures that all ex-slaves have full citizenship rights and deals with other post-Civil War issues.

★1868★ ULYSSES S. GRANT 18

CANDIDATE	PARTY	ELECTORAL VOTE	POPULAR VOTE
Ulysses S. Grant Schuyler Colfax	Republican	214	3,013,650
Horatio Seymour Francis Blair, Jr.	Democratic	80	2,708,744

Three former Confederate states are unable to vote in this election as they are not yet restored to the Union. Johnson's impeachment prevents the Democrats from nominating him. They pick Horatio Seymour instead. The Republican Party regroups, knowing they need a strong figure to defeat the Democrats who are also strong in the North. The Republicans back radical reconstruction for the South and pick the popular General Grant. The popular vote is close, but Grant easily wins the electoral vote.

1869

Transcontinental Railroad completed on May 10, 1869

They started building the railroad in 1863 during the war. The Central Pacific Railroad pushed from California eastward to Utah, run by a group of men known as "The Big Four"; Collis Huntington, Mark Hopkins, Charles Crocker, and Leland Stanford. These men have made their fortunes in the West and bankrolled the railroad to further their fortunes. The Union Pacific Railroad pushed westward from Omaha. The tracks meet at Promontory Summit, Utah. The country is finally connected, coast to coast. The trip from Omaha to Sacramento now takes only 12 days.

Grand Canyon explored

John Wesley Powell makes a wild trip down the Colorado River with four boats. After three months and a thousand miles, he reaches open country, finishing the first known trip through the Grand Canyon.

1870

★ 15ᵀᴴ AMENDMENT ★

Protects the voting right of ex-slaves.

1870

Southern states are slow to change

The South uses a legal loophole to require literacy tests to vote, essentially prohibiting former slaves from voting. States that balk at approving the 14th amendment are threatened with military occupation, causing many to question whether the amendment is fairly passed. The Ku Klux Klan emerges to terrorize former slaves.

First black U.S. Senator

Hiram R. Revels, a Mississippi Republican, is elected U.S. Senator by the state legislature, which is the normal election procedure at this time, to fill a vacant seat. Southern Democrats oppose his election, arguing that no black man was a citizen before the 1868 passage of the 14th Amendment, and the Constitution requires nine years of citizenship to qualify for the Senate. His supporters claim that the *Dred Scott* decision applied only to blacks of pure African blood, and Revels is of mixed black and white ancestry, so he has always been a citizen. He wins his case and becomes the first black United States Senator on February 25.

The *Wild West* is settled

With the war over, thousands of ex-soldiers head west to become cowboys, ranchers, and drifters. This movement is facilitated by the new transcontinental railroad and homestead acts that encourage new settlements. New inventions like the steel plow, windmill (for pumping water), and barbed wire (to fence livestock) open vast areas for farming and ranching. The huge herds of 50 million buffalo will soon vanish.

The rise of the robber barons

The late 1800s give rise to the so-called "robber barons" of industry who take advantage of new technologies, inventions, and discoveries to amass vast fortunes. They often use monopolistic practices to corner markets and drive out competition. This leads to the passage of anti-trust laws, and the rise of unions across the country to protect workers.

- John D. Rockefeller starts the Standard Oil Company in 1870 after oil is discovered in 1859.
- Jay Gould tries to corner the gold market with the help of President Grant, but instead causes the Panic of 1869.
- J.P. Morgan owns half of the country's railroads by 1900.
- James Duke corners the tobacco market.

The robber barons give back

Andrew Carnegie makes a fortune in steel but starts the trend of helping society with his money, giving away more than $350 million and founding thousands of public libraries. The Rockefellers create Rockefeller Center in New York City. Leland Stanford founds Stanford University. James Duke helps found Duke University. Henry Frick funds the Frick Museum in New York City.

1871 ─┤ **Georgia is the last state readmitted to the Union**
Georgia becomes the last state to ratify the Fifteenth Amendment in 1870. The following year, she is readmitted to the Union.

Great Chicago Fire

Mrs. O'Leary's cow starts a fire in her barn that quickly spreads and destroys $200 million of property and kills 300 people in Chicago.

Peshtigo Fire kills 1,000 on same day
On the same day as the Chicago Fire, the worst forest fire in American history sweeps northern Wisconsin and Michigan, destroying millions of dollars of property and timber.

1872 ─┤ **Yellowstone becomes the first National Park**
The government makes Yellowstone, located mostly in present-day Wyoming, the world's first National Park. Since it is located in territory that has not yet become part of any state, the federal government has to assume control.

★1872★ ULYSSES S. GRANT RE-ELECTED

CANDIDATE	PARTY	ELECTORAL VOTE	POPULAR VOTE
Ulysses S. Grant Henry Wilson	Republican	286	3,598,235
Horace Greeley G. Gratz Brown	Liberal Republican	66	2,834,761

The Republicans pick Henry Wilson to be Grant's new running mate. Liberal Republicans and Democrats back Horace Greeley on a Liberal Republican ticket. Their party wants civil service reform and improvements in conditions in the South. After the election but before the electors meet to cast their votes, Greeley dies. This frees his electors who vote for other candidates.

Susan B. Anthony casts a vote

She breaks the law by casting a vote in the presidential election and is arrested 2 weeks later.

1875 ─┤ **First Kentucky Derby run in Louisville**
The event will be held every year on the first Saturday in May as the first race in the coveted Triple Crown of horse racing—the Kentucky Derby, Preakness Stakes, and Belmont Stakes.

1876— **Custer's Last Stand**

In 1868, Civil War hero General George Custer had killed Chief Black Kettle at the Battle of Washita along with a hundred other Indians. In 1876, Custer is ambushed by the Sioux at Little Big Horn in Montana. Custer and his 250 men are wiped out.

⋆1876⋆   RUTHERFORD B. HAYES   19

CANDIDATE	PARTY	ELECTORAL VOTE	POPULAR VOTE
Rutherford B. Hayes William Wheeler	*Republican*	185	4,036,572
Samuel Tilden Thomas Hendricks	*Democratic*	184	4,284,020

In one of the most disputed elections in our history, Tilden beats Hayes in the popular vote and leads by 19 electoral votes with 20 votes in dispute in three states. After a lengthy legal battle, Hayes is awarded the twenty votes and becomes president. In return for agreeing to this outcome, the Democrats get federal troops removed from southern states, effectively ending Reconstruction. This is a huge setback to the recovery in the South and to the welfare of the freed slaves.

1877— **First telephone lines installed in Boston**
Alexander Graham Bell had patented the telephone a year earlier and tested it with his assistant Thomas Watson.

1878— **Thomas Edison receives patent for phonograph**

He later receives a patent for the first practical incandescent light bulb that is finally bright enough and long-lasting.

⋆1880⋆   JAMES A. GARFIELD   20

CANDIDATE	PARTY	ELECTORAL VOTE	POPULAR VOTE
James A. Garfield Chester A. Arthur	*Republican*	214	4,446,158
Winfield S. Hancock William English	*Democratic*	155	4,444,260

Hayes does not seek reelection, honoring his earlier promises. Ulysses Grant tries for the Republican spot and is the early favorite at their convention. Garfield is there as a delegate giving a speech in support of John Sherman for president, but soon finds himself nominated. The delegates are stalemated for 35 ballots, but Garfield edges out Grant on the next vote. The Democrats nominate Civil War General Winfield S. Hancock. The popular vote difference is razor-thin at only 1,898 votes, but Garfield easily wins the electoral count.

★1881★   CHESTER A. ARTHUR   21

President Garfield is shot on July 2 by Charles J. Guiteau after less than a year in office. Guiteau shouts "I am a Stalwart. Arthur is now President." Arthur is a member of the Stalwart faction of the Republican Party, but there is no apparent conspiracy, and the deranged Guiteau is hanged a year later. Garfield lingers until dying on September 19, and Arthur becomes president. Arthur becomes a champion of civil service reform and leaves office 4 years later with high marks.

Shootout at the O.K. Corral in Tombstone, Arizona

The Earp brothers and Doc Holliday shoot it out with the Clinton gang, killing three of the gang.

1882 — Chinese Exclusion Act signed

Chinese immigration exploded during the building of the Transcontinental Railroad. However, racism and the lack of jobs leads to calls to restrict their immigration. This law is supposed to last only ten years, but will be extended and stay in effect until 1943, and effectively bars all Chinese immigrants from entering the country.

1883 — Pendleton Civil Service Reform Act passes

Pushed by Arthur, it stipulates that government jobs should be awarded based on merit, not on connections or politics.

★1884★   GROVER CLEVELAND   22

CANDIDATE	PARTY	ELECTORAL VOTE	POPULAR VOTE
Grover Cleveland Thomas Hendricks	Democratic	219	4,874,621
James Blaine John Logan	Republican	182	4,848,936

The 1884 election is marred by a new level of personal attacks. Stories are leaked that Cleveland had fathered a child out of wedlock, while Blaine loses votes due to his alleged anti-Catholic sentiments which may have cost him the election. Cleveland wins by winning New York by the thinnest of margins, only 1,047 votes, giving him the needed electoral votes. He becomes the first Democrat president since 1856. The Republican convention produces the now famous *Sherman Pledge* made by General Sherman when he is pressured to run. He essentially states, "If drafted, I will not run; if nominated, I will not accept; if elected, I will not serve."

1884 — First roller coaster opens at Coney Island, NY

1885 — Washington Monument is dedicated

The 555-foot obelisk was started in 1848, but work stopped during the Civil War. When restarted in 1876, the same marble couldn't be found, so the finished tower is of two distinct colors. It is the tallest building in the world until the Eiffel tower is finished in 1887.

1886 — Apache Geronimo is arrested

He has been fighting the government since 1850. His arrest ends major Indian resistance in the country. Almost 250,000 Native Americans are now living on 187 reservations around the country.

An earthquake destroys Charleston, SC

The August 31 intraplate earthquake is one of most powerful ever to strike the eastern U.S. Two thousand buildings are damaged and 100 lives are lost.

Statue of Liberty dedicated

The French gift now welcomes visitors and immigrants from her island perch in New York harbor. The torch is 305 feet from the ground.

American Federation of Labor (AFL) is founded

Samuel Gompers founds first major labor union.

1887 — Interstate Commerce Act of 1887

The first federal law regulating private industry controls the railroad industry and curtail its monopolistic practices. It also creates the Interstate Commerce Commission.

★1888★   BENJAMIN HARRISON   23

CANDIDATE	PARTY	ELECTORAL VOTE	POPULAR VOTE
Benjamin Harrison Levi Morton	Republican	233	5,443,892
Grover Cleveland Allen Thurman	Democratic	168	5,534,488

Cleveland is running for a second term supporting a tariff reduction, while Harrison opposes the reduction. Cleveland wins the popular vote, but loses the election due to the loss of his home state of New York by only 1% of the vote. This is caused by dirty tricks by the Republicans who publish a letter from the British ambassador supposedly recommending Cleveland as the best candidate from the British point of view. This enrages the Irish-American voters who then vote for Harrison. Harrison also backs a high tariff which gains him votes.

1889 — Oklahoma Land Rush

At noon on April 22, a bugle sounds and 50,000 settlers rush into Oklahoma Territory to claim free land, resulting in more Indian relocation and eventual  statehood for Oklahoma. Each settler can claim 160 acres in exchange for living there and improving the land.

Johnstown Flood

A Pennsylvania dam collapses on May 31, sending twenty million tons of debris and water downstream to destroy the town of Johnstown, killing more than 2,000 people.

Kodak cameras go on sale

Photography is now available to every-one. The first camera takes round pictures on a 100-exposure roll of film.

1890 — Yosemite Valley becomes a National Park

 Naturalist John Muir convinces the government to officially protect the park. The valley features majestic granite peaks carved by ancient glaciers, including the iconic Half Dome and El Capitan.

Sherman Antitrust Act

The government prohibits monopolies in order to stimulate competition and lower prices.

Massacre at Wounded Knee Creek

U.S. troops accidently kill the influential Chief Sitting Bull while trying to arrest him. Two weeks later, the army surrounds Indians under Chief Big Foot at Wounded Knee Creek, South Dakota. The Indians are not hostile and have almost no weapons.

CHIEF SITTING BULL

Something happens and the U.S. troops open fire and kill more than 150 men, women and children. Twenty-five U.S. troopers are also killed, mostly by their own fire.

Western frontier closes

Though there was never an official frontier nor any way to know when it is "closed", the push westward changes around this time. The railroad has been built, the Indian resistance has ended, most free land has been given away, the gold rush is over, and civilization has reached most towns. Many fear American drive and ingenuity will end along with the frontier…but they don't know what the next century has in store.

1892

Ellis Island Immigration Station opens

Until its closure in 1954, more than 12 million immigrants will come through this station, located on an island in New York Harbor. It can process up to 5,000 immigrants each day. Most immigrants spend less than a day on the island. Those found with health problems are held in the island's hospital. Around 2% are denied admission to the U.S. due to health problems or criminal background. (Today, almost 40% of American citizens are descendents of immigrants who came through Ellis Island.)

⋆1892⋆   GROVER CLEVELAND   24

CANDIDATE	PARTY	ELECTORAL VOTE	POPULAR VOTE
Grover Cleveland Adlai Stevenson	Democratic	277	5,556,918
Benjamin Harrison Whitelaw Reid	Republican	145	5,176,108
James Weaver James Field	Populist	22	1,041,028

Cleveland becomes the only president to serve two non-consecutive terms, being the 22nd and 24th president. Currency policy is a major issue, and the new Populist Party makes a strong showing. Cleveland is against free coinage of silver, losing him support from western states. He also faces opposition from the New York Tammany organization. President Harrison's wife falls ill and dies two weeks before the election, putting a stop to further campaigning by all candidates.

1893

Cherokee Strip Land Run

The largest land rush in the history of the world takes place at Cherokee Strip in Oklahoma, on land purchased from the Cherokees for $8.5 million. More than 100,000 settlers wait at the starting line on September 16. When the gun fires at noon, they gallop out to claim their share of 7,000,000 acres. A smaller run in 1895 will be the last American land run.

1896

Plessy v. Ferguson

Another bad Supreme Court decision holds that segregation in businesses is legal under a doctrine of "separate but equal." This is used to justify much of the future segregation in the South until it is essentially overturned by the 1954 *Brown v. Board of Education* ruling.

★1896★   William McKinley   25

Candidate	Party	Electoral Vote	Popular Vote
William McKinley Garret Hobart	Republican	271	7,104,779
William Jennings Bryan Arthur Sewall	Democratic	176	6,502,925

The 1896 election heralds the disappearance of the old Democratic Party that favored small government and free trade. Bryan is strong in western and rural America, and among the Populist Party and silver backers. The Republicans spend five times what the Democrats spend, and hire speakers to canvas the country painting Bryan as a dangerous candidate. A big issue is whether to stay on the gold standard, or move to a silver standard pushed by Bryan, who feels it will expand the economy. McKinley's victory makes the gold standard and industrial growth important into the next century.

1897 — Yukon Gold Rush lures prospectors to Alaska

Gold is discovered along the Klondike River and thousands of Americans travel to Alaska to reach the goldfields.

1898 — Single-handed sail around the world in the *Spray*

Joshua Slocum becomes the first person to sail around the world single-handed when he returns to Rhode Island on his 36-foot sailboat *Spray*. He has spent three years sailing 46,000 miles westward around the world.

Spanish-American War starts

Hearst newspapers are accused of helping to incite unrest in Cuba in order to sell newspapers, so called "yellow journalism." The USS *Maine* blows up in Havana Harbor, Cuba on February 15, killing 266. War is declared by both sides in April. Admiral Dewey attacks and destroys the Spanish fleet in Manila, Philippines. Troops land in Cuba, including Teddy Roosevelt and his Rough Riders, and defeat the Spanish at the critical battle of San Juan Hill. The *Buffalo Soldiers* also see action, earning 5 Medals of Honor. These are the black regiments that were formed in 1866.

Treaty of Paris ends Spanish-American War

The war ends four months later. Cuba gains her independence, but the U.S. reserves the right to a base at Guantanamo Bay. The U.S. also gets control of Puerto Rico, Guam, and the Philippines for $20 million, and annexes Hawaii.

1899 **American Samoa acquired**
American gains control of Samoa in a treaty with Great Britain and Germany.

1 9 0 0

1900 **Galveston hurricane kills 8,000 people**
The September 8th hurricane completely destroys Galveston, Texas, the "Jewel of Texas." The storm will remain the worst natural disaster in U.S. history in terms of lives lost.

★1900★ WILLIAM MCKINLEY RE-ELECTED

CANDIDATE	PARTY	ELECTORAL VOTE	POPULAR VOTE
William McKinley Theodore Roosevelt	Republican	292	7,228,864
William Jennings Bryan Adlai Stevenson	Democratic	155	6,370,932

In a rematch of the 1896 election, McKinley again defeats Bryan. McKinley adds a new vice president, New York Governor Theodore Roosevelt. The current vice president, Garret Hobart, had died in 1899, leaving the office vacant until the election. The successful ending to the Spanish-American War and a return to prosperity ensures McKinley's victory.

★1901★ TEDDY ROOSEVELT 26

Anarchist Leon Czolgosz shoots President McKinley at the Pan-American Exposition in Buffalo, New York on September 6. McKinley appears to recover, but dies on September 14. His shooting leads to Secret Service protection being assigned to all future presidents. At 42, Roosevelt becomes the youngest U.S. President in history. He pushes a policy of business regulation.

Oil is discovered in Texas
An oil well at Spindletop near Beaumont, Texas explodes in a 100-foot geyser that won't be capped for 9 days. Texas enters the industrial age, and oil prices drop to 3 cents a barrel.

1903 **Panama Canal Zone is acquired by treaty**
Columbia refuses to ratify a proposed treaty covering the rights to a canal across Columbia, and President Roosevelt decides instead to help Panama set up a new government in return for a signed treaty for a canal across Panama.

1903

Wright Brothers fly

The Wright Brothers conduct the first heavier-than-air flight at Kill Devil Hill in North Carolina. The flight lasts 12 seconds and covers 120 feet. By 1905, their flights will last more than 30 minutes.

★**1904**★ TEDDY ROOSEVELT RE-ELECTED

CANDIDATE	PARTY	ELECTORAL VOTE	POPULAR VOTE
Theodore Roosevelt Charles Fairbanks	Republican	336	7,630,457
Alton Parker Henry Davis	Democratic	140	5,083,880

Roosevelt is easily picked as his party's candidate with the addition of the more conservative Fairbanks as running mate. The Republican platform calls for a protective tariff, a strong navy, and the gold standard. Both candidates have very similar campaign platforms, both believing in the gold standard and the importance of labor unions. In the end, Roosevelt's popularity gives him an enormous margin in his victory. He wins America's first Nobel Peace Prize in 1906 for helping to end the Russo-Japanese War.

1906

San Francisco Earthquake

A magnitude 7.9 earthquake strikes San Francisco at dawn. Most of the damage is done by fires started by the earthquake, fueled by breaks in natural gas lines, and with fighting hampered by breaks in water mains. Up to 3,000 die, and 4 square miles of the city are destroyed.

1907

Monongah mine explosion in West Virginia

A coal mine explosion in Monongah kills 362 miners, making it the worst mining disaster in U.S. history.

Great White Fleet circles the world

Roosevelt sends a fleet of 16 battleships around the world to project American military and naval power.

1908

FBI established as Bureau of Investigation

First Model-T automobile produced

Henry Ford makes an affordable car and works on improving the assembly line which ends up cutting production time to make one car from twelve hours to only 90 minutes. He promises customers "a car painted any color that he wants so long as it is black."

1908 — **Grand Canyon becomes a National Monument**
President Roosevelt declares the Grand Canyon a national monument. The 277-mile long canyon has been carved by the Colorado River over the last 17 million years.

★1908★   WILLIAM HOWARD TAFT   27

CANDIDATE	PARTY	ELECTORAL VOTE	POPULAR VOTE
William Howard Taft James Sherman	Republican	321	7,678,395
William Jennings Bryan John Kern	Democratic	162	6,408,984

Roosevelt most likely would have won this election, but he has promised not to run again. His party picks his Secretary of War, Howard Taft, to make the run. The Democrats try again with William Bryan, though the silver issue is not as important now. Bryan ends up with the worst loss of his three attempts.

1909 — **NAACP founded on February 12**
The National Association for the Advancement of Colored People (NAACP) is founded on February 12, 1909, the 100th anniversary of the birth of Abraham Lincoln.

Robert Peary reaches the North Pole
The Navy Commander is first to reach the North Pole, accompanied by 4 Inuit guides, and his black assistant, Matthew Henson. There will be continual debate over the next century over whether he actually made it to the Pole.

1910 — **Boy Scouts of America founded**

Robert Baden-Powell had started Scouting in England in 1907. W.D. Boyce visits England in 1909 and learns of scouting. He returns to the U.S. and founds the Boy Scouts of America the next year. It will grow to host over 4.5 million members, and claim presidents, executives, teachers, police officers, and astronauts as members.

CANDIDATE	PARTY	ELECTORAL VOTE	POPULAR VOTE
Woodrow Wilson Thomas Marshall	Democratic	435	6,296,284
Theodore Roosevelt Hiram Johnson	Progressive	88	4,122,721
William Howard Taft Nicholas Butler	Republican	8	3,486,242
Eugene V. Debs Emil Seidel	Socialist	0	901,551

The incumbent President Taft wins the Republican nomination, forcing Theodore Roosevelt to create his own Progressive Party. He tells the press he feels as strong as a "bull moose," earning his party the name, "Bull Moose Party." Wilson is nominated on the 46th ballot, thanks in part to the support of William Jennings Bryan. This is the first election where all 48 states cast votes, and the last election where the second place finisher is neither a Republican nor a Democrat. Taft's vice president, James Sherman, dies one week before the election, further dividing his party. Taft wins only eight electoral votes, the worst defeat ever for a sitting president and for the Republicans. Roosevelt has his own problems, surviving an assassination attempt on October 14 in Wisconsin, the bullet lodging in the 50-page speech in his pocket. Wilson wins the election in an electoral landslide.

Girl Scouts of America founded

Juliette Low meets Scout founder Robert Baden-Powell in England and returns to Savannah, Georgia to start the organization in the United States.

RMS *Titanic* sinks

The British passenger ship, *Titanic*, hits an iceberg and sinks, killing more than 1,400 people. The largest passenger ship in the world at 882 feet, she is on her maiden voyage from South-hampton, England with 2,223 people on board. She only has enough life-boats for one-half of the passengers,  and many are only half-filled leaving the sinking ship.

Wilson's early actions

Wilson had run on a progressive platform and promises to keep the U.S. out of any European war. He introduces a federal income tax and strengthens anti-trust laws. He also orders the Civil Service segregated, and nominates segregationists to cabinet posts.

1913 — **The Lincoln Highway connects the country**

The 3,389 mile route across the country connects Times Square in New York City with Lincoln Park in San Francisco, and is the first continuous road across the country. It will still take a motorist 20 to 30 days to drive across the country.

★ **16ᵀᴴ AMENDMENT** ★

Authorizes the collection of federal income tax.

★ **17ᵀᴴ AMENDMENT** ★

Changes the election of Senators from state legislatures to the voters of each state.

1914 — **World War I starts**

The June 28, 1914 assassination of Archduke Ferdinand in Sarajevo touches off a great world war. Austria-Hungary, Germany, Turkey, and Italy fight against the Allies consisting primarily of England, France, Belgium, Greece, and Russia. Italy eventually changes sides. Russia soon falls to Communism during the Bolshevik revolution and makes a separate peace with Germany. President Wilson declares American neutral. She will not enter the war until 1917. German forces sweep through Europe but stop at the Marne River, establishing a 4-year stalemate of trench warfare at its worst, including poison gas and the deaths of 200,000.

Panama Canal opens

George Goethals and over 50,000 men dig a canal across the 50-mile isthmus, fighting mud slides and yellow fever. An earlier French attempt had resulted in 22,000 worker deaths, while the American attempt loses 5,600 lives.

1915 — **Germans sink the *Lusitania***

A U-boat sinks the British RMS *Lusitania*, killing Americans on board and raising anti-German sentiment.

First phone service across the country

The first phone service is established between New York and San Francisco.

1916 — **Pancho Villa attacks the U.S.**

Pancho Villa is a Mexican Revolutionary General who has been robbing trains, and seizing Mexican haciendas to distribute to peasants. Upset at American support of his rivals, he leads 500 men in an attack on Columbus, New Mexico. Citizens and U.S. soldiers fight off the attack. President Wilson orders General Pershing to pursue Villa into Mexico. This *Pancho Villa Expedition* is unable to find Villa and returns home after nine months.

★1916★ WOODROW WILSON RE-ELECTED

CANDIDATE	PARTY	ELECTORAL VOTE	POPULAR VOTE
Woodrow Wilson Thomas Marshall	Democratic	277	9,126,868
Charles Hughes Charles Fairbanks	Republican	254	8,548,728

Europe is at war, but the U.S. is still not involved. The public is still neutral about entering the war, even though they support Britain and France. Wilson taps this sentiment with his slogan, "He kept us out of war." Republicans pull their party together and select moderate Supreme Court Justice Charles Hughes. The popular vote is close, but the electoral vote is razor-thin. Hughes will win if he carries California, but Wilson wins the state by only 0.4% to clinch the presidency.

First female member of Congress

Jeannette Rankin is elected a U.S. Representative from Montana. Montana had given women the vote in 1914.

1917 ### U.S. acquires Virgin Islands

U.S. buys what are now called the American Virgin Islands from Denmark for $25 million.

America enters World War I

U.S. tries to stay neutral, but German U-boats are sinking ships, including the *Housatonic,* resulting in the loss of American life. The secret "Zimmerman" telegram is decoded by the British revealing German plans for an alliance with Mexico, giving them back American land at war's end. Wilson declares war on April 6, calling it a war to "make the world safe for democracy." The U.S. Army increases from 200,000 to 4 million men. In Europe, General Pershing keeps American troops under U.S. control. At home, Wilson clamps down on civil liberties and freedom of the press.

1918 ### U.S. Marines win the Battle of Belleau Wood

U.S. Marines fight one of their costliest battles ever at Belleau Wood, France, finally pushing back a German attack.

Sergeant Alvin York receives Medal of Honor

The Tennessee sharpshooter attacks a machine gun nest, single-handedly killing 28 German soldiers and capturing 132 others. He receives the Distinguished Service Cross and the French Croix de guerre.

1918 — World War I ends

The armistice ending World War I is signed in a rail car in France, taking effect at 11am on 11/11/1918. The Germans are finally convinced that the Americans have unlimited resources, and know how  to fight. More than 10 million are killed in the war, including more than 110,000 Americans. This day will be commemorated in the U.S. as *Veterans Day*.

Spanish Flu epidemic devastates the world

 The great Spanish Flu epidemic sweeps the world during the war, killing up to 50 million people worldwide, including more than 500,000 Americans.

1919 —

> ★ 18ᵀᴴ AMENDMENT ★
> Prohibits the manufacture and sale of alcohol.

Wilson and the League of Nations

Wilson pushes his "14 points" for bringing world peace and establishing the League of Nations. He has little support from the opposition party, and his plans are never confirmed by the Senate. The Treaty of Versailles ending the war imposes severe terms on Germany which will lead directly to World War II. They are prohibited from having subs and planes, lose a lot of territory, and are saddled with a debt they can't repay. The treaty also redraws the maps of Europe and Africa, sowing the seeds for future unrest and conflict. On November 19, the United States Congress refuses to approve the treaty. The U.S. never joins the League of Nations which is disbanded in 1946.

Red scare sweeps America

With the Communist takeover of Russia, a fear of Communism sweeps America with the Attorney General rounding up 6,000 suspected Communists.

President Wilson suffers a stroke

He is left disabled until the end of his Presidency. The government essentially operates without a president for a year.

1920 —

> ★ 19ᵀᴴ AMENDMENT ★
> Gives women the right to vote.

Women get the right to vote

The 19th amendment gives women the right to vote. Suffragettes have worked towards this goal for decades. Susan B. Anthony is critical in getting the amendment passed.

1920 — *KDKA* first station to broadcast election results

⋆1920⋆   WARREN G. HARDING   29

CANDIDATE	PARTY	ELECTORAL VOTE	POPULAR VOTE
Warren G. Harding Calvin Coolidge	*Republican*	404	16,144,093
James Cox Franklin D. Roosevelt	*Democratic*	127	9,139,661

The war is over, the post-war economy is not doing well, and the League of Nations is still a contentious issue. Wilson is unpopular, and incapacitated after a stroke. Irish and German communities in America are upset at Wilson's policies. Women in all states can now vote for president. The Republicans consider running Teddy Roosevelt, but he dies in 1919 so they run the relatively unknown Senator Harding. The Democrats pick Ohio Governor Cox, and Franklin Roosevelt for the second spot. Harding campaigns against Wilson's policies and wins an enormous landslide victory and one of the largest popular vote margins in history. The Socialist candidate, Eugene V. Debs, receives almost one million votes even though he is in prison.

Roaring '20s

Helped by the prohibition of alcohol, the Twenties become a lawless decade since almost everyone violates prohibition. Speakeasies spring up serving illegal alcohol. Corruption exists at every level of government. Organized crimes takes over with leaders like Al Capone and John Dillinger. President Harding implements a "hands-off" policy with the economy and the stock market booms. His successor, Coolidge, will continue this hands-off approach. Jazz music takes off with singers like Louis Armstrong, and New York's Broadway offers great plays by playwrights like Eugene O'Neill and Noel Coward.

1921 — **Sales tax**

West Virginia becomes the first state with a sales tax.

1922 — **Lincoln Memorial is dedicated in D.C.**

The inside is inscribed with the words of his Gettysburg Address and Second Inaugural Speech, and contains a massive statue by Daniel Chester French.

Teapot Dome Scandal rocks the country

Secretary of the Interior Albert Fall is convicted of taking bribes from oil companies to secure lucrative government leases of petroleum reserves at Teapot Dome, Wyoming.

1922 | **First female U.S. Senator**

Rebecca Felton is appointed by the governor of Georgia to fill a vacant U.S. Senate seat, becoming the first female member of the Senate.

★1923★   CALVIN COOLIDGE   30

Harding dies suddenly from a heart attack and his vice president, Calvin Coolidge, takes over the presidency.

Hollywood arrives

A real estate developer erects a huge *Hollywoodland* sign in the hills of Los Angeles. The *"land"* is removed in 1949.

1924 | **Immigration Act of 1924**

Limits immigration to 2% of each nationality in America in 1880, discriminating against Far Eastern and East European immigrants. It will be in effect until the Immigration Act of 1965 which will focus on individuals more than quotas.

Indian Citizenship Act

The government gives U.S. citizenship and voting rights to all Native Americans born in the United States.

★1924★ CALVIN COOLIDGE RE-ELECTED

CANDIDATE	PARTY	ELECTORAL VOTE	POPULAR VOTE
Calvin Coolidge Charles Dawes	Republican	382	15,723,789
John Davis Charles Bryan	Democratic	136	8,386,242
Robert La Follette, Sr. Burton Wheeler	Progressive	13	4,831,706

The economy is booming, the war is long since over, and the voters are happy with the current administration. The Democratic Party is in disarray, needing 100 ballots to nominate the unknown but conservative Davis as their candidate. Liberal Democrats leave their party to back the Progressive Party candidate. This is the first national election in which Native-Americans can vote. Both major parties push a conservative agenda of smaller government, less regulation, and reduced taxes, but Coolidge wins in another landslide.

First elected female governor

Nellie Ross is elected governor of Wyoming, becoming the first elected female governor in the country. Wyoming had given women the right to vote in 1869.

1924 — **First Macy's Thanksgiving Day parade in New York City**

1925 — **Deadly Tri-State Tornado kills 695**

The deadliest tornado in our history (though this is unofficial) kills 695 in Missouri, Illinois, and Indiana. Its continuous path is the longest ever recorded, at more than 200 miles and lasting more than 3 hours.

Scopes Monkey Trial
A high school teacher, John Scopes, is accused of violating Tennessee law prohibiting the teaching of evolution. Scopes is represented by the ACLU and Clarence Darrow, and prosecuted by William Jennings Bryan. Scopes is found guilty, but the verdict is later overturned.

1926 — **First liquid fuel rocket**
Robert Goddard, the "father of rocketry", launches the world's first liquid-fuel rocket in Massachusetts.

1927 — **Charles Lindbergh flies the Atlantic**

He makes the first non-stop solo flight across the Atlantic, flying 3,600 miles from New York to Paris in the *Spirit of St. Louis*. The plane is on display now in the Space Museum in Washington, D.C.

***The Jazz Singer* opens in New York City**
It is the first full-length "talking" movie, starring Al Jolson. The audience loves it. The days of silent film are numbered.

★**1928**★   HERBERT HOOVER   31

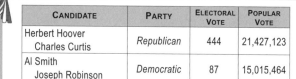

Candidate	Party	Electoral Vote	Popular Vote
Herbert Hoover Charles Curtis	Republican	444	21,427,123
Al Smith Joseph Robinson	Democratic	87	15,015,464

Coolidge decides not to run again as the economy continues to boom. Many influential Democrats decide not to run in an obvious losing cause, so their party picks New York Governor Al Smith as their candidate. He is hampered by his anti-prohibition stance, the well-known corruption of his home state, and the fact that he is a Roman Catholic. Many fear that the Pope would control any Catholic president. Hoover wins in a third consecutive Republican landslide.

1929 — **St. Valentine's Day Massacre**
Al Capone's gang massacres seven members of the rival Moran Gang on Valentine's Day in Chicago.

Stock market crashes on *Black Thursday*
The decade of speculation and buying stock on margin comes to a screeching halt on October 24, 1929. Collapsing prices mark the start of the decade-long Great Depression. Many lose their life savings as 5,000 banks will soon fail.

1930 — **Ninth planet Pluto is discovered**
Clyde Tombaugh discovers the new planet at Lowell Observatory in Arizona after a year of carefully comparing photographs of the night sky. Venetia Burney, an eleven-year-old English schoolgirl, is credited with suggesting the name for the new planet, Pluto. In 2006, astronomers will reclassify Pluto as a minor planet, reducing the official number of planets back to eight.

Smoot-Hawley Tariff Act
Though it is supposed to help Americans by increasing tariffs on imports, it only worsens the depression.

1931 — ***Star Spangled Banner* picked as anthem**
President Hoover signs a congressional resolution naming it the national anthem.

Empire State Building complete
Built in only 410 days, the 1250-foot tall Empire State Building edges out the Chrysler Building to become the world's tallest. It remains the world's tallest for forty years.

1932 — **"Bonus March" heads to Washington**
Twelve million people are out of work by 1932. Thousands of World War I vets march on Washington demanding their promised bonus pay from the war.

Amelia Earhart is first woman to fly the Atlantic nonstop
She had made an earlier flight as a passenger with two others. This flight was solo, going from Newfoundland to Northern Ireland in 15 hours.

Hoovervilles spring up all over the country
These homeless camps are named after the president many blame for their problems. Hoover resists using federal money to help the states, but his policies like the Smoot-Hawley Tariff only make things worse.

First elected female U.S. Senator
Hattie Caraway is the first woman actually elected, not appointed, to the Senate.

★1932★   FRANKLIN D. ROOSEVELT   32

CANDIDATE	PARTY	ELECTORAL VOTE	POPULAR VOTE
Franklin D. Roosevelt John Garner	Democratic	472	22,821,277
Herbert Hoover Charles Curtis	Republican	59	15,761,254

The depression hits the country hard. Voters blame Hoover for the crisis, or at least feel that he is unable to fix the problems. Roosevelt takes advantage of the crisis and promises that his "New Deal" will put the country back on its feet. Hoover warns that Roosevelt will increase taxes and the federal debt to pay for his social programs. But an unemployment rate over 20% makes voters willing to take the chance. Roosevelt picks "Happy Days are Here Again" as a campaign song. Ironically, those happy days won't show up for fifteen years. This is the first election in 56 years in which a Democratic candidate wins a majority of the popular vote. The pre-TV American public will almost never see the braces and wheelchair Roosevelt needs after contracting polio in 1921.

1933

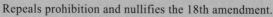

★ 20ᵀᴴ AMENDMENT ★

Sets the dates for the commencement of terms for newly elected members of Congress and the President.

★ 21ˢᵀ AMENDMENT ★

Repeals prohibition and nullifies the 18th amendment.

Albert Einstein flees Europe

The world-renown physicist arrives in the U.S. after fleeing Nazi Germany's persecution of Jews and intellectuals. He learns that the German government has banned Jews from teaching and has burned his books.

Assassination attempt on FDR

The president-elect is giving a speech in Miami when Guiseppe Zangara, an Italian anarchist, fires 5 shots at close range. All miss Roosevelt, but Chicago Mayor Anton Cermak is struck and later dies.

Wiley Post flies alone around the world

He becomes the first to make a solo round-the-world airplane trip, landing back in New York after almost eight days. He will die in 1935 in a plane crash in Alaska that will also kill humorist Will Rogers.

1935 ┤ **Dust storm strikes Washington, D.C.**

The Great Plains becomes a Dust Bowl due to severe drought, single crop-farming, and bad farming practices and policies. Farmers have plowed up grass lands to plant cash crops, exposing the soil to the sun and wind. Dust storms darken the skies for hours and leak into every house through the tiniest crack. More than 100 million acres lose most or all of their topsoil. During legislation in Washington on the need for a Soil Conservation Act, a dust storm from the Great Plains hits the city. The act passes later the same year.

Bad times breed Fascism and Communism

The world-wide depression creates a ripe breeding ground for the rise of the Nazis in Germany, Fascists in Spain and Italy, and the Communists in Russia and France.

FDR pushes his New Deal

FDR creates an astounding number of new government acts using his executive powers and the Democrat control of both houses of Congress. Many have unintended consequences that will prolong the depression instead of ending it, and make citizens dependent on the government. Many government projects take work away from the private sector and actually discourage new job formation. Social Security benefits are set to begin at age 65, which is just two years greater than the average life span in 1936 of 63 years. In 2011, the average life span will increase to 78 years.

- FHA: Federal Housing Administration guarantees home loans.
- FSA: Farm Security Administration helps poor farmers.
- CCC: Civilian Conservation Corps puts men to work building public structures.
- FCC: Federal Communication Commission monitors airwaves.
- WPA: Works Progress Administration puts people to work and funds the arts.
- SSA: Social Security Act provides benefits to retirees and the unemployed, and a lump-sum benefit at death.
- FLSA: Fair Labor Standards Act sets maximum work hours and minimum wages.
- FDIC: Federal Deposit Insurance Corporation guarantees deposits in banks.
- TVA: Tennessee Valley Authority builds dams to provide power and control floods.
- SEC: Securities and Exchange Commission monitors the securities market.
- Revenue Wealth Tax Act: Increases taxes on the rich up to 75% and increases estate taxes.

1935 —

The New Deal reaches too far

The National Industrial Recovery Act is declared unconstitutional. It was designed to stimulate recovery by permitting monopolies, setting minimum wages, and allowing collective bargaining.

The Agricultural Adjustment Act paid farmers to not grow crops, produce milk, or raise animals. This was paid for by taxing the producers. The Supreme Court declares the Act unconstitutional since it is illegal to tax one group and give that money to another.

Labor Day Hurricane

Devastating storm hits the Florida Keys, killing 400 people and destroying the Key West railroad. Its 892 mbar pressure reading when it touches land will remain the lowest in American history.

Huey "The Kingfish" Long killed by gunman

The U.S. Senator and former Louisiana Governor pushed a Share-Our-Wealth program to spread the wealth around.

Hoover Dam built

President Roosevelt dedicates Hoover Dam in Nevada (known as Boulder Dam at the time). The dam plays a vital part in the upcoming war by providing electricity to make aluminum needed for the airplanes that help win the war.

Italy invades Ethiopia

The attack highlights the weakness of the League of Nations. Italy and Ethiopia both belong, but that does nothing to stop the invasion or protect Ethiopia.

1936 —

Spanish Civil War

The liberal, Communist-leaning government is attacked by right-wind fascists, led by General Franco who is aided by Hitler and Mussolini. Hitler uses Spain as a testing ground for his new weapons and tactics. Russia backs the government, but the U.S. stays neutral during the 3-year war.

Jesse Owens humiliates Hitler

The black runner shatters Hitler's claims of Aryan superiority at the Berlin Olympics by winning 4 gold medals.

★1936★ Franklin Roosevelt re-elected

CANDIDATE	PARTY	ELECTORAL VOTE	POPULAR VOTE
Franklin Roosevelt John Garner	*Democratic*	523	27,752,648
Alf Landon Frank Knox	*Republican*	8	16,681,862

The Great Depression continues and FDR is still pushing his New Deal programs. The voters are willing to give him more time, even though unemployment is still above 16%. Roosevelt wins a lopsided victory, earning more electoral votes than any president except for Reagan in 1984.

1937 — Graf Zeppelin *Hindenburg* explodes upon landing

The German airship blows up and burns in New Jersey, killing 35 people, and effectively ending airship travel. The live coverage by Herbert Morrison will become famous.

Golden Gate Bridge opens in San Francisco

The new suspension bridge is the world's longest and will remain the longest until the 1964 construction of the Verrazano-Narrows Bridge in New York.

FDR threatens to pack the Supreme Court

The Supreme Court thwarts some of his policies so he threatens to add extra judges that will approve them. Fortunately, Congress does not approve of his plan.

Amelia Earhart disappears in the South Pacific

Her world circumnavigation attempt ends in tragedy. Her plane will never be found.

1938 — Chamberlin's "Peace for our Time"

In misguided appeasement, British Prime Minister Neville Chamberlin signs a treaty with Hitler, saying it will guarantee "Peace for our time." It gives Hitler control of the Sudetenland area of Czechoslovakia, which he then immediately occupies, burning synagogues, and sending Jews to concentration camps. A year later, Europe is at war.

War of the Worlds radio show scares the nation

Orson Welles plays a Halloween stunt on national radio by presenting H.G. Wells' novel, *The War of the Worlds*, as if it is real. He broadcasts simulated news flashes reporting aliens landing and using death rays to kill Americans. Hundreds of listeners panic, believing the alien attack is real.

1939

Spanish Civil War ends with General Franco victorious
He keeps Spain essentially neutral during World War II.

The movie *Wizard of Oz* opens in Hollywood

Judy Garland achieves immortality with her rendition of "Over the Rainbow." The film will become an American classic.

Hitler signs a non-aggression treaty with Russia
Hitler buys time, but makes secret plans with Russia to divide European countries between them, including Poland, Romania, Lithuania, Estonia, Latvia and Finland.

Hitler invades Poland to start World War II
In response, France and Britain declare war on Germany. America remains neutral though Roosevelt helps supply Britain under the authority of the Lend-Lease Act.

1940

Hitler occupies France

Hitler defeats France in a month, outflanking her vaunted Maginot Line. He divides France into a German-occupied North, and a free-French Vichy government in the South. On June 22, France is forced to sign the surrender documents in the same railcar used when Germany surrendered at the end of the first World War.

Mass evacuation at Dunkirk, France

The Nazis trap the British Army against the sea in Dunkirk and only a miraculous evacuation by small boats saves more than 300,000 soldiers.

The Battle of Britain saves England and the world

Hitler prepares to invade across the English Channel, but needs air superiority first. He spends the summer relentlessly bombing England, which is saved only by the valiant defense of the British RAF. Hitler postpones his invasion and turns his attention toward Russia. Churchill thanks those pilots with his famous saying, "Never was so much owed by so many to so few."

America First Committee tries to keep U.S. out of war
Charles Lindbergh leads isolationist, anti-war groups demanding all aid to Europe stopped and the U.S. kept out of the war.

★1940★ Franklin Roosevelt re-elected

CANDIDATE	PARTY	ELECTORAL VOTE	POPULAR VOTE
Franklin Roosevelt Henry Wallace	*Democratic*	449	27,313,945
Wendell Willkie Charles McNary	*Republican*	82	22,347,744

The war has started in Europe and is a major issue in the election. Unemployment is still high. Roosevelt becomes the first president to run for a third term, breaking with tradition, as he feels that only he has the necessary experience to handle the upcoming war, though he promises he will not involve the country in the war. The Republicans pick a businessman, Wendell Willkie, who is strongly in favor of giving Britain all the aid possible short of declaring war. Roosevelt's current vice president, John Garner, differs with FDR over his liberal policies, and Roosevelt picks Henry Wallace as a new running mate. Wallace is a liberal socialist who favors the USSR, but will fortunately be replaced before Roosevelt dies.

1941

Mount Rushmore is finished

Started in South Dakota in 1927 by Gutzon Borglum, it is finally finished by his son, Lincoln Borglum. Sixty-foot-high faces of George Washington, Thomas Jefferson, Theodore Roosevelt, and Abraham Lincoln are carved on the granite cliffs. The initial plans had called for each president to be carved from head to waist, but lack of funding stopped further carving. Thomas Jefferson was started on the other side of Washington, but unstable rock there forced the workers to move him to the other side.

Pearl Harbor - December 7

Carrier-launched Japanese aircraft attack the U.S. fleet at Pearl Harbor on the island of Oahu. The surprise attack sinks a number of ships and kills 2400 Americans. On the same day, the Japanese also occupy Wake Island, Guam, Singapore, the Philippines, and Hong Kong. FDR declares war on Japan. Germany and Italy then declare war on America. The "*Allies*" consist primarily of England, America, France, China, and the Soviet Union. They face the "*Axis*" forces of Germany, Italy, and Japan, although Hungary, Romania, Slovakia, and Bulgaria also join.

1942 — **Japanese internment camps ordered by FDR**
The U.S. government relocates Pacific coast Japanese-Americans to internment camps to protect them from anti-Japanese actions, and reduce chances for espionage.

Bataan Death March

Over 75,000 American and Filipino troops surrender at Bataan and Corregidor in the largest mass surrender in American history. The Japanese force the prisoners on a brutal march to POW camps that kills 7,000 prisoners. MacArthur escapes to Australia.

30 Seconds over Tokyo

Captain Jimmy Doolittle leads a flight of sixteen specially outfitted B-25's launched from the aircraft carrier USS *Hornet*. They drop bombs on Tokyo in a symbolic move that improves morale at home, and undermines Japanese leadership. The Japanese government had promised their people they would never be attacked. In retaliation, the Japanese massacre more than 250,000 Chinese civilians they accuse of helping the downed aviators.

Battle of the Coral Sea on May 4-8
Japanese and American naval forces fight the first naval battle between aircraft carriers, and the first naval battle where the ships of each side never see each other.

Battle of Midway on June 4-6

Trying to lure American carriers into a trap, the Japanese Navy attacks Midway, a small but strategic island in the middle of the Pacific. Americans have broken Japan's secret code and know the attack is coming. In one of the most decisive naval battles in history, the U.S. sinks four Japanese carriers and a heavy cruiser, while losing only one carrier and a destroyer. This defeat starts Japan on their slow retreat back to their mainland.

Battle of Stalingrad
In one of the bloodiest battles in history, the Germans fail to take Stalingrad, marking the end of their eastern advance into Russia. Two million die on both sides and the city is reduced to rubble. The Russian-German animosity pervades the war. Later, thousands of Germans flee toward advancing Americans rather than risk surrendering to the Russians.

1942 — **Battle of Guadacanal**

Allied forces land on the island of Guadacanal to deny its use to the Japanese threatening Allied supply routes.

1943 — **Germans surrender in North Africa**

The Allies surround the Axis forces in Tunisia and force the surrender of over 275,000 enemy troops. This enables the Allies to begin preparing for the invasion of Italy.

Allies land in Sicily, Italy

A large Allied assault takes the island and moves onto main-land Italy. Italy surrenders but the Germans keep fighting in Italy. Rome is not liberated until June 5, 1944. Mussolini is imprisoned but rescued by the Germans who need him to head the government. When Rome finally falls, Mussolini and his mistress are captured, shot, and hung upside down on meat hooks in a public square, before being stoned.

John F. Kennedy's PT-109 sinks

A Japanese destroyer rams and sinks the future president's torpedo boat in the Solomon Islands. Kennedy leads his men to safety and rescue six days later.

General Eisenhower picked to head invasion

Roosevelt names Dwight Eisenhower Supreme Allied Commander in Europe. He is responsible for the upcoming invasion and liberation of Europe.

1944 — **D-Day at Normandy, France on June 6**

The largest invasion force in history, with 7,000 ships supported by 11,000 planes, lands 150,000 troops at Utah, Omaha, Juno, Sword, and Gold beaches. The Germans still think the invasion will be at Calais. Months of fighting lie ahead as the Allies move eastward.

GI Bill passed by government

This pays for the education of returning servicemen.

America retakes Guam on July 21

Allied forces land and retake the island, an American possession captured by the Japanese after Pearl Harbor. During occupation, the Japanese had tortured and raped the locals. Guam celebrates Liberation Day every year on July 21.

Pilot George H.W. Bush shot down in the South Pacific

George H.W. Bush, the future 41st President, is shot down and survives in a raft until picked up by an American sub.

MacArthur returns to the Philippines

Fulfilling his earlier vow to the Filipino people that "I shall return," MacArthur wades ashore at Leyte Island to start the long battle to retake the islands.

1944 — Battle of Leyte Gulf

One of the biggest naval battles ever results in Japan's largest loss of ships and crew, and the use of kamikaze planes.

★1944★ FRANKLIN ROOSEVELT RE-ELECTED

CANDIDATE	PARTY	ELECTORAL VOTE	POPULAR VOTE
Franklin Roosevelt Harry S. Truman	Democratic	432	25,612,916
Thomas Dewey John Bricker	Republican	99	22,017,929

The war is beginning to wind down and Roosevelt remains popular, although many in his party are skeptical of his economic policies. There is stiff opposition to his current vice president and the party forces FDR to select Senator Truman as his new running mate. It is a fortunate pick, as events will soon reveal. New York Governor Dewey becomes his opponent. Roosevelt easily wins a record 4th term.

Battle of the Bulge

As Allies push the Germans back towards their homeland, the Germans stage a massive counterattack, resulting in one of the largest U.S. losses in the war. The Germans surround the town of Bastogne and demand surrender. The American Commander McAuliffe replies, "Nuts." The Americans hold the town until they are relieved.

Allies discover Nazi death camps throughout Europe

The extent of the Nazi systematic extermination of Jews and others considered "undesirable" is revealed as concentration camps are discovered by the advancing Allies. The *Holocaust* kills more than 11 million men, women, and children.

1945 — Yalta Conference in Ukraine

Stalin, Roosevelt, and Churchill meet to discuss the future of postwar Europe.

Iwo Jima

U.S. Marines take Iwo Jima in a bloody battle costing 6,800 American lives, and the lives of 20,000 Japanese defenders. It is the first invasion of a Japanese home island.

Battle of Okinawa

The largest Pacific amphibious assault secures Okinawa as an airbase for the upcoming invasion of Japan. The battle lasts 3 months and results in an enormous loss of life. Over 100,000 Japanese troops are killed or captured, and thousands of civilians are killed or commit suicide. This is a harbinger of what the invasion of the Japanese mainland will be like.

★1945★   HARRY S. TRUMAN   33

President Roosevelt dies on April 12 and Truman becomes president. He has a full plate, as he must end the war in Europe, and decide whether to use the atomic bomb on Japan. Then, he has a post-war world to handle along with the start of the Cold War. Fortunately for the country, Truman assumes the job and not Roosevelt's previous vice president, Wallace, who was taken off the ticket just the year before. Wallace is opposed to the Truman Doctrine and the Marshall Plan.

The Soviets take Berlin and Germany surrenders

Eisenhower decides to let the Russians take Berlin, saving tens of thousands of American lives. The bloody final battle results in 100,000 killed on each side. On April 30, Hitler and his wife, Eva Braun, commit suicide in their Berlin bunker and their bodies are cremated. Germans continue fighting westward to surrender to the Western Allies instead of the Soviets. Germany finally surrenders on May 8, 1945. Europe is finally at peace. The war with Japan continues.

Manhattan Project develops the A-Bomb

Working in secret, scientists in the U.S. develop the atomic bomb, employing up to 130,000 people in the process. It is successfully tested in New Mexico on July 16. Now, President Truman must decide how to use the weapon. America has only two working atomic bombs by August of this year. Based on fierce fighting seen in recent battles like Iwo Jima and Okinawa, it is felt that an invasion of the Japanese homeland will result in more than one million American casualties. After discussions on where and how to drop the bombs, Truman decides that with only two working bombs available, they must bomb the Japanese homeland.

Atomic bombs blast Hiroshima and Nagasaki

The *Enola Gay* drops the first atomic bomb on Hiroshima on August 6. The Japanese government still will not agree to the Allied terms of surrender, so the second atomic bomb is dropped on Nagasaki three days later. Together, they kill around 200,000 people.

Japan finally surrenders on August 15

The formal surrender is signed on the deck of the USS *Missouri* on September 2 in the presence of 250 Allied ships, and 2,000 planes overhead. World War II is finally over. General MacArthur takes over as Military Governor of Japan and wisely allows the Emperor to retain his throne. He drafts a new constitution that remains in effect to this day.

1945 ┤ ## Germany is divided

As pre-arranged, the Allies divide Germany into sectors—the Soviets control the Eastern half, and the Allies control the western portion. Berlin is stuck deep inside the Soviet sector and is itself divided into four parts—Soviet, French, American, and British.

War crime trials start in Nuremberg, Germany

 The Allies hold a series of tribunals to try Nazi leaders as war criminals. Some of the worst villains have already committed suicide, including Hitler, Heinrich Himmler, and Joseph Goebbels. Twelve defendants are sentenced to hang. Two of them escape hanging by committing suicide, including Hermann Göring the night before his hanging.

United Nations is established

The new organization is ratified in San Francisco by the five permanent members of the new Security Council—the United States, France, the Republic of China, the Soviet Union, and the United Kingdom.

1946 ┤ ### Philippines becomes an independent nation

On July 4, 1946, the American government signs a treaty with the Philippines that grants her independence. The U.S. retains a number of military bases, and pledges continued economic assistance.

First computer (ENIAC) unveiled

It has 17,000 vacuum tubes, 70,000 resistors, and 6,000 switches. Weighing 30 tons, it occupies 1800 square feet of space. Today, your laptop computer is probably 100 times more powerful.

First U.S. rocket to fly 50 miles into space

The United States launches a captured German V-2 rocket to an altitude of 69 miles.

1947 ┤ ### Jackie Robinson breaks race barrier

He becomes the first black major league baseball player, plays in six World Series, and is named MVP in 1949.

Truman forms the U.S. Air Force

The new force is created from the old Army Air Corps.

CIA established

Truman forms the National Security Council, the CIA (from the World War II OSS), and the Department of Defense (from the old Department of War).

1947 **Chuck Yeager breaks the sound barrier**
He becomes the first man to break the sound barrier in the experimental jet *X-1*, topping 807 mph.

1948 **Truman desegregates the military**
His Executive Order 9981 orders all armed forces integrated. He resorts to using an executive order because the southern Democrats would have blocked integration.

"Iron Curtain" falls over Europe
Germany and Berlin have been split since the war and the Allies rely on rail and highway lines across the Soviet sectors of Germany to supply Berlin. The Soviets still greatly outnumber the American forces in Europe. The 22,000 Allied troops in Berlin are surrounded by 1,500,000 Soviet troops. In 1948, the Soviets close

rail and highway access to Berlin to starve the civilians and force the Allies out of Germany. Their military assures the Kremlin that the Americans can never supply Berlin from the air. The U.S. responds with a year-long airlift to supply Berlin by flying more than 250,000 flights, often only minutes apart. They land more than 1.7 million tons of food, coal, and supplies. A year later, the Soviets lift the blockade.

Truman Doctrine
Truman warns the USSR that we will do whatever it takes to stop the spread of Communism. The Cold War starts, pitting Western democracies against the Communist Soviet Union and spread of communism.

Marshall Plan rebuilds Europe
America spends more than $13 billion to rebuild war-torn Europe and keep countries out of Communist control.

★1948★ HARRY S. TRUMAN RE-ELECTED

CANDIDATE	PARTY	ELECTORAL VOTE	POPULAR VOTE
Harry S. Truman Alben Barkley	*Democratic*	303	24,179,347
Thomas Dewey Earl Warren	*Republican*	189	21,991,292
Strom Thurmond Fielding Wright	*Dixiecrat*	39	1,175,930

The Republicans want Eisenhower, but he refuses. Southern Democrats form the Dixiecrats to push policies of racial segregation. Everyone picks Dewey to defeat the incumbent Truman, but Truman wins in one of our greatest upsets.

1949 — **NATO established to counter the Soviet threat**
The North American Treaty Organization is established, stating that an attack on a member will be considered an attack on them all. The Soviets get the atom bomb in 1949.

Chinese Nationalist Government is exiled to Taiwan
The communists under Mao Zedong force the Chinese Nationalist government to flee to the island of Taiwan where they form a new government under Chiang Kai-shek. The government in Taiwan continues to represent China in the United Nations until 1971 when the Communist government of mainland China takes her seat.

1950 **Korean War starts**
The Russians had declared war on Japan days before World War II ended in order to take over countries that Japan occupied during the war. When  Japan surrendered to the Soviet Union, the Russians took over North Korea. In 1950, North Korean Communists invade South Korea, intent on taking over the entire country. American and United Nations troops are sent in, commanded by General MacArthur. The North Koreans capture almost the entire South. General MacArthur lands forces behind the enemy lines at Inchon, catching the North Koreans off guard and they are pushed back almost all the way to China. This leads to the entry of 500,000 Chinese Communists into the war, and the Southern forces are forced to retreat south of Seoul.

Assassination attempt on President Truman
Two Puerto Rican Nationalists attempt to assassinate the President while he is living at the Blair House during White House renovation. They kill a White House policeman before the police kill one and wound the other.

1951 —

★ 22ND AMENDMENT ★
Limits presidents to two terms, or 10 years if serving a partial term.

General MacArthur removed from command
President Truman relieves MacArthur of command in Korea due to a number of public disagreements, primarily because of MacArthur's aggressive approach to the war.

1952 — **First thermonuclear bomb**
America explodes a hydrogen bomb 500 times more powerful than the Hiroshima blast.

Puerto Rico becomes a U.S. Commonwealth
Puerto Rico approves a new Constitution which is ratified by the U.S. Congress and signed by President Truman.

★1952★   DWIGHT D. EISENHOWER   34

CANDIDATE	PARTY	ELECTORAL VOTE	POPULAR VOTE
Dwight D. Eisenhower Richard Nixon	Republican	442	34,075,529
Adlai Stevenson John Sparkman	Democratic	89	27,375,090

This election takes place amidst the stalemated Korean War, increasing Cold War tensions, and anti-Communist investigations led by Senator McCarthy. The recently passed 22nd Amendment does not apply to the sitting president, so Truman is able to run again, but his sinking popularity and early primary losses cause him to drop out. Governor Stevenson of Illinois, grandson of the 1892 vice president, is selected by the Democrats. The Republicans favor the more conservative Robert Taft who wants to overturn many of Roosevelt's New Deal programs, but they select the war hero General Eisenhower as having the best chance to win. Ike campaigns with the popular slogan, "I Like Ike." Ike's running mate, Richard Nixon of California, is accused of accepting illegal gifts. In a televised speech known as the "Checkers" speech, he denies the charges and states that he will not return the dog Checkers that a supporter had given him because his children are so attached to it. Eisenhower wins in a landslide, ending 20 years of a Democratic White House.

1953 — Soviet leader Joseph Stalin dies
Nikita Khruschev takes over control of the USSR.

Soviet spies executed
The Rosenbergs are convicted of being Soviet spies and are executed.

Korean War ends
An armistice ends the war without a peace treaty ever being signed. The Communists don't want their freed POW's to stay in the South but rather be forcibly sent to the North. America pledges long-term aid and security, and our forces are still in South Korea today. More than 36,000 American lose their lives in this war, but millions of Chinese and North Korean soldiers, and Korean civilians die.

Dr. Jonas Salk invents polio vaccine

The vaccine ends a dreadful scourge that had even crippled Franklin Roosevelt. Polio will be essentially eradicated worldwide by the end of the century.

1954 **McCarthy Hearings**

Senator Joseph McCarthy holds hearings about communism in America. Anti-communist sentiment sweeps America and many careers are affected by the hysteria. Documents released later show that there were indeed Communists in the government, but many innocent people will have their lives destroyed.

Brown v. Board of Education
A Supreme Court decision declares that segregation in public schools is illegal.

Elvis Presley is aired for the first time
A Memphis, Tennessee radio station broadcasts "That's All Right" which some say is the first rock and roll hit.

Pledge of Allegiance changed
President Eisenhower officially adds "under God" to the Pledge of Allegiance.

1955 **McDonald's restaurant opens**
The first *McDonald's* opens in Des Plaines, Illinois.

Disneyland opens in Anaheim, California

Rock and Roll music takes off
The new music genre explodes with *Bill Haley and the Comets* release of "Rock Around the Clock" making it to Number 1 on the charts.

"In God We Trust" added to money
Congress orders the motto "In God We Trust" put on all U.S. currency, and makes it the official national motto.

Rosa Parks keeps her seat on the bus
The black woman is arrested for refusing to give up her seat to a white man, touching off a boycott and the civil rights movement that ultimately results in the Civil Rights Act that ends racial discrimination.

1956 **Interstate Highway Act**
The U.S. starts large-scale construction of interstate highways. Side effects include loss of railroads and right-of-ways that would be useful in the future, and the explosion of suburbs.

***Andrea Doria* sinks**
The liner *Andrea Doria* sinks off Nantucket after colliding with the Swedish liner *Stockholm*. Forty-six passengers die.

★1956★ DWIGHT EISENHOWER RE-ELECTED

CANDIDATE	PARTY	ELECTORAL VOTE	POPULAR VOTE
Dwight D. Eisenhower Richard Nixon	Republican	457	35,579,180
Adlai Stevenson Estes Kefauver	Democratic	73	26,028,028

Eisenhower and Nixon are picked to run again, and the Democrats pick Stevenson again. However, Stevenson lets the convention select his running mate, setting off a scramble to fill that spot. Stevenson's running mate in 1952, John Sparkman, is ignored due to his stance against racial integration. Senator Kennedy almost wins the nomination on the second ballot before the delegates pick Kefauver. There are concerns about Eisenhower's health, but his doctors clear him for running again. The country is prosperous and Ike has ended the Korean War, so he wins again in a landslide.

1957

Eisenhower signs Civil Rights Act of 1957
The first civil rights act since Reconstruction focuses on voting rights for blacks. The Democrat Senator from South Carolina, Strom Thurmond, sustains the longest one-person filibuster in history (24 hours) to try to block the bill. The act sets the scene for later civil rights legislation.

Integration enforced in the South
Federal troops are sent to Central High School in Little Rock, Arkansas to enforce integration.

Space Race begins
The Soviets launch the first satellite, *Sputnik*. Americans launch their first satellite a year later.

1958

NASA is formed to send America into space
The National Aeronautics and Space Administration selects the first seven Astronauts—Alan Shepard, Virgil Grissom, John Glenn, Scott Carpenter, Walter Schirra, Gordon Cooper, and Donald Slayton.

USS *Nautilus* reaches the North Pole
The first nuclear submarine travels under Arctic ice to become the first vessel to reach the North Pole on August 3.

1959

Castro takes over Cuba
Fidel Castro and his gang of rebels oust President Batista and make Cuba a Communist state propped up by the Soviet Union. He will rule Cuba into the next century.

1959 Saint Lawrence Seaway opens
The seaway connects the Atlantic Ocean to Lake Superior, using locks, canals, and the Saint Lawrence River.

Alaska and Hawaii become states
Alaska becomes the 49th state, and Hawaii follows soon thereafter as the 50th.

"The day the music died"
An airplane crash kills rock stars Buddy Holly, Ritchie Valens, and "Big Bopper" J.P. Richardson.

1960 First weather satellite Tiros I launched

★1960★   JOHN F. KENNEDY   35

CANDIDATE	PARTY	ELECTORAL VOTE	POPULAR VOTE
John F. Kennedy Lyndon Johnson	Democratic	303	34,220,911
Richard Nixon Henry Cabot Lodge, Jr.	Republican	219	34,108,157
Harry Byrd Strom Thurmond	Democratic	15	not on the ballot

Eisenhower cannot run again due to the terms of the 22nd amendment, so the Republicans pick his vice president, Richard Nixon, as their candidate, and Henry Cabot Lodge as his running mate for his foreign policy experience. Kennedy competes with Senate Majority Leader Johnson for the Democratic nomination. When Kennedy wins the nomination, he selects Johnson as his vice president to gain support from southern states. Nixon wastes time honoring his pledge to campaign in all 50 states—Hawaii and Alaska were just admitted as states. Kennedy's campaign is well-funded and well-run, and he directly addresses concerns about his Roman Catholic faith. His faith probably wins him more votes than it loses. Seventy million viewers watch the first televised presidential debate, in which a well-prepared and healthy-looking Kennedy bests the tired and pale-looking Nixon. Nixon does much better in the next three debates, but fewer people watch them. Kennedy wins the election with a popular margin of only 0.1%, but a wider margin in the Electoral College. However, ten states are decided by 2% or less of the vote, and there are charges that fraud in Illinois and Texas gave those states to Kennedy. If Nixon had won those two states, he would be president. Kennedy becomes the youngest elected president and ushers in a new generation of leaders.

1961

★ 23RD AMENDMENT ★
Grants Washington, D.C. representation in the Electoral College.

1961 — **Bay of Pigs disaster in Cuba**
U.S.-backed exiles invade Cuba but are killed or captured in a failed attempt to topple Castro.

First U.S. advisors arrive in South Vietnam

First American in space
Alan Shepard becomes the first American in space. The Russian Yuri Gagarin had become the first human in space the month before.

Freedom Riders
Thirteen men and women, both white and black, ride together on a bus from Washington, D.C. to New Orleans. They oppose southern laws that prevent whites and blacks from sitting together on buses. In Alabama, their bus is attacked and the riders beaten. In Mississippi, they are arrested and thrown into jail.

Berlin Wall divides the city
The Soviets build a solid wall to keep East Germans from escaping to the West, though the Soviets are brazen enough to call it an "Anti-Fascist Protection Rampart" supposedly to keep outside influences away from East Germany. Almost 200 people will die trying to escape to West Germany until the wall is torn down in 1989. The last time an escapee will be shot by a guard is in February of 1989.

1962 — **John Glenn orbits the Earth in *Friendship 7***
Kennedy's 1961 speech had challenged the U.S. to put a man on the moon, and this is the first step.

Cuban Missile Crisis
The USSR places nuclear missiles in Cuba but are spotted by American U-2 spy planes. The U.S. blockades Cuba and Kennedy forces the Soviets to back down. In exchange for removing the missiles, Kennedy agrees to remove missiles from Turkey, and never invade Cuba.

1963 — **"I Have a Dream" speech on August 28**
Martin Luther King delivers his famous "I Have a Dream" speech on the steps of the Lincoln Memorial in Washington, D.C. to over 200,000 civil rights supporters.

JFK assassinated on November 22

Lee Harvey Oswald shoots the president while he is riding in a Dallas motorcade, and Kennedy dies 30 minutes later. Oswald is arrested, but is killed days later by Jack Ruby.

⋆1963⋆ LYNDON B. JOHNSON 36

After Kennedy is shot in Dallas, his vice president, Lyndon Johnson, becomes president. Johnson is driven to the airport in an unmarked car and waits on board Air Force One for the arrival of Jackie Kennedy and her husband's casket. Upon her arrival, Johnson is administered the oath of office by federal judge Sarah Hughes. It is the only time a woman has administered

the oath, and the only time it has been done in an airplane. Nine minutes later, the plane departs for Washington, D.C.

1964

★ 24ᵀᴴ AMENDMENT ★
Prohibits the use of poll taxes to restrict voting rights.

Vietnam crisis heats up
Vietnam was divided in two in 1954 with the Communist Ho Chi Minh controlling the North, and Ngo Dinh Diem governing the South. The South is supported first by the French, and then by the United States. The North is propped up and supplied by China and the USSR.

Alaska Good Friday Earthquake
A devastating 9.2 earthquake hits Alaska on Good Friday, lasting for four minutes. It is the most powerful earthquake in North American history. The immediate shaking and resulting tsunami cause 130 deaths.

Civil Rights Act of 1964
President Johnson signs the Civil Rights Act that outlaws discrimination against blacks and women, ending segregation in schools and public places. It also protects voter registration. Martin Luther King receives the Nobel Peace Prize later this year.

Gulf of Tonkin incident

U.S. advisors are already in Vietnam. The North Vietnamese attack the USS *Maddox,* leading President Johnson to commit troops and resources. The U.S. bases its policies on the Domino Principle—the fear that if one nation falls to Communism, other nations will also fall like dominoes.

★1964★ LYNDON JOHNSON RE-ELECTED

CANDIDATE	PARTY	ELECTORAL VOTE	POPULAR VOTE
Lyndon Johnson Hubert Humphrey	Democratic	486	43,127,041
Barry Goldwater William Miller	Republican	52	27,175,754

Johnson is picked by his party, but has problems with Attorney General Robert Kennedy. The two have disliked each other ever since Kennedy tried to keep Johnson from being his brother's running mate in 1960. Kennedy wants the vice president spot, but Johnson announces that no cabinet member will be considered, and schedules Kennedy's speech on the last day of the convention to further diminish his influence. Johnson picks the liberal Hubert Humphrey as his running mate. The Republican Party is split, with conservatives favoring Barry Goldwater, a Senator from Arizona, and the moderates Nelson Rockefeller of New York. The conservatives support a low-tax, small government platform and oppose the social welfare programs of Johnson. Rockefeller is the front-runner for the Republican nomination until he remarries a new wife, 15 years younger, with four children, and who has just divorced her husband, leading to accusations of adultery. The scandal dies down, only to reemerge three days before the California primary when his new wife gives birth. He never recovers and Goldwater wins the nomination. Johnson wins in a landslide with a large popular vote margin. The election marks the first participation of the District of Columbia after the passage of the 23rd Amendment. It also is the first time Republicans win Georgia, and the first time they win three other southern states since Reconstruction. The election marks the emergence of the modern conservative movement, punctuated by Ronald Reagan's landslide victory in the California governor's race two years later.

1965 — Selma civil rights march

Troopers meet a civil rights march in Selma, Alabama with tear gas and billy clubs. Reverend Martin Luther King, Jr. leads thousands on a march from Selma to Montgomery.

Dominican Republic military action

President Johnson sends 42,000 soldiers to the Dominican Republic against the advice of his civilian advisers. He fears a Communist takeover of that country due to civil unrest. U.S. forces leave a year later. Forty-four American soldiers are killed during the occupation.

1965 **The Great Society**
President Johnson proposes the *Great Society*, involving a massive government commitment to Social Security, Medicaid, and Medicare.

President Johnson signs the Voting Rights Act
The Act bans literacy tests and similar barriers to voting, ensuring blacks will not be denied the right to vote.

Watts race riots
A routine arrest of a black driver by a white police officer touches off race riots in Los Angeles that kill 35 people.

1966 **Miranda ruling**
A Supreme Court ruling protects the rights of arrested citizens, resulting in the well-known Miranda Rights that must be read to all suspects.

First black Cabinet member
Robert Weaver becomes the first black cabinet member as head of Housing and Urban Development.

1967 **First Super Bowl**
Led by Bart Starr, the NFL Green Bay Packers defeat the AFL Kansas City Chiefs. The 2011 Super Bowl will be the most watched TV show in history.

Spacecraft fire kills three astronauts
Three NASA astronauts die in a spacecraft fire at Cape Canaveral; Gus Grissom, Edward White II, and Roger Chaffee.

★ **25ᵀᴴ AMENDMENT** ★
Defines the order and process of presidential succession.

First black Supreme Court Judge
Thurgood Marshall becomes the first black Supreme Court Justice.

Summer of Love
The Sixties see sexual freedom, the birth control pill, protest marches, drugs, and hippies.

1968 **More troops in Vietnam**
U.S. Troop strength in Vietnam rises to 500,000 troops.

Tet offensive in Vietnam
Though technically a victory for the U.S., this offensive by the North Vietnamese helps drive sentiment against the war. Up to 1,000 soldiers are dying each month.

1968

My Lai shooting
American troops kill innocent civilians in Vietnam.

Martin Luther King assassinated
Escaped convict James Earl Ray shoots King at a hotel in Memphis, Tennessee.

Robert Kennedy assassinated

An Arab nationalist, Sirhan Sirhan, shoots and kills presidential candidate Robert Kennedy as he campaigns in Los Angeles.

Intel Corporation starts

It soon becomes the leading developer of the microchip and the world's largest semiconductor chip maker.

Democratic National Convention riots
The Chicago convention is marked by huge anti-war demonstrations.

★1968★ RICHARD M. NIXON 37

CANDIDATE	PARTY	ELECTORAL VOTE	POPULAR VOTE
Richard M. Nixon Spiro Agnew	Republican	301	31,783,783
Hubert Humphrey Edmund Muskie	Democratic	191	31,271,839
George Wallace Curtis LeMay	American Independent	46	9,901,118

The 1968 election happens at a tumultuous time in our history. Civil Rights leader Martin Luther King, Jr. and presidential candidate Robert Kennedy have both been assassinated, and anti-war and race riots break out all over the country. Johnson announces he is suspending bombing in North Vietnam, and then withdraws from the race. His health is bad and he dies in 1973, two days after a new term would have ended. His popularity has also plummeted due to the ongoing war in Vietnam. Hubert Humphrey is picked as the Democratic candidate and runs on an anti-war platform. Nixon runs on a promise to restore law and order. Alabama Governor George Wallace also runs a strong campaign based on maintaining racial segregation. He picks retired General Curtis LeMay as his running mate, but LeMay makes a gaffe when he suggests we use nuclear weapons in Vietnam. The Democratic National Convention in Chicago is beset by violent anti-war protests. Nixon wins the election with a narrow popular vote margin, but wider electoral margin.

1968 — **Astronauts circle the Moon**

On Christmas Eve, the astronauts onboard Apollo 8 beam back a message of hope to Earth as they prepare to circle the moon several times before returning to Earth.

1969 — **Apollo 11 lands on the Moon—July 20, 1969**

Neil Armstrong and Edwin Aldrin walk on the moon, fulfilling President Kennedy's 1961 pledge. They leave a plaque that reads, "HERE MEN FROM THE PLANET EARTH FIRST SET FOOT UPON THE MOON JULY 1969 A.D. WE CAME IN PEACE FOR ALL MANKIND." 600 million people worldwide watch the event live on TV.

Woodstock Music Festival

Max Yasgur's farm in New York is the scene of a huge outdoor music festival attended by 400,000.

First messages sent on ARPANET

A UCLA programmer sends the first message on the Department of Defense network that will become the Internet.

1970 — **Apollo 13 mission aborted**

An explosion cripples the moon-bound spacecraft. Aided by radio instructions from Houston, the astronauts' ingenuity and endurance help them reach home safely.

Earth Day is first observed in the U.S.

U.S. Environmental Protection Agency (EPA) founded.

Cambodia invaded by U.S.

The invasion sparks huge student protests resulting in an accidental National Guard shooting resulting in the deaths of four Kent State students in Pennsylvania.

1971 — **Texas Instruments introduces first pocket calculator**

★ 26ᵀᴴ AMENDMENT ★

Changes the national voting age from 21 to 18.

"Pentagon Papers" are released

A former Marine releases confidential documents concerning the Vietnam War to the New York Times, further eroding public support for the war.

1972 — **President Nixon visits Communist China**

He opens trade relations on the first visit of an American president since the Communists took over.

1972┤ **Watergate break-in**

Nixon operatives break into the Democratic National Committee office at the Watergate building in Washington, D.C. This eventually leads to Nixon's resignation in two years. "Watergate" enters the national language, helping to name future scandals from Travelgate to Monicagate. The irony is that the break-in is completely unnecessary as Nixon easily wins reelection.

Munich Summer Olympics end in tragedy

American Mark Spitz wins 7 Olympic swimming medals. An Arab terrorist group kidnaps and murders 11 Israeli Olympians.

★1972★ RICHARD NIXON RE-ELECTED

CANDIDATE	PARTY	ELECTORAL VOTE	POPULAR VOTE
Richard Nixon Spiro Agnew	*Republican*	520	47,168,710
George McGovern Sargent Shriver	*Democratic*	17	29,173,222

The Democrats think that Ted Kennedy will be their candidate, but his role in the fatal accident at Chappaquiddick in 1969 ends his chances. Ed Muskie is another favorite, but George McGovern wins the nomination. McGovern's first pick for his running mate is Senator Thomas Eagleton. After the convention, he discovers that Eagleton had undergone electroshock therapy for depression and withheld this information. McGovern initially backs Eagleton completely, but doctors advise him that the condition could reoccur and endanger the country. Three days later, McGovern asks Eagleton to withdraw, and picks Shriver instead. However, his apparent indecision sinks his campaign. McGovern runs an anti-war campaign against incumbent Republican President Richard Nixon. Nixon wins in a landslide with one of the largest margins in history in the first election where the Republicans capture every Southern state.

Apollo 17 moon landing is America's last

Eugene Cernan, Ronald Evans, and Harrison Schmitt make the sixth lunar landing.

1973┤ **Paris Peace Treaty**

A treaty is signed to end the Vietnam War, but fighting continues and the U.S. resumes bombing in Cambodia.

Roe v. Wade **legalizes abortion**

This Supreme Court decision legalizes abortions in the first trimester. Texas District Attorney Henry Wade had defended Texas against Jane Roe's lawsuit about abortion.

1973 OPEC oil embargo

To punish countries that supported Israel in their recent war, the oil producing nations restrict oil exports. The cost of gasoline in the U.S. rises from 40 cents to above 55 cents a gallon, resulting in widespread shortages and conservation efforts such as reducing speed limits. Inflation continues throughout the decade with gold and gas prices soaring, and interest rates topping 12%.

Vice President Spiro Agnew resigns

Corruption charges force him from office. President Nixon picks Gerald Ford as the new vice president.

Endangered Species Act

President Nixon signs an environmental law to protect species identified as endangered by mankind's actions.

1974 New home run record on April 8, 1974

Atlanta Brave Henry Aaron breaks Babe Ruth's home run record when he hits his 715th home run.

President Richard Nixon resigns

He becomes the first president in history to resign. Investigations uncover his involvement in the Watergate scandal and his attempts to hamper the investigation. He admits to taping Oval Office conversations, but one of the critical tapes has an unexplained 18½ minute gap.

★1974★   GERALD FORD   38

Vice President Ford becomes president when Nixon resigns. He is the only president never to have been elected, since he was picked by Nixon to be vice president after Spiro Agnew resigned. Ford names Nelson Rockefeller as the new vice president.

President Ford pardons Nixon amid much criticism

He feels that the nation must leave the scandal behind.

1975 South Vietnam surrenders

The last U.S. civilians are evacuated from Saigon. Khmer Rouge forces take over Cambodia and embark on four years of terror, resulting in 1.5 million deaths. Saigon is eventually renamed Ho Chi Minh City.

1975 **President Ford survives 2 assassination attempts**
Lynette "Squeaky" Fromme botches an attempt in Sacramento, California, and Sara Jane Moore's shot misses two weeks later in San Francisco.

1976 **Viking 1 and 2 land on Mars**

They are the first landers to successfully complete their mission and transmit information back to Earth. Of 38 Soviet and U.S. launches of spacecraft for Mars, only 19 succeeded. Most of the failures were Soviet.

Woman admitted to military academies
The U.S. Naval Academy and West Point admit women for the first time.

★1976★   JIMMY CARTER   39

CANDIDATE	PARTY	ELECTORAL VOTE	POPULAR VOTE
Jimmy Carter Walter Mondale	Democratic	297	40,831,881
Gerald Ford Bob Dole	Republican	240	39,148,634

Gerald Ford narrowly beats out fellow Republican Ronald Reagan for the Republican nomination. After Reagan's stirring final speech, many delegates wish they had nominated him instead. Ford is still saddled with the effects of the Watergate scandal, and his subsequent pardoning of Nixon. Ford also misspeaks in the debate when he says that there is no Soviet domination of Europe. The Democrats select the relatively unknown former Georgia Governor Carter. He runs as an outsider and reformer. Carter wins a very close election, taking Wisconsin and Ohio by very slim margins. Winning those states would have given Ford the election. The 27 states won by Ford are the most ever won by a losing candidate.

1977 **Apple jump-starts the computer age**
Steve Wozniak and Steve Jobs release the Apple computer that really starts the computer age as business and homes start adopting computers. Earlier minicomputers like the Altair were mainly for hobbyists. The release of the Apple Macintosh and the IBM PC further advance home computers. Bill Gates forms Microsoft which becomes one of the largest companies in the world, and he becomes the world's richest man selling MS-DOS and Windows platforms, and applications like Word and Excel.

1977

The movie *Star Wars* debuts
The ground-breaking George Lucas epic is made for only $11 million and will earn over $800 million. It will receive six Academy Awards.

Elvis Presley dies suddenly in Memphis
However, many people will still report seeing him alive.

Trans-Alaska pipeline is finished
Its 800 miles of pipe will carry almost 16 billion barrels of oil by 2010.

Carter turns over the Panama Canal
Carter agrees to turn over the canal to Panama at a future date. He also pardons most Vietnam War draft evaders.

1978

Camp David Accords

Anwar El Sadat of Egypt and Menachem Begin of Israel sign an historic peace agreement at the White House, arranged by Jimmy Carter.

Jonestown mass suicide
Politicians investigate Reverend Jim Jones' People's Temple in Guyana. The paranoid Jones convinces his entire following to drink poisoned kool-aid in one of the largest mass suicides in history—more than 900 men, women, and children die.

1979

U.S. establishes diplomatic ties with Communist China

Three Mile Island nuclear reactor accident in Pennsylvania

A partial core meltdown is the worst accident in the U.S. nuclear industry's history. Radioactive gases are released but no one is killed or injured. The worst effect is turning public opinion against nuclear energy. The building of new reactors in the U.S. grinds to a halt.

Iranian hostages taken November 4
Radical Iranian students take sixty-six Americans hostage at our Embassy in Tehran. The U.S. had backed the Shah of Iran who was modernizing the country but was overthrown by the religious Ayatollah Khomeni. The hostages are held until January 20, 1981 when Reagan is inaugurated.

U.S.S.R. invades Afghanistan
The Soviets will occupy Afghanistan for ten years but fail to subdue the country and will be forced to retreat.

1980 Iranian rescue mission ends in disaster

Carter authorizes a daring helicopter mission into Iran to rescue the hostages but it ends in failure when a helicopter crashes in a desert storm, killing 8 soldiers.

Mount St. Helens explodes

The Washington volcano causes billions of dollars in damage and kills fifty-seven people. It is the deadliest volcano in American history. Its height is reduced by 1,312 feet.

The day before

After the eruption

U.S. boycotts Moscow Summer Olympics

In a response to the Soviet occupation of Afghanistan, the U.S. withdraws from the Moscow games. However, in the winter games at Lake Placid, NY, the U.S. hockey team defeats the superior Soviet squad, 4-3, giving the country a huge morale boost.

★1980★ RONALD REAGAN 40

Candidate	Party	Electoral Vote	Popular Vote
Ronald Reagan George H.W. Bush	Republican	489	43,903,230
Jimmy Carter Walter Mondale	Democratic	49	35,480,115
John Anderson Patrick Lucey	Independent	0	5,719,850

Incumbent Jimmy Carter fends off a challenge from Ted Kennedy, but is dogged by a bad economy, high inflation, and the ongoing Iranian hostage crisis. The Republicans pick Reagan, a former Hollywood actor of 53 films and two-term California governor, who almost was picked four years earlier. He believes in states' rights, lower taxes, and small government. Carter attacks Reagan as a right-wing radical who poses a threat to world peace and social welfare programs. The second presidential debate, held one week before the election, is a turning point. After the debate, the tight race opens up in Reagan's favor. Carter makes a few gaffes in the debate, at one point saying he relies on his 12-year old daughter for advice on nuclear arms policy. Republicans win control of the Senate for the first time in 28 years and begin the Reagan Revolution. His electoral college victory is the most lopsided ever for a non-incumbent.

1981 **President Reagan revitalizes America**

He is named "The Great Communicator" as he works to reduce the size of government. He lowers the top tax rates from 70% to 28%. His economic policies help produce a decade of reduced inflation, interest rates, and unemployment rates. His beliefs and speeches lead to a surge in patriotism.

President Reagan shot

John Hinckley almost kills the president in a shooting that severely wounds James Brady. Reagan survives the attempt, feeling God now has a specific purpose for him. He teams with Britain's Margaret Thatcher and Pope John Paul II, both of whom also survived assassination attempts, to help defeat Communism in Europe and bring down the Iron Curtain.

First space shuttle blasts off on April 12

Columbia blasts off from Cape Canaveral and returns to Earth two days later.

First female Supreme Court Justice

Sandra Day O'Conner becomes the first female Supreme Court Justice.

HIV and AIDS

The new scourge kills tens of thousands in the next decade. Reagan is accused of ignoring the problem, but both Democrat and Republican politicians avoid the issue. Annual federal spending on AIDS programs increases from $8,000,000 to $2,300,000,000. By 2010, more than 25 million worldwide will die from this disease, 500,000 in the U.S.

1982 **Vietnam Veterans Memorial**

A new polished black granite wall, designed by U.S. architect Maya Lin, is finished in Washington, D.C. containing the names of the 58,000 Americans who died in the war.

1983 **Evil Empire speech**

President Reagan delivers his famous speech calling the Soviet Union an "evil empire."

Pioneer 10 leaves the solar system

Launched in 1972, the satellite becomes the first spacecraft to leave our solar system. It will communicate until 2003.

Reagan announces SDI program

Reagan's push for the Strategic Defense Initiative (SDI) for space-based defense convinces the USSR that they cannot afford to compete against such a system and eventually leads to the Soviet collapse.

1983 ### First American woman in space

Sally Ride becomes the first American woman in space on board the shuttle *Challenger*.

Marines die in Lebanon blast

A terrorist explosion at a Marine barracks in Beirut, Lebanon kills 241 Marines. Islamic Jihad claims responsibility.

America invades Grenada

After a Marxist takeover of this Caribbean island, Reagan sends 8,000 troops to take control and rescue American students held there. Many debate whether the invasion is necessary, but it is a case of acting early to deter this and future Communist incursions into this part of the world.

1984 ### First woman on presidential ticket

Geraldine Ferraro becomes the first woman on a major presidential ticket in history, being named the vice presidential candidate for Walter Mondale. Their ticket is defeated by Ronald Reagan in a landslide.

★1984★ RONALD REAGAN RE-ELECTED

CANDIDATE	PARTY	ELECTORAL VOTE	POPULAR VOTE
Ronald Reagan George H. W. Bush	*Republican*	525	54,455,472
Walter Mondale Geraldine Ferraro	*Democratic*	13	37,577,352

The incumbent Reagan runs again with the same vice president, George H.W. Bush. The Democrats have more trouble. Walter Mondale, Jesse Jackson, and Gary Hart all vie for the nomination. Ted Kennedy decides not to run again, but not before making secret advances to Soviet Secretary Andropov in an attempt to discredit Reagan and his policies. Jackson makes racist remarks about Jews and loses backing. Hart lacks financing and stumbles in the televised debates. Mondale wins the nomination and picks Representative Geraldine Ferraro as his running mate, the first woman named on a major party's presidential ticket. He hopes to appeal to women voters. He runs a liberal campaign pushing for a nuclear freeze and calls Reagan's economic policies unfair. The election is never really in doubt. Reagan carries every state except Mondale's home state of Minnesota. He receives the highest number of electoral votes in history.

1986 ### Space shuttle *Challenger* explodes on takeoff

A faulty o-ring leads to an explosion that kills all seven astronauts, including teacher Christa McAuliffe.

1986

U.S. bombs Libya

Reagan determines Libya is behind a deadly Berlin disco bombing and orders American aircraft to bomb sites in Libya, almost killing leader Qaddafi in the process. Qaddafi's government has been financing and conducting anti-Western acts around the world for 2 decades, ignoring U.S. sanctions.

Reykjavik summit

Reagan and Gorbachev meet in Iceland to discuss disarmament. Reagan stands firm against the Soviet request to dismantle the Strategic Defense Initiative and the meeting is terminated.

Iran Contra scandal harms Reagan's legacy

In a scandal that almost destroys his presidency, information is released that details an American deal to give arms to Iran in return for the release of hostages held in Lebanon.

1987

"Mr. Gorbachev, tear down this wall!"

Reagan bluntly confronts the Soviets in a speech in front of the Berlin Wall. To the deafening cheers of Berliners, he implores Gorbachev to tear down the Berlin Wall.

Black Monday

The stock market falls 508 points in the largest percentage drop in history. It is caused by a number of factors, including program trading and speculation.

★1988★   GEORGE H. W. BUSH   41

CANDIDATE	PARTY	ELECTORAL VOTE	POPULAR VOTE
George H.W. Bush Dan Quayle	Republican	426	48,886,597
Michael Dukakis Lloyd Bentsen	Democratic	111	41,809,476

Ronald Reagan can't run again, so Vice President Bush becomes the Republican nominee. Democrats pick Massachusetts Governor Michael Dukakis. Democratic contender Gary Hart drops out after an affair with Donna Rice is revealed. Senator Kennedy declines to run, and Senator Joe Biden, accused of plagiarism in a speech, also drops out. Dukakis picks Texan Lloyd Bentsen as his running mate for his experience and to help in winning southern votes. Bush picks Dan Quayle of Indiana who becomes known for his verbal gaffes. Dukakis stages a disastrous photo-op wearing a tank commander's helmet, and is also hurt by the "Willie Horton" ads blaming him for releasing a convicted murderer who then commits rape. Bush benefits from a good economy, stability abroad, and Reagan's legacy, to easily win.

1988

First Hispanic Cabinet Member
President Reagan nominates the first Hispanic to serve in the cabinet, Lauro Cavazos, as Secretary of Education.

Pan Am Flight 103 destroyed
Libyan terrorists blow up Pan Am Flight 103 over Scotland, killing 270 people.

1989

Exxon Valdez runs aground

The tanker hits a reef in Prince William Sound, Alaska, and spills ten million gallons of crude oil causing great environmental damage.

First black governor elected in Virginia
Douglas Wilder is the nation's first elected black governor.

Berlin Wall and Iron Curtain fall

Helped by Reagan's policies, and Soviet leader Gorbachev's *glasnost* and *perestroika*, the Soviets relax their iron grip on Europe and jubilant Berliners tear down the Berlin Wall on November 9. This picture shows them on top of the wall in front of the Brandenburg Gate where Reagan spoke 2 years earlier. Over the next two years, the U.S.S.R. is dissolved into separate nation states.

U.S. invades Panama to capture fugitive General Noriega
The military dictator is accused by the U.S. of drug trafficking and racketeering, is tried in U.S. courts, and imprisoned.

1990

Hubble space telescope

The space shuttle deploys the most powerful telescope in history to help unlock secrets of the universe. It will be serviced 5 times by space shuttle missions and will still be working in 2011.

Picture from shuttle *Discovery*

Iraq invades Kuwait
Hoping to expand his oil resources, Saddam Hussein invades neighboring Kuwait and incites fears he could advance on Saudi Arabia. President Bush builds an international coalition to remove him from Kuwait.

1991

Operation Desert Storm
Congress approves war and President Bush orders Operation Desert Storm to retake Kuwait. A month of aerial bombing, including American stealth airplanes, leads to a short ground war lasting 100 hours. Iraq launches 39 missiles into Israel, killing 74 people. The U.S. deploys Patriot missiles to help shoot down these incoming missiles.

1991
Iraq war ends
The coalition forces drive Iraq from Kuwait, but President Bush stops short of destroying the entire Iraqi army. American losses are around 150 killed while Sadaam loses anywhere from 25,000 to 35,000 troops.

1992
Formal end to the cold war
President Bush and Russian President Yeltsin formally declare an end to the cold war.

Rodney King verdict sparks riots
Police officers accused of beating King in a year-earlier arrest are acquitted, touching off violent riots in Los Angeles that kill 54 people and damage $500 million of property.

Bosnia secedes from Yugoslavia
Years of war ensue with U.N. and U.S. involvement.

★ 27ᵀᴴ Amendment ★
Prevents any laws that affect Congressional salaries from taking effect until the next Congressional session.

1992   BILL CLINTON   42

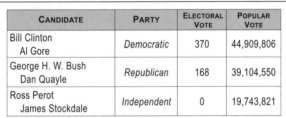

Candidate	Party	Electoral Vote	Popular Vote
Bill Clinton Al Gore	Democratic	370	44,909,806
George H. W. Bush Dan Quayle	Republican	168	39,104,550
Ross Perot James Stockdale	Independent	0	19,743,821

This three-way race has the strongest independent candidate since Teddy Roosevelt. Bush had 89% approval ratings after the Gulf War, but they are steadily falling. He raised taxes after promising he would not. His foreign policy experience is less important after the end of the Cold War. Several Democrats run for office, including Jerry Brown of California. His bid ends shortly after announcing in New York that he might pick Jesse Jackson as a running mate. The Jewish community still distrusts Jackson after earlier anti-Semitic remarks. Clinton wins the nomination and picks Al Gore of Tennessee as his running mate, bringing stronger family values and environmental experience to the race. Independent Texas billionaire Ross Perot promises to reduce debt and stop the NAFTA agreement. He gains support across the country and leads the race for two months. Clinton is accused of dodging the draft during the Vietnam War, using marijuana, which he famously says he "didn't inhale," and engaging in extramarital affairs. Clinton comfortably wins the election and, more importantly, the Democrats regain control of both houses of Congress.

1993 — **World Trade Center explosion**
Islamic extremists explode bombs in the basement of the World Trade Center in an attempt to destroy the building.

Branch Davidian standoff
A religious sect holds off the federal government at their compound near Waco, Texas. A government attack results in the death of 84 cult members and 4 agents.

Missile strike on Iraq
Clinton launches cruise missiles at several sites in Iraq in retaliation for an Iraqi assassination attempt on former President Bush.

American soldiers killed in Somalia
Islamic militia members ambush and kill 18 members of Task Force Ranger in Mogadishu, leading to a U.S. withdrawal from Somalia.

1994 — **North American Free Trade Agreement takes effect**
Canada, Mexico, and the United States sign the NAFTA agreement to improve trade between the nations.

***Contract with America* pays off for Republicans**
Republicans devise a "Contract with America" of pledges and promises, and gain control of both Senate and House for the first time in 40 years.

1995 — **Oklahoma City bombing**
U.S. extremist Timothy McVeigh explodes a home-made bomb by the federal building, killing 168 people. He will be executed on June 11, 2001.

U.S. establishes diplomatic ties with Vietnam

O.J. Simpson trial
The circus trial of former football star and actor O.J. Simpson for the murders of his ex-wife and her friend comes to an end. The jury acquits Simpson of the crime.

1996 — **Welfare Reform**
Pushed by a Republican Congress, President Clinton signs a Welfare Work bill that ends lifetime welfare benefits and requires work to continue benefits.

Pipe bomb explodes at the Atlanta Olympics
A domestic terrorist, Eric Rudolph, detonates the largest pipe bomb in our history at Centennial Olympic Park in Atlanta, killing two people and injuring 111.

★1996★ BILL CLINTON RE-ELECTED

CANDIDATE	PARTY	ELECTORAL VOTE	POPULAR VOTE
Bill Clinton Al Gore	Democratic	379	47,401,185
Bob Dole Jack Kemp	Republican	159	39,197,469
Ross Perot Patrick Choate	Reform	0	8.085,294

As an incumbent without competition, Clinton can focus on the election. The Republican Party is on a high after regaining control of Congress in the 1994 elections, but do not have an obvious candidate. They finally pick Bob Dole, whom Clinton depicts as an aged conservative—Dole is 73 compared to the 50-year-old Clinton. Dole highlights the perception by falling off a stage during an event, and forgetting that a baseball team has changed towns. He runs on a platform of reduced taxes and supply-side economics. Perot runs again, but garners only half the votes he got four years earlier. Clinton easily wins reelection in a manner almost identical to the 1992 election.

1998

African embassy bombings
Al-Qaeda terrorists explode bombs at U.S. embassies in Africa, killing more than 200.

Clinton caught in scandal
President Clinton is accused of having sex with intern Monica Lewinsky and then attempting to cover up the act. The House votes to impeach Clinton on charges of perjury and obstruction of justice.

1999

President Clinton acquitted of impeachment charges
Clinton is impeached by the House but acquitted by the Senate. President Andrew Johnson was also impeached and acquitted.

NATO attacks Yugoslavia
NATO forces attack Yugoslavia over ethnic cleansing charges during the Kosovo War.

Slovenia
Croatia
Bosnia Herzegovina
Serbia
Macedonia
FORMER YUGOSLAVIA

Columbine High School shooting
Two Colorado high school seniors use an arsenal of weapons to kill 12 students, a teacher, and then themselves.

Panama Canal transferred
Complete control of the Panama Canal is transferred to Panama following terms of the treaty signed by Carter in 1977.

2 0 0 0

2000—
Y2K disaster fizzles

Experts predict a disaster when clocks roll over from 1999 to 2000. This Y2K, or Millennium, bug would affect computer programs that represent the year with only two digits, thus possibly treating the new year '00' as 1900 and not 2000. However, no major problems occur.

Terrorists attack USS *Cole*

Al-Qaeda terrorists ram the USS *Cole* in Yemen with a small boat of explosives, killing 17 sailors and injuring 39. The Navy's rules of engagement prevent them from firing on the approaching vessel.

Damage to USS *Cole*

★2000★   GEORGE W. BUSH   43

CANDIDATE	PARTY	ELECTORAL VOTE	POPULAR VOTE
George W. Bush Dick Cheney	*Republican*	271	50,456,002
Al Gore Joe Lieberman	*Democratic*	266	50,999,897

The Republicans pick the 41st President's son, Texas Governor George W. Bush, as their candidate. Bill Clinton has served his maximum two terms, so his vice president, Al Gore, runs for the Democrats. Gore picks Joe Lieberman, the first Jewish-American chosen by a major party. Bush initially asks Secretary of Defense Dick Cheney to help him pick a vice president, but ends up selecting Cheney as his running mate. Cheney is also from Texas and electors can't cast both their votes to candidates from the same state, so Cheney changes his registration back to Wyoming. Bush's campaign is well-funded and he has obvious name recognition because of his father. Republicans run against the Clinton scandals, which Gore tries to ignore. Ralph Nader enters the race and eventually wins 2.7% of the popular vote, potentially affecting the outcome. The vote is extremely close but Gore concedes the race late in the night. He later recants as he learns that Florida, New Mexico, and Oregon are too close to call. Gore requests a hand recount of several Florida counties reporting voting irregularities. Both the Florida Supreme Court and the U.S. Supreme Court get involved. When the dust settles, Bush is declared winner on December 12. Bush wins all southern states, including Gore's home state of Tennessee, and Bill Clinton's home of Arkansas. Bush is the 4th president to receive fewer popular votes than the losing candidate.

2001

China illegally grounds U.S. plane

China intercepts and illegally detains a U.S. reconnaissance plane over international waters.

World Trade Centers destroyed—September 11, 2001

Islamic extremists hijack airplanes and fly them fully loaded into both World Trade Center towers in New York City, and the Pentagon in Washington, D.C. The Trade Center towers are both destroyed, but the Pentagon is only damaged. Heroic passengers attack the terrorists on a fourth plane causing it to crash in a Pennsylvania field, most likely sparing the White House. More than 3000 people are killed, and a world-wide war on terror is launched.

United States attacks Afghanistan

Intelligence identifies extremist Osama bin Laden as the mastermind of the 9/11 attack. After Afghanistan refuses to hand him over, the U.S. attacks in October and achieves victory two months later. Unfortunately, bin Laden escapes.

Patriot Act signed

President Bush signs the widely supported Patriot Act to remove restrictions on the law enforcement and intelligence services to allow them to better fight terrorism.

Enron files for bankruptcy

Enron, a leading energy company, had been falsifying their books and manipulating the market. Enron employees lose billions in their company retirement plan.

2002

Bush names the Axis of Evil

President Bush uses his State of the Union Address to label Iran, Iraq, and North Korea the new "Axis of Evil."

Steve Fossett circles the globe in a balloon

He completes the first solo balloon trip around the world.

Department of Homeland Security created

This new department is designed to help the U.S. fight terrorism and respond to natural disasters. It combines 22 existing agencies, including Immigration and Naturalization, the Coast Guard, and the Border Patrol.

2003

Space shuttle *Columbia* explodes

The shuttle explodes upon reentry due to missing heat tiles, killing all seven astronauts. The diverse crew included an Israeli astronaut and a woman from India.

2003 — **U.S. attacks Iraq in Second Gulf War**

After a decade of continued violations of the peace agreement ending the first Gulf War, and after evidence of WMD (weapons of mass destruction), the U.S. begins a bombing campaign against Iraq. Baghdad is captured after a ground war lasting only a few weeks with less than 200 Allies killed. The war will drag on until the end of the decade with roadside bombs and terrorist attacks killing thousands of U.S. soldiers.

President Bush signs $350 billion tax cut bill

Sadaam Hussein captured

On December 14, Sadaam is found hiding in an underground hole. He will be executed 3 years later by the Iraqis for his crimes against humanity.

2004 — **NATO gets new members**

NATO admits former Communist bloc countries to their organization, including Bulgaria, Estonia, Latvia, Lithuania, Romania, Slovakia, and Slovenia.

⋆2004⋆ GEORGE W. BUSH RE-ELECTED

CANDIDATE	PARTY	ELECTORAL VOTE	POPULAR VOTE
George W. Bush Dick Cheney	Republican	286	62,040,610
John Kerry John Edwards	Democratic	251	59,028,444

Bush and Cheney run again for the Republicans. Bush focuses on fighting terrorism and privatizing part of social security. Bush was transformed into a war president by the September 11, 2001 attacks, and his approval rating remained high through the invasion of Afghanistan and start of the invasion of Iraq. However, as the war drags on in Iraq and more soldiers are killed, his approval rating drops. Democrats have to pick a candidate from a large field. It narrows down to Howard Dean, John Kerry, John Edwards, and Richard Gephardt. Dean is hurt by a screaming cheer he makes at the Iowa caucus that is recorded. Kerry finally gets the nod and picks Edwards as his running mate. He emphasizes his Vietnam War experience, though later ads by the *Swift Vets* and *POWs for Truth* claim Kerry is exaggerating his war experience and combat wounds. Bush's National Guard service is brought into question with documents aired on CBS's *60 Minutes* which are later found to be fraudulent, resulting in the producer's dismissal. The election is not as contentious as 2000, but the victor is not determined until the Ohio results are finalized the next day. Kerry decides not to dispute Ohio, though he feels there are irregularities, even though the margin is 120,000 votes. Twelve million more votes are cast in 2004 than four years earlier, and this time, Bush wins both the electoral and popular vote.

2004

Indonesian tsunami kills 230,000

An underwater earthquake on December 26 creates massive waves that destroy coastal towns in one of the deadliest natural disasters in history. The 9.1 magnitude earthquake lasts longer than any on record, more than 8 minutes.

2005

Elections in Iraq

Iraq holds their first free elections in 50 years.

Hurricane Katrina devastates New Orleans

New Orleans sits well below the surrounding level of the Mississippi River and Lake Pontchartrain. When the surrounding levees failed, the city was flooded.

The huge hurricane hits New Orleans on August 29 and becomes the costliest in our nation's history. It floods most of New Orleans and kills 1,800. There is much finger pointing in the aftermath, as all levels of government failed, particularly the city and state.

2006

Democrats retake Congress

Nancy Pelosi becomes the first female Speaker of the House as Democrats retake the House and Senate.

2007

Virginia Tech shooting kills 32

A crazed shooter at Virginia Tech in Blacksburg kills 32 students. Ironically, the school is in a "gun free" zone.

Troop surge in Iraq is a success

Facing a deteriorating situation in Iraq, Bush orders an additional 20,000 troops into Iraq ("the surge") to provide stability and security. The surge is successful and violence decreases, allowing a transition of control back to the Iraqis.

2008

Michael Phelps sweeps the Beijing Olympics

He becomes the first athlete to win eight gold medals in one Olympics by winning all his swimming events. His eight gold medals tops Mark Spitz's 1972 record of seven. His Olympic medal count now totals sixteen.

Emergency Economic Stabilization Act passes

Faced with an economic crisis and possible collapse of major financial companies, Congress passes a massive $700 billion Troubled Asset Relief Program (TARP) to purchase failing bank assets. Following the vote, the Dow Jones Average falls 777 points in one day, its largest drop ever.

★2008★   BARACK H. OBAMA   44

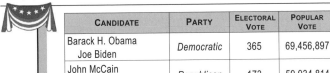

Candidate	Party	Electoral Vote	Popular Vote
Barack H. Obama Joe Biden	*Democratic*	365	69,456,897
John McCain Sarah Palin	*Republican*	173	59,934,814

This historic election returns a Democrat to the White House. It is the first time since 1952 that neither the incumbent president or vice president run again. This leaves the Republicans looking for a candidate. They finally pick Senator McCain, a respected former Vietnam POW. He selects the Governor of Alaska, Sarah Palin, as his running mate, the first time the Republicans have nominated a woman. She brings new energy to the campaign but many feel she is not qualified for the position. The Democrat nomination is a neck-and-neck race between Senator Hillary Clinton, former President Bill Clinton's wife, and Barack Obama, a black Senator from Illinois. Either will make history if elected. They fight each other until Obama finally clinches the nomination on June 3. He runs on a platform of change, though Clinton emphasizes Obama's inexperience during the primaries. The Republicans suffer from continued opposition to the conflict in Iraq, and low approval numbers for Bush. It is the first time two sitting senators run against each other, and the first time both candidates are born outside of the contiguous 48 states. The voter turnout is the highest in history and Obama easily wins the election.

2009 **$787 stimulus bill**

Obama signs the most expensive bill in the history of the country to try to pump money into the economy. However, the cost of the bill rises (to $862 billion), and unemployment keeps rising.

The government takes over private companies

Obama uses executive powers to place several auto and financial companies under government control.

Fort Hood shooting

A disgruntled Muslim U.S. Army officer kills 13 soldiers at Fort Hood in Texas. Political correctness has kept his superiors from removing him from the service.

2010 **Approval of Congress hits new low of 13%**

Nancy Pelosi's House and Harry Reid's Senate receive the lowest approval rating ever as just 13% of the American public approve of their work.

2010

Congress passes Health Care bill

After nationwide debates, Congress passes Obamacare, having to resort to controversial legislative procedures.

Offshore BP oil well disaster

An offshore oil well run by British Petroleum catches on fire, killing eleven workers and spilling thousands of barrels of oil into the Gulf until it is plugged months later.

Republicans win back the House

In an historic mid-term election, Democrats lose 63 seats in the House, the most lost since 1948, to give up control to the Republicans. They lose 6 Senate seats but retain control. Nancy Pelosi loses her position as Speaker of the House.

2011

Osama Bin Laden killed by U.S. Seals

In a daring night raid of four helicopters carrying 40 Navy Seals into a fortified compound in Pakistan, Bin Laden is killed. He has been hunted by our military ever since he orchestrated the September 11, 2001 terror bombings in New York and Washington. His body is taken for DNA verification, and then buried at sea.

The Future

It is up to every citizen to help write the future. Whether this country will endure, or whether it will join the other failed civilizations of history, depends on how well this and future generations heed the lessons of history, stay faithful to the concepts of the Constitution, and stay involved in their government.

History is a ribbon, always unfurling. History is a journey. And as we continue our journey, we think of those who traveled before us... and we see and hear again the echoes of our past: a general falls to his knees in the hard snow of Valley Forge; a lonely president paces the darkened halls and ponders his struggle to preserve the Union; the men of the Alamo call out encouragement to each other; a settler pushes west and sings a song, and the song echoes out forever and fills the unknowing air. It is the American sound. It is hopeful, big-hearted, idealistic, daring, decent, and fair. That's our heritage, that's our song. We sing it still. For all our problems, our differences, we are together as of old.

—*Ronald Reagan, 2nd Inaugural Address*

DIVINE PROVIDENCE HELPS THE NATION

You do not have to be a religious person to get a feeling that a higher power was there to help this country in her time of need. At a few critical points in her history, very unusual weather events were crucial in saving the country.

Boston weather saves the day

George Washington at Dorchester Heights
by Gilbert Stuart

The British fled eastward after the skirmishes at Lexington and Concord and occupied the city of Boston. Colonial militia started a siege of the city in April of 1775. Meanwhile, Ethan Allen and his Green Mountain boys had captured Fort Ticonderoga in New York, along with its cannon. Henry Knox, a Boston bookseller, proposed bringing those cannon back to Boston and, in November, he mounted an heroic 3-month effort to fetch the 60 cannon. He returned in February, 1776 with all the guns. Washington wanted to fortify Dorchester Heights that overlooked the British forces.

On March 4, more than 2000 colonial troops labored all night moving the cannon to the heights, concealing their movements behind bales of hay. The night was unseasonably mild, with clear skies and a full moon to help them in their work. A hazy fog below the heights hid the workers from the enemy. By early the next morning, their fortifications were sufficient to defend the hill. The British awoke to the sight of colonial cannon peering down on them from above. British General Howe exclaimed, "The rebels have done more in one night than my whole army would have done in a month," and estimated that at least 12,000 men must have been used to move the guns.

British Evacuation of Boston

The British immediately prepared a large force to attack Dorchester Heights at nightfall. As the first transports carrying British troops headed towards the heights, a strong wind arose, dissolving the warm day. It soon was a raging storm with hail, snow and sleet, smashing windows and blowing ships ashore. The attack was called off as the storms continued. On March 6, General Howe ordered the British to evacuate Boston. What a difference one day can make.

Fog saves the Colonial Army in New York

After the British left Boston, Washington moved his troops to New York. General Howe landed his troops on Staten Island and increased his strength to 32,000 men. Washington moved to Long Island but was soon outflanked and surrounded on Brooklyn Heights, his back

Delaware Regiment at the Battle of Long Island
by Domenick D'Andrea

to the East River. The British dug in instead of pressing for victory. The wind fortuitously stayed from the north, bottling up the British ships to the south. A southern breeze would have meant almost instant defeat.

Realizing his 9,000 men would soon be overwhelmed, Washington ordered a retreat across the river to Manhattan on the night of August 29, 1776. He secretly rounded up small boats to transport the men, telling them to prepare for an attack. Blustery winds died down around 11:00 pm, allowing the boats to start the journey. With muffled oars and strict orders for silence, the boats started their slow trips back and forth across the river. But by daybreak, a large portion of the army was still trapped on the wrong side of the river, and would soon be spotted and attacked by the British.

Here, Providence seemed to lend a hand again. Just at daybreak, an extremely heavy fog settled in, completely hiding the

Retreat at Long Island
by J. C. Armytage

troops in their retreat, even though the New York side of the river was clear. The fog lasted just long enough for the entire army to be rowed to safety—not a single man was lost. As the fog lifted, the astonished British saw empty colonial camps and could only wonder what had happened. Washington retreated across the Delaware River only to regroup in December with the surprise attack on the Hessians at Trenton, New Jersey in a turning point of the war.

A hurricane saves Washington, D.C.

During the War of 1812, the British sailed into Chesapeake Bay and landed 4,000 British troops that marched towards Washington. They quickly overwhelmed American troops facing them at the Battle of Bladensburg. President Madison was present at the battle and had to flee back to Washington. This defeat left the way open for the British troops to march into the capital on August 24. By then, the American government, including President Madison, had fled the city, but not before the President's wife, Dolley, had saved a number of paintings from the White House.

The British soldiers arrived and set fire to the White House, the Capitol, and many other public buildings, after dining in the empty White House. They were under orders not to burn any private buildings. They continued setting fires throughout the next day. Suddenly, an enormous storm, complete with a tornado, and of an intensity

The British Burn Washington

rarely seen in the area, struck the center of the capital. It blew roofs off buildings, smashed trees, and even tossed cannon in the air. But it also dropped continual rain on the city, extinguishing the fires, and saving the city from further harm. The shattered British forces left Washington and retreated to their ships. Our government returned to work.

Burned Capitol Building

The books destroyed at the Library of Congress would be restored by Thomas Jefferson's sale of his personal library the next year. The British would retreat to Baltimore and bombard Fort McHenry which was at the entrance to Baltimore Harbor. The bombardment would be the inspiration for Francis Scott Key to write *The Star-Spangled Banner.*

GEORGE WASHINGTON
The Father of Our Country

When King George asked an American in London what Washington would do after the war, the man answered that he would probably go back home to his Virginia farm. "If he does that," said the astonished king, "he will be the greatest man in the world."

—*King George*

First in war, first in peace and first in the hearts of his countrymen, he was second to none in the humble and endearing scenes of private life. Pious, just, humane, temperate and sincere—uniform, dignified and commanding—his example was as edifying to all around him as were the effects of that example lasting. . . . Correct throughout, vice shuddered in his presence and virtue always felt his fostering hand. The purity of his private character gave effulgence to his public virtues. . . . Such was the man for whom our nation mourns.

—*Henry Lee at Washington's funeral, 1799*

Chapter 2

U.S. PRESIDENTS

✤

PRESIDENTIAL ELECTIONS are held every four years in November with the victor being inaugurated early the next year. The following information lists the years the president served in office, starting with the year they were elected (not inaugurated), except for cases when a president died, was killed in office, or resigned. The state of birth is shown along with their dates of birth and death. The history timeline in the preceding chapter lists more details about each Presidential election.

GEORGE WASHINGTON

Virginia
Feb 22, 1732 - Dec 14, 1799

1

1789-1796

Washington was tall, strong, and one of the richest colonists. He had fought alongside the British during the Indian wars and served in the House of Burgesses. He was picked by the Continental Congress to lead the American troops against the British, and it was only his fierce determination and belief in his new country that kept the rag-tag Continental Army together. After the war, he left public life but was unanimously selected to be the new country's first President. He wisely turned down requests to act as its King. As the first President, he had an enormous responsibility to set the precedents that would guide America in the future. He had no government buildings—he had only the Constitution. He declined a third term, feeling that a President should only serve two terms. Sadly, he died a few years after leaving office.

JOHN ADAMS
Massachusetts
Oct 30, 1735 - Jul 4, 1826

2
1796-1800

Adams was Washington's vice president. He had been instrumental in the founding of the new country and had long supported the concept of an independent nation and the signing of the Declaration of Independence, but he was not as popular as Washington or Jefferson. He was a strong Federalist and was constantly fighting anti-Federalists like Jefferson. His passage of the Alien and Sedition Laws of 1789 met with great disapproval and increased the fear of a strong central government. He died on the 50th anniversary of the signing of the Declaration, on July 4, 1826—the same day that Jefferson died.

THOMAS JEFFERSON
Virginia
Apr 13, 1743 - Jul 4, 1826

3
1800-1808

The builder of Monticello in Virginia and the founder of the University of Virginia, Jefferson was crucial in the creation of the Declaration of Independence. He was a member of the Virginia House of Burgesses and the Continental Congress, Governor of Virginia, Secretary of State, and vice president under Adams. He was one of the most accomplished and talented Presidents in our history. He was a strong believer in state and individual rights. His term in office was highlighted by three key events—the purchase of the Louisiana territory from the French; the backing of the Lewis and Clark expedition that explored the new territory; and the rise of the American Navy that successfully fought the Barbary pirates in Africa. He died on the same day as John Adams, July 4, 1826, 50 years after the signing of the Declaration.

U.S. TRIVIA	Presidential Trivia
	Which presidents were born or died on the Fourth of July?

Born: Calvin Coolidge on July 4, 1872.

Died: Three of the first five presidents died on July 4: Thomas Jefferson and John Adams on July 4, 1826, the fiftieth anniversary of the signing of the Declaration; and James Monroe on July 4, 1831.

JAMES MADISON

Virginia
Mar 16, 1751 – Jun 28, 1836

4

1808-1816

Madison believed in many of the same principles as Jefferson. He was instrumental in the creation of the Constitution and, along with John Jay and Alexander Hamilton, wrote the Federalist Papers to help convince the nation to adopt the Constitution. Madison had introduced the Bill of Rights which was crucial in getting final ratification from all thirteen states. Maritime conflict with Britain led to the War of 1812 and he, along with his wife Dolly, were forced to flee the new capital of Washington when the British invaded. He was unpopular, but the successful conclusion of the war with Britain helped restore his legacy. Washington was the Father of his Country, but Madison was the Father of the Constitution.

JAMES MONROE

Virginia
Apr 28, 1758 – Jul 4, 1831

5

1816-1824

Monroe presided over 8 years of peace. He purchased Florida from Spain, made the Canadian border peaceful, and issued the Monroe Doctrine declaring the Western Hemisphere off-limits to European powers. He also helped pass the Missouri Compromise which outlawed slavery north of the Mason-Dixon line. He was the last of three consecutive Virginian Presidents. He helped further Jefferson's beliefs in state and individual rights.

JOHN QUINCY ADAMS

Massachusetts
Jul 11, 1767 – Feb 23, 1848

6

1824-1828

Son of the 2nd President, John Adams, John Quincy was a lawyer who held a number of positions prior to the Presidency. He helped write the Monroe Doctrine under the previous President. The election in 1824 produced no clear winner, and the House of Representatives had to decide between Adams and Andrew Jackson. Henry Clay supported Adams and the dispute resulted in the creation of two political parties. After leaving the White House, Adams served in Congress for seventeen years until he died on the floor of the House. He spent his last years opposing slavery.

Andrew Jackson

South Carolina
Mar 15, 1767 - Jun 8, 1845

7
1828-1836

Jackson fought the British during the Revolution as a 13-year-old boy and was taken prisoner and permanently scarred by a British officer's sword. As a General during the War of 1812, he soundly defeated the British at the Battle of New Orleans. He had a large following and became the first real President of the "people." He exercised federal authority and prevented the recharter of the Bank of the United States. He also vetoed more bills than all the previous presidents put together.

Martin van Buren

New York
Dec 5, 1782 - Jul 24, 1862

8
1836-1840

Van Buren helped organize the Democrat Party that Andrew Jackson brought to power in 1828. He ran a political machine in New York before becoming President. After becoming President, he was faced with the financial Panic of 1837, and formed the basis of the Treasury Department.

William H. Harrison

Virginia
Feb 9, 1773 - Apr 4, 1841

9
1840-1841

The Whig party nominated the 68-year-old Harrison but didn't count on him giving a 3-hour inauguration speech in the rain. Harrison died one month later—the shortest term of any President. His father, Benjamin Harrison, had been a signer of the Declaration of Independence. He was succeeded by his vice president, John Tyler. Harrison's election heralded in a new era of national politics as the Whigs ran an organized campaign which pictured Harrison as a war hero at the Battle of Tippecanoe. The Whigs pushed the slogan "Tippecanoe and Tyler, too" at their rallies.

JOHN TYLER | 10

Virginia
Mar 29, 1790 - Jan 18, 1862

1841-1844

Assuming office after the untimely death of President Harrison, Tyler became the first vice president to take over for an elected President. The Whigs most likely would not have nominated him for vice president if they had known this would happen as Tyler's policies were not consistent with the Whig party platform. He vetoed a bill for the Bank of the U.S. causing almost the entire original cabinet to resign. His main accomplishment was the annexation of Texas which became a state in 1845. After leaving the White House, he supported state's rights and joined the Confederate Congress.

JAMES POLK | 11

North Carolina
Nov 2, 1795 - Jun 15, 1849

1844-1848

Perhaps one of the most under-rated Presidents, Polk came from obscurity to beat the well-known Henry Clay and head a fairly successful presidency. He presided over one of the most expansionist eras in the country. He led the country in the Mexican-American War which resulted in the addition of territory from Texas to California. He also resolved the Oregon Territory dispute with Great Britain, and acquired full rights to what became Oregon, Washington and Idaho. He served only one term and died 3 months after leaving office.

ZACHARY TAYLOR | 12

Virginia
Nov 24, 1784 - Jul 9, 1850

1848-1850

Taylor was the first career Army officer to become President. He had been fighting since 1812 and became a national hero fighting the Mexicans in 1846 and 1847, crushing a larger army under Santa Anna at Buena Vista. He was unskilled at politics and soon ran into trouble over the issue of slavery and the admission of California as a free state. He was the last President to actually own slaves while in office. He died of unknown causes halfway through his term.

Millard Fillmore

New York
Jan 7, 1800 - Mar 8, 1874

13
1850-1852

Fillmore was born in a log cabin and, upon President Taylor's death, became the last Whig to be President. He signed the Compromise of 1850 and the Fugitive Slave Act which favored the South but angered the North and helped keep the country divided. He kept the French from annexing the Hawaiian Islands. After leaving the White House, he later opposed President Lincoln.

Franklin Pierce

New Hampshire
Nov 23, 1804 - Oct 8, 1869

14
1852-1856

Pierce was a reluctant dark-horse candidate who received the Democratic nomination after 35 stalemated ballots. He had served in the House and Senate, but had retired to private life before being thrust back into politics. His support of the 1850 Compromise and the Fugitive Slave Act alienated the North, and the passage of the Kansas-Nebraska Act created new problems. A plan to buy Cuba from Spain was successfully opposed by anti-slavery interests. His presidency is usually viewed as one of the most ineffective in history, and his reputation was further tarnished by his support for the Confederacy.

James Buchanan

Pennsylvania
Apr 23, 1791 - Jun 1, 1868

15
1856-1860

Born in a log cabin and the only bachelor President, Buchanan was also one of the oldest. He was unable to handle the slavery issue and his attempts at compromise only alienated both sides and earned him a position as one of our worst Presidents.

U.S.	Presidential Trivia
Trivia	Which presidents have been elected with fewer popular votes than their opponents?

George W. Bush (2000), Benjamin Harrison (1888), Rutherford Hayes (1876), John Q. Adams (1824)

ABRAHAM LINCOLN

Kentucky
Feb 12, 1809 - Apr 15, 1865

16
1860-1865

Born in a log cabin in Kentucky, Lincoln overcame adversity to become one of the greatest U.S. Presidents. He was a lawyer, state legislator, and national representative, but lost his two attempts to became a Senator. He campaigned against slavery and won the presidential election without a majority, or a single southern state—they started seceding as soon as he was elected. His entire presidency was consumed by the Civil War. His overriding goal was to preserve the Union at any cost. His Gettysburg Address encapsulated his vision for America. His perseverance won the war, preserved the Union, and ended slavery. Unfortunately, he was assassinated just 6 days after General Lee surrendered his Army.

ANDREW JOHNSON

North Carolina
Dec 29, 1808 - Jul 31, 1875

17
1865-1868

Johnson became vice president in 1864 and was thrust into the Presidency when Lincoln was shot. Lacking formal education, he was previously a Tennessee Senator, and the only southern Senator to keep his seat when the south seceded. He opposed Republicans who wanted to crush the southern states, and was impeached but acquitted by only one vote. After leaving office, he returned to the Senate and continued to fight Reconstruction policies.

ULYSSES S. GRANT

Ohio
Apr 27, 1822 - Jul 23, 1885

18
1868-1876

Raised on a farm and educated at West Point, Grant was picked by Lincoln to head the Northern armies after his victories at Vicksburg and Chattanooga. He used brute force to finally defeat the South, suffering enormous casualties in the process. He was picked by the Republicans for president even though he had no political experience. He made a number of mistakes early in office and assisted in events that led up to the Panic of 1873. His two terms were marred by corruption and incompetence, though he continued to fight for the civil rights of freed slaves.

RUTHERFORD B. HAYES
Ohio
Oct 4, 1822 - Jan 17, 1893

19
1876-1880

Picked in part for his honesty after the corrupt Grant administration, Hayes had served in the military and was Governor of Ohio when picked for President. His election was hotly disputed as he lost the popular vote. A compromise with the Democrats gave him the 20 disputed votes needed to become President. The price of this compromise was the end of the military occupation of the South, the end of Reconstruction, and the subsequent loss of voting rights for former southern slaves.

JAMES A. GARFIELD
Ohio
Nov 19, 1831 - Sep 19, 1881

20
1880-1881

As the last "log cabin" president, Garfield started out as a teacher and college president. He was a Union officer and a member of Congress for 18 years. The Republican convention deadlocked for 35 ballots before the dark-horse Garfield got the nomination. Unfortunately, an assassin killed him after only four months in office.

CHESTER A. ARTHUR
Vermont
Oct 5, 1829 - Nov 18, 1886

21
1881-1884

Garfield's vice president was associated with the New York political machine and many feared he would bring that to the White House. But he changed course and worked for the good of the country. His support of the Civil Service Reform Act led to federal employment based on examinations and merit, not political connections.

GROVER CLEVELAND
New Jersey
Mar 18, 1837 - Jun 24, 1908

22
1884-1888

A self-taught lawyer and governor of New York, Cleveland had fought corruption in his own Democrat party before becoming president. He helped protect civil service and fought against a high import tariff. He also created the Interstate Commerce Commission and started to modernize the navy.

BENJAMIN HARRISON
Ohio
Aug 20, 1833 - Mar 13, 1901

23
1888-1892

Grandson of the 9th President, Harrison had been a lawyer and Union army officer. His was the first administration to spend one billion dollars, and his McKinley Tariff was one of the most protective ever. The Sherman Antitrust Act was passed but his office did little to enforce its terms. Six states were admitted during his tenure.

GROVER CLEVELAND
New Jersey
Mar 18, 1837 - Jun 24, 1908

24
1892-1896

Cleveland was the only man to be elected President for two non-consecutive terms. His first successor, Benjamin Harrison, could not overcome the economic conditions to win a second term. Cleveland quickly inherited the Panic of 1893, a depression across the entire country that ruined the Democrat party. Cleveland supported the gold standard and used government forces to crush the Pullman Strike of 1894.

WILLIAM MCKINLEY
Ohio
Jan 29, 1843 - Sep 14, 1901

25
1896-1901

A supporter of high tariffs, McKinley pushed the gold standard and represented big business. Pressure grew to interfere in Cuba, fed by yellow journalism from some major newspapers. The USS *Maine* was sunk in Havana and war broke out. The Spanish-American War ended quickly and the U.S. acquired Puerto Rico, Guam, and the Philippines from Spain, and also annexed Hawaii in 1898. He named the hero Teddy Roosevelt as his vice president in the 1900 election, a move that would soon have consequences since Roosevelt was not as pro-business as McKinley. McKinley was shot and killed by an anarchist in 1901.

Teddy Roosevelt
New York
Oct 27, 1858 – Jan 6, 1919

26
1901-1908

Teddy Roosevelt had served in many positions prior to becoming President, including governor of New York. He was multifaceted, similar to Thomas Jefferson, being a scientist, hunter, and family man. He was a strong reformer but popular enough to earn a spot on Mount Rushmore. He personally led the Rough Riders to victory in the Spanish-American War. When he took over for president, he became the youngest President ever at 42. He attacked business trusts, started major conservation projects, and established the United States Forest Service. He acquired the Panama Canal Zone and sent the Great White Fleet of battleships around the world to project American power. Roosevelt helped negotiate the end to the Russo-Japanese War, becoming the first American Nobel Peace Prize winner.

William Howard Taft
Ohio
Sep 15, 1857 – Mar 8, 1930

27
1908-1912

Roosevelt had promised not to run for a third term, and he was succeeded by his Secretary of War, William Taft. Taft continued Roosevelt's policies of fighting trusts and reforming the civil service, but alienated his friends. Roosevelt finally took to publicly attacking him. Taft lost his bid for a second term. He later became the tenth Chief Justice of the United States, the only President to hold both positions.

U.S.
TRIVIA

Presidential Trivia

Which presidents did not finish their elected term of office and why?

Assassinated: Abraham Lincoln (1865), James Garfield (1881), William McKinley (1901), John Kennedy (1963)

Resigned: Richard Nixon (1974)

Died from illness: William Harrison (1841), Zachary Taylor (1850), Warren Harding (1923), Franklin Roosevelt (1945)

Assassination attempts: Andrew Jackson (1835), Theodore Roosevelt (1912), FDR (1933), Harry Truman (1950), Gerald Ford (1975-twice), Ronald Reagan (1981)

WOODROW WILSON

Virginia
Dec 28, 1856 - Feb 3, 1924

28
1912-1920

Teddy Roosevelt, upset by Taft's performance, tried to win the Republican nomination, and won the majority of the primaries before being outmaneuvered at the convention with the nomination going to Taft. Roosevelt formed a new Progressive party resulting in splitting the national vote, giving the election to the Democrat Wilson with only 42% of the popular vote. Wilson had been a history professor, president of Princeton, and governor of New Jersey. After his election, he launched a number of progressive programs, including the Federal Reserve Act, Federal Trade Commission Act, the Clayton Antitrust Act, the Federal Farm Loan Act, and a progress federal income tax. He also helped segregate federal agencies.

Wilson barely won re-election in 1916, campaigning on keeping the U.S. out of war. But German submarine warfare and a secret German alliance with Mexico finally forced a declaration of war against Germany. Wilson re-instituted the draft, took over the railroads, promoted labor unions, and suppressed anti-war movements. He pushed his Fourteen-Points vision of a peaceful post-war world, helped shape the Treaty of Versailles, and pushed for the creation of a League of Nations. However, he alienated his opposition, refused to compromise, and finally was stopped by a stroke. The U.S. never joined the League of Nations.

WARREN G. HARDING

Ohio
Nov 2, 1865 - Jul 2, 1923

29
1920-1923

Running on a platform similar to Teddy Roosevelt's, Harding came into office promising a return to normalcy. He favored big business, but his term became embroiled in corruption. Upon his return from a trip to Alaska, he died under suspicious circumstances in San Francisco.

U.S.	Presidential Trivia
TRIVIA	Which president was never elected to the office?

Gerald Ford: When Spiro Agnew resigned in 1973, President Nixon picked Gerald Ford for his Vice President. When Nixon resigned in 1974, Ford became President.

CALVIN COOLIDGE
Vermont
Jul 4, 1872 - Jan 5, 1933

30
1923-1928

As governor of Massachusetts, Coolidge reduced the number of departments from 118 to 18. He took over the high office favoring big business, stating "The business of America is business." He ran an efficient administration, and business prospered as he continued his laissez-faire policies. He ran a budget surplus each year and reduced top tax rates from 73% to 25%, enabling his reelection the following year. Even though he was popular, he decided not to run for re-election in 1928, and left office while times were good.

HERBERT HOOVER
Iowa
Aug 10, 1874 - Oct 20, 1964

31
1928-1932

Hoover had no previous elected office experience. He used his engineering background to eliminate waste in the government. However, the 1929 Stock Market Crash heralded in a decade-long depression, and Hoover's efforts were for naught. His inability to turn the country around was seen very unfavorably by voters. Homeless camps around the country came to be called "Hoovervilles."

FRANKLIN D. ROOSEVELT
New York
Jan 30, 1882 - Apr 12, 1945

32
1932-1945

Educated at Harvard, Roosevelt was crippled with polio before serving two terms as New York governor. He launched a 4-term project of transforming America during the height of the Depression. A liberal social reformer, he used the hard times to justify his actions. His government programs were designed to provide jobs and security, but also created a government dependence that still exists. He formed numerous agencies and spent billions, but ten years of effort did not end the Depression. However, he recognized the danger of German and Japanese aggression, and did what he could to help the Allies, particularly by implementing the Lend-Lease Act. After the Pearl Harbor attack, he worked with Churchill and Stalin to plot the war's course and plan the post-war world. He died suddenly in 1945 before the war ended. He was the only president to serve 4 terms, leading to an Amendment limiting the president to two terms.

HARRY S. TRUMAN

Missouri

May 8, 1884 - Dec 26, 1972

33

1945-1952

Roosevelt's death thrust his vice president into a mass of problems—ending the war, dealing with post-war Russia, and the atomic bomb. Truman dealt with these problems in a straight-forward manner, approving the use of the atomic bomb to end the war. He successfully dealt with the Russians in a divided Germany, established NATO, and upset Thomas Dewey in the 1948 election. He ratified the U.N. charter and used the Marshall Plan to help Europe recover. He oversaw the Korean War and relieved General MacArthur for insubordination.

DWIGHT D. EISENHOWER

Texas

Oct 14,1890 - Mar 28, 1969

34

1952-1960

The leader of Allied forces in World War II had never held public office, but his popularity thrust him into public office. Communism was on the march, with North Vietnam falling to Communists, and the Russians crushing the Hungary uprising, but Americans were content to regain prosperity after the lean years of the Depression and the war. Civil rights became a major issue and Eisenhower ordered troops to Little Rock, Arkansas to protect school children.

JOHN F. KENNEDY

Massachusetts

May 29, 1917 - Nov 22, 1963

35

1960-1963

The first president born in the 20th century, he was a war hero and part of the Kennedy dynasty. He outshone his opponent, Richard Nixon, in the first televised presidential debate, and narrowly won victory. He was the first Catholic president which had worried many Americans. His book, *Profiles in Courage*, won a Pulitzer Prize. He backed the disastrous Bay of Pigs invasion of Cuba, and faced the placing of Russian missiles in Cuba. The world was brought to the brink of nuclear war, but the blockade of Cuba turned back the Russians, and the missiles were removed from Cuba. His challenge to put a man on the moon by the end of the decade inspired the effort that placed Neil Armstrong on the moon in 1969. While in Dallas on November 22, 1963, he was killed by Lee Harvey Oswald—an event that shocked the world.

LYNDON B. JOHNSON
Texas
Aug 27, 1908 - Jan 22, 1973

36
1963-1968

The eighth vice president to take over for a dead president, Johnson was sworn into office on a plane ready to return to Washington after the assassination in Texas. He was a seasoned politician who had vehemently opposed Kennedy in the 1960 Democratic primaries, but was placed on the ticket to help secure Southern votes and leverage Johnson's considerable influence. After winning re-election in 1964, he pushed his plan for a "Great Society" resulting in a number of social programs like Medicare and Medicaid. He signed the historic Civil Rights Act of 1964, overcoming stubborn opposition, mainly from southern Democrats. However, his escalation of the war in Vietnam let to riots at home and a decline in popularity which led him to withdraw from the 1968 election.

RICHARD NIXON
California
Jan 9, 1913 - Apr 22, 1994

37
1968-1974

Nixon was Eisenhower's vice president, but lost to Kennedy in one of the closest races in history. He lost a race for California governor two years later and retired from politics until his 1968 bid for the presidency. Opposition to the Vietnam War continued, but he had success in other foreign policy efforts, being the first president to visit Communist China leading to an agreement with that country. He also signed an anti-ballistic missile treaty with the USSR in 1972. However, a bungled 1972 break-in at Democratic Headquarters at the Watergate building eventually led to his downfall. Ironically, he easily won that election and needed no help from any underhanded methods. Troops started withdrawing from Vietnam the next year but the nation became engrossed with the Watergate hearings and revelations of secret White House tapes including a crucial tape that was missing 18½ minutes of audio. The Supreme Court ordered his tapes released and he resigned in 1974 to avoid impeachment.

GERALD FORD

Nebraska
Jul 14, 1913 - Dec 26, 2006

38
1974-1976

Gerald Ford was the only President who was never elected. Nixon had appointed him vice president when Spiro Agnew left office due to corruption charges. When Nixon resigned, Ford took over the top job. A college football player, he had been a Representative in Congress for twenty years. He started office by pardoning Richard Nixon for all his crimes, a move that most likely helped heal the country, but brought sharp criticism. He signed the Helsinki Accords with the Soviets, and presided over the final U.S. withdrawal from Vietnam.

JIMMY CARTER

Georgia
Oct 1, 1924 -

39
1976-1980

The first president from the deep South since the Civil War, Carter used televised debates to overcome his relative obscurity. An intelligent former Navy officer, Carter owned a large peanut farm in Georgia and was governor of Georgia in 1970. He created the Department of Energy but signed over control of the Panama Canal to Panama, a move that angered many. His 1978 Camp David Accords worked towards Middle East peace between Egypt and Israel. However, soaring inflation and rising oil prices greatly harmed the economy. In 1979, the Iranians seized the American Embassy in Tehran, starting a hostage crisis that would not end until the inauguration of Ronald Reagan. The Soviets invaded Afghanistan, prompting a grain embargo and a boycott of the 1980 Moscow Olympics. Barely beating Ted Kennedy for the Democratic nomination in 1980, he was soundly defeated by Ronald Reagan.

U.S.	Presidential Trivia
TRIVIA	Which presidents have been related to each other?

Fifth Cousin (1): Theodore Roosevelt/Franklin D. Roosevelt.

Second Cousin (1): James Madison/Zachary Taylor.

Grandfather/Grandson (1): William H. Harrison/Benjamin Harrison.

Father/Son (2): John Adams/John Quincy Adams, George H. W. Bush/George W. Bush.

RONALD REAGAN

Illinois
Feb 6, 1911 – Jun 5, 2004

40
1980-1988

Reagan started as a Hollywood actor making more than 40 movies before serving as governor of California. He brought an upbeat belief in the greatness of America to the office, based on conservative and traditional values. He became known as "The Great Communicator." His term started with the release of the Iranian hostages on the day of his inauguration. A failed assassination attempt several months into office left him with the belief that God had spared him for some great task. He nominated the first female Supreme Court judge, Sandra O'Connor. His trickle-down economic policies and huge tax cuts (top rates fell from 70% to 28%) spurred a decade-long expansion of the economy. His conservative policies and aggressive expansion of the military led to a landslide victory in 1984, winning every state except one. He used the military to bomb Libya, invade Grenada, and confront the Soviets whenever possible. He demanded that Gorbachev tear down the Berlin Wall, and kept funding the space defense program, ultimately leading to the collapse of the Soviet Union without a shot being fired. The later years of his term were marred by the Iran Contra crisis but he left office on a high note.

GEORGE H. W. BUSH

Massachusetts
June 12, 1924 –

41
1988-1992

Bush had been the youngest Navy pilot in World War II. He was shot down in the Pacific and rescued by a submarine. He became the first sitting vice president to be elected president since Martin van Buren. He had experience in government and had been director of the CIA. He started his term carrying on many of the policies of Reagan but had to fight a Democrat Congress. He won election on a promise of no new taxes, but his major tax increases soon cost him support. The Soviet Union collapsed during his tenure and he put together a successful international coalition in the Gulf War to remove Sadaam Hussein from Kuwait after Sadaam had invaded that country. But Bush's failure to restore the economy and his lack of support for true conservative ideals cost him the next election.

BILL CLINTON

Arkansas

Aug 19, 1946 -

42
1992-2000

Clinton won only 43% of the popular vote due to the candidacy of Ross Perot. Clinton had been governor of Arkansas and a Rhodes Scholar. Coming into office, he passed the "Don't ask, don't tell" policy to allow gays in the military, but suffered a setback when his wife, Hillary, was unable to push new health care measures. He lost control of both houses of Congress in 1994, causing him to moderate his policies, but, banking on his personal popularity, won re-election in 1996. Clinton was caught in a sex scandal involving an intern at the White House, and his subsequent lies to a Grand Jury resulted in impeachment hearings. He was acquitted on charges, but the affair tainted his presidency. Clinton had served two terms, so his vice president, Al Gore, was the 2000 Democratic nominee.

GEORGE W. BUSH

Connecticut

Jul 6, 1946 -

43
2000-2008

The son of the 41st president, George W. Bush was a Harvard MBA, National Guard pilot, and Texas governor. The 2000 election was so close it would not be decided for weeks. Gore won the popular vote, but vote counting problems in Florida left the electoral vote undecided. Incorrect and miscounted ballots, and prematurely announced results clouded the election. The Supreme Court finally decided the outcome. Before Bush's first year was over, Islamic terrorists attacked New York and Washington on September 11, 2001, and Bush's presidency was redefined. When Afghanistan refused to turn over the attack's planner Osama Bin Laden, Bush attacked the country. Two years later, the U.S. invaded Iraq to finish the job started ten years earlier. The U.S. was still involved in both countries at the end of his 2nd term in 2008. He passed extensive tax cuts and withdrew from the Kyoto protocol on Global Warming. He was continually attacked about his policies on enhanced interrogation and the Patriot Act. He narrowly beat Senator Kerry in 2004. His administration was denounced for its handling of Hurricane Katrina, though state and local governments were also to blame. The Democrats gained control of both houses of Congress in 2006, and the end of his presidency was marked by a worsening economy.

BARACK H. OBAMA

Hawaii
Aug 4, 1961 -

44

2008-

Barack Obama made history by becoming America's first black president after serving as an Illinois and U.S. Senator. A financial crisis, triggered in part by problems with home mortgages and foreclosures, forced the passage of costly economic stimulus and job creation acts. Obama had complete Democrat control of both houses of Congress, so acts could pass Congress without fear of a presidential veto. He came to the office on a wave of enthusiasm about his ability to change Washington, but his initial popularity was put to the test by the debate over the new healthcare bill that was finally passed by a divided Congress. He also ran into difficulty fulfilling other campaign promises, such as the closing of the Guantanamo Bay detention facility, and removing troops from Iraq and Afghanistan. The Congress under Harry Reid and Nancy Pelosi sank to new lows of popularity and the elections of 2010 resulted in the Democrats losing control of the House and almost losing the Senate. Obama received a surge of support by the country in 2011 when the terrorist Osama bin Laden was killed by U.S. troops in Pakistan after a 9-year search.

At what point shall we expect the approach of danger? By what means shall we fortify against it?— Shall we expect some transatlantic military giant, to step the Ocean, and crush us at a blow? Never!-All the armies of Europe, Asia and Africa combined, with all the treasure of the earth (our own excepted) in their military chest; with a Bonaparte for a commander, could not by force, take a drink from the Ohio, or make a track on the Blue Ridge, in a trial of a thousand years.

At what point then is the approach of danger to be expected? I answer, if it ever reach us, it must spring up amongst us. It cannot come from abroad. If destruction be our lot, we must ourselves be its author and finisher. As a nation of freemen, we must live through all time, or die by suicide.

—Abraham Lincoln, 1838

Chapter 3

U.S. MAPS

❧

THE ORIGINAL 13 STATES made up less than 10% of the total land area of the future country. Some of the original states had claims to additional territory, but most of the continent was still claimed by various European nations, including England, France, Spain, and Russia. The United States had received a huge parcel of land, the Northwest Territory, in the treaty that ended the Revolutionary War, and the founders knew they had to set up procedures to handle the admission of new states as the nation grew. The procedures in the Northwest Ordinance and the Constitution would govern how those new states were to be admitted.

The path to our manifest destiny of 50 states would be long and tortuous. It involved wars, treaties, purchases, conflicts with the Native Americans, the discovery of gold, and, most importantly, the resolution of the slavery issue. The growth of the new Union was reflected in how the country was referenced, changing from "the United States *are*" to "the United States *is*."

Northwest Ordinance of 1787

The Northwest Ordinance of 1787, passed under the Articles of Confederation, established the policy used, with minor exceptions, for admitting future states. Its guidelines included:

- Congress appoints a territorial governor, territorial secretary, and three judges.

- When there are 5,000 free adult males in each territory, they can elect a general assembly legislature. (Remember women don't have the vote yet and slavery still existed.)

- When the population reaches 60,000, they can write their constitution and apply for statehood.

- New states are admitted on equal footing with old states.

- Slavery was prohibited in the Northwest territory.

Article 4 of the Constitution

The Constitution was written after the Northwest Ordinance was passed. Article 4 broadly covers admission of new states, with the important guarantee that state governments have a republican form of government. It stated:

> New States may be admitted by the Congress into this Union; but no new States shall be formed or erected within the Jurisdiction of any other State; nor any State be formed by the Junction of two or more States, or parts of States, without the Consent of the Legislatures of the States concerned as well as of the Congress...The United States shall guarantee to every State in this Union a Republican Form of Government...

The Enabling Act of 1802

The first in a number of acts formalizing the statehood process for qualifying states. It set the precedent for the creation of future states. This specific act authorized Ohio to start the transition towards statehood as they had reached the required population of 60,000.

Flag Act of 1818

This set the current policy of a fixed 13 stripes on our national flag, with one star for each state. Previously, the number of stripes had also increased with each state, resulting in the 15-stripe "Star-Spangled Banner" that inspired our national anthem. Each new star is added to the flag on the 4th of July following the admission of the new state.

Other acts affecting territories and states

Missouri Compromise (1820): Prohibited slavery in the former Louisiana Territory north of latitude 36°30', except for Missouri.

Compromise of 1850: Admitted California as a free state, prohibited slavery in Washington, D.C., and allowed Utah and New Mexico to decide their own slave status.

Kansas-Nebraska Act (1854): This created the territories of Kansas and Nebraska, repealed the Missouri Compromise of 1820, and allowed territories to determine their own slavery status. This led to years of the *Bleeding Kansas* wars as settlers fought over her slavery status, killing 50 in the process.

THE GROWTH OF AMERICA

Native American Tribes

The map shows some of the major tribes prior to European settlement. These are also hundreds of smaller ones. You'll recognize future state and city names among the tribe names. Columbus had mistakenly called the natives "Indians" thinking he had reached the East Indies.

1	Delaware (1787)	**8**	South Carolina (1788)
2	Pennsylvania (1787)	**9**	New Hampshire (1788)
3	New Jersey (1787)	**10**	Virginia (1788)
4	Georgia (1788)	**11**	New York (1788)
5	Connecticut (1788)	**12**	North Carolina (1789)
6	Massachusetts (1788)	**13**	Rhode Island (1790)
7	Maryland (1788)		

The 13 colonies become states when their state legislatures ratify the new Constitution. Several states do not ratify until they have been assured that a Bill of Rights will be included. Delaware takes the title as "The First State." Massachusetts also claims what is present-day Maine, and Kentucky and West Virginia are part of Virginia. The treaty ending the Revolution gives the U.S. the Northwest Territory.

14 Vermont (1791)	**16** Tennessee (1796)
15 Kentucky (1792)	**17** Ohio (1803)

Jefferson doubles the size of the country by purchasing the Louisiana Territory from France. Kentucky separates from Virginia and becomes the 15th state, and Ohio becomes the first state from the Northwest Territory.

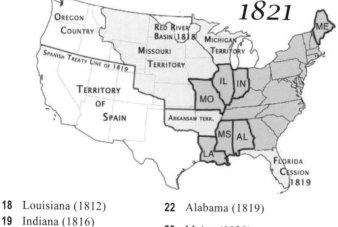

18 Louisiana (1812)	**22** Alabama (1819)
19 Indiana (1816)	
20 Mississippi (1817)	**23** Maine (1820)
21 Illinois (1818)	**24** Missouri (1821)

The Louisiana Territory is renamed the Missouri Territory when Louisiana becomes a state. It then becomes an unorganized territory when Missouri becomes a state. Arkansas is originally spelled "Arkansaw" before the spelling is later changed. Maine is admitted as a free state to balance the new slave state Missouri. The 1819 Adams-Onis Treaty grants Florida and surrounding area to the U.S. The Anglo-American Convention of 1818 gives the Red River Basin to the U.S. since it is south of the new border with Canada at latitude 49°.

25	Arkansas (1836)	29	Iowa (1846)
26	Michigan (1837)	30	Wisconsin (1848)
27	Florida (1845)		
28	Texas (1845)	31	California (1850)

The treaty ending the Mexican war in 1848, along with a payment of $18 million, gives the U.S. control of the Mexican Cession area. Texas (a slave state) has to wait to become a state until a Northern non-slave state can also be added. The 1846 Oregon Treaty sets the 49th parallel as our border with Canada.

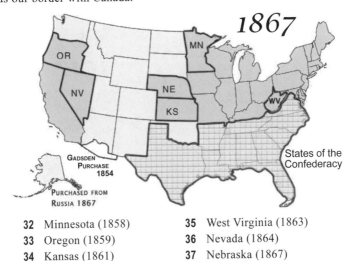

32	Minnesota (1858)	35	West Virginia (1863)
33	Oregon (1859)	36	Nevada (1864)
34	Kansas (1861)	37	Nebraska (1867)

As a result of the Kansas-Nebraska Act, Kansas draws up an anti-slavery constitution and is allowed into the Union as a free state. Nebraska has to wait until after the Civil War to be admitted as a free state. West Virginia votes itself independent of Virginia (which it had been a part of) and applies for statehood with the Union. The U.S. gets the Gadsden area from Mexico for $10 million in 1854, and purchases Alaska from Russia for $7.2 million in 1867.

38	Colorado (1876)	**42**	Washington (1889)
39	North Dakota (1889)	**43**	Idaho (1890)
40	South Dakota (1889)	**44**	Wyoming (1890)
41	Montana (1889)	**45**	Utah (1896)

Utah enters the Union with a large population that is 90% Mormon. Wyoming women had been given the right to vote which almost kept Wyoming from acquiring statehood. North and South Dakota achieve statehood on the same day, but are recorded in alphabetical order.

46	Oklahoma (1907)	**48**	Arizona (1912)
47	New Mexico (1912)		

Attempts to split the Oklahoma Territory into two states, a regular U.S. state and the Native American state of Sequoyah, fall short. A combined Oklahoma is admitted to the Union. New Mexico and Arizona fulfills the promise of Manifest Destiny as the United States now spreads continuously from sea to sea.

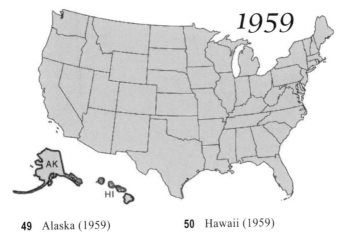

49 Alaska (1959)   **50** Hawaii (1959)

The Alaska territory, bought from the Russians in 1867 for $7.2 million, finally becomes the largest state in the Union. Hawaii had been annexed to the United States in 1898 and becomes the last state in 1959—the United States now has a fifty-star flag.

Regions and rivers of America
The map above shows the major rivers of the country, and the names of the general regions used to describe parts of the country. The names overlap and represent general areas and not exact collections of states. The Mississippi and Missouri rivers are the longest, each being over 2,000 miles long.

Continental Divide
The vertical line running through the Rocky Mountains divides the two major watersheds of the continental United States. All rivers to the west of the divide drain into the Pacific Ocean, while all rivers to the east drain into the Atlantic Ocean or Gulf of Mexico.

States, capitals(★), major cities, and time zones

How many city nicknames can you recognize in this list?

Beantown	Big Apple	Big Easy
Motor City	Music City	City of Angels
Windy City	City by the Bay	Gateway to the West
Steel City	Mile High City	City of Brotherly Love

Pittsburgh	*Denver*	*Philadelphia*
Chicago	*San Francisco*	*St. Louis*
Detroit	*Nashville*	*Los Angeles*
Boston	*New York*	*New Orleans*

U.S. Territories and Possessions

These islands are overseen directly by the United States government and are not part of any U.S. state.

Puerto Rico	Wake Island
U.S. Virgin Islands	Kingman Reef
Northern Mariana Islands	Navassa Island
American Samoa	Palmyra Atoll
Johnston Atoll	Midway Islands
Baker, Howland, Jarvis Islands	Guam

PACIFIC
TIME ZONE
3PM

MOUNTAIN
TIME ZONE
4PM

CENTRAL
TIME ZONE
5PM

ALASKA
TIME ZONE
2PM

HAWAII

HAWAIIAN
TIME ZONE
1PM

National Parks, Monuments, and attractions

Washington, D.C.
FDR Memorial, Korean War Veterans Memorial, Lincoln Memorial, National Mall, Thomas Jefferson Memorial, Vietnam Veterans Memorial, Washington Monument, White House, U.S. Capitol, World War II Memorial, Smithsonian Museum

Philadelphia, Pennsylvania
Liberty Bell, Independence Hall

New York City
Statue of Liberty, Ellis Island, Empire State Building

United States facts *(Source: CIA Factbook 2011)*

Highest point (50 states): Mt. McKinley, AK (20,320 ft.)

Highest point (48 states): Mt. Whitney, CA (14,494 ft.)

Lowest point: Death Valley, CA (-282 ft.) 100 miles from Whitney

Square Area (50 states): 3,794,101 sq. mi. (3rd largest in world)

Population (2011): 313,232,044 (3rd largest in world) White: 79%; Black: 13%; Asian: 4.4%; Hispanic: 15% (overlaps w/others)

Largest Metropolitan Areas: New York (19,300,000) Los Angeles (12,675,000) Chicago (9,134,000)

Religion: Protestant: 51%, Catholic: 24%, Mormon: 1.7%, Jewish: 1.7%, Buddhist: 0.7%, Muslim: 0.6%, other/none: 20.3%

Signing of the Mayflower Compact
Plymouth Harbor—November 11, 1620
by Jean Leon Gerome Ferris

We on this continent should never forget that men first crossed the Atlantic not to find soil for their ploughs but to secure liberty for their souls.

—*Robert J. McCracken*

America is much more than a geographical fact. It is a political and moral fact—the first community in which men set out in principle to institutionalize freedom, responsible government, and human equality.

—*Adlai Stevenson*

Signing of the Constitution of the United States
Independence Hall, Philadelphia—September 17, 1787
by Howard Chandler Christy

Chapter 4

OUR FOUNDING DOCUMENTS

❧

OUR FORM OF GOVERNMENT can trace its roots back through English law, the Magna Carta of 1215, and the civilizations of Rome and Greece. The early settlers of the new land knew the importance of the rule of law, and soon produced documents protecting individual rights and ensuring that the will of the people would always be heard. Some of America's most important documents are the Mayflower Compact, the Declaration of Independence, the Northwest Ordinance of 1787, and the U.S. Constitution. The full text of all these is included, except the Northwest Ordinance which is an important but often overlooked document establishing the procedures for territories to achieve statehood.

Declaration of Independence BY JOHN TRUMBULL

This famous painting (also on the cover) depicts the Declaration being presented to the Continental Congress by the drafting committee on June 28, 1776. Trumbull included 42 of the 56 signers of the Declaration in the picture. The 18x12-foot painting hangs in the U.S. Capitol and is reproduced on the back of the $2 bill. It does *not* depict the actual signing of the document.

Documents Grow Longer as Government Grows

Mayflower
Compact
1 page

Declaration of Independence
1 big page

U.S. Constitution
4 pages

2010 Health Bill
2,100 pages

U.S. Tax
Code
16,845 pages

MAYFLOWER COMPACT

PILGRIMS   NOVEMBER 11, 1620

> Before the colonists landed at Plymouth, Massachusetts in 1620, they
> all signed a document since known as the Mayflower Compact. This
> social contract established the right of the people to form a new gov-
> ernment in the new land based on the consent of those same people.
> This eventually led to the Declaration of Independence and the Amer-
> ican Constitution more than 150 years later. The *Mayflower* was sup-
> posed to land in Northern Virginia which explains their reference to
> Virginia in this document.

In the name of God, Amen. We whose names are underwrit-
ten, the loyal subjects of our dread Sovereign Lord King James,
by the Grace of God of Great Britain, France and Ireland, King,
Defender of the Faith, etc.

Having undertaken, for the Glory of God and advancement of
the Christian Faith and Honour of our King and Country, a Voyage
to plant the First Colony in the Northern Parts of Virginia, do by
these presents solemnly and mutually in the presence of God and
one of another, Covenant and Combine ourselves together into a
Civil Body Politic, for our better ordering and preservation and
furtherance of the ends aforesaid; and by virtue hereof to enact,
constitute and frame such just and equal Laws, Ordinances, Acts,
Constitutions and Offices, from time to time, as shall be thought
most meet and convenient for the general good of the Colony,
unto which we promise all due submission and obedience.

In witness whereof we have hereunder subscribed our names at
Cape Cod, the 11th of November, in the year of the reign of our
Sovereign Lord King James, of England, France and Ireland the
eighteenth, and of Scotland the fifty-fourth. Anno Domini 1620.

I sought for the greatness and genius of America in her commodious
harbors and her ample rivers, and it was not there. In the fertile fields
and boundless prairies, and it was not there. In her rich mines and her
vast world commerce, and it was not there. Not until I went into the
churches of America and heard her pulpits, aflame with righteousness, did I understand the secret of her genius and power. America
is great because she is good, and if America ever ceases to be good,
America will cease to be great.

—*attributed to Alexis de Tocqueville*

Declaration of Independence

Second Continental Congress   July 4, 1776

> The colonies had been fighting with British forces for a year when the Continental Congress met in Philadelphia to formally declare their separation from England. A draft, composed primarily by Thomas Jefferson, was presented on June 28 and approved on July 4. British forces were landing in New York and threatening Philadelphia, so there was no time to lose. The final document was sent to the printing presses, and copies were rushed by land and sea to all the colonies. The original, signed copy is in the Washington National Archives.

In CONGRESS, July 4, 1776
The Unanimous Declaration of the Thirteen United States of America

When in the Course of human events it becomes necessary for one people to dissolve the political bands which have connected them with another and to assume among the powers of the earth, the separate and equal station to which the Laws of Nature and of Nature's God entitle them, a decent respect to the opinions of mankind requires that they should declare the causes which impel them to the separation.

We hold these truths to be self-evident, that all men are created equal, that they are endowed by their Creator with certain unalienable Rights, that among these are Life, Liberty and the pursuit of Happiness. — That to secure these rights, Governments are instituted among Men, deriving their just powers from the consent of the governed, — That whenever any Form of Government becomes destructive of these ends, it is the Right of the People to alter or to abolish it, and to institute new Government, laying its foundation on such principles and organizing its powers in such form, as to them shall seem most likely to effect their Safety and Happiness. Prudence, indeed, will dictate that Governments long established should not be changed for light and transient causes; and accordingly all experience hath shewn that mankind are more disposed to suffer, while evils are sufferable than to right themselves by abolishing the forms to which they are accustomed. But when a long train of abuses and usurpations, pursuing invariably the same Object evinces a design to reduce them under absolute Despotism, it is their right, it is their duty, to throw off such Government, and to provide new Guards for their future security. — Such has been the patient sufferance of these Colonies; and such is now the necessity which constrains them to alter their former

Systems of Government. The history of the present King of Great Britain is a history of repeated injuries and usurpations, all having in direct object the establishment of an absolute Tyranny over these States. To prove this, let Facts be submitted to a candid world.

He has refused his Assent to Laws, the most wholesome and necessary for the public good. He has forbidden his Governors to pass Laws of immediate and pressing importance, unless suspended in their operation till his Assent should be obtained; and when so suspended, he has utterly neglected to attend to them.

He has refused to pass other Laws for the accommodation of large districts of people, unless those people would relinquish the right of Representation in the Legislature, a right inestimable to them and formidable to tyrants only.

He has called together legislative bodies at places unusual, uncomfortable, and distant from the depository of their Public Records, for the sole purpose of fatiguing them into compliance with his measures. He has dissolved Representative Houses repeatedly, for opposing with manly firmness his invasions on the rights of the people.

He has refused for a long time, after such dissolutions, to cause others to be elected, whereby the Legislative Powers, incapable of Annihilation, have returned to the People at large for their exercise; the State remaining in the mean time exposed to all the dangers of invasion from without, and convulsions within.

He has endeavoured to prevent the population of these States; for that purpose obstructing the Laws for Naturalization of Foreigners; refusing to pass others to encourage their migrations hither, and raising the conditions of new Appropriations of Lands.

He has obstructed the Administration of Justice by refusing his Assent to Laws for establishing Judiciary Powers. He has made Judges dependent on his Will alone for the tenure of their offices, and the amount and payment of their salaries.

He has erected a multitude of New Offices, and sent hither swarms of Officers to harass our people and eat out their substance. He has kept among us, in times of peace, Standing Armies without the Consent of our legislatures. He has affected to render the Military independent of and superior to the Civil Power.

He has combined with others to subject us to a jurisdiction foreign to our constitution, and unacknowledged by our laws; giving his Assent to their Acts of pretended Legislation:

For Quartering large bodies of armed troops among us: For protecting them, by a mock Trial, from punishment for any Murders which they should commit on the Inhabitants of these States:

For cutting off our Trade with all parts of the world: For imposing Taxes on us without our Consent: For depriving us in many cases, of the benefit of Trial by Jury: For transporting us beyond Seas to be tried for pretended offences:

For abolishing the free System of English Laws in a neighbouring Province, establishing therein an Arbitrary government, and enlarging its Boundaries so as to render it at once an example and fit instrument for introducing the same absolute rule into these Colonies

For taking away our Charters, abolishing our most valuable Laws and altering fundamentally the Forms of our Governments: For suspending our own Legislatures, and declaring themselves invested with power to legislate for us in all cases whatsoever.

He has abdicated Government here, by declaring us out of his Protection and waging War against us. He has plundered our seas, ravaged our coasts, burnt our towns, and destroyed the lives of our people. He is at this time transporting large Armies of foreign Mercenaries to compleat the works of death, desolation, and tyranny, already begun with circumstances of Cruelty & Perfidy scarcely paralleled in the most barbarous ages, and totally unworthy the Head of a civilized nation.

He has constrained our fellow Citizens taken Captive on the high Seas to bear Arms against their Country, to become the executioners of their friends and Brethren, or to fall themselves by their Hands.

He has excited domestic insurrections amongst us, and has endeavoured to bring on the inhabitants of our frontiers, the merciless Indian Savages whose known rule of warfare, is an undistinguished destruction of all ages, sexes and conditions.

In every stage of these Oppressions We have Petitioned for Redress in the most humble terms: Our repeated Petitions have been answered only by repeated injury. A Prince, whose character is thus marked by every act which may define a Tyrant, is unfit to be the ruler of a free people.

Nor have We been wanting in attentions to our British brethren. We have warned them from time to time of attempts by their legislature to extend an unwarrantable jurisdiction over us. We have reminded them of the circumstances of our emigration and settlement here. We have appealed to their native justice and magnanimity, and we have conjured them by the ties of our common kindred to disavow these usurpations, which would inevitably interrupt our connections and correspondence. They too have been deaf to the voice of justice and of consanguinity. We must, therefore, acquiesce in the necessity, which denounces our Separation, and hold them, as we hold the rest of mankind, Enemies in War, in Peace Friends.

We, therefore, the Representatives of the united States of America, in General Congress, Assembled, appealing to the Supreme Judge of the world for the rectitude of our intentions, do, in the Name, and by Authority of the good People of these Colonies, solemnly publish and declare, **That these united Colonies are, and of Right ought to be Free and Independent States,** that they are Absolved from all Allegiance to the British Crown, and that all political connection between them and the State of Great Britain, is and ought to be totally dissolved; and that as Free and Independent States, they have full Power to levy War, conclude Peace, contract Alliances, establish Commerce, and to do all other Acts and Things which Independent States may of right do. — **And for the support of this Declaration, with a firm reliance on the protection of Divine Providence, we mutually pledge to each other our Lives, our Fortunes, and our sacred Honor.**

John Hancock

NEW HAMPSHIRE
Josiah Bartlett
Wm Whipple
Matthew Thornton

DELAWARE
Cæsar Rodney
Geo Read
Tho M:Kean

CONNECTICUT
Roger Sherman
Sam.el Huntington
Wm Williams
Oliver Wolcott

PENNSYLVANIA
Robt Morris
Benjamin Rush
Benj Franklin
John Morton
Geo Clymer
Jas. Smith
Geo Taylor
James Wilson
Geo. Ross

GEORGIA
Button Gwinnett
Lyman Hall
Geo Walton

NEW JERSEY
Rich Stockton
Jno Witherspoon
Fras Hopkinson
John Hart
Abra Clark

VIRGINIA
George Wythe
Richard Henry Lee
Th Jefferson
Benja Harrison
Ths Nelson jr.
Francis Lightfoot Lee
Carter Braxton

SOUTH CAROLINA
Edward Rutledge
Thos Heyward Junr.
Thomas Lynch Junr.
Arthur Middleton

MARYLAND
Samuel Chase
Wm Paca
Thos Stone
Charles Carroll of Carrollton

NEW YORK
Wm Floyd
Phil. Livingston
Frans Lewis
Lewis Morris

NORTH CAROLINA
Wm Hooper
Joseph Hewes
John Penn

RHODE ISLAND
Step Hopkins
William Ellery

MASSACHUSETTS
Sam.l Adams
John Adams
Robt Treat Paine
Elbridge Gerry

NORTHWEST ORDINANCE OF 1787

CONGRESS OF THE CONFEDERATION   **JULY 13, 1787**

In one of its last official acts, the Confederation passed the Northwest Ordinance earlier in the same year that they passed the Constitution. This document was of upmost importance to the subsequent expansion of the country as it set the general procedures for statehood. The 1783 Peace Treaty had granted a large territory to the new country, consisting of present-day Ohio, Indiana, Illinois, Michigan, Wisconsin, and Minnesota. However, there were no procedures in place to handle new states. On July 13, the Congress passed this new ordinance which set the rules for establishing new states in this territory, as well as prohibiting slavery in those states. It also encouraged schools, protected property rights, guaranteed religious freedom, and protected the rights of Native Americans. All new states would be admitted as equals with existing states. Excerpts from the Ordinance follow:

That there shall be appointed from time to time by Congress, a governor, whose commission shall continue in force for the term of three years, unless sooner revoked by Congress; he shall reside in the district, and have a freehold estate therein in 1,000 acres of land, while in the exercise of his office...There shall also be appointed a court to consist of three judges, any two of whom to form a court, who shall have a common law jurisdiction, and reside in the district, and have each therein a freehold estate in 500 acres of land while in the exercise of their offices; and their commissions shall continue in force during good behavior...

The governor, for the time being, shall be commander in chief of the militia, appoint and commission all officers in the same below the rank of general officers; all general officers shall be appointed and commissioned by Congress...

So soon as there shall be five thousand free male inhabitants of full age in the district, upon giving proof thereof to the governor, they shall receive authority, with time and place, to elect a representative from their counties or townships to represent them in the general assembly...

As soon as a legislature shall be formed in the district, the council and house assembled in one room, shall have authority, by joint ballot, to elect a delegate to Congress, who shall have a seat in Congress, with a right of debating but not voting during this temporary government.

And, for extending the fundamental principles of civil and religious liberty...and for their admission to a share in the federal councils on an equal footing with the original States, at as early periods as may be consistent with the general interest...

Art. 1. No person, demeaning himself in a peaceable and orderly manner, shall ever be molested on account of his mode of worship or religious sentiments, in the said territory.

Art. 2. The inhabitants of the said territory shall always be entitled to the benefits of the writ of habeas corpus, and of the trial by jury; of a proportionate representation of the people in the legislature; and of judicial proceedings according to the course of the common law...No man shall be deprived of his liberty or property, but by the judgment of his peers or the law of the land; ...

Art. 3. Religion, morality, and knowledge, being necessary to good government and the happiness of mankind, schools and the means of education shall forever be encouraged. The utmost good faith shall always be observed towards the Indians; their lands and property shall never be taken from them without their consent; and, in their property, rights, and liberty, they shall never be invaded or disturbed, unless in just and lawful wars authorized by Congress; but laws founded in justice and humanity, shall from time to time be made for preventing wrongs being done to them, and for preserving peace and friendship with them...

Art. 5. There shall be formed in the said territory, not less than three nor more than five States; and the boundaries of the States, as soon as Virginia shall alter her act of cession, and consent to the same, shall become fixed....

And, whenever any of the said States shall have sixty thousand free inhabitants therein, such State shall be admitted, by its delegates, into the Congress of the United States, on an equal footing with the original States in all respects whatever, and shall be at liberty to form a permanent constitution and State government: Provided, the constitution and government so to be formed, shall be republican, and in conformity to the principles contained in these articles; and, so far as it can be consistent with the general interest of the confederacy, such admission shall be allowed at an earlier period, and when there may be a less number of free inhabitants in the State than sixty thousand.

Art. 6. There shall be neither slavery nor involuntary servitude in the said territory, otherwise than in the punishment of crimes whereof the party shall have been duly convicted: Provided, always, That any person escaping into the same, from whom labor or service is lawfully claimed in any one of the original States, such fugitive may be lawfully reclaimed and conveyed to the person claiming his or her labor or service as aforesaid...

United States Constitution

Constitutional Convention	March 4, 1789

After the Revolutionary War, it became obvious that the Articles of Confederation were not capable of running the new country. Its national government was too weak to hold the country together. There was no provision for taxation or handling the national debt. Its form of weak central government was only natural due to the country's recent problems with, and separation from, the British monarchy.

A Constitutional Convention met in Philadelphia in May of 1787 to amend the Articles of Confederation, but decided instead that an entirely new document was needed. A new plan from Virginia called for a 3-branch government, but there were concerns about a legislative body based solely on population. A compromise led to the creation of a bicameral body with a House based on population, and a Senate with equal representation from each state. The Three-Fifths Compromise counted slaves as only 3/5 of a person for determining representation, but this was mainly to reduce the influence of southern states.

By September of 1787, they had produced a draft of a new Constitution. It received the required ratification by nine states on June 21, 1788, and became effective on March 4, 1789. It was the first time that a nation's people had peacefully decided on their new form of government, and the document they produced is the oldest written constitution still in effect. Only 12 states initially signed the Constitution. Rhode Island did not even attend the convention as she was the smallest state and felt that the new government would take away too much of her power as a state. The Constitution is now the supreme law of the land. Note: The original text is shown below with sections that have been changed or superseded by amendments shown in ***bold italic***. There is one grammar mistake that has been copied from the original document. See if you can find it (it is not an old or British spelling like chuse).

We the People of the UNITED STATES, in Order to form a more perfect Union, establish Justice, insure domestic Tranquility, provide for the common defence, promote the general Welfare, and secure the Blessings of Liberty to ourselves and our Posterity, do ordain and establish this Constitution for the United States of America.

Article I

Section 1. All legislative Powers herein granted shall be vested in a Congress of the United States, which shall consist of a Senate and House of Representatives.

Section 2. The House of Representatives shall be composed of Members chosen every second Year by the People of the several States, and the Electors in each State shall have the Qualifications requisite for Electors of the most numerous Branch of the State Legislature.

No Person shall be a Representative who shall not have attained to the Age of twenty five Years, and been seven Years a Citizen of the United States, and who shall not, when elected, be an Inhabitant of that State in which he shall be chosen.

Representatives and direct Taxes shall be apportioned among the several States which may be included within this Union, according to their respective Numbers, which shall be determined by adding to the whole Number of free Persons, including those bound to Service for a Term of Years, and excluding Indians not taxed, three fifths of all other Persons. (Modified by 14 amendment.) The actual Enumeration shall be made within three Years after the first Meeting of the Congress of the United States, and within every subsequent Term of ten Years, in such Manner as they shall by Law direct. The Number of Representatives shall not exceed one for every thirty Thousand, but each State shall have at Least one Representative; and until such enumeration shall be made, the State of New Hampshire shall be entitled to chuse three, Massachusetts eight, Rhode Island and Providence Plantations one, Connecticut five, New York six, New Jersey four, Pennsylvania eight, Delaware one, Maryland six, Virginia ten, North Carolina five, South Carolina five and Georgia three.

When vacancies happen in the Representation from any State, the Executive Authority thereof shall issue Writs of Election to fill such Vacancies.

The House of Representatives shall chuse their Speaker and other Officers; and shall have the sole Power of Impeachment.

SECTION 3. The Senate of the United States shall be composed of two Senators from each State, *chosen by the Legislature thereof,* (modified by the 17th Amendment) for six Years; and each Senator shall have one Vote.

Immediately after they shall be assembled in Consequence of the first Election, they shall be divided as equally as may be into three Classes. The Seats of the Senators of the first Class shall be vacated at the Expiration of the second Year, of the second Class at the Expiration of the fourth Year, and of the third Class at the Expiration of the sixth Year, so that one third may be chosen every second Year; *and if Vacancies happen by Resignation, or otherwise, during the Recess of the Legislature of any State, the Executive thereof may make temporary Appointments until the next Meeting of the Legislature, which shall then fill such Vacancies.* (modified by the 17th amendment)

No person shall be a Senator who shall not have attained to the Age of thirty Years, and been nine Years a Citizen of the United States, and who shall not, when elected, be an Inhabitant of that State for which he shall be chosen.

The Vice President of the United States shall be President of the Senate, but shall have no Vote, unless they be equally divided.

The Senate shall chuse their other Officers, and also a President pro tempore, in the absence of the Vice President, or when he shall exercise the Office of President of the United States.

The Senate shall have the sole Power to try all Impeachments. When sitting for that Purpose, they shall be on Oath or Affirmation. When the President of the United States is tried, the Chief Justice shall preside: And no Person shall be convicted without the Concurrence of two thirds of the Members present.

Judgment in Cases of Impeachment shall not extend further than to removal from Office, and disqualification to hold and enjoy any Office of honor, Trust or Profit under the United States: but the Party convicted shall nevertheless be liable and subject to Indictment, Trial, Judgment and Punishment, according to Law.

SECTION 4. The Times, Places and Manner of holding Elections for Senators and Representatives, shall be prescribed in each State by the Legislature thereof; but the Congress may at any time by Law make or alter such Regulations, except as to the Place of Chusing Senators.

The Congress shall assemble at least once in every Year, and such Meeting shall be *on the first Monday in December,* (superseded by the 20th amendment) unless they shall by Law appoint a different Day.

SECTION 5. Each House shall be the Judge of the Elections, Returns and Qualifications of its own Members, and a Majority of each shall constitute a Quorum to do Business; but a smaller number may adjourn from day to day, and may be authorized to compel the Attendance of absent Members, in such Manner, and under such Penalties as each House may provide.

Each House may determine the Rules of its Proceedings, punish its Members for disorderly Behavior, and, with the Concurrence of two-thirds, expel a Member.

Each House shall keep a Journal of its Proceedings, and from time to time publish the same, excepting such Parts as may in their Judgment require Secrecy; and the Yeas and Nays of the Members of either House on any question shall, at the Desire of one fifth of those Present, be entered on the Journal.

Neither House, during the Session of Congress, shall, without the Consent of the other, adjourn for more than three days, nor to any other Place than that in which the two Houses shall be sitting.

SECTION 6. *The Senators and Representatives shall receive a Compensation for their Services, to be ascertained by Law, and paid out of the Treasury of the United States.* (modified by the 27th Amendment.) They shall in all Cases, except Treason, Felony and Breach of the Peace, be privileged from Arrest during their Attendance at the Session of their respective Houses, and in going to and returning from the same; and for any Speech or Debate in either House, they shall not be questioned in any other Place.

No Senator or Representative shall, during the Time for which he was elected, be appointed to any civil Office under the Authority of the United States which shall have been created, or the Emoluments whereof shall have been increased during such time; and no Person holding any Office under the United States, shall be a Member of either House during his Continuance in Office.

SECTION 7. All bills for raising Revenue shall originate in the House of Representatives; but the Senate may propose or concur with Amendments as on other Bills.

Every Bill which shall have passed the House of Representatives and the Senate, shall, before it become a Law, be presented to the President of the United States; If he approve he shall sign it, but if not he shall return it, with his Objections to that House in which it shall have originated, who shall enter the Objections at large on their Journal, and proceed to reconsider it. If after such Reconsideration two thirds of that House shall agree to pass the Bill, it shall be sent, together with the Objections, to the other House, by which it shall likewise be reconsidered, and if approved by two thirds of that House, it shall become a Law. But in all such Cases the Votes of both Houses shall be determined by Yeas and Nays, and the Names of the Persons voting for and against the Bill shall be entered on the Journal of each House respectively. If any Bill shall not be returned by the President within ten Days (Sundays excepted) after it shall have been presented to him, the Same shall be a Law, in like Manner as if he had signed it, unless the Congress by their Adjournment prevent its Return, in which Case it shall not be a Law.

Every Order, Resolution, or Vote to which the Concurrence of the Senate and House of Representatives may be necessary (except on a question of Adjournment) shall be presented to the President of the United States; and before the Same shall take Effect, shall be approved by him, or being disapproved by him, shall be repassed by two thirds of the Senate and House of Representatives, according to the Rules and Limitations prescribed in the Case of a Bill.

SECTION 8. The Congress shall have Power To lay and collect Taxes, Duties, Imposts and Excises, to pay the Debts and provide for the common Defence and general Welfare of the United States; but all Duties, Imposts and Excises shall be uniform throughout the United States;

To borrow money on the credit of the United States;

To regulate Commerce with foreign Nations, and among the several States, and with the Indian Tribes;

To establish an uniform Rule of Naturalization, and uniform Laws on the subject of Bankruptcies throughout the United States;

To coin Money, regulate the Value thereof, and of foreign Coin, and fix the Standard of Weights and Measures;

To provide for the Punishment of counterfeiting the Securities and current Coin of the United States;

To establish Post Offices and Post Roads;

To promote the Progress of Science and useful Arts, by securing for limited Times to Authors and Inventors the exclusive Right to their respective Writings and Discoveries;

To constitute Tribunals inferior to the supreme Court;

To define and punish Piracies and Felonies committed on the high Seas, and Offenses against the Law of Nations;

To declare War, grant Letters of Marque and Reprisal, and make Rules concerning Captures on Land and Water;

To raise and support Armies, but no Appropriation of Money to that Use shall be for a longer Term than two Years;

To provide and maintain a Navy; To make Rules for the Government and Regulation of the land and naval Forces;

To provide for calling forth the Militia to execute the Laws of the Union, suppress Insurrections and repel Invasions;

To provide for organizing, arming, and disciplining, the Militia, and for governing such Part of them as may be employed in the Service of the United States, reserving to the States respectively, the Appointment of the Officers, and the Authority of training the Militia according to the discipline prescribed by Congress;

To exercise exclusive Legislation in all Cases whatsoever, over such District (not exceeding ten Miles square) as may, by Cession of particular States, and the acceptance of Congress, become the Seat of the Government of the United States, and to exercise like Authority over all Places purchased by the Consent of the Legislature of the State in which the Same shall be, for the Erection of Forts, Magazines, Arsenals, dock-Yards, and other needful Buildings; And

To make all Laws which shall be necessary and proper for carrying into Execution the foregoing Powers, and all other Powers vested by this Constitution in the Government of the United States, or in any Department or Officer thereof.

SECTION 9. The Migration or Importation of such Persons as any of the States now existing shall think proper to admit, shall not be prohibited by the Congress prior to the Year one thousand eight hundred and eight, but a tax or duty may be imposed on such Importation, not exceeding ten dollars for each Person.

The privilege of the Writ of Habeas Corpus shall not be suspended, unless when in Cases of Rebellion or Invasion the public Safety may require it.

No Bill of Attainder or ex post facto Law shall be passed.

No capitation, or other direct, Tax shall be laid, unless in Proportion to the Census or Enumeration herein before directed to be taken. *(Clarified by the 16th Amendment.)*

No Tax or Duty shall be laid on Articles exported from any State.

No Preference shall be given by any Regulation of Commerce or Revenue to the Ports of one State over those of another: nor shall Vessels bound to, or from, one State, be obliged to enter, clear, or pay Duties in another.

No Money shall be drawn from the Treasury, but in Consequence of Appropriations made by Law; and a regular Statement and Account of the Receipts and Expenditures of all public Money shall be published from time to time.

No Title of Nobility shall be granted by the United States: And no Person holding any Office of Profit or Trust under them, shall, without the Consent of the Congress, accept of any present, Emolument, Office, or Title, of any kind whatever, from any King, Prince or foreign State.

SECTION 10. No State shall enter into any Treaty, Alliance, or Confederation; grant Letters of Marque and Reprisal; coin Money; emit Bills of Credit; make any Thing but gold and silver Coin a Tender in Payment of Debts; pass any Bill of Attainder, ex post facto Law, or Law impairing the Obligation of Contracts, or grant any Title of Nobility.

No State shall, without the Consent of the Congress, lay any Imposts or Duties on Imports or Exports, except what may be absolutely necessary for executing it's inspection Laws: and the net Produce of all Duties and Imposts, laid by any State on Imports or Exports, shall be for the Use of the Treasury of the United States; and all such Laws shall be subject to the Revision and Controul of the Congress.

No State shall, without the Consent of Congress, lay any duty of Tonnage, keep Troops, or Ships of War in time of Peace, enter into any Agreement or Compact with another State, or with a foreign Power, or engage in War, unless actually invaded, or in such imminent Danger as will not admit of delay.

ARTICLE II

SECTION 1. The executive Power shall be vested in a President of the United States of America. He shall hold his Office during the Term of four Years, and, together with the Vice President chosen for the same Term, be elected, as follows:

Each State shall appoint, in such Manner as the Legislature thereof may direct, a Number of Electors, equal to the whole Number of Senators and Representatives to which the State may be entitled in the Congress: but no Senator or Representative, or Person holding an Office of Trust or Profit under the United States, shall be appointed an Elector.

The Electors shall meet in their respective States, and vote by Ballot for two persons, of whom one at least shall not be an Inhabitant of the same State with themselves. And they shall make a List of all the Persons voted for, and of the Number of Votes for each; which List they shall sign and certify, and transmit sealed to the Seat of the Government of the United States, directed to the President of the Senate. The President of the Senate shall, in the Presence of the Senate and House of Representatives, open all the Certificates, and the Votes shall then be counted. The Person having the greatest Number of Votes shall be the President, if such Number be a Majority of the whole Number of Electors appointed; and if there be more than one who have such Majority, and have an equal Number of Votes, then the House of Representatives shall immediately chuse by Ballot one of them for President; and if no Person have a Majority, then from the five highest on the List the said House shall in like Manner chuse the President. But in chusing the President, the Votes shall be taken by States, the Representation from each State having one Vote; a quorum for this Purpose shall consist of a Member or Members from two-thirds of the States, and a Majority of all the States shall be necessary to a Choice. In every Case, after the Choice of the President, the Person having the greatest Number of Votes of the Electors shall be the Vice President. But if there should remain two or more who have equal Votes, the Senate shall chuse from them by Ballot the Vice-President. (superseded by the 12th Amendment.)

The Congress may determine the Time of chusing the Electors, and the Day on which they shall give their Votes; which Day shall be the same throughout the United States.

No person except a natural born Citizen, or a Citizen of the United States, at the time of the Adoption of this Constitution, shall be eligible to the Office of President; neither shall any Person be eligible to that Office who shall not have attained to the Age of thirty-five Years, and been fourteen Years a Resident within the United States.

In Case of the Removal of the President from Office, or of his Death, Resignation, or Inability to discharge the Powers and Duties of the said Office, the same shall devolve on the Vice President, and the Congress may by Law provide for the Case of Removal, Death, Resignation or Inability, both of the President and Vice President, declaring what Officer shall then act as President, and such Officer shall act accordingly, until the Disability be removed, or a President shall be elected. (modified by the 20th and 25th Amendments.)

The President shall, at stated Times, receive for his Services, a Compensation, which shall neither be increased nor diminished during the Period for which he shall have been elected, and he shall not receive within that Period any other Emolument from the United States, or any of them.

Before he enter on the Execution of his Office, he shall take the following Oath or Affirmation:

"I do solemnly swear (or affirm) that I will faithfully execute the Office of President of the United States, and will to the best of my Ability, preserve, protect and defend the Constitution of the United States."

SECTION 2. The President shall be Commander in Chief of the Army and Navy of the United States, and of the Militia of the several States, when called into the actual Service of the United States; he may require the Opinion, in writing, of the principal Officer in each of the executive Departments, upon any subject relating to the Duties of their respective Offices, and he shall have Power to Grant Reprieves and Pardons for Offenses against the United States, except in Cases of Impeachment.

He shall have Power, by and with the Advice and Consent of the Senate, to make Treaties, provided two thirds of the Senators present concur; and he shall nominate, and by and with the Advice and Consent of the Senate, shall appoint Ambassadors, other public Ministers and Consuls, Judges of the supreme Court, and all other Officers of the United States, whose Appointments are not herein otherwise provided for, and which shall be established by Law: but the Congress may by Law vest the Appointment of such inferior Officers, as they think proper, in the President alone, in the Courts of Law, or in the Heads of Departments.

The President shall have Power to fill up all Vacancies that may happen during the Recess of the Senate, by granting Commissions which shall expire at the End of their next Session.

SECTION 3. He shall from time to time give to the Congress Information of the State of the Union, and recommend to their Consideration such Measures as he shall judge necessary and expedient; he may, on extraordinary Occasions, convene both Houses, or either of them, and in Case of Disagreement between them, with Respect to the Time of Adjournment, he may adjourn them to such Time as he shall think proper; he shall receive Ambassadors and other public Ministers; he shall take Care that the Laws be faithfully executed, and shall Commission all the Officers of the United States.

SECTION 4. The President, Vice President and all civil Officers of the United States, shall be removed from Office on Impeachment for, and Conviction of, Treason, Bribery, or other high Crimes and Misdemeanors.

ARTICLE III

SECTION 1. The judicial Power of the United States, shall be vested in one supreme Court, and in such inferior Courts as the Congress may from time to time ordain and establish. The Judges, both of the supreme and inferior Courts, shall hold their Offices during good Behavior, and shall, at stated Times, receive for their Services a Compensation which shall not be diminished during their Continuance in Office.

SECTION 2. *The judicial Power shall extend to all Cases, in Law and Equity, arising under this Constitution, the Laws of the United States, and Treaties made, or which shall be made, under their Authority; to all Cases affecting Ambassadors, other public Ministers and Consuls; to all Cases of admiralty and maritime Jurisdiction; to Controversies to which the United States shall be a Party; to Controversies between two or more States; between a State and Citizens of another State; between Citizens of different States; between Citizens of the same State claiming Lands under Grants of different States, and between a State, or the Citizens thereof, and foreign States, Citizens or Subjects.* (modified by the 11th Amendment.)

In all Cases affecting Ambassadors, other public Ministers and Consuls, and those in which a State shall be Party, the supreme Court shall have original Jurisdiction. In all the other Cases before mentioned, the supreme Court shall have appellate Jurisdiction, both as to Law and Fact, with such Exceptions, and under such Regulations as the Congress shall make.

The Trial of all Crimes, except in Cases of Impeachment, shall be by Jury; and such Trial shall be held in the State where the said Crimes shall have been committed; but when not committed within any State, the Trial shall be at such Place or Places as the Congress may by Law have directed.

SECTION 3. Treason against the United States, shall consist only in levying War against them, or in adhering to their Enemies, giving them Aid and Comfort. No Person shall be convicted of Treason unless on the Testimony of two Witnesses to the same overt Act, or on Confession in open Court.

The Congress shall have power to declare the Punishment of Treason, but no Attainder of Treason shall work Corruption of Blood, or Forfeiture except during the Life of the Person attainted.

ARTICLE IV

SECTION 1. Full Faith and Credit shall be given in each State to the public Acts, Records, and judicial Proceedings of every other State. And the Congress may by general Laws prescribe the Manner in which such Acts, Records and Proceedings shall be proved, and the Effect thereof.

Section 2. The Citizens of each State shall be entitled to all Privileges and Immunities of Citizens in the several States.

A Person charged in any State with Treason, Felony, or other Crime, who shall flee from Justice, and be found in another State, shall on demand of the executive Authority of the State from which he fled, be delivered up, to be removed to the State having Jurisdiction of the Crime.

No Person held to Service or Labour in one State, under the Laws thereof, escaping into another, shall, in Consequence of any Law or Regulation therein, be discharged from such Service or Labour, But shall be delivered up on Claim of the Party to whom such Service or Labour may be due. (superseded by the 13th Amendment.)

Section 3. New States may be admitted by the Congress into this Union; but no new States shall be formed or erected within the Jurisdiction of any other State; nor any State be formed by the Junction of two or more States, or parts of States, without the Consent of the Legislatures of the States concerned as well as of the Congress.

The Congress shall have Power to dispose of and make all needful Rules and Regulations respecting the Territory or other Property belonging to the United States; and nothing in this Constitution shall be so construed as to Prejudice any Claims of the United States, or of any particular State.

Section 4. The United States shall guarantee to every State in this Union a Republican Form of Government, and shall protect each of them against Invasion; and on Application of the Legislature, or of the Executive (when the Legislature cannot be convened) against domestic Violence.

Article V

The Congress, whenever two thirds of both Houses shall deem it necessary, shall propose Amendments to this Constitution, or, on the Application of the Legislatures of two thirds of the several States, shall call a Convention for proposing Amendments, which, in either Case, shall be valid to all Intents and Purposes, as part of this Constitution, when ratified by the Legislatures of three fourths of the several States, or by Conventions in three fourths thereof, as the one or the other Mode of Ratification may be proposed by the Congress; Provided that no Amendment which may be made prior to the Year One thousand eight hundred and eight shall in any Manner affect the first and fourth Clauses in the Ninth Section of the first Article; and that no State, without its Consent, shall be deprived of its equal Suffrage in the Senate.

ARTICLE VI

All Debts contracted and Engagements entered into, before the Adoption of this Constitution, shall be as valid against the United States under this Constitution, as under the Confederation.

This Constitution, and the Laws of the United States which shall be made in Pursuance thereof; and all Treaties made, or which shall be made, under the Authority of the United States, shall be the supreme Law of the Land; and the Judges in every State shall be bound thereby, any Thing in the Constitution or Laws of any State to the Contrary notwithstanding.

The Senators and Representatives before mentioned, and the Members of the several State Legislatures, and all executive and judicial Officers, both of the United States and of the several States, shall be bound by Oath or Affirmation, to support this Constitution; but no religious Test shall ever be required as a Qualification to any Office or public Trust under the United States.

ARTICLE VII

The Ratification of the Conventions of nine States, shall be sufficient for the Establishment of this Constitution between the States so ratifying the Same.

Done in Convention by the Unanimous Consent of the States present the Seventeenth Day of September in the Year of our Lord one thousand seven hundred and Eighty seven and of the Independence of the United States of America the Twelfth.

In Witness whereof We have hereunto subscribed our Names.

Go Wafhington
PRESIDENT AND DEPUTY FROM VIRGINIA

DELAWARE	NEW HAMPSHIRE	PENSYLVANIA
Geo. Read	*John Langdon*	*B Franklin*
Gunning Bedford, Jr.	*Nicholaf Gilman*	*Thomaf Mifflin*
John Dickinfon	MARYLAND	*Robt Morrif*
Richard Baffett	*Jamef McHenry*	*Geo. Clymer*
Jaco. Broom	*Dan of St Tho Jenifer*	*Thof FitzSimonf*
VIRGINIA	*Danl Carroll*	*Jared Ingerfoll*
John Blair	CONNECTICUT	*Jamef Wilfon*
Jamef Madifon Jr.	*Wm Saml Johnfon*	*Gouv Morrif*
NEW JERSEY	*Roger Sherman*	MASSACHUSETTS
Wil Livingfton	NORTH CAROLINA	*Nathaniel Gorham*
David Brearley	*Wm Blount*	*Rufuf King*
Wm Paterfon	*Richd Dobbf Spaight*	SOUTH CAROLINA
Jona. Dayton	*Hu Williamfon*	*J. Rutledge*
GEORGIA	NEW YORK	*Charlef Cotefworth Pinckney*
William Few	*Alexander Hamilton*	*Charlef Pinckney*
Abr Baldwin		*Pierce Butler*

ATTEST: *William Jackfon*, SECRETARY

Amendments to the Constitution

Congress   1791 - Today

The Constitution allowed for changes or additions to be made using state-approved amendments. Several states were concerned about the potential power of the new federal government, and agreed to ratify the new Constitution only if some changes were made to protect state and individual rights. These became the first ten amendments to the Constitution, commonly referred to as the Bill of Rights. The dates shown below are the dates the amendments were ratified by the states. Amendments must be approved by 2/3 of Congress and 3/4 of the states.

Bill of Rights - Amendments 1 to 10

Amendment I   1791

Freedom of religion, speech, press, peaceful assembly

Congress shall make no law respecting an establishment of religion, or prohibiting the free exercise thereof; or abridging the freedom of speech, or of the press; or the right of the people peaceably to assemble, and to petition the Government for a redress of grievances.

Amendment II   1791

Right to bear arms

A well regulated Militia, being necessary to the security of a free State, the right of the people to keep and bear Arms, shall not be infringed.

Amendment III   1791

No quartering of soldiers

No Soldier shall, in time of peace be quartered in any house, without the consent of the Owner, nor in time of war, but in a manner to be prescribed by law.

Amendment IV   1791

Protection against unreasonable searches and seizures

The right of the people to be secure in their persons, houses, papers, and effects, against unreasonable searches and seizures, shall not be violated, and no Warrants shall issue, but upon probable cause, supported by Oath or affirmation, and particularly describing the place to be searched, and the persons or things to be seized.

Amendment V   1791

No self-incrimination or double jeopardy, right to Grand Jury

No person shall be held to answer for a capital, or otherwise infamous crime, unless on a presentment or indictment of a Grand Jury, except in cases arising in the land or naval forces, or in the Militia, when in actual service in time of War or public danger; nor shall any person be subject for the same offense to be twice put in jeopardy of life or limb; nor shall be compelled in any criminal case to be a witness against himself, nor be deprived of life, liberty, or property, without due process of law; nor shall private property be taken for public use, without just compensation.

Amendment VI — 1791

Right to speedy trial, confrontation of witnesses

In all criminal prosecutions, the accused shall enjoy the right to a speedy and public trial, by an impartial jury of the State and district wherein the crime shall have been committed, which district shall have been previously ascertained by law, and to be informed of the nature and cause of the accusation; to be confronted with the witnesses against him; to have compulsory process for obtaining witnesses in his favor, and to have the Assistance of Counsel for his defence.

Amendment VII — 1791

Right to a trial by jury for civil cases

In Suits at common law, where the value in controversy shall exceed twenty dollars, the right of trial by jury shall be preserved, and no fact tried by a jury, shall be otherwise re-examined in any Court of the United States, than according to the rules of the common law.

Amendment VIII — 1791

Protection from cruel and unusual punishment

Excessive bail shall not be required, nor excessive fines imposed, nor cruel and unusual punishments inflicted.

Amendment IX — 1791

Extent of enumerated rights in Constitution

The enumeration in the Constitution, of certain rights, shall not be construed to deny or disparage others retained by the people.

Amendment X — 1791

Undelegated powers reside in the states and the people

The powers not delegated to the United States by the Constitution, nor prohibited by it to the States, are reserved to the States respectively, or to the people.

End of Bill of Rights

AMENDMENT XI   1795

JUDICIAL LIMITS

The Judicial power of the United States shall not be construed to extend to any suit in law or equity, commenced or prosecuted against one of the United States by Citizens of another State, or by Citizens or Subjects of any Foreign State.

AMENDMENT XII   1804

CHOOSING THE PRESIDENT AND VICE PRESIDENT

The Electors shall meet in their respective states, and vote by ballot for President and Vice President, one of whom, at least, shall not be an inhabitant of the same state with themselves; they shall name in their ballots the person voted for as President, and in distinct ballots the person voted for as Vice President, and they shall make distinct lists of all persons voted for as President, and of all persons voted for as Vice President and of the number of votes for each, which lists they shall sign and certify, and transmit sealed to the seat of the government of the United States, directed to the President of the Senate;

The President of the Senate shall, in the presence of the Senate and House of Representatives, open all the certificates and the votes shall then be counted;

The person having the greatest Number of votes for President, shall be the President, if such number be a majority of the whole number of Electors appointed; and if no person have such majority, then from the persons having the highest numbers not exceeding three on the list of those voted for as President, the House of Representatives shall choose immediately, by ballot, the President. But in choosing the President, the votes shall be taken by states, the representation from each state having one vote; a quorum for this purpose shall consist of a member or members from two-thirds of the states, and a majority of all the states shall be necessary to a choice. And if the House of Representatives shall not choose a President whenever the right of choice shall devolve upon them, before the fourth day of March next following, then the Vice President shall act as President, as in the case of the death or other constitutional disability of the President.

The person having the greatest number of votes as Vice President, shall be the Vice President, if such number be a majority of the whole number of Electors appointed, and if no person have a majority, then from the two highest numbers on the list, the Senate shall choose the Vice President; a quorum for the purpose shall consist of two-thirds of the whole number of Senators, and a majority of the whole number shall be necessary to a choice. But no person constitutionally ineligible to the office of President shall be eligible to that of Vice President of the United States.

Amendment XIII   1865

Abolishment of slavery

1. Neither slavery nor involuntary servitude, except as a punishment for crime whereof the party shall have been duly convicted, shall exist within the United States, or any place subject to their jurisdiction.

2. Congress shall have power to enforce this article by appropriate legislation.

Amendment XIV   1868

Citizenship rights
Apportionment of representatives; oaths

1. All persons born or naturalized in the United States, and subject to the jurisdiction thereof, are citizens of the United States and of the State wherein they reside. No State shall make or enforce any law which shall abridge the privileges or immunities of citizens of the United States; nor shall any State deprive any person of life, liberty, or property, without due process of law; nor deny to any person within its jurisdiction the equal protection of the laws.

2. Representatives shall be apportioned among the several States according to their respective numbers, counting the whole number of persons in each State, excluding Indians not taxed. But when the right to vote at any election for the choice of electors for President and Vice President of the United States, Representatives in Congress, the Executive and Judicial officers of a State, or the members of the Legislature thereof, is denied to any of the male inhabitants of such State, being twenty-one years of age, and citizens of the United States, or in any way abridged, except for participation in rebellion, or other crime, the basis of representation therein shall be reduced in the proportion which the number of such male citizens shall bear to the whole number of male citizens twenty-one years of age in such State.

3. No person shall be a Senator or Representative in Congress, or elector of President and Vice President, or hold any office, civil or military, under the United States, or under any State, who, having previously taken an oath, as a member of Congress, or as an officer of the United States, or as a member of any State legislature, or as an executive or judicial officer of any State, to support the Constitution of the United States, shall have engaged in insurrection or rebellion against the same, or given aid or comfort to the enemies thereof. But Congress may by a vote of two-thirds of each House, remove such disability.

4. The validity of the public debt of the United States, authorized by law, including debts incurred for payment of pensions and bounties for services in suppressing insurrection or rebellion, shall not be

questioned. But neither the United States nor any State shall assume or pay any debt or obligation incurred in aid of insurrection or rebellion against the United States, or any claim for the loss or emancipation of any slave; but all such debts, obligations and claims shall be held illegal and void.

5. The Congress shall have power to enforce, by appropriate legislation, the provisions of this article.

AMENDMENT XV   1870

VOTING RIGHTS EXTENDED
TO EX-SLAVES AND ALL RACES AND COLORS

1. The right of citizens of the United States to vote shall not be denied or abridged by the United States or by any State on account of race, color, or previous condition of servitude.

2. The Congress shall have power to enforce this article by appropriate legislation.

AMENDMENT XVI   1913

CONGRESS GIVEN RIGHT TO COLLECT INCOME TAX

The Congress shall have power to lay and collect taxes on incomes, from whatever source derived, without apportionment among the several States, and without regard to any census or enumeration.

AMENDMENT XVII   1913

SENATORS ELECTED BY POPULAR VOTE

The Senate of the United States shall be composed of two Senators from each State, elected by the people thereof, for six years; and each Senator shall have one vote. The electors in each State shall have the qualifications requisite for electors of the most numerous branch of the State legislatures.

When vacancies happen in the representation of any State in the Senate, the executive authority of such State shall issue writs of election to fill such vacancies: Provided, That the legislature of any State may empower the executive thereof to make temporary appointments until the people fill the vacancies by election as the legislature may direct.

This amendment shall not be so construed as to affect the election or term of any Senator chosen before it becomes valid as part of the Constitution.

Amendment XVIII   1919

Prohibits Manufacture, Sale and Transportation of Alcohol

1. After one year from the ratification of this article the manufacture, sale, or transportation of intoxicating liquors within, the importation thereof into, or the exportation thereof from the United States and all territory subject to the jurisdiction thereof for beverage purposes is hereby prohibited.

2. The Congress and the several States shall have concurrent power to enforce this article by appropriate legislation.

3. This article shall be inoperative unless it shall have been ratified as an amendment to the Constitution by the legislatures of the several States, as provided in the Constitution, within seven years from the date of the submission hereof to the States by the Congress.

Amendment XIX   1920

Women Given the Right to Vote

The right of citizens of the United States to vote shall not be denied or abridged by the United States or by any State on account of sex.

Congress shall have power to enforce this article by appropriate legislation.

Amendment XX   1933

Defines Terms of President and Congress

1. The terms of the President and Vice President shall end at noon on the 20th day of January, and the terms of Senators and Representatives at noon on the 3d day of January, of the years in which such terms would have ended if this article had not been ratified; and the terms of their successors shall then begin.

2. The Congress shall assemble at least once in every year, and such meeting shall begin at noon on the 3d day of January, unless they shall by law appoint a different day.

3. If, at the time fixed for the beginning of the term of the President, the President elect shall have died, the Vice President elect shall become President. If a President shall not have been chosen before the time fixed for the beginning of his term, or if the President elect shall have failed to qualify, then the Vice President elect shall act as President until a President shall have qualified; and the Congress may by law provide for the case wherein neither a President elect nor a Vice President elect shall have qualified, declaring who shall then act as President, or the manner in which one who is to act shall be selected, and such person shall act accordingly until a President or Vice President shall have qualified.

4. The Congress may by law provide for the case of the death of any of the persons from whom the House of Representatives may choose a President whenever the right of choice shall have devolved upon them, and for the case of the death of any of the persons from whom the Senate may choose a Vice President whenever the right of choice shall have devolved upon them.

5. Sections 1 and 2 shall take effect on the 15th day of October following the ratification of this article.

6. This article shall be inoperative unless it shall have been ratified as an amendment to the Constitution by the legislatures of three-fourths of the several States within seven years from the date of its submission.

Amendment XXI   1933

Repeals 18th Amendment; legalizes alcohol again

1. The eighteenth article of amendment to the Constitution of the United States is hereby repealed.

2. The transportation or importation into any State, Territory, or possession of the United States for delivery or use therein of intoxicating liquors, in violation of the laws thereof, is hereby prohibited.

3. The article shall be inoperative unless it shall have been ratified as an amendment to the Constitution by conventions in the several States, as provided in the Constitution, within seven years from the date of the submission hereof to the States by the Congress.

Amendment XXII   1951

Limits President to two terms in office

1. No person shall be elected to the office of the President more than twice, and no person who has held the office of President, or acted as President, for more than two years of a term to which some other person was elected President shall be elected to the office of the President more than once. But this Article shall not apply to any person holding the office of President, when this Article was proposed by the Congress, and shall not prevent any person who may be holding the office of President, or acting as President, during the term within which this Article becomes operative from holding the office of President or acting as President during the remainder of such term.

2. This article shall be inoperative unless it shall have been ratified as an amendment to the Constitution by the legislatures of three-fourths of the several States within seven years from the date of its submission to the States by the Congress.

Amendment XXIII   1961

Gives Presidential vote to District of Columbia

1. The District constituting the seat of Government of the United States shall appoint in such manner as the Congress may direct: A number of electors of President and Vice President equal to the whole number of Senators and Representatives in Congress to which the District would be entitled if it were a State, but in no event more than the least populous State; they shall be in addition to those appointed by the States, but they shall be considered, for the purposes of the election of President and Vice President, to be electors appointed by a State; and they shall meet in the District and perform such duties as provided by the twelfth article of amendment.

2. The Congress shall have power to enforce this article by appropriate legislation.

Amendment XXIV   1964

Outlaws poll tax

1. The right of citizens of the United States to vote in any primary or other election for President or Vice President, for electors for President or Vice President, or for Senator or Representative in Congress, shall not be denied or abridged by the United States or any State by reason of failure to pay any poll tax or other tax.

2. The Congress shall have power to enforce this article by appropriate legislation.

Amendment XXV   1967

Sets Presidential disability and succession rules

1. In case of the removal of the President from office or of his death or resignation, the Vice President shall become President.

2. Whenever there is a vacancy in the office of the Vice President, the President shall nominate a Vice President who shall take office upon confirmation by a majority vote of both Houses of Congress.

3. Whenever the President transmits to the President pro tempore of the Senate and the Speaker of the House of Representatives his written declaration that he is unable to discharge the powers and duties of his office, and until he transmits to them a written declaration to the contrary, such powers and duties shall be discharged by the Vice President as Acting President.

4. Whenever the Vice President and a majority of either the principal officers of the executive departments or of such other body as Congress may by law provide, transmit to the President pro tempore of the Senate and the Speaker of the House of Representatives their written declaration that the President is unable to discharge the powers

and duties of his office, the Vice President shall immediately assume the powers and duties of the office as Acting President.

Thereafter, when the President transmits to the President pro tempore of the Senate and the Speaker of the House of Representatives his written declaration that no inability exists, he shall resume the powers and duties of his office unless the Vice President and a majority of either the principal officers of the executive department or of such other body as Congress may by law provide, transmit within four days to the President pro tempore of the Senate and the Speaker of the House of Representatives their written declaration that the President is unable to discharge the powers and duties of his office. Thereupon Congress shall decide the issue, assembling within forty eight hours for that purpose if not in session. If the Congress, within twenty one days after receipt of the latter written declaration, or, if Congress is not in session, within twenty one days after Congress is required to assemble, determines by two thirds vote of both Houses that the President is unable to discharge the powers and duties of his office, the Vice President shall continue to discharge the same as Acting President; otherwise, the President shall resume the powers and duties of his office.

AMENDMENT XXVI   1971

SETS VOTING AGE TO 18 YEARS

1. The right of citizens of the United States, who are eighteen years of age or older, to vote shall not be denied or abridged by the United States or by any State on account of age.

2. The Congress shall have power to enforce this article by appropriate legislation.

AMENDMENT XXVII   1992

LIMITS CONGRESSIONAL PAY INCREASES

No law, varying the compensation for the services of the Senators and Representatives, shall take effect, until an election of Representatives shall have intervened.

The 27th amendment was first proposed in 1789 and took 203 years to be ratified. Michigan was the 38th state to ratify the amendment in 1992. There have been over 10,000 amendments introduced in Congress, and there are still four amendments that have passed Congress and are awaiting ratification by the states. The Equal Rights Amendment (ERA) was never ratified and has expired.

❦

The Constitution is not an instrument for government to restrain the people, it is an instrument for the people to restrain the government—lest it come to dominate our lives and interests.

—*Patrick Henry*

Inauguration of
George Washington
April 30, 1789
New York City
by Ramon de Elorriaga

Humanity has won its
battle. Liberty now has
a country.
　—*Marquis de Lafayette*

Inauguration of
Abraham Lincoln
March 4, 1861
Washington, D.C.

The ballot is stronger
than the bullet.
　—*Abraham Lincoln*

To live under the
American Constitution
is the greatest political
privilege that was ever
accorded to the human
race.
　—*Calvin Coolidge*

Inauguration of
Barack Obama
January 20, 2009
Washington, D.C.

The orderly transfer of authority as called for in the Constitution routinely takes place, as it has for almost two centuries,
and few of us stop to think how unique we really are. In the
eyes of many in the world, this every-four-year ceremony we
accept as normal is nothing less than a miracle.
　—*Ronald Reagan*

Chapter 5

HOW OUR GOVERNMENT WORKS

❧

MOST OF THE INFORMATION in this section is taught at every level in our public school system. People applying for citizenship need to know this information, and all natural-born citizens should as well.

WHAT THE FOUNDERS WERE THINKING

The founders of this country were very aware of how other forms of government had fared throughout the world, going back to ancient Greece and Rome. They knew the tyranny of monarchs and tyrants, just as they realized the tyranny of pure democracies. The founders were products of the Age of Enlightenment, the Renaissance, and an increased reliance on science and reason. They were also descendants of settlers fleeing religious persecution, so they knew the danger of state religion and intolerance. They shared an almost universal belief in a God, whether they were Deists or devout Christians. These views manifested themselves in the Declaration of Independence and the Constitution, and their entire approach to the new country.

What does the Preamble to the Constitution mean?

Gouverneur Morris attended the Convention as a delegate from Pennsylvania. He had strong beliefs opposing slavery in the states, and helped write parts of the Constitution. He is best remembered, however, for writing the Preamble to the Constitution. The Preamble assigns no powers, nor does it directly stipulate any function of government. It does, however, describe the principles behind the document, and has even been used by the courts to help establish the meaning of the Constitution and the intent of the Founding Fathers.

The phrases in the short preamble were carefully chosen to convey the intent of the men crafting this historic document. Just the inclusion of the words "We the People" was historic. The phrases of the preamble are:

We the People of the United States
This was the first country in the world to form a government based on the consent of the people.

in Order to form a more perfect Union
The Articles of Confederation were ineffective, primarily due to lack of power in the central government, and the founders knew they could never produce a perfect nation, just a "more" perfect one.

establish Justice
The new nation had to be based on equal justice for all citizens. The people can enjoy their freedom and rights, but they are not free to violate the rights of others.

insure domestic Tranquility
The Confederation had been unable to control domestic unrest and the founders knew the new government had to be able to control the country.

provide for the common defence
The new country would be threatened on all sides, and the states all needed to band together to stand any chance of success.

promote the general Welfare
The founders knew that government's role was not to guarantee success or happiness, but to provide the framework required to make it happen.

and secure the Blessings of Liberty to ourselves and our Posterity
The founders had fought for their liberty, and knew they were creating a government that should last for centuries.

do ordain and establish this Constitution
"Ordaining" this document implies a higher power similar to the reference in the Declaration to unalienable rights flowing from a Creator.

for the United States of America.
This closing clause formalizes the name for the new nation: The United States of America.

What Kind of Government Do We Have

The United States was formed as a **Federal Constitutional Republic**. It is democratic, but it is not a democracy. This distinction is very important. These three words mean:

Federal: comprised of states united by a central government.

Constitutional: bound by a formal constitution adopted by the citizens and only changed with their consent.

Republic: run by representatives elected by the citizens rather than by direct vote, and not run by a monarch or dictator.

America is not a true democracy

It is democratic in the sense that the citizens can all vote for their officials. It is a representative democracy in the sense that the citizens elect officials who actually create and pass the laws. However, it is not a pure democracy, nor is it a pure representative democracy. In a pure democracy, a majority may impose their will over the minority with nothing to protect those minorities. What makes America work is the protection of the Constitution. A constitutional republic protects the unalienable rights and liberties of all its citizens, including any minority. A majority cannot simply exercise their will over the minority by simply voting their desires—that is mob rule. Laws passed in this country must be both approved by the voters, and be constitutional. The Constitution is the supreme law of the land.

It is critical for every citizen to understand the importance of the Constitution, and not assume that a majority may pass any law they desire. It is interesting that the word "democracy" does not appear anywhere in either the Declaration or the Constitution.

The founding fathers knew the dangers of a pure democracy and also knew the importance of a strong Constitution. Alexander Hamilton, arguing in 1788 for the approval of the Constitution, said:

> It has been observed that a pure democracy, if it were practicable, would be the most perfect government. Experience has proved that no position is more false than this. The ancient democracies in which the people themselves deliberated never possessed one good feature of government. Their very character was tyranny; their figure deformity.

As so clearly stated in the Declaration of Independence, our rights are unalienable and come from our Creator, not from any government. Any government that thinks they must pass laws to "give" rights to individuals will be the same government that "takes" those rights away. The government's only purpose is to protect the rights each person already possesses. Allowing a majority vote to violate anyone's unalienable rights is no different than allowing a tyrant or dictator to do the same.

A quotation often attributed to Alexander Tytler states, "A democracy cannot exist as a permanent form of government. It can only exist until a majority of voters discover that they can vote themselves largesse out of the public treasury." Our government today is perilously close to this tipping point.

The government often mischaracterizes itself as a democracy. President Wilson called World War I the war "to make the world safe for democracy," and President Roosevelt called America "the great arsenal of democracy." An accurate description of the perils of a pure democracy was outlined in the *1928 U.S. Training Manual*:

> **Democracy:** A government of the masses. Authority derived through mass meeting or any other form of "direct" expression. Results in mobocracy. Attitude toward property is communistic—negating property rights. Attitude toward law is that the will of the majority shall regulate, whether it be based upon deliberation or governed by passion, prejudice, and impulse, without restraint or regard to consequences. Results in demagogism, license, agitation, discontent, anarchy.

The Creation of the Constitution

The *Articles of Confederation*, created at the start of the Revolution, proved to be completely unusable in running the new country. A convention was convened to fix the Articles, but the founders ended up creating a novel new form of government. It was not a straight forward or easy process. There were strong arguments on all sides. There was a basic split between those favoring a strong central government, and those favoring state and individual rights. Some of the more important compromises during the debating included:

1. **Great Compromise of 1787:** The rights of small and large states were balanced by creating a Senate with equal state representation, and a House with representation proportional to population.

2. **Bill of Rights:** The concerns of several states about an overly strong central government led to the promise of the creation of the Bill of Rights (the first ten amendments) to protect the rights of states and individuals. The Constitution was finally ratified because of this promise.

3. **Slavery:** Slaves could be imported only until 1808, but the Fugitive Slave Clause allowed southern owners to reclaim runaway slaves. To keep southern states from acquiring too much power in the new House, slaves were counted as 3/5 of a person in determining state representation.

4. **Electoral College:** The president would be elected by electors in the Electoral College, and not by a direct vote.

The ultimate innovation was the process of how the Constitution was to be changed. The Constitution stipulated that it can only be changed by a formal process of "amendments," and provided the mechanism to make those changes in a manner that is difficult enough to ensure it will be used only when absolutely necessary. And the tenth amendment itself states that any powers not specifically granted to the federal government by the Constitution revert to the states or to the people. There have been twenty-seven amendments to date, although there have been over 10,000 amendments proposed.

Once the Constitution was finished and approved by the members, it had to be sent to the thirteen states for ratification. It was decided that only nine states had to ratify the new document for it to take effect. New Hampshire became the ninth state to ratify the Constitution on June 21, 1788, and the new nation finally had a government. The Constitution defined the structure of the new government, and protected the rights of its citizens, but it was up to the early leaders to actually put that government into action.

On April 30, 1789, George Washington was inaugurated as the first president in New York City. He has been the only unanimous selection for president. He was essential in setting the tone for our government since the Constitution did not detail every specific process, position, or department. Washington named cabinet positions, created a national bank, established a precedent for dealing with Congress, and stuck with his belief that a president should not serve more than 2 terms.

Lord Acton of England wrote of the Constitution,

> They had solved with astonishing ease and unduplicated success two problems which had heretofore baffled the capacity of the most enlightened nations. They had contrived a system of federal government which prodigiously increased national power and yet respected local liberties and authorities, and they had founded it on a principle of equality without surrendering the securities of property or freedom.

Three Equal Branches

Our particular republic government was created with another crucial safeguard—its three separate, but equal, Executive, Legislative, and Judicial branches. The Constitution was very clear on this separation of powers. Each branch has very specific duties, responsibilities, and limits.

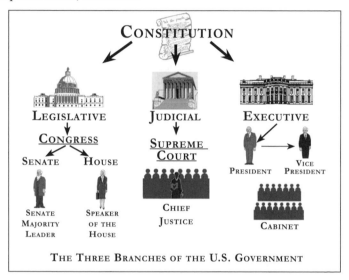

THE THREE BRANCHES OF THE U.S. GOVERNMENT

Executive branch

This branch consists of the President, Vice President and 15 cabinet level departments. The president and vice president are elected every four years. The president appoints Supreme Court justices and Cabinet members who all have to be approved by the Senate. The executive branch is in charge of ensuring laws are carried out, collecting taxes, and keeping the country safe. The president submits the federal budget to Congress every year. Most of the work is accomplished by the various departments, such as the Attorney General, State Department, Defense Department, etc. The president can sign bills given to him for signature and make them law, or veto the bill, which then requires a 2/3 vote in Congress to overcome the veto. The president also serves as Commander-in-Chief of the military. To be eligible for president, a candidate must be 35 years or older, a natural-born citizen, and have lived in the U.S. for at least 14 consecutive years. Since the passage of the 22nd amendment, the president can serve only two terms in office.

Legislative Branch

The Senate and the House of Representatives are collectively known as Congress. This branch is responsible for creating, passing, and funding the laws of the country, and approving presidential nominations and Cabinet selections. After passing laws, they send them to the President for approval or veto. The president has limited powers to use the military, but wars can only be declared by Congress. There are no term limits now for any member of Congress, and some have served for decades—Senator Byrd served for 51 years. Sixteen Senators have gone on to become president.

Senate

The Senate consists of 100 Senators, two from each state. Senators serve six-year terms, with 1/3 of them being elected every two years. They are elected to represent the entire state. The Senate gives equal representation to each state regardless of their population. The Vice President acts as *President of the Senate,* casting the deciding vote in case of ties. The *president pro tempore* presides in his absence. The Senate Majority Leader normally controls the Senate. The Senate can approve treaties, confirm judges and Cabinet picks, and confirm impeachments. Senators must be 30 years of age, a citizen of the U.S. for the previous nine years, and a resident of the state they represent.

House of Representatives

The House has representatives from each state, the number varying with the population of the state. The members elect their leader, the Speaker of the House. The party not in control elects a Minority Leader. The House is more representative of the interests of smaller groups of citizens, and represent small congressional districts around the country. Serving 2-year terms, they have to stay in touch with their constituents back home and continue to earn their support. A Representative must be 25 years or older, a citizen for seven years before the election, and a resident of the state of their election, but not necessarily the district to which they are elected. The Apportionment Act of 1911 fixed the total number of representatives at 435. The exact number allocated to each state is calculated after the National Census is taken every ten years. Some states may lose representatives and some may gain, but the total number remains fixed at 435. The House originates all revenue bills and elects the president in case of an electoral tie.

Judicial Branch

The judiciary consists of the U.S. Supreme Court (the highest court in the land) and all the lower federal courts. It hears cases to interpret the constitutionality of legislation. There are nine justices on the Supreme Court, appointed by the president for their lifetime, but confirmed by the Senate. The Chief Justice of the United States, one of the nine judges, heads the Supreme Court. The Executive Branch enforces the laws, but the Judicial Branch ensures that the laws are constitutional. Our Constitution and our laws are the backbone of our system of government. We are a nation that honors the "rule of law." Every citizen, no matter what position they hold, how rich they are, or what their social status is, must obey the law—it is equal justice for all.

Checks and balances keep the government honest

The founders crafted the government to include a separation of powers to prevent any one branch or any one person from seizing control of the government or causing harm to its citizens. The president's power is kept in check by Congress which can turn down his appointments, override his veto, or impeach him. Congress passes laws that the president can veto, though they can override the veto with enough votes. Or their laws may be declared unconstitutional by the Supreme Court. Congress has to approve Supreme Court judges and can attempt to amend the Constitution, but this requires approval of two-thirds of Congress and three-fourths of all the states.

Sometimes the checks do not work as they should, particularly when one party controls the White House and both houses of Congress. One attempt to upset the balance occurred in 1937 when Franklin Roosevelt proposed enlarging the Supreme Court by adding more hand-picked justices who would rule in favor of some of his more radical programs. But a different "check" saved the day when Congress refused to approve FDR's request.

❦

If no one is to be accounted as born into a superior station, if there is to be no ruling class, and if all possess rights which can neither be bartered away nor taken from them by any earthly power, it follows as a matter of course that the practical authority of the Government has to rest on the consent of the governed.

—*Calvin Coolidge*

The Executive Cabinet

The "Cabinet" refers to the heads of the various departments that exist in the Executive Branch of the government. George Washington appointed four cabinet members—Secretary of State, Secretary of the Treasury, Secretary of War, and Attorney General. Today, there are 15 members who head their corresponding departments. These positions are filled by the President with Senate approval. Besides running their respective departments, the Cabinet members advise and assist the President. The Departments, with the year they were formed, are:

Agriculture (1862): helps promote our agriculture at home and abroad, researches new crops, manages food programs like Food Stamps, and ensures the safety of our food.

Commerce (1903): promotes international trade, works to prevent unfair trade and business practices, forecasts the weather, regulates patents, and conducts the census every ten years.

Defense (1789): originally named the War Department, manages all military forces, including Navy, Army, and Air Force.

Education (1979): administers federal education programs, handles student loans, and works to eliminate discrimination in education.

Energy (1977): researches and encourages the development of energy and energy conservation, oversees nuclear energy and nuclear weapons, and regulates energy allocation.

Health and Human Services (1953): administers Social Security, Medicare, and Medicaid, manages social programs for the needy, conducts medical research, and ensures safety of drugs and non-meat food products.

Homeland Security (2002): formed from 22 separate agencies after the 9/11 attacks, it protects the country from terrorist attacks and natural disasters. It includes the Coast Guard, Immigration, Customs and Border protection, and the Secret Service.

Housing and Urban Development (1965): encourages affordable housing and community development, administers fair housing laws, oversees and insures mortgages.

Interior (1849): manages federal land, forests, monuments, and parks, runs federal dams, encourages resource conservation, and manages U.S. territories.

Justice (1789): enforces federal laws, supervises federal marshals, administers immigration laws, and runs federal prisons.

Labor (1913): protects workers' rights, gathers employment statistics, and improves working conditions.

State (1789): handles U.S. foreign policy; negotiates treaties; represents U.S. internationally; supervises foreign embassies and consulates.

Transportation (1966): sets transportation policy for the nation including land, sea, and air.

Treasury (1789): regulates banks, prints money, collects Federal income taxes (IRS), and prints stamps for Post Office.

Veterans Affairs (1989): handles government programs and hospitals that assist veterans and their families, and operates national cemeteries.

Other cabinet-level positions

There are other cabinet level positions that are not officially cabinet departments. Presidents can decide which positions are accorded cabinet-level status. Currently, they include:

Chief of Staff: responsible for the White House staff and managing the president's schedule.

Environmental Protection Agency (EPA): protects the health and environment of the country.

Office of Management and Budget (OMB): helps the president prepare the federal budget.

U.S. Trade Representative: helps promote economic growth and open-market policies.

Ambassador to the U.N.: leader of the U.S. delegation to the United Nations.

Council of Economic Advisers: advises the president on matters of domestic and international economic policy.

Vice President of the United States: A cabinet-level position.

Other well-known agencies

United States Postal Service (USPS): an independent government agency that provides postal service to the entire country. Authorized by the Constitution, it is not paid for by taxes.

Federal Bureau of Investigation (FBI): an agency of the Department of Justice whose job it is to defend against terrorism and uphold the country's criminal laws.

Central Intelligence Agency (CIA): a civilian agency that reports to the Director of National Intelligence. It collects information about foreign governments and individuals, and advises our government on intelligence issues.

National Security Agency: Department of Defense intelligence agency that collects and analyzes foreign communications.

PRESIDENTIAL SUCCESSION

There is a clear path of succession outlined in the Constitution, the 25th Amendment, and the Presidential Succession Act of 1947. If the president dies, resigns, is impeached, or is incapacitated for any reason, the duties of the office pass to the next person in the line of succession. The list includes the Vice President, leaders of both houses of Congress, and all 15 cabinet members. The rules of succession were used when Nixon resigned from office, when Reagan was shot, and when presidents have died in office. This peaceful and clearly-defined process displays the strength of our system. Where many countries experience turmoil, uncertainty, and even violence whenever a leader dies, America peacefully moves on. After the first three positions, the order is determined by the year the department was formed, the older departments being higher in the list. Today, the line of succession is:

1. **Vice President**
2. **Speaker of the House**
3. **President pro tempore of the Senate**
4. **Secretary of State**
5. **Secretary of the Treasury**
6. **Secretary of Defense**
7. **Attorney General**
8. **Secretary of the Interior**
9. **Secretary of Agriculture**
10. **Secretary of Commerce**
11. **Secretary of Labor**
12. **Secretary of Health and Human Services**
13. **Secretary of Housing and Urban Development**
14. **Secretary of Transportation**
15. **Secretary of Energy**
16. **Secretary of Education**
17. **Secretary of Veterans Affairs**
18. **Secretary of Homeland Security**

Joint Chiefs of Staff

A group of senior military officers appointed by the President who advise the President, Secretary of Defense, National Security Council, and the Homeland Security Council on matters of national defense. Besides a chairman and vice chairman, the group consists of the leaders of the Army, Navy, Air Force, and Marine Corps. The Pentagon in Arlington, Virginia, houses the Department of Defense. It is the world's largest office building with 6.5 million square feet of floor area.

THE FEDERAL BUDGET

The spending budget for the country is prepared by the president and submitted to Congress every year. The federal fiscal year goes from October 1 to September 30 of the following year. The 2010 budget was $3.6 trillion, more than double what it was in 1999. Shown another way, that's: **$3,600,000,000,000**. Remember this every April 15th when you have to send in your annual income tax payment. Social security, Medicare, and Medicaid spending consumed more than twice what was spent by the Defense Department. The 2010 budget included the following items: *(Source: Government Accountability Office)*

$695 billion   **Social Security**

$663 billion   **Dept of Defense**

$571 billion   **Other mandatory programs**

$453 billion   **Medicare**

$331 billion   **Other**

$290 billion   **Medicaid**

$164 billion   **Interest on national debt**

$ 78 billion   **Dept of Health & Human Services**

$ 72 billion   **Dept of Transportation**

$ 52 billion   **Dept of Veterans Affairs**

$ 51 billion   **Dept of State and International**

$ 47 billion   **Dept of Housing & Urban Development**

$ 46 billion   **Dept of Education**

$ 42 billion   **Dept of Homeland Security**

$ 11 billion   **Disasters**

STATES' RIGHTS AND POWERS

The Supremacy Clause of Article VI of the Constitution essentially declares federal law supreme over any laws of the states. However, this applies only if the federal acts are constitutional. The federal government can print money, declare war, create an army, and make treaties. But the 10th Amendment reserves to the states all powers that are not delegated to the federal government by the Constitution. Powers that are exercised by the states today include: issuing licenses, conducting state elections, ratifying Constitutional amendments, providing education and local services such as fire and police, and approving land use. But they are prohibited from other actions, such as printing their own money.

THE ELECTORAL COLLEGE

When Americans vote every four years for president, they are not actually directly electing that person. Instead, the voters of each state vote for "electors" who then cast the actual vote for the president and vice president later. The only vote

Electoral votes based on 2010 census

that counts is the electoral vote. Presidents can win the electoral vote but lose the popular vote. This has happened four times in our history, most recently in 2000 when George W. Bush beat Al Gore in the electoral count, but lost the popular vote.

Each state is represented by the same number of electors as that state has Representatives and Senators in the U.S. Congress. Some less populated states have only three electors, while California has the most with fifty-five. Today, the total number is fixed at 538, which includes one vote for each of the 435 Representatives, one vote for each of the 100 Senators, and 3 votes for the District of Columbia. The number of Representatives has been fixed at 435 since the Apportionment Act of 1911.

States have different rules on how the electors for that state must vote. Most states require that all electoral votes for that state be cast for the presidential candidate that wins the popular vote in that state.

Though many have talked about removing the Electoral College from the election process and relying on just the popular vote, there are important reasons to keep this method.

- It is a cornerstone of federalism in this country. It helps protect the rights of small states and prevents a few large urban population centers from deciding the fate of the country.
- It is one more barrier between our present, successful form of government, and mob rule.
- It reduces or eliminates the need for recounts in more than one or two states in close elections, as was seen in Florida in 2000. Examine the timeline in this book to see how close the popular vote has been in the past. If that was the sole method used to select the president, the vote counts from every state could easily be challenged, and recounts ordered in every state.
- It has worked for over 200 years.

The founders provided further protection for states by requiring that Constitutional amendments to change the electoral process require three-fourths of the states to approve. The smaller states would almost certainly never agree to that.

When are elections?

Local and state elections generally have their elections at the same time that the national government has theirs, which is the Tuesday following the first Monday in November. It was originally set to this date to be after the crops had all been harvested, thus allowing farmers to have the time to  travel and vote in the election. It was set on Tuesday, not Monday, so no voters would have to start travel on Sunday. There are other local and special elections held throughout the year in the states. National elections are held every two years in even-numbered years. Those years divisible by four (such as 2012 and 2016) are also presidential elections. The new president is sworn into office the following January, as stipulated in the 20th amendment.

Who can vote?

Generally, you must be a U.S. citizen who is 18 years or older, and a legal resident of the state you are voting in. There are restrictions on current or former felons. And, most importantly, you must register to vote—you can't just show up on Election Day.

Registering for the Selective Service

All males must register with the Selective Service System within 30 days of their 18th birthday. This information will be used if the country ever re-institutes the military draft.

THE HISTORY OF VOTING IN AMERICA

The new federal government in the 1700s was elected by only 15-20% of the total population, due mainly to voting restrictions against women, slaves, and those not owning land. But as the country grew and conditions changed, the Constitution allowed the system to adapt. Over the following two centuries, voting rights expanded as restrictions were gradually removed. States are still responsible for determining who votes, but amendments to the Constitution and legal decisions bar states from denying the right to vote to certain groups of citizens. Unfortunately, in the aftermath of the Civil War, many states adopted various methods to restrict the rights of ex-slaves to vote, including literacy tests and poll taxes. But all the restrictions have been slowly peeled away.

- **Property-owning requirements**: These were dropped by most states shortly after the birth of the country.

- **Race and color:** Slaves had been freed after the Civil War, and the 15th amendment in 1870 gave the vote to men of all races and colors.

- **Sex**: The 19th amendment in 1920 gave all women the vote. Women had been voting in certain states, primarily in the West, for years before this amendment. Women in Wyoming had been voting since 1869. In an interesting twist, women actually ran for president in 1872 and 1884. Even though they were not allowed to vote, there were no laws preventing them from running for president.

- **District of Columbia**: The 23rd amendment in 1961 restored presidential voting rights to Washington, D.C. residents.

- **Poll tax:** The 24th amendment in 1964 prohibited states from denying the right to vote in federal elections due to failure to pay a poll tax. Several southern states had adopted poll taxes starting in 1889.

- **Age:** The 26th amendment in 1971 barred states from denying voting rights to anyone 18 years of age or older. States
  can still individually grant voting rights to younger voters.

- **Election of Senators:** The 17th amendment in 1913 changed
  the election of Senators from being made by the State Legislatures to being made directly by the people.

- **Literacy tests:** These were adopted by several southern
  states in the late 1800s to deny the vote to freed slaves. When
  the tests were found to exclude too many white voters, the
  southern states changed the law, adding a loophole allowing whites failing the test to still vote. The change allowed
  citizens whose father or grandfather could vote in 1867 to
  be allowed to vote (this is the origin of the phrase: *grandfather clause*). Since slaves had not been given the right to
  vote until 1870, this prohibited their descendants use of this
  allowance. The Supreme Court declared literacy tests unconstitutional in 1915, but they were still in use until outlawed
  by the Voting Rights Act of 1965.

- **Native Americans:** As a group, they finally received full citizenship rights in 1924 when the Indian Citizenship Act gave
  them the right to vote in federal elections. A number of western states would still obstruct their ability to vote for decades.

Our country has a checkered history of fulfilling the dream of
its Declaration of Independence that "all men are created equal."
The important point is that these rights were eventually granted
using procedures set up by the Constitution. And our country's
record should be viewed in the context of other countries in the
world—many of which still prohibit its citizens from voting at all,
or treat women or other groups as second-class citizens.

POLITICAL PARTIES

George Washington was first elected before he formally belonged to a political party, but the presidential elections after
that pitted members of one party against another (and sometimes
against each other). A number of political parties have come and
gone, including the Whigs and the Federalists, but today we basi-
cally have a two-party system consisting of the Republican Party
and the Democratic Party. Many other parties run candidates,
with the strongest showings usually belonging to the Libertarian,
Green, and Constitution parties. Ross Perot ran as an Independent

in 1992 and 1996, winning millions of popular votes and possibly changing the outcome of those elections.

There is nothing in the Constitution about political parties. The original method of electing the vice president was to name the candidate receiving the highest number of votes president, and name as vice president the candidate getting the second highest number of votes. However, this could lead to a president having a vice president from a different party, as in 1796, or, in the case of the 1800 election, the candidate running for vice president could actually get as many votes as his presidential running mate. The confusion of the 1800 election led to the adoption of the 12th amendment modifying how vice-presidents were elected. From that point forward, the presidential elections have consisted of president/vice-president pairs of candidates running against each other.

Major political parties in America today

There are two dominant political parties in the country today that have been shaping American politics for more than 150 years—the Democratic Party and the Republican Party.

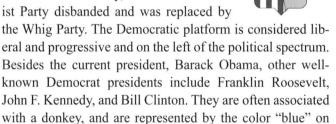

Democratic Party: The 1790s saw the Democratic-Republican Party form to face the Federalist Party. This eventually becomes the Democratic Party, while the Federalist Party disbanded and was replaced by the Whig Party. The Democratic platform is considered liberal and progressive and on the left of the political spectrum. Besides the current president, Barack Obama, other well-known Democrat presidents include Franklin Roosevelt, John F. Kennedy, and Bill Clinton. They are often associated with a donkey, and are represented by the color "blue" on political maps.

Republican Party: This party was started in 1854 as an anti-slavery party before the Civil War. Their platform is conservative and on the right side of the political spectrum. Well-known Republican presidents include Abraham Lincoln, Dwight Eisenhower, George Bush, and Ronald Reagan. They are associated with an elephant, called the *GOP* (Grand Old Party), and are represented by the color "red" on political maps.

Primaries and the national conventions

Since 1832, the major parties had used national conventions as the method of selecting their best candidates for president and vice president. These would usually consist of party officials meeting to determine who they thought the best candidate was. This made it difficult to gauge the actual popular support for any candidate. Starting in 1910, the parties started holding primary elections in a number of states. These elections selected the delegates that would go to the national convention to vote for their candidate. The parties follow this procedure today, though each party and state handle the process differently. Normally each state has a primary election for each party early in the same year as the presidential election. These primary elections are usually open only to registered voters of that party. Some states hold more informal *caucuses* to select candidates.

The elected delegates meet at their national convention later that year to cast their votes for their party's candidate. Normally, if no candidate gets the required number of votes on the first ballot, the delegates are free to vote for anyone. Conventions in the past have held up to 100 ballots before finally selecting a candidate. These stalemates often result in a relatively unknown *"dark horse"* candidate finally winning the vote. The conventions also formalize their party's platform, which is their formal stand on the important issues of the day.

STATE AND LOCAL GOVERNMENTS

The state and local governments generally duplicate the federal structure, though there are local variations. This creates a very orderly structure as laws and rulings can move from the top of the structure down to the local level, and other issues, such as legal disputes over certain laws, can travel back up the structure, all the way to the Supreme Court if needed. The general structure throughout the country is:

Type	Location	Executive	Legislative	Judicial
National	Washington, D.C.	President	U.S. Senate U.S. House	Supreme Court Federal Courts
State	State Capitol	Governor	State Senate State House	State courts
City	City Hall	Mayor	City Council	Municipal courts

Responsibilities of a U.S. Citizen

Being a United States citizen gives you some of the most valued rights in the world. You can vote, bring family to this country, travel with a U.S. passport, run for federal office, get a federal job, enjoy the rights guaranteed to you under the Constitution, receive help from the federal government, and be protected by that government and its military anywhere in the world. And what are your responsibilities? Not many, but they are important:

- Serve on a jury when called
- Vote
- Serve your country when required
- Obey the laws
- Pay taxes
- Respect the rights, beliefs, and opinions of others
- Defend the Constitution

United States Oath of Allegiance

Citizens born in this country often take it for granted how special their country is. Immigrants fleeing repressive governments and oppressive conditions don't have that problem, and most likely appreciate their responsibilities as well. Oaths of Allegiance have been used since the Revolutionary War. Naturalized citizens must take the following oath before they can become a citizen. Every native-born citizen should be prepared to take the same oath.

I hereby declare, on oath,

that I absolutely and entirely renounce and abjure all allegiance and fidelity to any foreign prince, potentate, state, or sovereignty of whom or which I have heretofore been a subject or citizen;

that I will support and defend the Constitution and laws of the United States of America against all enemies, foreign and domestic; that I will bear true faith and allegiance to the same;

that I will bear arms on behalf of the United States when required by the law;

that I will perform noncombatant service in the Armed Forces of the United States when required by the law;

that I will perform work of national importance under civilian direction when required by the law; and that I take this obligation freely without any mental reservation or purpose of evasion; so help me God.

American Holidays

The celebration of common holidays is important to this country. These celebrations help unite an increasingly diverse population in shared activities that serve as links to the past. This ensures that we never forget the people and events that made this country, and the sacrifices that have been made by our ancestors. Holidays mark the passage of time, and frame each year with indelible markers. Unfortunately, they often have become just excuses for 3-day vacation weekends, or time off from work, which is why we need to be reminded of their meanings. Halloween is not devil worship but a rite of passage for children, and a time that adults can dress up and laugh at themselves. Thanksgiving, in particular, is woven into American life as a time for all families to gather and give thanks for the bounty this country has given them. It has no religious connotations and can be celebrated by everyone. The following list includes Federal holidays, some state holidays, and unofficial holidays and observances.

April Fools Day (April 1): Known as *All Fools Day*, this is a time to play pranks and practical jokes on friends and relatives.

Christmas (December 25): An important Christian holiday celebrating the birth of Jesus Christ. Almost all schools have a 2-week recess around Christmas. It has also become an important secular holiday with Christmas trees and gift giving.

Columbus Day (2nd Monday in October): Celebrates Columbus' arrival in the new world on October 12, 1492.

Earth Day (April 22): Celebrated since 1970 to promote interest in cleaning up the earth's soil, air, and water.

Easter (1st Sunday after 1st full moon after spring equinox): A Christian holiday celebrating the resurrection of Jesus Christ. Along with Christmas, it is the most important Christian holiday. Many attend sunrise services and hide colored Easter eggs.

Father's Day (3rd Sunday in June): Celebrated since 1909 and made an official holiday in 1966, it is a day to honor fathers.

Flag Day (June 14): Celebrates the adoption of the American Flag in 1777 by the Continental Congress. Citizens are encouraged to fly the national flag on this day.

Groundhog Day (February 2): Celebrated since 1887. If the groundhog Punxsutawney Phil emerges from his burrow in Pennsylvania and sees his shadow, there will be six more weeks of winter weather.

Halloween (October 31): The night before All Hallows Day, it is celebrated by children dressing in costumes and "trick or treating" around their neighborhood to receive candy. It also involves carved pumpkins, haunted houses, and scary tales.

Independence Day (July 4): Our most important holiday celebrates the signing of the Declaration of Independence in 1776. It is celebrated by parades and massive firework demonstrations.

Labor Day (1st Monday in September): Celebrates the labor movement in America and marks the end of summer vacations.

Lincoln's Birthday (February 12): A legal holiday in some states honoring the 16th President's birthday in 1809. Never a federal holiday, it is often combined with the Washington's Birthday celebration and called President's Day.

Martin Luther King, Jr. Day (3rd Monday in January): Celebrates the birth of the slain civil rights leader, January 15, 1929.

Memorial Day (last Monday of May): Honors Americans who have given their lives fighting for their country. It was on May 30 until moved to this day in 1968. Americans usually use it to celebrate the first day of summer vacations.

Mother's Day (2nd Sunday in May): President Wilson started this day of thanks in 1914. Besides giving cards and flowers, wise husbands also take their wives out to dinner.

National Arbor Day (last Friday in April): Started in 1970 to encourage tree planting across the country.

New Years Eve (December 31): This is normally marked by parties and celebrations at midnight to mark the end of the Gregorian calendar year. The most famous celebration is at Times Square in New York City. New Years Day is a holiday normally filled with parades and football games.

Pearl Harbor Remembrance Day (December 7): Honors the military personnel who died in the surprise attack on December 7, 1941, resulting in the U.S. entering World War II.

Presidents' Day*: see Washington's Birthday.* Presidents' day is not an official holiday.

Thanksgiving Day (4th Thursday in November): Started by colonial settlers in New England in 1621 to give thanks for their harvest, it is a traditional day of family gatherings and turkey dinners. It also has the heaviest air travel of the year. President Lincoln declared Thanksgiving to be the last Thursday in November. This was observed until President Roosevelt moved it to the second to last Thursday of November to allow for more shopping days before Christmas. The ensuing national furor resulted in some states ignoring the new date until Congress finally passed a 1941 law setting the official date as the fourth Thursday.

Valentine's Day (February 14): Named after St. Valentine, a day for loved ones to give each other cards, candy, and flowers.

Veterans Day (November 11): Honors all veterans of the armed forces. Originally called Armistice Day, it calls for a moment of silence at 11:00 am commemorating the start of the World War I armistice on 11/11/1918 at 11:00 am.

Washington's Birthday (3rd Monday in February): The birthday of the first president is February 22. The holiday was moved to its present day in 1968, and sometimes called Presidents' Day.

Heritage Days

A number of celebrations are not official holidays, but honor the heritage or country of origin of various groups. These include:

Native American Heritage Day (Friday after Thanksgiving): Celebrates the culture and traditions of Native Americans.

Chinese New Year (varies): The start of a new year in the Chinese calendar is usually marked by large parades and celebrations.

Cinco de Mayo (May 5): The victory of the Mexican Army over the French in 1862 is marked by parades and parties, often larger in the United States than in Mexico. It does not celebrate Mexican Independence, which was on September 16, 1810.

Kwanzaa (December 26): Established in 1966 for African-Americans to celebrate their heritage, it lasts for seven days.

Mardi Gras (varies, the day before Ash Wednesday): *Mardi Gras* is French for "Fat Tuesday" describing the last day of overeating before beginning the fasting period of Lent the next day. First celebrated in this country in Mobile, Alabama in 1703, it is marked by a week of wild celebrations and parades, epitomized by the New Orleans celebration.

Rosh Hashanah (varies): A Jewish holiday marking the start of a new year in the Jewish calendar, usually in September or October.

St. Lucia's Day (December 13): A Scandinavian holiday that honors Saint Lucia. It is usually celebrated by processions of girls in white robes carrying candles or with crowns of candles.

St. Patrick's Day (March 17): An Irish holiday celebrating St. Patrick who brought Christianity to Ireland and drove the snakes from that island. It is marked in this country by parties, wearing of something green, and the greening of everything including the Chicago River. Nineteen presidents, including Barack Obama, and 36 million Americans claim Irish ancestry.

HISTORY OF THE AMERICAN FLAG

George Washington and the Continental  Army were laying siege to Boston at the start of 1776. On January 1st, he flew the Grand Union flag at his headquarters.

GRAND UNION FLAG

Later that year, Betsy Ross is purported  to have created the first flag containing 13 5-pointed stars, and 13 stripes. That flag was not made official until June 14, 1777 (later celebrated as Flag Day) when the Continen- BETSY ROSS FLAG tal Congress passed the Flag Act.

Over the following years, Congress passed  acts to alter the appearance of the flag to allow for the admission of new states. The Act of 1794 provided for 15 stars and 15 stripes on the flag. This was the "Stars and Stripes" STAR-SPANGLED BANNER celebrated in the Star-Spangled Banner.

Since 1818, the design has been fixed with 13  stripes and a star for each state. A 48-star flag was flown from 1912 until 1959 when Alaska and Hawaii were admitted. This is the longest time any one flag design has been used. 48-STAR FLAG

Since 1959, we have had the modern flag con-  sisting of 13 stripes and 50 stars, one for each state. This is the flag the astronauts left on the moon on July 20, 1969. The colors used in the flag are the same as those in the Great TODAY'S 50-STAR FLAG Seal. The meaning of those colors was reported to Congress as: *"White signifies purity and innocence, Red, hardiness & valour, and Blue...signifies vigilance, perseverance & justice."*

Flag Act of 1818

This set the current policy of 13 stripes with one star for each state (before this act, the number of stripes had increased with each state). The new star would be added to the flag on the next 4th of July following the admission of the new state.

United States Flag Etiquette

U.S. Code, Title 4, Chapter i

Pledge of Allegiance

The pledge was written in 1892 by Francis Bellamy to celebrate the 400th anniversary of the voyage of Christopher Columbus. The pledge is recited at public events and in schools. The words "under God" were added in 1954. The pledge should be spoken while at attention, facing the flag, with the right hand over the heart. Non-religious headwear should be removed and held with the right hand. Uniformed personnel should face the flag and salute.

> I pledge allegiance
> To the flag of the United States of America
> And to the republic for which it stands,
> One nation under God,
> Indivisible, with liberty and justice for all.

Time and occasions for display of flag

- Normally display the flag from sunrise to sunset. If displayed at night, it must be properly illuminated. Do not display the flag if the weather is bad, unless you use an all-weather flag. The flag is often raised at 8:00 am and lowered at sunset on military bases and ships not underway.

- Hoist and lower the flag briskly and ceremoniously.

- You can display the flag everyday, especially on holidays or special days declared by the President.

- Display the flag daily at public institutions, at schools during school days, and at polling places on election days.

Position and manner of display

- In parades, the flag should be on the right, or in front.

- No other flag shall be flown above or to the right of the American flag, including the U.N. flag.

- The American flag, when displayed with crossed staffs, should be on the flag's right in front of any other staffs.

- 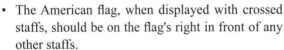 In any grouping of staffs with state or local flags, the American flag should be in the center and the highest.

- When flown with other state or local flags on the same halyard, the American flag is always at the top.

- When flown with state or local flags on adjacent staffs, the American flag is raised first and lowered last. No other flag can be to the right of the American flag or above it.

- When flags of two or more nations are displayed, they should be of the same size and flown from separate staffs of the same height. International usage forbids the display of the flag of one nation above that of another nation in time of peace.

- When displayed from a horizontal staff on the side of a building, place the union (blue square) towards the peak.

 • Against a wall or in a window, the union should be at the top to the observer's left.

- When displayed over the middle of the street, suspend it vertically with the union to either the north or east.

- Indoors, a flagpole should be at the front of any audience behind any speaker in a position of prominence to the speaker's right (audience's left). Any other flags on poles should be displayed on the other side of the speaker.

Flag flown at half-staff (half-mast)

- The President may order flags flown at half-staff upon the deaths of principal figures in the government, or on similar days of mourning.

- To raise, first hoist the flag to the peak, and then lower halfway.

- To lower, first raise the flag to the peak and then lower to the bottom.

- On Memorial Day, the flag is displayed at half-staff until noon, then raised to the top of the staff.

On a casket

- Place the flag with the union (blue square) at the head over the left shoulder. Do not lower the flag into the grave.

Inside a building

- When the flag is suspended across a corridor or lobby in a building with only one main entrance, it should be suspended vertically with the union of the flag to the observer's left upon entering.

Respect for the American flag

- No disrespect should ever be shown to the American flag.
- The flag should not be dipped to any person or thing.
- Never fly upside down except as a distress signal.
- The flag should never touch anything beneath it, such as the ground, the floor, water, or merchandise.
- The flag should not be torn or soiled.
- Never place any mark, letter, or drawing on the flag.
- Flags no longer fit for display should be destroyed in a dignified way, preferably by burning.

The flag should not be used for:

- Wearing apparel, bedding, or drapery.
- For bunting or decoration.
- As covering for a ceiling.
- Holding or carrying anything.
- Advertising on temporary items like napkins.
- Costumes or uniforms, except a flag patch may be affixed to uniforms, and lapel flag pins can be worn on *left* lapel.
- Covering any part of a car, railroad car, or boat.

Conduct during hoisting, lowering, or passing

- All persons in uniform should render the military salute.
- Members of the Armed Forces, and veterans not in uniform, may render the military salute.
- Others should face the flag and stand at attention with their right hand over the heart, holding any removed headgear.
- Citizens of other countries stand at attention.
- Render conduct toward the flag in a moving column at the moment the flag passes.

Conduct during the National Anthem

- Uniformed individuals salute at the first note and maintain that position until the last note.
- Military members, and veterans who are not in uniform, may also render the military salute.
- All others should face the flag and stand at attention with their right hand over the heart, holding any removed headgear.
- If no flag is present, face the music while showing this respect.

FOLDING THE AMERICAN FLAG

Since the American flag should not be carried flat, it needs to be folded for transportation or storage. It should be properly folded when removed from the flagpole at the end of the day. During funeral services held by military personnel, they will remove the flag from the casket, fold it properly, and present it to the next of kin.

1. Start by holding the flag parallel to the ground.

2. Fold lengthwise.

3. Fold lengthwise again, ensuring that the blue field of stars covers both sides.

4. Starting at the striped end, fold the corner up to form a triangle and pull tight.

5. Fold this triangle toward the blue field, forming another triangle.

6. Continue folding the triangles toward the blue field, approximately 12 folds in total. You should end up with a small triangle of blue stars. Tuck the loose end under the fold to form a tight package.

Honoring Our Flag and Country

John McCain   1988

> Senator John McCain was shot down over Vietnam in 1967 and
> spent more than five years in a Vietnamese prison. He recounted
> this story about fellow pilot and prisoner-of-war Mike Christian.
> This story will make you fully appreciate the power of our flag,
> and the sacrifices our fighting men and women make to honor that
> symbol and their country. McCain had refused an offer for an early
> release in 1968 because he did not want to leave before prisoners
> that had been there longer. That decision resulted in five more years
> of captivity and repeated torture.

Let me tell you what I think about our Pledge of Allegiance,
our flag and our country. I want to tell you about when I was a
prisoner of war.

I spent five years in the Hanoi Hilton. In the early years of our
imprisonment, the North Vietnamese kept us in solitary confine-
ment or two or three to a cell. In 1971, the North Vietnamese
moved us from these conditions of isolation into large rooms with
as many as 30 to 40 men to a room. This was, as you can imagine,
a wonderful change . . . and a direct result of the efforts of millions of Americans, led by people like Nancy and Ronald Reagan,
on behalf of a few hundred POWs, 10,000 miles from home.

One of the men moved into my cell was Mike Christian. Mike
came from a small town near Selma, Ala. He didn't wear a pair
of shoes until he was 13 years old. At 17, he enlisted in the U.S.
Navy. He later earned a commission. He became a naval flying
officer and was shot down and captured in 1967. Mike had a
keen and deep appreciation for the opportunities this country
-- and our military -- provide for people who want to work and
want to succeed.

The uniforms we wore in prison consisted of a blue short-
sleeved shirt, trousers that looked like pajama trousers and rubber
sandals that were made out of automobile tires. (I recommend
them highly; one pair lasted my entire stay.) As part of the change
in treatment, the Vietnamese allowed some prisoners to receive
packages from home. In some of these packages were handkerchiefs, scarves and other items of clothing. Mike got himself a
piece of white cloth and a piece of red cloth and fashioned himself
a bamboo needle. Over a period of a couple of months, he sewed
the American flag on the inside of his shirt.

Every afternoon, before we had a bowl of soup, we would hang Mike's shirt on the wall of our cell and say the Pledge of Allegiance. I know that saying the Pledge of Allegiance may not seem the most important or meaningful part of our day now, but I can assure you that for those men in that stark prison cell, it was, indeed, the most important and meaningful event of our day.

One day, the Vietnamese searched our cell and discovered Mike's shirt with the flag sewn inside and removed it. That evening they returned, opened the door of the cell, called for Mike Christian to come out, closed the door of the cell and, for the benefit of all of us, beat Mike Christian severely for the next couple of hours. Then they opened the door of the cell and threw him back inside.

He was not in good shape. We tried to comfort and take care of him as well as we could. The cell in which we lived had a concrete slab in the middle on which we slept and four naked light bulbs in each corner of the room. After things quieted down, I went to lie down to go to sleep. As I did, I happened to look in the corner of the room. Sitting there, beneath that dim light bulb, with a piece of white cloth, a piece of red cloth, another shirt and his bamboo needle, was my friend, Mike Christian.

Sitting there, with his eyes almost shut from his beating, making another American flag. He was not making the flag because it made Mike Christian feel better. He was making that flag because he knew how important it was for us to be able to pledge our allegiance to our flag and country.

Duty, honor, country. We must never forget those thousands of Americans who, with their courage, with their sacrifice and with their lives, made those words live for all of us.

THE NATIONAL MOTTO

UNITED STATES CONGRESS   1956

The motto *"In God We Trust"* had been used on U.S. coins since 1864. In 1954, the words "under God" were added to the Pledge of Allegiance. Congress approved the new National Motto in 1956, and it was added to paper currency the next year.

IN GOD WE TRUST

THE MEANING OF OUR FLAG

HENRY WARD BEECHER   1863

A clergyman in the mid-19th century, Beecher was involved in social reform and anti-slavery movements as well. Unfortunately, he is most likely better known for his well-publicized adultery trial in 1875. He believed in the right of women to vote and fought attempts to restrict Chinese immigration. And he loved his nation's flag.

If one asks me the meaning of our flag, I say to him: It means just what Concord and Lexington meant, what Bunker Hill meant. It means the whole glorious Revolutionary War. It means all that the Declaration of Independence meant. It means all that the Constitution of our people, organizing for justice, for liberty and for happiness, meant.

Under this banner rode Washington and his armies. Before it Burgoyne laid down his arms. It waved on the highlands at West Point. When Arnold would have surrendered these valuable fortresses and precious legacies, his night was turned into day and his treachery was driven away by beams of light from this starry banner.

It cheered our army, driven out from around New York, and in their painful pilgrimages through New Jersey. This banner streamed in light over the soldiers' heads at Valley Forge and at Morristown. It crossed the waters rolling with ice at Trenton, and when its stars gleamed in the morning with a victory, a new day of hope dawned on the despondency of this nation.

Our Flag carries American ideas, American history and American feelings. Beginning with the Colonies, and coming down to our time, in its sacred heraldry, in its glorious insignia, it has gathered and stored chiefly this supreme idea: divine right of liberty in man. Every color means liberty; every thread means liberty; every form of star and beam or stripe of light means liberty - not lawlessness, but organized, institutional liberty - liberty through law, and laws for liberty!

This American Flag was the safeguard of liberty. Not an atom of crown was allowed to go into its insignia. Not a symbol of authority in the ruler was permitted to go into it. It was an ordinance of liberty by the people, for the people. That it meant, that it means, and, by the blessing of God, that it shall mean to the end of time!

The American's Creed

WILLIAM TYLER PAGE   1918

> The creed was written for a contest and adopted by the U.S. House of Representatives in 1918. The winner, William Page, took the $1000 prize money, bought Liberty bonds, and gave them to his church.

I believe in the United States of America, as a government of the people, by the people, for the people; whose just powers are derived from the consent of the governed; a democracy in a republic; a sovereign Nation of many sovereign States; a perfect union, one and inseparable; established upon those principles of freedom, equality, justice, and humanity for which American patriots sacrificed their lives and fortunes.

I therefore believe it is my duty to my country to love it, to support its Constitution, to obey its laws, to respect its flag, and to defend it against all enemies.

The National Bird

The Bald Eagle was adopted by Congress as the national bird in 1782 and placed on the Great Seal. The eagle won out over other birds, including the Wild Turkey purportedly favored by Benjamin Franklin. The eagle is now the symbol of the United States. The Bald Eagle is native only to North America and symbolizes courage, strength, and freedom. Its head is covered in white feathers and is not really bald. The numbers of bald eagles in the lower 48 states dropped dangerously in the mid 20th century to as few as 400 pairs, but the bird received federal protection and, along with a reduction in pesticide use and hunting, has rebounded to more than 10,000 pairs in the mainland America, and over 50,000 in Alaska.

Service flags honor our military

Service flags are official banners that can be displayed by families who have family members serving on active duty in the United States military. The banner displays a red border around a white interior, with a blue star for each family member on duty. A gold star indicates a member that died during service. Mothers whose children have died during service have formed the Gold Star Mothers Club.

GREAT SEAL OF THE UNITED STATES

The Great Seal was first used in 1782. The front (obverse) is the national coat of arms used on passports, military insignia, and flags. The reverse is now used on the back of the one-dollar bill.

Front of the Great Seal

An American Bald Eagle supports a shield of thirteen stripes representing the original 13 colonies. Unlike the flag, the out-

ermost stripes are white, not red, in keeping with heraldic rules. The stripes support a blue bar (chief) that contains no stars. This blue chief represents Congress support-ed by the states. The eagle holds a bundle of 13 arrows in its left talon and an olive branch with 13 leaves and 13 olives in its right, all repre-senting the original colonies. The olives represent peace, while the arrows represent America's readiness for war. The eagle's head is turned towards the olive branch, symbolizing America's preference for peace.

The motto *E Pluribus Unum* alludes to the union of states: "Out of Many, One." The constellation of 13 stars above the eagle's head, arranged to form a small star, represents a new country tak-ing its place among the powers of the world. The color white sig-nifies purity and innocence; red represents hardiness and valor; and blue signifies perseverance and justice.

Reverse of the Great Seal

The pyramid represents strength and duration, and is composed of 13 layers to represent the colonies. The eye and the motto

"Annuit Coeptis" refer to the inter-vention of providence in favor of America. The date MDCCLCCVI (1776) on the pyramid is the date of the Declaration of Independence, and "Novus Ordo Seclorum" signi-fies the beginning of the new Amer-ican era, roughly meaning "A New Order of the Ages."

Liberty Bell

The 2000-pound Liberty Bell was cast in 1752 in England, but after it was delivered to Philadelphia, it developed cracks and was twice recast by John Pass and John Stow. It bears the inscription *"Proclaim LIBERTY throughout all the Land unto all the inhabitants thereof."* The bell was reportedly rung from the Independence Hall tower when the Declaration of Independence was read aloud in public for the first time on July 8, 1776. It developed a crack that grew large enough by 1846 that they stopped ringing the bell, though it was rung on D-Day during World War II. The bell is now located in its own pavilion across from Independence Hall in Philadelphia.

Think you know your money?

Fill in the name of the person found on each bill and coin before turning to the next page to see pictures of the current money. No fair peeking in your wallet!

Coins

1¢ _____

5¢ _____

10¢ _____

25¢ _____

50¢ _____

$1.00 _____

Currency

$1 _____

$2 _____

$5 _____

$10 _____

$20 _____

$50 _____

$100 _____

AMERICAN MONEY

1¢ - penny
Abraham Lincoln

5¢ - nickel
Thomas Jefferson

10¢ - dime
Franklin Roosevelt

25¢ - quarter
George Washington

50¢ - half-dollar
John Kennedy

$1 - dollar
Sacagawea

$1 George Washington

$2 Thomas Jefferson

$5 Abraham Lincoln

$10 Alexander Hamilton

$20 Andrew Jackson

$50 U.S. Grant

$100 Benjamin Franklin

Forgot what to call it? Try...

bacon, beans, Benjamin($100), bills, bread, buck($1), buckaroos, cabbage, cash, chump change, clams, C-notes($100), coconuts, dinero, do-re-mi, double sawbuck ($20), doubloons, dough, fin($5), grand($1000), green, greenbacks, jack, Jackson($20), lettuce, loot, moolah, pocket money, quid, sawbuck($10), scratch, shekels, silver, simoleons, spending money, stash, wad, wampum...or just plain old dollars and cents.

ARMED FORCES OF THE UNITED STATES

The U.S. Armed Forces consist of the Army, Air Force, Navy, Marines, and Coast Guard. The Marines are a part of the U.S. Navy, and the Coast Guard is under Homeland Security, except in times of war when it reports to the Navy. There are almost 1.5 million personnel in the services today with another 1.5 million in the Reserve, broken down approximately as:

Army	548,000	Marine Corps	203,095
Navy	332,000	Air Force	323,000
Coast Guard	42,000		

The table below lists the titles and insignias for the enlisted, warrant officers, and commissioned officers of each service. Don't get caught insulting some Chief by calling him an Ensign.

PAY GRADE	ARMY	AIR FORCE	NAVY	MARINES	COAST GUARD
E-1	Private *no insignia*	Airman Basic *no insignia*	Seaman Recruit *no insignia*	Private *no insignia*	Seaman Recruit
E-2	Private 2	Airman	Seaman Apprentice	Private 1st Class	Seaman Apprentice
E-3	Private 1st Class	Airman 1st Class	Seaman	Lance Corporal	Seaman
E-4	Corporal	Senior Airman	Petty Officer 3rd Class	Corporal	Petty Officer 3rd Class
E-5	Sergeant	Staff Sergeant	Petty Officer 2nd Class	Sergeant	Petty Officer 2nd Class

Pay Grade	Army	Air Force	Navy	Marines	Coast Guard
E-6	Staff Sergeant	Technical Sergeant	Petty Officer 1st Class	Staff Sergeant	Petty Officer 1st Class
E-7	Sergeant 1st Class	Master Sergeant	Chief Petty Officer	Gunnery Sergeant	Chief Petty Officer
E-8	Master Sergeant	Senior Master Sergeant	Senior Chief Petty Officer	Master Sergeant	Senior Chief Petty Officer
E-9	Sergeant Major	Chief Master Sergeant	Master Chief Petty Officer	Master Gunnery Sergeant	Master Chief Petty Officer
E-9 special	Sergeant Major of the Army	Chief Master Sergeant of the Air Force	Master Chief Petty Officer of the Navy	Sgt. Major of the Marine Corps	Master Chief Petty Officer of Coast Guard
W-1	Warrant Officer 1	n/a	n/a	Warrant Officer 1	n/a

PAY GRADE	ARMY	AIR FORCE	NAVY	MARINES	COAST GUARD
W-2	Chief Warrant Officer 2	n/a	Chief Warrant Officer 2	Chief Warrant Officer 2	Chief Warrant Officer 2
W-3	Chief Warrant Officer 3	n/a	Chief Warrant Officer 3	Chief Warrant Officer 3	Chief Warrant Officer 3
W-4	Chief Warrant Officer 4	n/a	Chief Warrant Officer 4	Chief Warrant Officer 4	Chief Warrant Officer 4
W-5	Chief Warrant Officer 5	n/a	Chief Warrant Officer 5	Chief Warrant Officer 5	n/a
O-1	Second Lieutenant — GOLD	Second Lieutenant — GOLD	Ensign	Second Lieutenant — GOLD	Ensign
O-2	First Lieutenant — SILVER	First Lieutenant — SILVER	Lieutenant, Junior Grade	First Lieutenant — SILVER	Lieutenant Junior Grade
O-3	Captain	Captain	Lieutenant	Captain	Lieutenant
O-4	Major — GOLD	Major — GOLD	Lieutenant Commander	Major — GOLD	Lieutenant Commander

PAY GRADE	ARMY	AIR FORCE	NAVY	MARINES	COAST GUARD
O-5	Lieutenant Colonel SILVER	Lieutenant Colonel SILVER	Commander	Lieutenant Colonel SILVER	Commander
O-6	Colonel	Colonel	Captain	Colonel	Captain
O-7	Brigadier General	Brigadier General	Rear Admiral Cmmodore	Brigadier General	Rear Admiral
O-8	Major General	Major General	Rear Admiral	Major General	Rear Admiral
O-9	Lieutenant General	Lieutenant General	Vice Admiral	Lieutenant General	Vice Admiral
O-10	General	General	Admiral	General	Admiral

American military deaths in war—all causes
(Source: U.S. Army Military History Institute)

Revolution	25,000
War of 1812	20,000
Mexican War	13,300
Civil War - North	360,000
Civil War - South	260,000
Spanish American War	2,500
World War I	116,700
World War II	407,300
Korean War	36,900
Vietnam War	58,200
Persian Gulf War	258
Afghanistan (ongoing)	1,600+
Iraq (ongoing)	4,500+

Size of military units

Unit	Approximate Size	Composition	Typical Commander
Army	100,000	2+ corps, HQ	General
Corps	30,000+	2+ divisions	Lt. General
Division	15,000+	3 brigades, HQ, support units	Maj. General
Brigade	4,500+	3+ regiments, HQ	Brig. General
Regiment	1,500+	2+ battalions, HQ	Colonel
Battalion	700	4+ companies, HQ	Lt. Colonel
Company	175	4 platoons, HQ	Captain
Platoon	40	4 squads	Lieutenant
Squad	10		Staff Sergeant

U.S. Military Awards

The awards listed are the highest military awards given, including the service cross and distinguished service awards. They are listed in general order of precedence and order worn. Some awards have different names and medals for each service, so we show the award for just one of the services. There are many more awards given, including service and achievement awards.

1. Medal of Honor
Our nation's highest military decoration bestowed on those who distinguished themselves through "conspicuous gallantry and intrepidity at the risk of his or her life above and beyond the call of duty while engaged in an action against an enemy of the United States." Over 3,450 have been given since 1862, many posthumously. (Air Force shown)

2. Service Cross
Each service has a unique Service Cross award given for extraordinary heroism above and beyond the call of duty while engaged in combat, but not qualifying for a Medal of Honor. (Navy medal shown)

3. Distinguished Service Medal
Each service has their own Distinguished Service Medal that is given for "exceptionally meritorious service to the Government in a duty of great responsibility." It is the highest medal that can be given for non-combat actions. (Army medal shown)

4. Silver Star
The Silver Star is given for gallantry in action against an enemy. The recipient must have distinguished himself or herself by extraordinary heroism.

5. Defense Superior Service Medal
This medal is a senior Department of Defense military decoration given to members who perform "superior meritorious service in a position of significant responsibility."

6. Legion of Merit
A military decoration given for exceptionally meritorious conduct in the performance of outstanding services and achievements. It can be given to U.S. military personnel, or foreign military or political figures. Like the Medal of Honor, it can be worn around the neck.

7. Distinguished Flying Cross
The Flying Cross is awarded to any member of the military for "heroism or extraordinary achievement while participating in an aerial flight, subsequent to November 11, 1918."

9. Bronze Star Medal
The Bronze Star is after the Soldier's Medal in precedence, but it is a more common medal. It is awarded for bravery, acts of merit, or meritorious service. It has been in existence since 1944.

Purple Heart
Not a top medal for heroism, the Purple Heart may be the medal best-known by the public. It is the oldest award still given to the military, started by Washington in 1782, and is awarded to any member who has been wounded or killed while fighting the enemy.

NATIONAL GUARD

The National Guard is the U.S. reserve military force. Its members are citizen soldiers, holding regular civilian jobs while serving part time in the Guard. It consists of the Army National Guard and the Air National Guard. The units are organized by states and ter- ritories, and report to their state governor, or territorial adjutant general, who can call them up for active duty for domestic emergencies. The members can also be assigned to active duty in the federal armed forces if required. The Guard has almost 500,000 members.

LABOR IN AMERICA

The labor movement in the United States started early in the 19th century as various groups worked to protect the wages and conditions of workers. By the end of the century, organized labor would help end inhumane work conditions, low wages, and child labor.

1869 — **Knights of Labor founded**
The group is organized to unionize workers to give them negotiating powers with their companies. Wage cuts and bad working conditions lead to strikes throughout the country.

1874 — **Massachusetts' Ten Hour Act**
Legislation sets work limits for women and children.

1877 — **Molly Maguires arrested and executed**
This Pennsylvania secret association of coal miners is involved in the burning of buildings and murder.

Great Strike of 1877
Railroad workers strike after wages are cut 10%. The strike turns violent with battles between militia and striking workers. Federal troops are sent in to end the violence.

1885 — **Knights of Labor strike the railroads**
Strikes are successful against Jay Gould's railroads. Strikes will increase the next year to 1,400 across the country, mostly focused on setting an 8-hour working day.

1886 — **Haymarket Square Riot in Chicago**
The Knights of Labor get involved in violent riots, along with other unions and anarchists. The subsequent bombings and shootings kill eight and result in the arrest of anarchists.

American Federation of Labor (AFL) founded
Samuel Gompers founds the group to fight for shorter work hours and higher wages. It consists mainly of skilled workers, excluding unskilled workers, blacks, and women.

1890 — **Sherman Antitrust Act**
Enables government to break up monopolies and labor strikes.

1894 — **Pullman Strike**
Eugene V. Debs leads a strike against the railroads in protest of wage cuts by the Pullman Palace Car Company. President Cleveland sends in federal troops to break the strike. The rise of large corporations leads to unrest as the disparity between rich and poor increases. Women and children are still working in large numbers for extremely low wages. A large influx of immigrants also keeps wages depressed.

1911 — **New York Garment district fire kills 150 workers**
The International Ladies' Garment Workers Union pushes for stricter safety standards in the wake of the tragedy.

1922 — **Great Railroad Strike of 1922**
A nationwide strike starts after the Railroad Labor Board votes to cut hourly wages to seven cents. The railroads use strikebreakers to fill hundreds of thousands of vacated jobs. The hostilities end with federal legislation against the strikers.

1933 — **National Industrial Recovery Act (NIRA)**
The New Deal act encourages collective bargaining, sets maximum work hours and minimum wages, and restricts child labor. It is declared unconstitutional two years later.

Congress of Industrial Organizations (CIO) started
John Lewis starts a new group to organize labor. He supports FDR's New Deal, and Lewis' United Mine Workers Union becomes a major contributor to Roosevelt. Membership will grow to 4 million by 1937.

1935 — **Wagner Act**
This establishes the National Labor Relations Board which protects labor from unfair business practices.

1938 — **Fair Labor Standards Act**
Sets a 40-hour work week, restricts child labor, and sets a minimum wage of 40 cents an hour. Economists later determine that Roosevelt's New Deal policies actually prolonged the Depression by interfering with the free market.

1947 — **Taft Hartley Act**
A Republican Congress passes the act over Truman's veto. The anti-labor law outlaws closed shops, forbids union political contributions, and calls for 60-day cooling-off periods before strikes. There is a public backlash against unions with many feeling that the New Deal has helped them too much.

1955 — **AFL and CIO merge to form AFL/CIO**
Union membership peaks at 35% of the workforce.

1964 — **Leader of Teamster's Union jailed**
Jimmy Hoffa is the target of federal investigation for corruption. Teamster's Union is ejected from AFL.

1965 — **Cesar Chavez starts United Farm Workers Union**
He leads a 4-year strike and international boycott of grapes.

2010 — **Union membership reaches 70-year low**
2010 union membership reaches 70-year low at 11.9%. Government union members now account for more than half of union membership. Some states pass laws limiting the power of public unions. Some of the problems include:
• Taxpayers pay the employees' salaries, which is then used to finance the public union. The unions can then donate money (the taxpayer's money) to politicians of their choice.
• Public union employees can essentially influence the election of the very officials who give them their jobs and decide on their benefits.

BASIC ECONOMIC CONCEPTS

The success of the United States over the last 2½ centuries owes a lot to her form of government, her protection of personal freedoms, and her economic system. Important concepts are:

Capitalism: The means of production are privately owned and operated for profit. Production decisions are made based on the potential profits. Risk takers are often rewarded by large profits, but there is also no guarantee against failure and bankruptcy.

Free market system (market economy): Production, pricing, and distribution of goods and services are determined by the interactions of buyers and producers, with minimal government intervention, mainly in collecting taxes, enforcing contracts, and ensuring public safety. Prices are determined by the intersection of supply and demand curves (see below). Producers are not forced to make specific products, nor sell them at any specific price. Government attempts to circumvent this relationship, using price controls, subsidies, quotas, or rent controls, almost always results in failure. The free market is the optimal way to allocate scarce resources, which include time, labor, material, and money.

Laissez-faire: French meaning "leave it alone." This advocates minimal government intervention and taxation, usually only in enforcing contract and safety laws.

Economic terms

Every citizen should have a basic understanding of economics, and how companies, workers, wages, and prices are related. Too many important decisions are being made by our politicians that involve the consequences of economic policy. Common terms are:

Bond prices vs. interest rates: Bonds typically pay a certain interest rate based on their face value. When interest rates rise, bond prices fall, and when interest rates fall, bond prices rise.

Depression: More severe than a recession, there have been only three real depressions; the Great Depression of the 1930s, and smaller ones in 1837 and 1873. A depression is usually accompanied by a decline in the GDP by more than 10%.

Debt ceiling: The maximum amount of debt the government can assume. Congress must vote to raise this ceiling before borrowing more. It has raised the ceiling seven times in the last ten years, so it is obvious that Congress is very unclear on the concept of a ceiling, which is meant to limit excessive spending.

Commons: Resources that are commonly held or shared among multiple groups, or by the country or world as a whole. They are not privately held so cannot be fenced in or similarly controlled. The oceans and the atmosphere are good examples.

Compound interest: Adding interest earned on savings back to the principal so that it will grow with interest as well. Saving just $5 a day during your working years could grow to over $200,000 if left in a compound interest account paying just 5%.

Federal Deposit Insurance Corporation (FDIC): A federal program insuring deposits at banks up to $250,000 per person.

Federal Reserve: The Federal Reserve System acts as the central bank for the country.

Gross domestic product (GDP): The total value of all goods and services produced in a country, used as a general indicator of their standard of living. The United States GDP in 2009 was $13 trillion, equating to a per capita GDP of $46,859.

Laffer Curve: A theoretical representation of the relationship between total tax revenue and tax rates. While not precise, it depicts an optimal tax rate that will maximize revenue. Either raising or lowering the tax rate from this point will decrease revenue.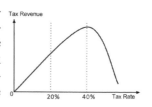

Misery Index: An indicator of how the public feels about the state of the economy, normally calculated by adding the unemployment rate to the rate of inflation. It reached an all-time high of 21.98 in 1980, and is around 11.5 in 2011.

Opportunity cost: The related cost involved every time decisions are made between one option and another. Almost all choices in life involve determining the best use of one's limited time, money, or resources. The opportunity cost when you choose one job is the value of the job you passed up.

Present value: What a future sum of money or stream of income would be worth today, taking into account projected interest rates. For example, the winner of a lottery can choose between $20 million spread out over 10 years, or a lump sum payment today of $10 million which would be the calculated present value of the total prize.

Prime rate: The interest rate banks charge their best customers, usually linked to a U.S. Treasury security interest rate.

Recession: This occurs when the GDP declines for 2 quarters in a row, or when unemployment rises 1.5% in 12 months. The country officially entered a recession in late 2007.

Rule of 72: A simple method to roughly determine how long any given interest rate will take to double your money. Divide 72 by the interest rate to determine the number of years. Dividing 72 by an interest rate of 6% equals 12. This means that it will take 12 years of 6% interest to double your money.

Social Security Tax (FICA): Social Security and Medicare are paid for by your FICA taxes withheld from your salary at a rate of 15.3% total, split by you and your employer. This is on top of your federal and state income tax, property tax, and sales tax.

Supply and demand curves: Graphs depicting the basic relationship of supply and demand in a free market economy. The final price of any good will be at the intersection of the two curves, where the quantity demanded by the consumer at that price equals the quantity that the supplier is willing to provide at that same price. The graph can be used to show some basic laws:

1. Increase demand (move demand curve to the right) and keep supply constant—prices rise and quantity sold increases.

2. Decrease demand (move demand curve to the left) and keep supply constant—prices fall and quantity sold decreases.

3. Increase supply (move supply curve to the right) and keep demand constant—prices fall and quantity sold increases.

4. Decrease supply (move supply curve to the left) and keep demand constant—prices rise and quantity sold decreases.

Unemployment rate: The percentage of the work force presently out of work but actively looking for a job. There is always unemployment due to seasonal workers, people changing jobs, and those experiencing life changing events. A rate of 4% is considered full employment. If the unemployed stop looking for work, the rate goes down, so the real unemployment rate is probably higher than the published rate.

———————— ❧ ————————

The government's view of the economy could be summed up in a few short phrases: If it moves, tax it. If it keeps moving, regulate it. And if it stops moving, subsidize it.

—*Ronald Reagan*

Poor Richard, 1739

AN
Almanack

- Be slow in chusing a Friend, slower in changing.
- Humility makes great men twice honourable.
- Early to bed and early to rise, makes a man healthy wealthy and wise.
- Fish & Visitors stink in 3 days.
- Tis easy to see, hard to foresee.
- God helps them that help themselves.
- The rotten Apple spoils his Companion.
- Don't throw stones at your neighbours, if your own windows are glass.
- Creditors have better memories than debtors.
- He that cannot obey, cannot command.
- Well done is better than well said.
- The worst wheel of the cart makes the most noise.
- Sell not virtue to purchase wealth, nor Liberty to purchase power.
- Wish not so much to live long as to live well.
- He that falls in love with himself, will have no Rivals.
- Well done, is twice done.
- Tart Words make no Friends: a spoonful of honey will catch more flies than a Gallon of Vinegar.
- Make haste slowly.
- A true Friend is the best Possession.
- No gains without pains.
- Many complain of their Memory, few of their Judgment.

PHILADELPHIA:
Printed and sold by *B. FRANKLIN*, at the New Printing-Office near the Market.

Chapter 6

WHAT IS AMERICA?

❧

IT IS DIFFICULT TO DETERMINE EXACTLY what makes America great or what American exceptionalism means. Our country's unique birth was unburdened by centuries of warfare and despotic rule. Our founders created a nation that protected the freedom of every individual to pursue their dreams. This also means they have the freedom to fail, but without that freedom, there would be no winners. The superlative athletes listed below all succeeded because someone else had to lose. But this helped create the very drive to succeed and overcome obstacles that made them winners.

In attempting to describe America, one needs to look at the myriad influences that help create each of us. This includes history, family, sports, arts, customs, literature, holidays, traditions, politics, inventions, and education. Only then can one begin to understand our national psyche.

America is a nation of vision, enterprise, and achievement. It pushed a railroad across the continent in only a few years, won World War II, and put a man on the moon. The "*Can Do*" spirit exists everywhere. Americans prize individualism, self-reliance, ingenuity...and absolutely treasure their freedom and independence.

WHAT IS AN AMERICAN?

It is impossible to describe a typical American, other than to say that they are not typical. America is one giant melting pot.

- We are a nation of inventors, diplomats, soldiers, farmers, artists, writers, scientists, explorers, doctors, nurses, and teachers.
- We are a nation of Christians, Jews, Buddhists, Muslims, Hindus, deists, and atheists.
- We are a nation of conservatives, liberals, libertarians, and independents.

- We are a nation of whites, blacks, Native Americans, Hispanics, Asians, and Arabs.
- We are a nation of generational groups—the greatest generation, silent generation, baby boomers, generation X, generation Y, and now, generation Z.
- We are a nation of regional groups—Southerners, mid-Westerners, New Englanders, New Yorkers, Alaskans, Texans, and Californians.
- We are a nation of immigrants from every country in the world.

We are so diverse that our most common trait is our diversity. What is important is that all Americans have common ground to bind them as a people. Among other things, this includes a common language and educational experience. You can't recognize an American by their looks, but you can recognize them by their beliefs and their actions.

Central Pacific and Union Pacific railroads meet
Promontory Summit, Utah - May 10, 1869

Where did we come from?

We have always been a nation of immigrants. Even the Native Americans are descendants of tribes that crossed the Bering Strait thousands of years ago. The Vikings came and went one thousand years ago. Columbus ignited one hundred years of exploration by French, English, Spanish, and Dutch adventurers. Finally, English settlers searching for treasure or fleeing religious persecution came to stay at Jamestown and Plymouth. French and Russian trappers continued their influences, while Spanish missionaries traversed the West. The descendants of the early settlers multiplied and moved westward while immigrants from around the world kept landing on our shores.

- Some were brought here by force—African slaves sold against their will to Southern farmers.
- Some came here to escape something— persecution, war, repression, famine, disease.
- Some came here looking for something—opportunity, jobs, food, land, freedom.
- Native Americans were already here and would be displaced by the relentless push westward.

Millions of Irish fled the potato famine in Ireland to come to the New World so they could find food to stay alive. Chinese workers came to California to help build the great railroad. Two million Scandinavians left their homes to come in search of opportunity, settling in the Great Lakes area. Descendants of German immigrants make up almost one-fifth of our current population. Italians came looking for work. Russians arrived, escaping repression, discrimination, and hardship back home. Later, thousands would arrive from Southeast Asian, fleeing chaos and Communism.

Whatever the reason, they arrived by the millions, bringing their skills, tastes, customs, religions, and languages. But they also assimilated into their new land. They learned our language and our customs, and were soon full participants in the American dream. Many were disliked at first, accused of taking jobs or often just because they were different. But they persevered and became "American." They used their old skills to start new businesses. They moved to parts of the country that reminded them of their homeland, or that contained relatives from back home. They became part of this country, and many would soon be asked to fight and die for that new land. They celebrated their heritage...but they became Americans.

In all, between 1840 and 1920, more than 30 million immigrants came to this country, most of them arriving in New York City. More than 40% of the American population today are descendants of immigrants who passed through the Ellis Island Immigration Station after its 1892 opening.

What have Americans accomplished?

American success stories are everywhere, giving us all hope and inspiration to keep striving in our lives. Many are rags-to-riches stories of overcoming immense odds to finally succeed. Others are stories of individuals making the right choices at the right time, or fully using their natural talents. Knowing the accomplishments of fellow Americans helps connect the citizens in every corner of this country, and remind them of what this relatively new nation has accomplished, and what it can accomplish. It is the greatness of the American system that fostered and encouraged these accomplishments.

Any list of the "greatest" of anything is open to widespread and heated debate. The following lists are meant to give a general idea of the best or most memorable in each category and are not definitive top-10 lists. In keeping with that spirit, the lists are usually in alphabetical order.

LITERATURE FROM AMERICA'S WRITERS

Americans have been writing ever since the early days of the colonies. The *Federalist Papers* and Thomas Paine's *Common Sense* were important in the creation of the nation. The writers moved from pamphlets to religious writing to creating unique poetry and novels. Writers like Jack London developed a style of realism, while others chronicled the historic events of the country. Some of the American writers that have contributed over the centuries include the following names.

Mark Twain
born Samuel Clemens

Louisa May Alcott *(1832–1888)*: Little Women

Pearl Buck *(1892–1973)*: The Good Earth

Rachel Carson *(1907–1964)*: Silent Spring

James Fenimore Cooper *(1789–1851)*: Last of the Mohicans; Deerslayer

Stephen Crane *(1871–1900)*: The Red Badge of Courage

Emily Dickenson *(1830–1886)*: Because I Could Not Stop for Death; I Died for Beauty

Ralph Waldo Emerson *(1803–1882)*: Self-Reliance; Concord Hymn

William Faulkner *(1897–1962)*: Death of a Salesman; As I Lay Dying; Sanctuary; The Sound and the Fury

F. Scott Fitzgerald *(1896–1940):* The Great Gatsby; This Side of Paradise

Robert Frost *(1874–1963):* The Road Not Taken; Stopping by Woods on a Snowy Evening

Nathaniel Hawthorne *(1804–1864):* The House of the Seven Gables; The Scarlet Letter

Joseph Heller *(1923–1999):* Catch-22

Ernest Hemingway *(1899–1961):* The Sun Also Rises; A Farewell To Arms; For Whom the Bell Tolls; The Old Man and the Sea

O. Henry *(1862–1910):* The Gift of the Magi

Washington Irving *(1783–1859):* Rip Van Winkle; Legend of Sleepy Hollow

Jack Kerouac *(1922–1969):* On the Road

Sinclair Lewis *(1855–1951)* (first American Nobel Prize winner for literature): Elmer Gantry; Main Street; Babbitt

Jack London *(1876–1916):* Sea Wolf; Call of the Wild; To Build a Fire

Henry Wadsworth Longfellow *(1807–1882):* Paul Revere's Ride; The Song of Hiawatha

Alfred Mahan *(1840–1914)*: The Influence of Sea Power upon History

Herman Melville *(1819–1891):* Moby Dick; Billy Budd

Margaret Mitchell *(1900–1949)*: Gone with the Wind

Thomas Paine *(1737–1809):* Common Sense; The Rights of Man

Edgar Allen Poe *(1809–1849):* The Raven; The Gold Bug; Annabel Lee

Ayn Rand *(1905–1982):* Atlas Shrugged; The Fountainhead

J.D. Salinger *(1919–2010):* The Catcher in the Rye

Carl Sandburg *(1878–1967):* Abraham Lincoln; Chicago

Upton Sinclair *(1878–1968):* The Jungle

John Steinbeck *(1902–1968)*: The Grapes of Wrath; Of Mice and Men; Cannery Row; The Pearl; East of Eden

Harriet Beecher Stowe *(1811–1896):* Uncle Tom's Cabin

Henry David Thoreau *(1817–1862):* Walden; Civil Disobedience

Mark Twain *(1835–1910):* Tom Sawyer; Huckleberry Finn; Life on the Mississippi; The Prince and the Pauper

Kurt Vonnegut *(1922–2007):* Cat's Cradle; Slaughterhouse-Five

Walt Whitman *(1819–1892):* Leaves of Grass; Song of Myself; O Captain! My Captain!

Tennessee Williams *(1911–1983)*: A Streetcar Named Desire; Cat on a Hot Tin Roof; The Glass Menagerie; The Night of the Iguana

Thomas Wolfe *(1900–1938):* Look Homeward Angel; You Can't Go Home Again

AMERICAN INVENTIONS LEAD THE WORLD

Thomas Alva Edison
holder of 1,093 U.S. patents

These items are from Encyclopedia Britannica's 2003 list of great inventions. Of the 321 world-wide inventions, half belonged to the United States. The United States comprises only a fraction of the world's population and is one of the newest countries, so you have to credit its free market system that encourages risk-taking but rewards success. Some were related to the government-funded space program, but the inventions were usually made by individuals and companies. Some inventors were extremely prolific, like Thomas Edison with 1093 patents. Many truly changed the world with their ideas.

Medicine/Health: *artificial heart; bifocals; defibrillator; pacemaker; laser vision correction; magnetic resonance imaging (MRI); oral contraceptives; Prozac; respirator; sunscreen; synthetic skin; tampon; Viagra*

Food: *Aspartame; beverage can; can opener; cereal flakes; chewing gum; Coca-cola; food irradiation; frozen foods; genetic engineering; hybrid corn; potato chips; prepared baby food; saccharin; sliced bread; supermarket; tea bag*

Technology: *air conditioning; airplanes; artificial diamond; assembly line; Astroturf; ATM; atomic bomb; auto airbag; bar code; barbed wire; brassiere; camera; carbon-14 dating; cash register; computer; computer mouse; corrugated cardboard; cotton gin; crayons; credit card; digital wristwatch; dishwasher; disposable diapers; electric guitar; electric iron; electric motor; electric razor; electric stove; e-mail; escalator; fiberglass; gas lawn mower; hand-held calculator; integrated circuit; Internet; jeans; jukebox; Kevlar; laser; laundromat; light bulb; light-emitting diode (LED); liquid crystal display (LCD); liquid-fueled rocket; loudspeaker; LP record; mechanical reaper; microwave oven; miniature golf; mobile home; mobile telephone; Morse code; motion-picture animation; movie camera; nuclear reactor; nylon; oil well; paper towel; parking meter; passenger elevator; phonograph; photocopying; photographic film; photography; Post-it Notes; radio; refrigerator; repeating rifle; revolver; revolving door; roller coaster; safety pin; safety razor; satellite; Scotch tape; sewing machine; skateboard; skyscraper; slot machine; smoke detector; stapler; steamboat; steel plow; Teflon; telegraph; telephone; television; tractor; traffic lights; transistor; tube lipstick; TV remote control; typewriter; video games; videotape; virtual reality; vulcanized rubber; washing machine; wire coat hanger; zipper*

AMERICAN MUSIC

America has also served as a melting pot for music, but also has contributed several very unique music genres to the world. It is heavily influenced by African-American blues and gospel music, but has been tempered and transformed by the diverse nature of America. The genres continue to evolve and overlap. Many of the following styles overlap or are subgenres of other groups.

Louis Daniel Armstrong
The great jazz musician *Satchmo*

Folk: Many unique American music genres spring from what is called *roots music*. This covers a wide range from bluegrass to Native American. Popular folk music experienced a revival in the 1950s and 1960s with singers like the Kingston Trio.

Bob Dylan, Burl Ives, Joan Baez, Judy Collins , New Christie Minstrels, Pete Seeger, Peter, Paul and Mary, The Kingston Trio, The Limelighters, Weavers, Woody Guthrie

Minstrel: Another "roots" genre that appeared in the 1830s, accompanying traveling minstrel shows and using the newly popular banjo. It is often identified with slavery and the Old South. It is important in the development of bluegrass, blues, and country music. Hundreds of minstrel shows toured the country, often featuring white actors in blackface. The best-known composer was Stephen Foster whose songs included:

Camptown Races; Oh! Susanna; Swanee River; My Old Kentucky Home; Beautiful Dreamer

Jazz: Influenced by New Orleans and former slaves, it is uniquely American. Scott Joplin made ragtime music famous with his hits *The Entertainer* and *Maple Leaf Rag*.

Count Basie, Dave Brubeck, Charlie Parker, Miles Davis, John Coltrane, Billy Holliday, Max Roach, Dizzy Gillespie, Duke Ellington, Scott Joplin, Thelonious Monk, Ella Fitzgerald, Louis Armstrong

Big Band/Swing: Popular in the 1930s and 1940s as a form of jazz played with lots of musicians playing saxophones, trumpets, and trombones. Many singers, such as Frank Sinatra, got their start with big bands, and their singing style was called Swing or Jazz.

Benny Goodman, Glenn Miller, Frank Sinatra, Tommy Dorsey, Duke Ellington, Bing Crosby, Count Basie, Artie Shaw

Country: A unique blend of Appalachia, gospel, bluegrass, and western influences.
Dolly Parton, Johnny Cash, Carrie Underwood, Chet Atkins, Garth Brooks, Willie Nelson, Merle Haggard, Buck Owens.

Classical: American classical music is heavily influenced by the unique music styles of this country, including folk, jazz, and blues. Some of the well-known works instantly bring to mind images of America, from New York to the Grand Canyon.
Aaron Copland, George Gershwin, Ferde Grofé, Yo-Yo Ma

Patriotic Music and Marches: Patriotic music has been part of our culture since the country was founded. Its hymns, national songs, and marches encourage national unity, particularly in times of war. The most famous composer is John Philip Sousa.
America the Beautiful; Over There; Yankee Doodle; God Bless America; Star Spangled Banner; This Land is Your Land; Stars & Stripes Forever; Battle Hymn of Republic; My Country, 'Tis of Thee

Rhythm and Blues (R&B): A broad category that also includes jazz, gospel, soul music, and what is called Motown music.
Alicia Keys, Aretha Franklin, Barry White, Beyoncé, Curtis Mayfield, Diana Ross, Dionne Warwick, Donna Summer, Dusty Springfield, Gladys Knight, Isley Brothers, Jackie Wilson, Jackson 5, Janet Jackson, Jennifer Hudson, Kelly Clarkson, Lionel Richie, Mariah Carey, Marvin Gaye, Michael Jackson, Otis Redding, Patti LaBelle, Pointer Sisters, Prince, Ray Charles, Rihanna, Sam & Dave, Sly & the Family Stone, Smokey Robinson, Stevie Wonder, Stylistics, Supremes, Teddy Pendergrass, Temptations, Tina Turner, Toni Braxton, Whitney Houston

Rock and Roll: Starting in the 1950s and engulfing the world, this category now covers a huge number of sub-genres. Many performers listed elsewhere could also be listed under Rock and Roll. The list is endless, but here are a few.
Beach Boys, Bill Haley and the Comets, Buddy Holly, The Byrds, Carly Simon, Doors, Drifters, Eagles, Elvis Presley, Grateful Dead, James Brown, Janis Joplin, Jefferson Airplane, Jimi Hendrix, Jimmy Buffett, Kingsmen, Little Richard, Lynyrd Skynyrd, Madonna, Sam Cooke, Simon and Garfunkel

Musicals & Movies: Musicals and movies have showcased hundreds of famous songs and soundtracks, using composers like John Williams, Henry Mancini, and Rogers & Hammerstein.
Annie Get Your Gun, Carousel, Chorus Line, Grease, Guys & Dolls, Hair, Jaws, Meet Me in St. Louis, My Fair Lady, Oklahoma!, Over Here!, Pink Panther, Porgy & Bess, Singin' in the Rain, Show Boat, South Pacific, Star Wars, The King and I, The Music Man, The Sound of Music, Wizard of Oz, West Side Story

AMERICAN ACTORS AND ACTRESSES

John Wayne
Starred in 142 movies

America brought radio, movies, and TV to the world, and made Hollywood the home of entertainment. The yearly Academy Awards ceremony sends images of movies, actors, and actresses around the world. The participants are also from around the world, but America's contribution tops all countries. And this doesn't include the great directors and producers that make America their home. The industry grosses billions of dollars every year, while producing hundreds of movies. Some of the stars are:

Al Pacino, Alec Baldwin, Andy Griffith, Angelina Jolie, Ava Gardner, Barabara Stanwyck, Barbra Streisand, Bette Davis, Bob Hope, Brad Pitt, Bruce Lee, Bruce Willis, Burt Lancaster, Buster Keaton, Cameron Diaz, Cary Grant, Charlton Heston, Christopher Reeves, Christopher Walken, Clark Gable, Clint Eastwood, Cuba Gooding Jr., Demi Moore, Denzel Washington, Diane Keaton, Drew Barrymore, Dustin Hoffman, Eddie Murphy, Frank Sinatra, Fred Astaire, Gary Cooper, Gene Hackman, Gene Kelly, George Clooney, Ginger Rogers, Grace Kelly, Gregory Peck, Gwyneth Paltrow, Halle Berry, Harrison Ford, Henry Fonda, Humphrey Bogart, Jack Benny, Jack Lemmon, Jack Nicholson, James Cagney, James Dean, Jamie Foxx, Jennifer Garner, Jimmy Stewart, Joaquin Phoenix, Jodie Foster, John Malkovich, John Travolta, John Wayne, Johnny Depp, Judy Garland, Julia Roberts, Katharine Hepburn, Kevin Bacon, Kevin Costner, Kevin Spacey, Kirk Douglas, Kirsten Dunst, Kurt Russell, Lauren Bacall, Leonardo DiCaprio, Mae West, Marilyn Monroe, Marlon Brando, Marx Brothers, Matt Damon, Matthew Perry, Meg Ryan, Mel Gibson, Meryl Streep, Michael Douglas, Michelle Pfeiffer, Morgan Freeman, Nancy Kwan, Nicolas Cage, Orson Welles, Patrick Swayze, Paul Newman, Queen Latifah, Reese Witherspoon, Renee Zellweger, Richard Gere, Rita Hayworth, Robert De Niro, Robert Downey Jr., Robert Duvall, Robert Redford, Robin Williams, Samuel L Jackson, Sandra Bullock, Sean Penn, Sharon Stone, Shirley Temple, Spencer Tracy, Steve Martin, Steve McQueen, Susan Sarandon, Sylvester Stallone, Tobey Maguire, Tom Cruise, Tom Hanks, Tommy Lee Jones, Uma Thurman, Will Smith.

WORLD-CLASS ATHLETES

The United States has produced outstanding athletes in every sport. And "outstanding" means more than just the number of victories, points, or statistics—these athletes are often world-class in their attitude and approach to life. Some athletes are left off this list for lacking that balance in their lives. The sports below are primarily professional or Olympic sports. Sports are important in America at every level, with high school and college sports being dominant in many parts of the country not close to a professional franchise. The high school and college tradition of Homecoming is linked to football games in autumn. College football leads to bowl games in January, and the pro football season ends with the Super Bowl. The Baseball World Series has been going on for more than 100 years. Other athletes rely on the Olympic games every four years for their major competition.

Jim Thorpe
All-around athlete

Baseball

Hank Aaron: On the All-Star team for 20 straight years, he broke Babe Ruth's home run record when he hit #715 in 1974.

Ty Cobb: He set 90 major league records in a career that ended in 1928, and still holds the career batting average record of .366.

Joe DiMaggio: A three-time MVP winner and 13-time All-Star player, he still holds the hitting streak record at 56 games.

Lou Gehrig: Yankee first baseman who holds the record for career grand slams (23) and, for a time, most consecutive games. His 1939 emotional farewell after being fatally diagnosed with ALS (now called Lou Gehrig's disease) earned him admiration as he called himself "the luckiest man on the face of the earth."

Mickey Mantle: The Yankee who played in 16 All-Star games and holds World Series records including total home runs (18).

Willie Mays: Considered the best all-around player, he tied the record of 24 All-Star games, and hit 660 home runs, including 4 in one game.

Stan Musial: 24-time All-Star player who played 22 seasons and was named MVP three times (some years had 2 All-Star games).

Jackie Robinson: The first black Major League baseball player in 1947. He played in 6 World Series and was the first black MVP.

Babe Ruth: The best-known baseball player, he may also be the greatest. He held the single season home run record (60) for 34 years, and the total home run record of 714 for 47 years.

Ted Williams: Playing his entire career as left fielder for the Boston Red Sox, he led the league in hitting six times, and had a .482 on-base percentage.

Basketball

Kareem Abdul-Jabbar: He led UCLA to 3 championships before turning pro. When he retired, he was the all-time leader in points scored, games played, blocked shots, and defensive rebounds.

Larry Bird: Led the Celtics to several titles and won two NBA Finals MVP and three regular-season MVP awards.

Wilt Chamberlain: One of the most dominant players in history, and still the only player to score 100 points in one game.

Michael Jordan: A virtually unanimous pick as greatest basketball player ever. In addition to his scoring records, he also became the first player to have 200 steals and 100 blocks in one season. He led the Chicago Bulls to six NBA titles.

Bill Russell: Helped lead the Boston Celtics to eleven NBA championships during thirteen years in the 1950s and 1960s.

Biking

Lance Armstrong: Fighting testicular cancer, Lance won a record seven consecutive Tour de France races.

Boxing

Muhammad Ali: Three-time heavyweight champion, he was a flamboyant boxer who won a boxing gold medal at the 1960 Olympics. He had classic title fights against Joe Frazier and George Foreman. He retired with 56 wins in 61 fights.

Joe Louis: The heavyweight champ from 1937 to 1949, he may be the best of all-time. He won 65 bouts, most by KO, with only 3 losses. He was possibly the first black hero in the United States. The German champ Schmeling gave Louis his first loss in 1936, becoming a Nazi symbol of supposed Aryan superiority. Their 1938 rematch was one of the most famous boxing matches of all time, held in Yankee Stadium before 70,000 fans. Louis won the fight in less than 3 minutes before a battered Schmeling gave up.

Rocky Marciano: The only heavyweight boxer to retire undefeated at 49-0 with 43 KOs. He had only one opponent who even lasted the full fifteen rounds.

Sugar Ray Robinson: Fighting mainly as a welterweight or middleweight, Robinson achieved 173 wins in 200 total fights before retiring in 1965.

Football

Jim Brown: Often picked as the best player of all time, he holds the Cleveland Brown season rushing record of 1,863 yards.

Peyton Manning: Winner of NFL MVP 4 times and holder of many records including most seasons with 4,000 passing yards.

Joe Montana: As quarterback, he led the 49ers to four Super Bowl titles and consistently led the league in passer ratings.

Jerry Rice: Possibly the greatest player in NFL history and a Pro-Bowl pick 13 times, this wide receiver holds the record for touchdowns with 208.

Barry Sanders: An explosive runner still holding many records, he retired early within striking distance of the rushing record.

Johnny Unitas: A record-setting quarterback for the Colts in the 1950s and 1960s, he holds the record for throwing a touchdown pass in 47 consecutive games.

Golf

Bobby Jones: Jones was the most successful amateur golfer ever until he retired at 28. He won 13 major championships and founded the Masters Tournament after he retired.

Jack Nicklaus: Winner of a record 18 major championships, his last when he was 46.

Arnold Palmer: A popular golfer who helped bring attention to the sport while winning seven major championships.

Tiger Woods: One of the most successful golfers ever with 14 major wins, he is the youngest player to win the Grand Slam. Marital problems in 2010 led to a major disruption in his career.

Horse Racing

Even horses reflect the American spirit and capture our imagination.

Man o'War: This horse won 20 of 21 races, and lived for 30 years after a short but brilliant racing career.

Seabiscuit: This unlikely winner captured America's imagination by beating the popular War Admiral by four lengths in the 1938 "Match of the Century", listened to by 40 million Americans.

Secretariat: The greatest horse ever with a 22-pound heart and records at Belmont and the Kentucky Derby. He won the Triple Crown in 1973, winning Belmont by a staggering 31 lengths.

Swimming

Duke Kahanamoku: A Hawaiian swimmer who won 5 Olympic medals and is credited with spreading the sport of surfing.

Michael Phelps: The greatest American swimmer with 16 Olympic medals including 14 gold medals won in two games including all 8 events at the 2008 Beijing Olympics.

Mark Spitz: Winner of 11 Olympic medals, including 7 gold medals in one game, a record until broken by Phelps in 2008.

Johnny Weissmuller: Winner of five Olympic gold medals, he went on to star as Tarzan in Hollywood movies.

Tennis

Arthur Ashe: Winner of three Grand Slams, and the only black man to win singles title at Wimbledon, U.S. Open, and Australian Open.

Chris Evert: Winner of 18 Grand Slam single championships and holder of the best win-loss singles record in history.

Billie Jean King: Winner of titles in 16 Grand Slam women's doubles, 12 Grand Slam singles, and 11 Grand Slam mixed doubles.

Serena Williams: One of the greatest women's tennis players ever, she holds 27 Grand Slam titles.

Track and Field

Michael Johnson: The only male to win both 200m and 400m events at the same Olympics, he won four Olympic gold medals.

Jackie Joyner-Kersee: Named greatest female athlete of her century, she won 6 Olympic medals in the long jump and heptathlon.

Carl Lewis: One of the best all around track stars, he won ten Olympic medals in games from 1984 to 1996.

Jesse Owens: The black runner who stunned the Nazis at the 1936 Berlin Olympics by winning four gold medals and demolishing Hitler's claim of a master Aryan race.

Wilma Rudolph: The fastest woman in the world at the time, she won three gold medals at the 1960 Rome Olympics.

Jim Thorpe: A natural, all-around Native-American athlete, he played baseball and football, and won two gold medals at the 1912 Stockholm Olympics in the pentathlon and decathlon.

Winter Sports

Bonnie Blair: A speedskater winner of five Olympic gold medals.

Peggy Fleming: Gold medal figure skater at the 1968 Olympics.

Eric Heiden: Speed skater who won 5 Olympic gold medals in 1980, the only athlete in history to win gold in all speed skating events at one Olympics.

Michelle Kwan: An Olympic medalist and the most decorated figure skater in U.S. history.

1960 and 1980 men's hockey teams: Both amateur teams scored huge upset wins over highly favored, seasoned Soviet teams. The 1960 win was the first American Olympic hockey gold medal ever. The 1980 victory over the best team in the world has been called the greatest upset in sports history.

American Cooking

America is not traditionally known for a single cooking style. Immigrants from all over the world added their cooking styles to America's diverse culture. Though many of America's unique plants and animals were taken back to Europe by early explorers, its cuisine was influenced by those plants and animals, including corn, cranberries, maple syrup, blueberries, pecans, avocados, squash, beans, peanuts, pumpkins, tomatoes, and turkey. The resulting cuisine is a mixture of cultures, ingredients, geography, and hardships associated with settling the continent.

American Lobster
Homarus americanus

Regional differences

Soul food/Southern: Pork, barbecued ribs, grits, white gravy, chicken fried steak, fried chicken, black eyed peas, collard greens, hush puppies (fried cornbread), corn dogs, blue crab.

Creole/Cajun: Influenced by the French in the Louisiana Territory. Seafood gumbo, jambalaya, crawfish, chicory coffee.

New England: lobster, cod, clams, mussels, chowder, baked beans, cranberries, maple syrup.

Philadelphia: Philly cheesesteak, soft pretzels.

Chicago: Chicago style pizza.

Midwestern: meat, mashed potatoes, meatloaf, catfish—all usually mildly seasoned.

Southwest: chili peppers, enchiladas, burritos, tacos, tortillas, salsa, chili con carne, fajitas.

California/Northwest: salmon, oysters, artichokes, abalone, avocados, garlic, Dungeness crab, sourdough french bread.

Uniquely American

Thanksgiving dinner: Turkey, dressing, mashed potatoes, peas, cranberry sauce, sweet potatoes.

Sandwiches: two pieces of bread filled with peanut butter, jelly, tuna fish, turkey, ham, or cheese. Hero sandwiches, Reuben sandwiches, submarine sandwiches, and the classic Philly cheesesteak.

American breakfast: eggs, bacon, ham, pancakes, syrup, waffles, toast, grits, hash browns, sausage, cereals, oatmeal, French toast.

Peanut butter. Milk. Frozen dinners and doughnuts of every kind.

Fast Foods: Burgers, hot dogs, milk shakes, root beer floats, popcorn, pizza, french fries, potato chips.

Seafood: Dungeness crabs, blue crabs, lobster, crawfish, salmon, oysters, clams, catfish.

Healthy/Organic: more stores and restaurants offer organic food, and consumers are buying more locally grown produce.

ARCHITECTS CHANGE AMERICA'S FACE

America transformed herself by selecting the best of the old architectural styles while innovating with bold new visions. Not bound by centuries of tradition, the country's architecture is dominated by function, not form, as early settlers built with materials on hand, creating log cabins and sod houses. But they soon created unique structures, such as Boston's State House (1713) and Jefferson's Monticello (1784). Regional influences are seen everywhere, from French Creole in New Orleans, to Native American and Mexican influences in the Southwest, and Victorian mansions in San Francisco. Some of the more notable structures are listed.

Chrysler Building
New York City

White House Washington, DC	**Golden Gate Bridge** San Francisco, CA
Rotunda Charlottesville, VA	**Monticello** Charlottesville, VA
House of Burgesses Williamsburg, VA	**Guggenheim Museum** New York, NY
Brooklyn Bridge New York, NY	**Massachusetts State House** Boston, MA
Thomas Jefferson Memorial Washington, DC	**Lincoln Memorial** Washington, DC
Washington Monument Washington, DC	**Chrysler Building** New York, NY
Empire State Building New York, NY	**United Nations Building** New York, NY
Rockefeller Center New York, NY	**Dulles Airport** Washington, D.C.
Transamerica Pyramid San Francisco, CA.	**Gateway Arch** St. Louis, MO
Sears Tower Chicago, NY	**Hearst Castle** San Simeon, CA
Hotel Del Coronado San Diego, CA	**World Trade Centers** New York, NY
Grand Central Station New York, NY	**Old Faithful Inn** Yellowstone Park
Frank Lloyd Wright's **Falling Water House** Pennsylvania	**Ahwahnee Hotel** Yosemite, CA

FAMOUS AMERICAN SHIPS

Old Ironsides
USS Constitution

Our country's founders, realizing that a strong navy was critical to the continued survival of the nation, started building that navy during the Revolutionary War. The U.S. Navy now commands the seas and our history is full of famous vessels. They range from a 38-foot sailing ship displacing 40 tons, to a 1,123-foot nuclear aircraft carrier displacing 95,000 tons and carrying 70 powerful jet airplanes.

America: The 101-foot sailboat won a 1851 race at the Isle of Wight. The *America's Cup* is the oldest active trophy in sports.

USS *Arizona*: The battleship *Arizona* sank when Pearl Harbor was attacked in 1941. She is now a U.S. memorial in the harbor.

USS *BonHomme Richard:* While defeating the British ship *Serapis,* John Paul Jones stated "I have not yet begun to fight."

USS *Constitution:* During the War of 1812, cannonballs bounced off her sides earning her the name of *Old Ironsides.* In Boston Harbor now, she is the oldest commissioned warship

USS *Enterprise:* The first American nuclear aircraft carrier and the eighth U.S. Naval vessel to bear the name. The seventh was the most decorated U.S. ship of World War II.

CSS *Hunley*: A Confederate submarine that sank the USS *Housatonic* at Charleston, becoming the first submarine to sink a ship.

USS *Intrepid:* The first American carrier to have steam catapults. Now a floating museum in New York Harbor.

USS *Maine:* The battleship that blew up in Havana harbor, sparking the Spanish-American War.

Mayflower: The 100-foot long sailing ship that brought 102 passengers to Plymouth Rock in 1620.

USS *Monitor:* John Ericsson created this ironclad just in time to stop the first Confederate ironclad, *Virginia*, from destroying the Union fleet. She was the first of many ironclad ships.

USS *Nautilus:* The first American nuclear submarine launched in 1954, it was also the first to travel under the North Pole.

PT-109: Future President John Kennedy's PT boat in World War II that was cut in two by an enemy ship.

Susan Constant, Discovery, **and** *Godspeed:* The three sailing vessels that brought the English settlers to Jamestown, Virginia.

USS *Thresher*: An American nuclear submarine that sank at sea with loss of all hands in 1963.

Turtle: World's first submarine, built by David Bushnell and unsuccessfully used against the British in New York in 1776.

FAMOUS AMERICAN PLANES AND SPACECRAFT

Americans turned to the skies as the 20th century dawned. After moving from propeller-driven planes to jet airplanes capable of flying faster than the speed of sound, they turned to space and landed a man on the moon in 1969, while sending almost 2,000 craft into space. Here are some of the more famous planes and spacecraft.

Blackbird
Lockheed SR-71

Apollo 11: Made the first manned landing on the moon, allowing Neil Armstrong to become the first human on the moon in 1969.

Blackbird (SR-71): The stealth supersonic aircraft developed by Lockheed in 1964, capable of Mach 3 speeds at high altitudes.

Challenger: The space shuttle that blew up during launch in 1986.

Columbia: The first space shuttle launched on April 12, 1981. It flew 27 missions before disintegrating during re-entry in 2003.

Enola Gay: The B-29 bomber that dropped the first atomic bomb on Hiroshima, Japan in 1945.

Explorer 1: First U.S. satellite launched in 1958.

Freedom 7: Carried the first American, Alan Shepherd, into space on May 5, 1961.

Memphis Belle: The famous B-17F bomber that became the first to complete 25 combat missions over Germany in 1943.

Spirit of St. Louis: Charles Lindbergh's small airplane that made the first solo non-stop flight across the Atlantic Ocean.

Spruce Goose: The largest seaplane ever with a wingspan of 319 feet, it was built of plywood during the war and only flew once.

Starship Enterprise: The famous, but fictional, spaceship from *Star Trek*. It will be at least the 9th American vessel with that name.

U-2: The 1955 Lockheed spy plane that flew at 70,000 feet, safely above most enemy missiles and fighters.

Voyager: Flown by two pilots for 9 days in 1986, it was the first plane to fly around the world without stopping or refueling.

Voyager 1: Launched in 1977, the satellite has left the Solar System and is the farthest craft from Earth.

Wright Flyer: The Wright Brothers' creation that made the first heavier-than-air flight in 1903 in North Carolina.

X-1: This Bell Aircraft jet carried Chuck Yeager as he became the first person to fly faster than the speed of sound in 1947.

MOVIES CAPTURE AMERICA'S SPIRIT

Gary Cooper
Marshal Kane in *High Noon*

Movies offer a unique view of our history. They can immerse the viewer into the events that shaped this country in a way no book can accomplish, while reaffirming the spirit, determination, and heroism of the men and women accomplishing those deeds. America leads the world in producing movies. The list is endless, but some of the more notable films are listed. If you haven't seen them already, you may want to see what you have missed.

1776: The founders debate and finally sign the Declaration of Independence.

Apollo 13: The aborted mission to the Moon that ends in triumph.

Best Years of our Lives: World War II veterans return home to a world that has completely changed.

Boys Town: Father Flanagan starts a town to help troubled boys.

Coal Miner's Daughter: The story of country music star Loretta Lynn.

Dave: A presidential impersonator assumes the office of President.

Davy Crockett: America's most famous frontiersman fights and dies at the Alamo.

Driving Miss Daisy: Exploring race relations in the South.

Field of Dreams: An Iowa farmer turns his cornfields into a baseball field to await the 1919 Chicago White Sox team.

Far and Away: An Irish immigrant makes it in the new World.

Forrest Gump: A simple southern boy grows up making history without knowing it.

Giant: Cattle, oil, and sex against the backdrop of Texas.

Glen Miller Story. The famous big band leader who disappeared during World War II.

Glory: The first black regiment fights for glory in the Civil War.

Gone with the Wind: Love amidst the devastation of the Civil War in the South.

Grapes of Wrath: The Depression forces an Oklahoma family to migrate to California in search of work.

Great Escape, The: Allied prisoners plan a daring escape from a German prisoner-of-war camp.

High Noon: Courage in a western town in the face of four outlaws gunning for a fight.

Hoosiers: The improbable basketball championship of a small Indiana high school in 1951.

Independence Day: Aliens threaten our way of life until courageous men and women fight back.

In the Heat of the Night: A visiting black detective investigates a murder in a small, racist southern town.

It's a Wonderful Life: The holiday feel-good classic of a man given a second chance to see how wonderful his life has been.

Johnny Tremain: A Boston patriot at the start of the American Revolution.

Last of the Mohicans: A graphic depiction of colonial involvement in the French and Indian War in 1757.

Man Who shot Liberty Valance, The: Terror and revenge in the Wild West.

Miracle: The inspiring and true triumph of the 1980 U.S. Olympic hockey team.

Miracle on 34th Street: A department story Santa might be the real thing, if you really believe…

Mr. Smith Goes to Washington: A small town innocent goes to Congress and finally overcomes all odds against him.

Music Man, The: A con man convinces a small town to buy instruments for their children.

National Treasure: Treasure hunters find clues, hidden in old American landmarks, to an enormous treasure.

October Sky: A young schoolboy dreams of space and builds a rocket.

Oklahoma!: Conflict between the ranchers and cattlemen on the plains of Oklahoma.

Our Town: Life in a small New Hampshire town in the early 1900s.

Patriot, The: The Revolutionary War forces a planter to fight for freedom.

Patton: The outspoken General who won the Battle of the Bulge.

Pride of the Yankees, The: Lou Gehrig's rise to baseball fame.

Rocky: The inspiring success story of the boxer Rocky Balboa.

Roots: A ground-breaking TV movie following the life of a slave and his descendants.

Rudy: The inspiring true story of Daniel "Rudy" Ruettiger, who overcomes all obstacles to play Notre Dame football.

Sands of Iwo Jima: A John Wayne classic ending with the brutal fight for control of Iwo Jima by the U.S. Marines.

Saving Private Ryan: Soldiers on a mission to find Private Ryan after the D-Day landing.

Seabiscuit: The inspirational story of a courageous race horse.

Sergeant York: One of the most decorated American soldiers of World War I.

She Wore a Yellow Ribbon: A classic John Ford western with breathtaking views of the Southwest.

Singin' in the Rain: Hollywood moves from silent movies to talkies with great dancing and singing, and Gene Kelly's unforgettable dance in the rain.

Stagecoach: A classic western epic about a stagecoach ride and the Ringo Kid should give you a feel of the western frontier.

Stand and Deliver: The true story of a Los Angeles math teacher inspiring his students to greatness.

To Kill a Mockingbird: A Southern lawyer defends a black man accused of raping a white woman.

Top Gun: Carrier pilots are trained to be aces in the desert fighter pilot school.

Yankee Doodle Dandy: George M. Cohan's life story.

RELIGION IN AMERICA

The United States is one of the more religious of the developed countries. Initially formed by settlers fleeing religious persecution in Europe, the country's founders ensured that the new Constitution guaranteed freedom of religion without establishing any official state religion. The approximate breakdown of the country in 2007 by religion, according to the CIA Factbook, is show below. One should keep these figures in mind when discussing

St. John's Episcopal Church Richmond, Virginia

religious tolerance in America, and comparing this country to others in the treatment of minority religions by the dominant religions.

Protestant:	51.0%
Catholic:	24.0%
Mormon:	1.7%
Jewish:	1.7%
Buddhist:	0.7%
Muslim:	0.6%
Other (unaffiliated, agnostic):	20.3%

ART IN AMERICA

American art is as varied as everything else in the country. Early painters strove to document the new country with scenes of historical interest and portraits of famous people. The Hudson River School of painting arose in 1820 producing scenes of sweeping landscapes. The ever-westward push of the frontier gave painters new majestic landscapes, unique geographical features, and iconic subjects in cowboys and Native Americans. Later painters portrayed American urban life and values. The twentieth century brought more changes with a focus on the Southwest, emergence of Harlem Renaissance painting, government-funded art during the Depression, and modern abstract art.

Paul Revere   *John Hancock*

John Singleton Copley (1738-1815)

Made famous by his battle scenes and portrait paintings of famous people.

Thomas Jefferson   *The Athenaeum Portrait*

Gilbert Stuart (1755-1828)

Painted portraits of early leaders, including six presidents and a famous unfinished portrait of George Washington.

Washington Crossing the Delaware

Emanuel Leutze (1816-1868)

A German-American painter of patriotic American history scenes, he is best known for this iconic painting of a battle that changed the course of the Revolutionary War.

Looking Down Yosemite Valley

Albert Bierstadt (1830-1902)

Famous for his sweeping panoramas of the American West. Two of his works hang in the U.S. Capitol.

Tropical Scenery

Frederic Church (1826-1900)

Church, a landscape painter in the Hudson River School, included spiritual dimensions in his works.

Fur Traders Descending the Missouri

George Caleb Bingham (1811-1879)

Painted life along the frontier of the Missouri River, as well as political events. He was also a Union general during the Civil War.

Breezing Up (A Fair Wind)

Winslow Homer (1836-1910)

A landscape painter famous for his marine subjects. He was the foremost painter of his time, and also illustrated Civil War battles.

The Smoke Signal   *The Bronco Buster*

Frederic Remington (1861-1909)

A painter, illustrator, and sculptor who depicted the cowboys, soldiers, and Indians of the American West.

John Audubon (1785-1851)

A French Caribbean immigrant, Audubon painted the birds of America. His beautiful book, *The Birds of North America*, contained drawings of 700 birds and is still considered the greatest picture book ever made.

White Gerfalcons

Dempsey and Firpo

George Bellows (1882-1925)

As an early American realist painter, Bellows graphically depicted urban life, particularly of New York City.

Freedom from Want   *Freedom of Speech*

Norman Rockwell (1894-1978)

A painter and illustrator who depicted scenes of American life, drawing for Boy's Life and the Saturday Evening Post.

Whistler's Mother

James Whistler (1834-1903)

A painter known for his subtle drawings, and famous for his *Whistler's Mother.*

The Tetons and the Snake River

Ansel Adams (1902-1984)

Photographer known for his black-and-white pictures of the west, particularly Yosemite Valley.

Ram's Head White Hollyhock and Little Hills

Georgia O'Keeffe (1887-1986)

Developed a unique style of representing natural objects like flowers, rocks and shells, particularly from the Southwest.

American Gothic

Grant Wood (1891-1942)
Well-known painter of Midwest scenes; famous for his iconic *American Gothic* depiction of a farmer and his daughter. The name comes from the Gothic Revival style of the house.

Christina's World

Andrew Wyeth (1917-2009)
Known as a realist painter, he loved to paint the land and people of Pennsylvania and the Northeast.

Andy Warhol (1928-1987)
A pop art painter and illustrator known for his expression "15 minutes of fame."

Campbell's Soup 1

AMERICAN FOLK HEROES

America's history is full of folk heroes that have become part of the American psyche and myth. Some are completely fictional, while others are real people who have become legends over the years as their deeds are embellished.

Huckleberry Finn

Fictional folk heroes

Alfred Bulltop Stormalong: A giant sailor with a ship so large it has hinged masts to avoid scraping the moon.

Bigfoot: Also known as Sasquatch, this is a large ape-like creature reportedly seen in the forests of the Pacific Northwest.

John Henry: A steel-driver builder of railroads, Big John beat the new steam-powered drill but died in the process.

Paul Bunyan: The big lumberjack who dug the Grand Canyon and Great Lakes, and owned Babe, the big Blue Ox.

Pecos Bill: A giant cowboy who could ride tornadoes and used a rattlesnake for a lasso.

Rip Van Winkle: A character in a Washington Irving story who falls asleep for twenty years only to wake and find everything changed.

Uncle Sam: A personification of the United States, with white hair and a top hat, pointing and saying "Uncle Sam wants you!"

Tom Sawyer and Huckleberry Finn: Mark Twain's characters that depicted life on the Mississippi River in the 19th century.

Real folk heroes

Annie Oakley: A sharpshooter in Buffalo Bill's Wild West Show who could split a playing card from the side at 90 feet. Travelling in Europe before World War I, she was requested by the new German Kaiser, Wilhelm II, to shoot the ashes off a cigar in his mouth. She obliged. After the war with Germany started, she sent a letter to the Kaiser, requesting another shot. He never replied.

Betsy Ross: The woman credited with sewing the first American Flag in 1776 and making the stars five-sided instead of six.

Black Bart: This Old West stagecoach robber was known as a gentleman bandit for leaving poems after his robberies.

Buffalo Bill: A scout and buffalo hunter in the wild west, he started a famous Wild West Show.

Calamity Jane: A frontierswoman who was friends with Wild Bill Hickok while fighting the Indians.

Casey Jones: This heroic train engineer died slowing his train before crashing, killing himself but saving the passengers.

Daniel Boone: A frontiersman who helped settle Kentucky by crossing the Cumberland Gap. He was a legend while still alive.

Davy Crockett: A Tennessee frontiersman, he also served in Congress and died fighting the Mexican Army at the Alamo.

Francis Marion: The "Swamp Fox" constantly harassed the British forces fighting in the South during the Revolution.

Hatfields and McCoys: Two feuding families in Appalachia whose fights killed at least 12 family members.

James "Grizzly" Adams: A mountain man, Adams trained grizzly bears, including "Ben" who lived in a San Francisco zoo.

John Paul Jones: Fighting the HMS *Serapis* during the Revolutionary War, he famously said, "I have not yet begun to fight!"

Johnny Appleseed: Born in Massachusetts, he planted apple trees throughout Ohio, Indiana and Illinois.

Lizzie Borden: A New England spinster accused of the hatchet murder of her father and stepmother, but later acquitted.

Mike Fink: A legendary keelboater on the Mississippi, Fink was an archrival of Davy Crockett.

Molly Pitcher: A Revolutionary War heroine credited with firing the cannons at the Battle of Monmouth while under fierce enemy fire.

P.T. Barnum: A showman and entertainer, Barnum started the famous Barnum and Bailey Circus.

Paul Revere: Making the famous 1775 midnight ride to warn the colonials of the approaching British troops, he became a legend.

Pocahontas: An Indian chief's daughter who helped the settlers at Jamestown, Virginia, later marrying John Rolfe.

Wild Bill Hickok: As a gunfighter in the Wild West, Hickok gained fame as a lawman but was finally killed while playing poker.

Will Rogers: Humorist, writer, and actor, Rogers starred in 71 movies, and wrote numerous newspaper columns.

Wyatt Earp: A Western lawman best known for the Gunfight at the O.K. Corral along with his brothers and Doc Holliday.

INFAMOUS OUTLAWS

Bonnie Elizabeth Parker
1910 - 1934

Even the bad guys have an effect on our culture. Unfortunately, time diminishes the seriousness of their crimes, and they often obtain a cult following. Even in their day, they were often treated as celebrities. Many arose during Prohibition, and flourished during (and often were caused by) the Depression. Many gangsters were killed in the same year, 1934. Most have also been the subject of Hollywood movies. For better or worse, here are some of them.

Billy the Kid: A frontier outlaw who shot several men but became a hero after his capture and execution by Sheriff Pat Garrett in 1881.

Bonnie and Clyde: This outlaw pair robbed banks during the Depression, capturing the public's imagination. They killed several officers, and were finally ambushed and killed in 1934.

Butch Cassidy and the Sundance Kid: Butch (born Robert Parker) and the Sundance Kid (born Harry Longabaugh) were members of the Wild Bunch Gang who robbed banks and trains, and hid out in the Hole-in-the-Wall in Wyoming. They fled to South America where they supposedly were surrounded and killed in Bolivia.

Al Capone: Capone operated in Chicago during Prohibition, involved in smuggling, prostitution, and bootlegging. A public figure protected by charitable donations and extensive bribery, he ordered the 1929 St. Valentine's Day Massacre of rival gang members. Convicted of tax evasion, he was imprisoned for life.

D.B. Cooper: An American legend who hijacked a plane between Portland and Seattle in 1971, received $200,000 in ransom, and then parachuted out of the plane. He has never been found.

John Dillinger: Responsible for killing more than 10 men, robbing more than 20 banks, and escaping from jail twice. The notorious gangster was shot and killed during his arrest in 1934.

"Pretty Boy" Floyd: A bank robber who killed several people while operating in the Midwest and was finally killed in 1934.

Jesse James: A Confederate accused of atrocities against Union soldiers. He was active after the Civil War, robbing trains, banks, and stagecoaches. He was killed in 1882 by Robert Ford.

"Machine Gun" Kelly: A prohibition gangster who used a Thompson submachine gun. Arrested in 1933, he was jailed for life.

"Baby Face" Nelson: A bank robber and murderer who escaped from prison using a wooden pistol before being shot in 1934.

WORST U.S. DISASTERS

*Surface Barometric Pressure
Galveston, Texas
September 8, 1900*

The United States has been struck by a number of disasters since its inception, both man-made and natural. The following lists the top disasters in terms of lives lost, not counting losses during wars. Other disasters have caused more damage but resulted in fewer lives lost. It should be noted that a similar list of global disasters would have losses in the hundreds of thousands and millions—we wouldn't even make the top 50 list. If you include epidemics in this list, the 1918 Spanish Flu epidemic killed more than 500,000 Americans.

Year	Lives	Event
1900	6,000 - 12,000	***Galveston Hurricane.*** The massive storm that destroyed Galveston, Texas remains the deadliest natural disaster in North American history.
1906	3000 - 6,000	***San Francisco Earthquake and Fire.*** Most damage was caused by the fire that followed the earthquake.
1928	3,000	***Okeechobee Hurricane, Florida.*** After striking the Caribbean, the storm slammed Florida and caused Lake Okeechobee to breach its dike, flooding hundreds of square miles.
2001	2,973	***September 11, 2001 Terror Attacks.*** Terrorists fly jets into New York's Twin Towers, destroying both towers. They also fly another jet into the Pentagon, killing 184 but causing less damage.
1889	2,209	***Johnstown Flood:*** The South Fork Dam fails and sends 20 million tons of water downstream to destroy Johnstown, Pennsylvania.
1893	2,000	***Chenière Caminada Hurricane.*** The storm surge from this powerful hurricane devastates Chenière Caminada Island on the coast of Louisiana.

2005	1,836	***Hurricane Katrina***: Huge damage to New Orleans, Mississippi, Alabama and Florida.
1865	1,700	***Sultana Explosion:*** Steamboat carrying returning Civil war soldiers blows up and sinks in Mississippi river.
1980	1,700	***Heat Wave:*** Central and southern states struck by extremely high temperatures.
1871	1200 - 2,500	***Peshtigo Fire:*** This Upper Wisconsin fire remains the worst forest fire in U.S. history. It happened on the same day as the more famous Chicago Fire killed hundreds.
1904	1,021	***General Slocum:*** Fire causes steamship to sink in New York Harbor, killing most of the church group that was on board.
1893	1,000 - 2,000	***Sea Islands Hurricane:*** Huge storm hits Georgia and South Carolina in the same year as the deadly Chenière Caminada Hurricane.

ANNUAL CAUSES OF DEATH IN AMERICA

The Center for Disease Control collects statistics on deaths in America. The following table lists the top ten causes for 2007. The list may help put other deaths in perspective. Deaths from HIV/AIDS have fallen dramatically and are below 18,000/year, though up to a million Americans may be infected with HIV and over 600,000 Americans have died from AIDS.

Disease	Annual deaths
Heart disease:	616,067
Cancer:	562,875
Strokes:	135,952
Lower respiratory diseases:	127,924
Accidents (42,000 from autos):	123,706
Alzheimer's disease:	74,632
Diabetes:	71,382
Influenza and Pneumonia:	52,717
Nephritis related:	46,448
Septicemia:	34,828

FINANCIAL PANICS AND CRASHES

Run on Seamen's Saving Bank
1857

It is easy to think that current financial problems haven't happened before, but our country has a long history of financial crisis, and the recovery from those declines. Many were caused by the continually repeating cycle of boom and bust as the markets finally adjust to the problems caused by the excesses of the boom years.

Panic of 1819: Triggered by the end of the War of 1812 boom and the revival of European agriculture. Crop prices fall, banks fail, and houses are foreclosed.

Panic of 1837: The boom of land sales in the West is followed by bust when the government requires purchases be made in gold or silver. Deflation strikes, and hundreds of banks close.

Panic of 1857: Grain prices fall due to an increase in Russian wheat exports after the Crimean War. Banks fail, including several due to management fraud. Western land sales stop, and the Dred Scott decision affects western expansion.

Panic of 1873: The Jay Cooke banking house fails, resulting in a severe stock market decline. The overbuilding of American railroads and the opening of Suez Canal also contribute.

Panic of 1893: The National Cordage Company fails, followed by many banks. Gold reserves decrease, and silver coinage rises.

Panic of 1901: Triggered by railroad competition between James Hill and E.H. Harriman. Railroad stocks also collapse.

Panic of 1907: The failure of United Copper Company triggers the failure of other trust companies. J.P. Morgan helps end the crisis by getting other bankers to help raise cash. This leads to the formation of the Federal Reserve System in 1913.

Crash of 1929: Black Thursday (Oct 24) ends the Roaring Twenties. Inflated stock prices, margin buying, and concerns about the Smoot-Hawley Tariff bill lead to this crash. The Depression starts the next year and stock prices don't recover until 1954.

Crash of 1987: Black Monday (Oct 19) sees the Dow Jones fall 508 points to 1738, a huge percentage drop. Program trading is partly responsible, leading to new regulations on trading.

Crash of 2008: Subprime loan defaults bring down several large financial institutions resulting in worldwide failures and stock market declines. A number of banks fail and the government steps in to rescue others. The Dow Jones falls 18% in one week.

COLORFUL SAYINGS

The American language is full of colorful sayings, idioms, and metaphors. Many are regional in their origin and indicative of the character of their creators. The first group of sayings is taken from our national pastime of baseball, showing how much this sport has become intertwined with our culture.

Sayings and idioms from baseball

in the ballpark: approximate; in the general acceptable range

batting a thousand: getting everything correct

playing in the big leagues: at the highest level; working with the pros in any field

bush league: amateurish; not professional

cleanup hitter: someone who comes in to finish the job; the best person to accomplish the task

curveball: something unexpected and usually bad; a surprise that somehow has to be handled

double header: two similar events on the same day

grand slam: the ultimate; accomplishing the most difficult feat, often in four parts

play hardball: to act in a tough manner; to be ruthless

hit it out of the park: to accomplish a great success; to perform a task perfectly

home run: a success; something achieving its goal

out of left field: unexpected; from a new direction or point of view

major league: working or playing at the highest level

in the ninth ending: running out of time; near the end

off base: by surprise; out of line; inappropriate

pinch hit: to substitute for someone or something

play ball: to go along with someone or something; to start a task

softball questions: questions that are easy to answer

rain check: a chance or ticket to see or do the same event at a future time, or purchase a product in the future at the current price (fans at rained-out games get a ticket for a future game)

shutout: scoring no runs; achieving none of one's goals

step up to the plate: take your turn; accept your responsibility and face a possibly unpleasant task

strike: a miss or failure, often used in a context where two misses are permitted, but the third strike means failure

swing for the fences: to take a risk to make a big gain at one time (in baseball, this means swinging hard for a home run) *switch-hitter:* someone or something capable of performing two different tasks (switch-hitters can bat left or right handed)

that's the ball game: it's all over, often with a bad ending

touch base: to stay in touch; check in and share information

triple play: something accomplishing three simultaneous tasks (in baseball, this was a defensive play resulting in three outs)

whiff: to attempt something and fail; to miss the ball; strike out

whole new ball game: starting all over again; facing the same task but starting from scratch

Other American sayings and idioms

as the crow flies: in a direct line

at the end of your rope: out of options

barking up the wrong tree: to be misled

bats in the belfry: someone who is crazy

beat around the bush: avoid facing the problem

birds of a feather: people that have similar tastes

birthday suit: not wearing any clothes

bite the bullet: accept the situation as it is and get it done

bite the dust: to die, fail, or collapse

bite the hand that feeds you: harming one who is helping you

bottom dollar: last money

break the ice: break the silence and start

bring home the bacon: bring home earned money

burn the candle at both ends: working hard day and night

by the skin of your teeth: just barely escape or avoid

*catch forty wink*s: take a short nap

caught red-handed: discovered in the act

caught with your pants down: surprised and unprepared

chip on your shoulder: to be in a bad mood

clean as a whistle: having no problems or guilt

dead as a doornail: worn out or hopeless

don't count your chickens before they hatch: don't count on an event happening before it actually happens

don't put all your eggs in one basket: don't risk everything at one time but rather spread the risk out

eat crow: to eat your word or take back something you said

eleventh hour: to happen at the very last moment

every cloud has a silver lining: there is good even in bad things

face the music: confront an unpleasant situation or consequence

faster than greased lightning: really, really fast

fit as a fiddle: healthy

fly off the handle: get angry

fork it over: hand something over

get the lead out: to hurry up

get up on the wrong side of the bed: to be irritable or grumpy

get your feathers ruffled: get upset.

go off half-cocked: starting without all the information needed

grass is always greener on the other side of the fence: thinking that things are better somewhere else, or that someone else is better off, even though this is often not the case

head man; big cheese; top dog; big banana; head honcho; numero uno: the person in charge

Horatio Alger story: a rags to riches story of success (named after the writer who wrote stories of overcoming adversity)

kick the bucket: to die

kill two birds with one stone: achieving two goals with one action

know the ropes: know how to accomplish something

lay an egg: make a mistake

let the cat out of the bag: divulge a secret

let your hair down: relax

life of Riley: an easy life with no worries

like two peas in a pod: just alike.

lock, stock and barrel: everything

make a mountain out of a molehill: make a big deal about something that is not important

make ends meet: make enough money to pay your bills

Mutt and Jeff: any pair of a tall and a short man, Mutt being the tall one (from an early comic strip)

nip it in the bud: stop something early before it gets started

no spring chicken: not young anymore.

nothing to be sneezed at: something important or noteworthy

old stamping ground: a place one used to hang out (also old stomping ground)

on cloud nine: very happy

on the house: paid for by someone else or the establishment

out of the frying pan into the fire: to go from a bad situation to an even worse one

over a barrel: in a difficult position with no way out

paint the town red: to go out on the town and party hard

pass the buck: pass responsibility

pig in a poke: something that looks attractive at first glance but is a bad purchase

play hookey: to skip school or work

plumb tuckered out: really tired.

pull one's leg: to make fun of someone

put the cart before the horse: to do things in the wrong order

put the screws to: pressure someone to get something done

put up your dukes: get ready to fight

rack one's brain: think really hard

raining cats and dogs: raining really hard

read between the lines: get extra meaning out of something that isn't obvious

read my lips: pay attention to what I am saying

read someone the riot act: severely reprimand someone

shoot the bull: to talk, usually in idle chatter

sit on the fence: to be undecided

skeleton in the closet: secrets from one's past

smell a rat: realize there is something suspicious

spill the beans: tell secrets

steal one's thunder: grab attention before they have a chance to

straight from the horse's mouth: hear from the original source

take the bull by the horns: directly confront a problem and do something

talk turkey: to be up-front or talk details

the handwriting on the wall: a warning of danger or doom

three sheets to the wind: drunk or out of it

through the grapevine: received via gossip

throw in the towel: give up

'till the cows come home: to take forever to do something

to go the whole 9 yards: to give it everything you have

to pull strings: use personal connections to get something done

up to snuff: of sufficient quality

watched pot never boils: paying too much attention to the progress of something makes it seem to take forever

wet behind the ears: someone inexperienced

where there's a will, there's a way: if you want something bad enough, you will figure out a way to get it

white elephant: an unwelcome or unattractive gift

whole ball of wax; whole enchilada: everything

THE AMERICAN CAN-DO SPIRIT

Americans just don't understand the phrase "I can't." From the time the first settlers touched foot on this continent, they have overcome every obstacle placed in their way, using ingenuity, hard work, and sometimes a little luck. They were not bound by Old World limits. They were all "created equal" and there was nothing stopping any of them from achieving their goals. Often slow to rouse, they were unstoppable once they had their goal in mind. We must strive to make sure that increasing dependence on government programs and assistance does not eradicate the *can-do* spirit that made this country. The accomplishments listed here were mammoth projects undertaken over time, requiring lots of money, people, and sacrifice—similar to the Pyramids or the Great Wall of China. But these tasks were accomplished by a fledgling new nation over the space of 200 years. They are marvels to behold and show what Americans can accomplish.

Transcontinental Railroad (1869): The historic link connecting the East and West coasts was finished on May 10, 1869 with the driving of the final, golden spike. It took only 6 years to build, part of which was during the Civil War. The Central Pacific Railroad moved eastward from California, while the Union Pacific pushed westward from Council Bluffs, Iowa. The building was supported by Congressional land grants and payments for each mile completed, igniting competition that encouraged each company to lay track as fast as possible. When the two lines met at Promontory Point, Utah, each had actually graded for track miles past the meeting point. The Central Pacific set a record that still stands by laying 10 miles of track in one day.

Route and elevation change of railroad

Panama Canal (1914): Considered one of the most difficult engineering tasks ever, the 50-mile canal was finished in 1914. It cut the journey from New York to San Francisco from 14,000 miles to less than 6,000. However, the cost was staggering—the French lost 21,000 workers, mainly from disease, trying to build a canal in the 1880s. Dr. Walter Reed identified the mosquito as the carrier of yellow fever. Using that information to control the disease, and deciding to construct the canal using a series of locks, George Goethals led the team that finally finished the canal, but he still incurred a further loss of 5,600 workers.

Empire State Building (1931): Not as large a project as the others mentioned, it is listed because of the speed of construction and relative safety (only 5 workers died). This 102-story building took only 410 days to build with over 3,000 workers toiling away with 57,000 tons of steel. Its 1250-foot height held the record for tallest building for 42 years after its completion on May 1, 1931. And this was all managed without computers.

Hoover Dam (1936): Originally known as Boulder Dam, this mammoth structure blocks the Colorado River at the Arizona/Nevada border. Built during the Great Depression and finished 2 years ahead of time, it cost over one hundred lives, including the first death, surveyor J.G. Tierney, and the last death, his son Patrick. It

Generators at the powerhouse

was the largest concrete structure ever built at the time, needing 3 million cubic yards of concrete, and using many untested techniques, such as using cooling pipes to remove excess heat from the curing concrete. The dam created Lake Mead and provides electricity for the surrounding states. The electricity produced by the new dam also helped win World War II, as it was required in huge amounts for making aluminum for airplane and ship construction.

Manhattan Project (1944): With the help of the UK and Canada, the U.S. launched a massive program to develop the first atomic bomb during World War II. President Franklin had been warned in 1939 that the Nazis might be developing nuclear weapons. The crash program cost almost $2 billion dollars starting in 1942, and employed 130,000 people at 30 sites. The first test bomb was exploded in July, 1945, and the first two usable bombs, nicknamed *Little Boy* and *Fat Man,* were dropped on Japan in August. The stakes had never been higher: if the Nazis or Soviets had gotten the bomb first, they would have used it to rule the world.

"Fat Man" atomic bomb

"Little Boy" atomic bomb

Winning World War II (1945): This was America at its finest. From an almost standing start, America outproduced the world and became the "arsenal of democracy." During the war, U.S. factories produced over 300,000 planes, 6 million M1 carbines, 2.6 million machine guns, 2.3 million trucks, 22 aircraft carriers, 349 destroyers, and over 33 million tons of merchant ships. Everyone chipped in with more than 2 million American women working in factories by the war's end. The size of the military exploded during the war from 350,000 to almost 13 million. We won the war…and then we came home.

Landing on the Moon (1969): Spurred by President Kennedy's

challenge to land a man on the moon by the end of the decade, NASA launched an all-out effort to fulfill that goal. Starting with the one-man Mercury capsules that launched Alan Shepard into space on May 5, 1961, it progressed through the two-man Gemini spaceships, to the three-man Apollo spacecraft. Finally, on July 20, 1969, as the whole world watched on television, Apollo 11 landed on the moon and Neil Armstrong became the first human to step on its surface. And, as a testimony to the freedom of the American system, the entire effort was done in full view on public radio and television, unlike the secretive Soviet space program. The total cost was likely around $100 billion, and up to one-half a million people would ultimately be involved.

Saturn V rocket launching Apollo 11

Alaska Pipeline (1977): Finished in 1977, this oil pipeline covers the 800 miles from the Prudhoe Bay oil field to the shipping terminals at Valdez, Alaska. The pipe is up to 4 feet in diameter and was approved after the oil crisis of the 1970s. The builders had to overcome extreme cold, unfriendly terrain, frozen ground, and environmental concerns about the fragile tundra.

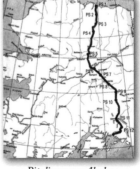

Pipeline across Alaska

GETTING TO KNOW AMERICA

 Foreigners visiting our country, and naturalized citizens that are new to America, may have problems fully understanding and appreciating this large and diverse nation. Even natural-born citizens often live their lives without fully exploring the richness of America. Here are a few uniquely American experiences that you may enjoy if you haven't already. There are hundreds more...this is just a starter list. You'll understand your country better with each experience. They are listed in no particular order.

☐ *Watch the movie "Singin' in the Rain".* This is classic Americana with great singing and dancing.

☐ *Volunteer at a soup kitchen.* Help feed the needy. Try it during Thanksgiving.

☐ *Enroll in adult education:* Take some extra classes, or get your high school or college diploma if you haven't already.

☐ *Get up before dawn.* Go someplace special like a beach or lake to watch the sun come up.

☐ *Take the train.* Take a short trip, or go all the way across the country. Travel in style the way everyone used to.

☐ *Drive cross-country.* Take a road trip. Go with family or friends. You can take old Route 66 across part of the south, or take Interstate highways north or south. Stop for meals at local diners (not fast food places) and listen to local radio stations.

☐ *Camp overnight in a National Park or National Forest.* You can camp close to your car or hike in. See the beauty of our parks and forests while getting backing to nature.

☐ *Visit colonial sites that were important in our early days.* The list is almost endless: Jamestown, Yorktown, Williamsburg, Plymouth, Mount Vernon, Independence Hall, Charleston, Boston, Valley Forge.

☐ *Visit Civil War battlefields.* See what the brave soldiers endured during that war. Be sure you don't miss Gettysburg,

☐ *Visit a working farm.* Find one that will let you help out. See how most of the country lived 200 years ago.

☐ *Memorize a poem.* Pick your favorite, or one of the classic American poems in this book.

☐ ***Serve your country in the military or Peace Corps.*** If you are too old, there are lots of other ways to volunteer to help out.

☐ ***Watch a local 4th of July Parade.*** Or better yet, march in one.

☐ ***Watch your local 4th of July fireworks show.*** The bigger the better. Share the experience with your family and neighbors.

☐ ***Visit a church service if you haven't, or go to a church of a different denomination.*** Our country was settled by many who were fleeing religious persecution. Find out more about your fellow citizen's beliefs.

☐ ***Invite someone to your Thanksgiving dinner.*** Open your home to someone who may be without friends or family this day.

☐ ***Read this book.*** Get to know the basic information and be sure you can pass the Citizenship Test yourself.

☐ ***Give hand-made gifts.*** It saves resources, gives you a hobby, and will make a much more meaningful gift.

☐ ***Give presents to someone in need.*** Use Christmas or any other time of the year to deliver presents to those in need.

☐ ***Learn a foreign language.*** This gives you perspective and may come in handy some day during your travels.

☐ ***Collect American coins or stamps.*** It doesn't have to cost much—you can start with your pocket change. U.S. postage stamps tell the history of our country.

☐ ***Fly the American flag at your house.*** You can fly it every day, or just on national holidays.

☐ ***Buy produce at your local farmer's market.*** This supports your local growers, reduces energy consumption, and gives you some healthy choices.

☐ ***Visit a military cemetery on Memorial Day.*** This can be a very moving experience, particularly for your family. Place small American flags on the graves.

☐ ***Dress up on Halloween.*** Trick-or-treat with your children, or dress up for work. It's a great day to make fun of yourself.

☐ ***Bake an apple pie from scratch.*** As they say, there is nothing more American than apple pie.

☐ ***Attend your city council meeting.*** Participate if you can, or just observe. You may find issues that will be of personal interest.

☐ *Volunteer to help a local church, high school or similar or-ganization.* They all need volunteer help to properly provide services, particularly with all the budget cuts.

☐ *Visit New England when the leaves are changing colors.* It will take your breath away. Some papers and news programs actu-ally publish forecasts of color changes.

☐ *Visit Disneyland or Disney World.* Go with your kids, or just go yourself. It is impossible not to have a good time and you will also get a good flavor of America.

☐ *Swim in each ocean.* At least put your feet in the water. And you can also paddle in the Gulf of Mexico.

☐ *Swim in the Great Salt Lake.* You won't believe how easy it is to float.

☐ *Visit New Orleans.* See the French Quarter, listen to the Preser-vation Hall Band, eat a beignet, and drink some chicory coffee.

☐ *Visit Philadelphia.* Have a Philly cheesesteak for lunch, then see Independence Hall and the Liberty Bell.

☐ *Visit San Francisco.* Ride the cable car, walk the Golden Gate Bridge, eat local Dungenous crabs and sourdough bread.

☐ *Visit Seattle.* Take a trip to the top of the Space Needle, drink some great coffee, and ride a ferry on Puget Sound.

☐ *Go to a baseball game.* A baseball game encapsulates America. Sit in the bleachers. Watch fathers and sons enjoy the clas-sic American game. Have a hot dog and a beer. Witness the unique duel between pitcher and hitter. They often face each other in what seems like a fight to the death. The difference between the hero and the loser is often only a matter of inches.

☐ *Attend a local sports game.* High school and college sports, par-ticularly football and basketball, can be very thrilling.

☐ *Mail packages of goodies to soldiers overseas.* Get names from websites that help our military, and pack a box of food and essentials that they will love. Drop in a note from you or your children to let them know we appreciate what they are doing.

☐ *Visit Washington D.C..* Spend several days just seeing the monuments and memorials, and that's without going inside the Smithsonian Museum. Don't miss some less-visited but impressive spots like the Library of Congress.

☐ *Visit the Grand Canyon.* It is truly awe inspiring.

☐ *See Mt. Rushmore.* Marvel at the ambition of the men that dared to carve these faces on a mountainside.

☐ *Pay for a meal for a soldier in uniform.* It doesn't have to be anything more than a burger and fries...make sure they know you appreciate their sacrifice. You can do it at the airport or anywhere you run into men or women in uniform.

☐ *Watch a rocket launch at Cape Canaveral.* Hard to schedule but well worth the effort. The force of the large rockets is a humbling experience.

☐ *Take a ferry to the island of your choice.* Santa Catalina, Nantucket, Martha's Vineyard, Bainbridge Island, Mackinac Island...you have lots to pick from. Experience slow island time and island self-sufficiency.

☐ *Visit Ellis Island and the Statue of Liberty.* See where many of your ancestors may have entered this country, and marvel at France's beautiful gift to this country.

☐ *Go to the top of the Empire State Building.* You just have to do this, even if you are not meeting your lost love there.

☐ *Get your picture taken next to a Continental Divide sign.* You can straddle the line dividing the rivers flowing to the Pacific from those flowing to the Atlantic.

☐ *Participate in your local political party.* Government works only when citizens get involved, and you will be a better citizen for the effort.

☐ *Help out at a polling station on election day.* They always need more volunteers. Watching our peaceful exchange of power every election and the participation of our citizens is a very patriotic event.

☐ *Visit a county fair.* Find a local or nearby country fair and spend an afternoon with your family.

☐ *Memorize the names of all the states.* It is easier than you think and may win you a bet some day. Use the map in this book and picture each state and its neighbors on the map in your mind.

☐ *Go fishing.* Find a nearby lake, river, or ocean. You don't have to catch anything, just go. If you have kids, take them. It is a great way to slow down the frantic pace of everyday life.

Let's roll.

—*Todd Beamer, 9/11/2001*

Chapter 7

AMERICAN HEROES

❧

AMERICAN HISTORY IS FULL OF THE STORIES of the men and women that helped make this country great. Some heroes are well known or already in the list of presidents. Others are relatively unknown, but their actions have had enormous effects. An unusually large number of gifted men lived in the colonies in the 1700s, helping to direct our country to successful nationhood.

SOME OF OUR FOUNDING FATHERS

Samuel Adams *(1722-1803)*: A cousin of John Adams, he was one of the most vocal supporters of American independence. He defied the British on taxation, was a leader of the Sons of Liberty, and organized the Boston Tea Party in 1773. He subsequently signed the Declaration of Independence.

Samuel Adams
by John Johnston

Charles Carroll *(1737-1832)*: A Catholic leader in Maryland and one of the largest landowners in the Colonies, Carroll strongly opposed British actions. He helped organize resistance to the tea tax resulting in the burning of the ship Peggy Stewart during what became known as the Annapolis Tea Party. He later signed the Declaration of Independence and then helped draft the Bill of Rights. When he died in 1832, he was the last surviving signer of the Declaration, and one of the wealthiest men in America.

The Burning of the Peggy Stewart
by Francis Mayer

John Dickinson *(1732-1808)*: A lawyer educated in England,

Dickinson wrote many of the most important documents of the time, including the 1765 Declaration of Rights and the 1776 Articles of Confederation. He penned other documents condemning British taxes and supporting the right of the colonists to bear arms. He played a vital role at the Constitutional Convention in supporting the Great Compromise

John Dickinson
by Charles Peale

that finally broke the deadlock by allowing for a House with proportional representation, and a Senate with two Senators per state.

Benjamin Franklin *(1706-1790)*: Franklin was the quintessential American—inventor, writer, scientist, diplomat, and patriot. America would be a very different place without him. Besides experimenting with electricity, he researched the Gulf Stream and started a library system. He helped produce the Declaration of Independence, Articles of Confederation, and the

Franklin's Return to Philadelphia, 1785
by Jean Leon Gerome Ferris

Constitution. He was vital in getting French help to win the Revolution. His speech on the final day of the Constitutional Convention helped win overwhelming support from the delegates. He was the first Postmaster General and wrote Poor Richard's Almanac.

Elbridge Gerry *(1744-1814)*: A signer of the Declaration who refused to sign the Constitution without a Bill of Rights, Gerry was worried that democracy would not work. While governor of Massachusetts, he redrew political boundaries resulting in salamander-shaped districts to help his party. This forever placed his name in our language, "gerrymander." He died while serving as Madison's vice president.

"The Gerry-Mander"
by Elkanah Tisdale

Alexander Hamilton *(1755-1804)*: Hamilton was crucial in the founding of our nation. Born in the British West Indies, he had one of the best minds of all founding fathers. He strongly believed in a strong central government and had a firm grasp of finances. He wrote the majority of the Federalist Papers that were vital in convincing the public of the importance of the Constitution. He was the first Secretary of the Treasury and implemented the necessary financial systems that allowed the new country to prosper, such as having the federal government assume the war debts of the

Alexander Hamilton in Uniform
by Alonzo Chappel

states. Hamilton's belief in a strong federal government was at odds with Jefferson's belief in state and individual rights. Hamilton was killed in a duel with his rival Aaron Burr.

John Hancock *(1737-1793)*: As President of the Continental Congress, he signed his name in large print on the Declaration to ensure that King George would see it. He, along with Samuel Adams, were the targets of the British attack on Lexington in 1775.

Benjamin Harrison *(1726-1791)*: A signer of the Declaration of Independence, Harrison also pushed for the Bill of Rights as a requirement for signing the Constitution. His son, William Harrison, became president, as well as his grandson, Benjamin Harrison.

Patrick Henry *(1736-1799)*: The famous Virginian orator whose immortal "Give me liberty, or give me death" speech in a Richmond church helped galvanize resistance to the British crown. He continually fought for American rights and realized that military action would be required against Britain. He was Virginia's first governor and actually fought against the adoption of the Constitution without a Bill of Rights.

Patrick Henry Before the Virginia House of Burgesses
by Peter Rothermel

John Marshall *(1755-1835)*: A young officer in the Revolution who

took no part in the Declaration or Constitution. He was the 4th Chief Justice of the Supreme Court, and longest-serving one, from 1801 to 1835. He helped develop the American legal system. His views were critical in establishing the judiciary as a co-equal branch of government, and helping to clarify the relationship between the federal government and the states, upholding the supremacy of federal law over state law. He

John Marshall
by Henry Inman

gave an opinion in more than 500 cases and solidified the Supreme Court's position as interpreter of the Constitution.

George Mason *(1725-1792)*: Mason helped create Virginia's Constitution and Declaration of Rights, models for our Constitution and Declaration of Independence. He helped Jefferson create the Northwest Ordinance prohibiting slavery in new states, and refused to sign the Constitution without a bill of rights and a ban on slavery. He was vindicated when the Bill of Rights was finally added but never lived to see the end of slavery.

Gouverneur Morris *(1752-1816)*: Morris was active in the Constitutional Convention but felt that the President and Senators should have life terms. However, his most famous contribution was writing the opening lines of the Preamble, "We, the people of the United States, in order to form a more perfect union…"

Thomas Paine *(1736-1809)*: Paine wrote the widely-read pamphlet "Common Sense", crucial in gaining popular support for the Revolution. He later wrote *The Rights of Man*. Late in his life, he was spurned by the other founders due to his anti-religion views. John Adams said of Paine, "Without the pen of the author of Common Sense, the sword of Washington would have been raised in vain."

Thomas Paine
by Auguste Milliere

Edmund Randolph *(1753-1813)*: The young Virginia governor showed up in 1787 to revise the Articles of Confederation with a new Virginia Plan outlining an entirely new form of government, including an executive, legislative, and judicial branch. He turned against the Constitution until the Bill of Rights was added. He later became the first Attorney General.

OTHER HEROES IN OUR HISTORY

Thousands of Americans have exhibited courage, strength, and resolution in the hundreds of years since our founding. Some have simple stories of instant decisions to act, saving lives or helping to change history. Others struggled a lifetime to achieve greatness and earn our undying respect. Many were just ordinary people doing extraordinary things. Here are just a few.

Susan B. Anthony: This leading civil rights leader played a key role in getting women voting rights. She co-founded the Women's Temperance Movement, but died before the 19th amendment gave women the vote. She was placed on the 1979 dollar coin.

Clara Barton: Barton, a schoolteacher, rushed to tend to the wounded at the start of the Civil War, and risked her life tending to soldiers during the entire war. When the war ended, she helped search for the graves of Union soldiers who died at Andersonville Prison. In 1881, she founded the American Red Cross.

Nellie Bly: A journalist, adventurer, and inventor who completed a  trip around the world in 1890 that took only 72 days, beating Jules Verne's *Around the World in 80 Days* trip. She had previously written a book called *Ten Days in a Mad-House*, chronicling conditions in a mental institution where she was admitted after pretending to be insane. Later in life, she was a leading female industrialist.

Andrew Carnegie: A Scottish self-educated immigrant who opened a steel plant in 1875 and built one of the largest companies in the country, Carnegie Steel. He took his fortune and started more than 2500 libraries, and Carnegie Hall in 1891.

Sergeant William Carney: This 23-year-old former slave joined the Union Army and led the 54th Massachusetts against Fort Wagner in South Carolina. The regiment was composed of black troops organized after the Emancipation proclamation. Hit several times, Carney ensured the Union flag never touched the ground as his forces retreated, losing almost half their  strength. He was the first black to receive the Medal of Honor.

George Washington Carver: Born a slave at the end of the Civil War, the baby George and his mother were kidnapped by Night Riders. His owner, Moses Carver, tracked down the kidnappers and gave them a horse in exchange for George's return. Moses never found George's mother, so he raised him and got him an education. George became a famous scientist and inventor. He convinced farmers in the South to plant crops other than cotton, particularly peanuts which he used to make more than 100 products. He was instrumental in combating the stereotypes of an inferior black race.

Four Chaplains: These U.S. Army chaplains aboard the USAT *Dorchester* lost their lives when the ship was torpedoed by the Germans during World War II. They helped soldiers board lifeboats and even gave up their own life jackets to help others. As the ship sank, they were seen with joined arms singing hymns. They were: Methodist Reverend George L. Fox, Rabbi Alexander D. Goode, Roman Catholic Priest John P. Washington, and Reformed Church in America Reverend Clark V. Poling.

César Chávez: A Mexican-American migrant farm worker, he co-founded United Farm Workers. The activist organized strikes and boycotts in the '60s in California, including a boycott of all table grapes, to raise awareness of the plight of migrant workers. César Chávez Day is a holiday in several states.

Chief Sitting Bull: The influential Sioux chief led the Indian tribes during the conflicts in the last half of the 19th century. Though the Sioux were responsible for Custer's Last Stand in 1876, Chief Sitting Bull was not directly involved. Sitting Bull worked for Buffalo Bill Cody's Wild West Show before returning to North Dakota. The government was concerned about his involvement in the Indian Ghost Dance movement and ordered him arrested. During his arrest, he was shot and killed.

Walt Disney: Walt moved to Los Angeles and, against all odds, made *Mickey Mouse* a universal hit in 1928, followed by the 1937 release of the *Snow White* animated movie. More movies followed and, in 1955, he opened the world-famous Disneyland park. His movies, characters, and amusement parks are now woven into the American psyche, and part of childhood.

Dorothea Lynde Dix: An American activist who served as Superintendent of Army Nurses during the Civil War. She actively lobbied for the creation of mental asylums in America.

General Jimmy Doolittle: He led a bombing raid of 16 specially outfitted B-25 bombers, launched from the USS *Hornet*, that struck Tokyo on April 18, 1942. The first attack on mainland Japan was a huge morale booster. The Japanese people had been promised by their government that their homeland would never be attacked. The crews ditched their aircraft over China, and 11 crewmen were killed or captured. There were two immediate consequences. The Japanese killed almost 250,000 Chinese civilians in retaliation for helping the downed flyers, and the attack encouraged Japan to attack Midway Island two months later, leading to the disaster that was a turning point in the war.

Frederick Douglass: This former slave rose to prominence before the Civil War as a orator, statesman, and social reformer. His skills were a direct rebuttal to claims that the slaves were inferior. He wrote several books, continually fought against slavery, and supported women's suffrage.

Corporal Jason Dunham: A Marine fighting in Iraq in 2004  who threw himself on top of a live enemy grenade to protect his fellow Marines. Mortally wounded, he received the Medal of Honor posthumously—the first Marine to receive that Medal for fighting in Iraq. A new destroyer, DDG-109, was named in his honor, the USS *Jason Dunham.*

William Eaton: The officer in charge of U.S. forces in Tripoli fighting the Barbary pirates in 1804. Stephen Decatur had earlier destroyed the captured USS *Philadelphia* in Tripoli harbor. Eaton led a force of ten Americans (including Marines), several hundred Arabs, and a thousand camels. He made a 600-mile trip from Alexandria to capture Derne, a town near Tripoli, suppressing a mutiny, and holding off counter-attacks until a peace treaty with Tripoli was signed.

William Eaton
by Rembrandt Peale

Thomas Edison: A high school dropout, Edison became the greatest inventor in the world with more than 1,000 patents, including the phonograph, light bulb, and movie projector. He always insisted "Genius is 1 percent inspiration and 99 percent perspiration." He also claimed that he hadn't failed 1,000 times to find the proper light bulb filament, he just found 1,000 materials that would not work.

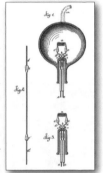

Light bulb patent
1880

Private Guy Gabaldon: An 18-year-old Marine on Saipan in 1944 who would sneak out at night on his own initiative to get Japanese soldiers to surrender without fighting. He rounded up almost 1,500 prisoners before being wounded. He knew that for every prisoner he took, he was saving American lives. He received the Navy Cross for his heroism.

Nathan Hale. The young school teacher joined the Colonial Army to fight the British. When the British captured New York City, Nathan volunteered to go behind the lines as a spy for Washington. He wrote his observations in Latin and hid them in his shoes. He was stopped by British sentries and ordered hung by General

Howe the next day. Hale's last words were "I only regret that I have but one life to lose for my country."

Mary "Molly Pitcher" Hays: Mary was often called Molly when she followed her husband, John, into war during the  Revolution, aiding in cooking and washing. At the Battle of Monmouth in the hot summer of 1778, Molly helped the troops by carrying pitcher after pitcher of water from a nearby stream, earning her the nickname "Molly Pitcher." When her husband was hurt, she spent the rest of

Molly Pitcher
by J. C. Armytage

the day loading and firing the heavy gun. George Washington rewarded her the next day by giving her a non-commissioned officer position.

Bob Hope: Hope, a comedian and actor, starting entertaining troops around the world starting in 1941, during peace and during war. Named an "honorary veteran" by Congress, Hope said he would not trade those tours with the troops for his entire career. He died in 2003 at the age of 100.

Samuel Houston: He led the Texans that defeated Santa Anna at San Jacinto in 18 minutes, leading to independence for Texas. He was then President of the Republic of Texas, U.S. Senator, and governor of Texas. As governor, he faced a dilemma when Texas seceded from the Union in 1861. He refused to swear loyalty to the Confederacy, and resigned his position. He also refused to fight fellow Texans over the issue, so he retired to Huntsville, Texas.

Helen Keller: Deaf and blind from childhood, she went  on to graduate from college, author books, receive numerous awards, and even star in a movie. She is the subject of the play and film, *The Miracle Worker*. She was a socialist who campaigned for rights for women and those with disabilities.

Daniel Inouye: As President pro tempore of the U.S. Senate, the Japanese-American Senator from Hawaii is the highest-ranking Asian-American in U.S. history, being fourth in the chain of command.  He received the Medal of Honor during World War II for heroic efforts fighting the Germans in Italy. Under attack by three entrenched German machine guns, he was shot in the stomach but continued to attack and destroyed the first machine gun. Refusing medical treatment, he destroyed the second machine gun. Crawling toward the third machine gun nest, he raised his arm to throw a grenade when a German shot nearly severed his arm, leaving the live grenade still clutched in his now-useless hand. Inouye pried the grenade from his severed hand and managed to toss it using his left hand, destroying the final machine gun. The field hospital amputated the remainder of his right arm. He has been a U.S. Senator representing Hawaii since 1963.

Jack Jouett: Considered the Paul Revere of the South, Jouett was a member of the Virginia Militia in 1781 when the British occupied much of that state. He heard Colonel Tarleton's 250-man cavalry ride by one night on their way to capture Thomas Jefferson and other leaders in Charlottesville. Though he was 40 miles from Charlottesville, he jumped on his horse and sped over back roads to warn Jefferson in time to escape capture.

Martin Luther King: The leading black leader of the civil rights movement in America. He led peaceful protests in the South before giving his famous "I Have a Dream" speech in 1963. He worked tirelessly for equality for all Americans. He received the Nobel Peace Prize before he was assassinated in 1968.

Marquis de Lafayette: The French nobleman made the American cause his own. He served without pay with the colonial army. He was wounded at the Battle of Brandywine and suffered through the winter at Valley Forge. He helped provide the French support that was crucial for our ultimate victory and was instrumental in the final defeat of Cornwallis at Yorktown, Virginia. He was granted U.S. citizenship during his lifetime.

Marquis de Lafayette
by Joseph-Désiré Court

Robert E. Lee: He graduated from West Point and served in the U.S. Army for 32 years before joining the Confederacy

when Virginia seceded from the Union. He became the Commander of the Confederate Army of Northern Virginia, and the war's most famous General, admired by both sides. President Lincoln had offered him command of the Union Army, but Lee could not fight against his home state of Virginia. His defeat at

Robert E. Lee and Traveller

Gettysburg was the beginning of the end for the South. After the war, he urged reconciliation, and served as President of Washington and Lee University.

Audie Murphy: Murphy was raised in a poor family and dropped out of school in the fifth grade. In 1942, he tried to enlist but

was turned down three times for being too young, too short, or too underweight. He was finally accepted and went on to become the most decorated soldier in the war, winning 33 medals, including the Medal of Honor when he held off a German attack, killing 250 enemy soldiers and destroying six tanks. After the war, he returned home to act in more than 40 movies.

Rosa Parks: A black secretary who refused a bus driver's order in 1955 to give up her seat to a white passenger in Montgomery, Alabama. Her action ignited the Montgomery Bus Boycott and she became an icon of the Civil Rights Movement. She later received the Presidential Medal of Freedom from President Clinton in 1996.

Lt. Cdr. Edward O'Hare: He single-handedly saved the carrier *Lexington* in 1942 by shooting down five Japanese bombers attacking the ship. He received the Congressional Medal of Honor, but was killed in action two years later. Chicago named their airport in his honor.

Harriet Quimby: The first woman pilot in the U.S. in 1911, and the first woman to fly a plane across the English Channel. She also authored several screenplays. She died in 1912 in a flying accident in Massachusetts when she and her co-pilot were ejected from their plane at an altitude of 1,500 feet.

Wilma Rudolph: Born prematurely at 4.5 pounds, she caught infantile paralysis as a young girl, leaving her twisted leg  in a brace. She survived scarlet fever, whooping cough, chickenpox, and measles. But she was determined to be a runner and shed her brace to begin running. In the 1960 Rome Olympics, she became the first American woman to win three gold medals in track and field at one game, earning the title "fastest woman in the world." In her last relay race, she actually dropped the baton, picked it up, and still won the race.

Sacajawea: A Shoshone woman who helped guide the Lewis and Clark Expedition from 1804 to 1806 on their trip to the west coast. She was instrumental in the success of their mission. The U.S. Mint issued a dollar coin in her honor in 2000.

Squanto: A Patuxet Indian, he was kidnapped in 1614 by English explorers and taken to Europe. He returned to America only to find his tribe had been wiped out by disease. He helped the Pilgrims survive their first years by teaching them how to fish and plant crops. He died in 1622.

Captain Chesley Sullenberger: The veteran pilot successfully landed his passenger jet in the Hudson River in 2009 after all the engines failed on takeoff. Not a single passenger was lost. This was the first time in 50 years of commercial jet flights that a water landing had been made without fatalities.

Chuck Yeager: The military test pilot was the first to break the sound barrier in the X-1 aircraft on October 14, 1947. He had broken his ribs and had trouble closing the cockpit door, but got the chance after the Bell test pilot (non-military) demanded $150,000 for the attempt. Yeager took the job as part of his normal $283 a month Army salary.

Pat Tillman: A college football star and pro safety with the Arizona Cardinals. After the 9/11 terrorist attacks, he left his multi-million dollar football career and joined the Army to do the right thing. He was killed in Afghanistan in 2004 by what turned out to be friendly fire.

Harriet Tubman: Born a slave in Maryland, she walked north to freedom in 1849. She spent the next years leading other slaves to freedom using the Underground Railroad, constantly putting her life at risk and earning the name of "Moses." She also worked in South Carolina as a spy for the Union. When the war ended, she continued helping other people and was active in the suffrage movement.

Booker T. Washington: Born in slavery, Booker was freed  after the Civil War and gave himself his last name of Washington. He was the leading figure in the black community from 1890 to 1915, and was the first black to be invited to the White House when Teddy Roosevelt invited him for dinner. He wrote 14 books, including his autobiography *Up From Slavery*, and helped blacks get educated and maintain their right to vote. He led the newly created Tuskegee Institute in Alabama on its way to become a world-renown educational center.

Alvin York: The most famous American soldier of World War I. When his patrol was ambushed by the Germans, York coolly shot 28 Germans and convinced 132 to surrender, and walked the whole lot of them back to Allied lines. He was awarded the Medal of Honor and went back home to resume farming.

Betty Zane: The sixteen-year-old girl was trapped in Fort Henry, surrounded by enemy British and Indian forces in 1782. The colonials were running out of gunpowder. She volunteered to run outside the fort in front of the enemy forces to get gunpowder from a nearby cabin. On her return, the enemy real-  ized what she was doing and opened fire on her. She avoided being hit, and her gunpowder helped defeat the enemy forces.

UNSUNG HEROES WHO CHANGED HISTORY

The future impact of one's actions is almost impossible to determine at the time. It is often only through the lens of history that the full consequences can be determined. These men and women altered the course of history with their actions, done not because they were told to do so, but because they felt it was the right thing to do. And sometimes it is the small things that make the big differences. They shared an unwavering commitment to their country.

Henry Knox: This Boston bookseller convinced General Washington in 1776 to let him go to Fort Ticonderoga to bring back 60 heavy cannon to help force the British from Boston. Against all odds, he and his  men dragged the guns back and, overnight, they were quietly moved into place at Dorchester Heights towering above the British. The British were forced to pull out of Boston and head South. The course of the war was changed due to Knox's initiative.

Harriet Beecher Stowe: She authored Uncle Tom's Cabin, an  1852 book that exposed the evils of slavery to the country, and to the world. It was extremely important in influencing the events leading up to the Civil War. When President Lincoln met the author, he quipped "So you're the little woman who wrote the book that started this great war!"

Robert Morris: One of only two men to have signed all three founding documents—the Declaration of Independence, Articles of Confederation, and the Constitution. By the simple act of using his personal credit to help finance Washington's troops so they could defeat the Hessians at Trenton, he helped win the war. He continued to help finance the war effort, but  eventually ended up in debtor's prison. Without his actions, the country may never have been founded.

Haym Solomon: A Polish Jew who embraced the colonial cause before the Revolution. A member of the Sons of Liberty, he was arrested twice by the British as a spy. He worked with Robert Morris to help finance the war. When Cornwallis was trapped at Yorktown, Washing-

ton was unable to march south from New York because he was out of money to pay and provision his troops. Haym raised the required money and the rest is history. He continued to help raise the money required to keep the new nation alive.

Andrew Higgins: The founder of Higgins Industries in New

Orleans created a novel design for a flat bottomed landing craft used for amphibious landings in the Pacific and Normandy. It was called the LCVP, or Higgins Boat, and could carry 36 men. His company made more than 20,000 of these craft. General Eisenhower called Higgins "...the man who won the war for us...If Higgins had not designed and built those LCVPs, we never could have landed over an open beach."

Dr. Norman Borlaug: An agronomist, he received his Ph.D. in plant pathology and genetics in 1942. He developed high-

yield, disease-resistant wheat varieties that allowed Mexico, India, and other countries to double their yields. He is credited with saving a billion people from starvation—that's billion with a 'b'. "The Father of the Green Revolution" received a Nobel Prize and Congressional Gold Medal.

Jonas Salk and Albert Sabin: Diseases have crippled and killed for hundreds of years, from the Black Plague to the recent avian flu. Causes and cures have been found for scourges like Yellow Fever and Smallpox. Polio outbreaks increased in the 20th century, para-

lyzing thousands of people including Franklin Roosevelt. Dr. Jonas Salk announced a vaccine in 1955, and Dr. Albert Sabin developed an oral vaccine a few years later. Worldwide cases of polio dropped from hundreds of thousands to less than a thousand.

Dr. Jonas Salk   *Dr. Albert Sabin*

THE BERLIN AIRLIFT—1948-1949

The Berlin Airlift is an amazing story of three unlikely and under-appreciated heroes who together changed the fate of Europe and perhaps the world. It embodies much of what makes America great. After World War II ended, the Allies split Germany and Berlin into sectors—the Soviets controlled half of Germany and Berlin, and America, France, and Britain controlled the rest. The Soviets had suffered over

350,000 casualties in the fight for Berlin, losing almost 2,000 tanks as well, while over 100,000 Germans were killed. The Red Army ravaged Berlin with a vengeance, raping over 120,000 women. The Germans would never trust them again. Berlin was located deep within the Soviet sector, so the American supply convoys had to use roads and railroads which ran through the Soviet sector.

The Soviets wanted all of Germany…in fact, they wanted all of Europe. Stalin had publicly stated that he thought the Americans would leave Germany soon and that he wanted it to be a totally Communist country. The 4-country council that ran Berlin was marked by continual Soviet obstruction. The Soviets already controlled Hungary, Latvia, Lithuania, Estonia, Romania, Bulgaria, Yugoslavia, Albania, and Poland, and in February of 1948, they seized control of Czechoslovakia. Now they wanted the Americans out of Berlin. In June, 1948, they closed down all supply routes into Berlin. They were sure that the lack of food and coal would force the Berlin citizens to flock to the Soviet side, resulting in the Americans and British leaving Berlin.

The Americans had few options. Their military forces had been severely depleted after the War—the 20,000 friendly troops in Berlin were surrounded by one and a half million Soviet troops. The only thing that probably saved them from instant annihilation is that America had the atomic bomb, and the Soviets did not. Many in our government wanted to pull out of Germany completely. Others thought we should prepare the atomic bomb to use on Russia, and Truman even made preparations to move the required airplanes to Europe. Either solution would have resulted in catastrophe. If Germany had fallen to the Communists then, it is highly likely that the Soviets would have kept moving until they controlled all of Europe. The world was at a dangerous crossroads. This is where the three unlikely heroes step in…

General Lucius Clay

The Military Governor of the U.S. Occupation Zone in Germany from 1947 to 1949, Clay fought against U.S. government and military officials who wanted to evacuate Berlin and give it to the Soviets. He knew that any perceived weakness of American resolve would result in the Germans giving in to the Soviets, leading to the rest of Europe falling to Communism. He believed in the importance of direct assistance to Europe to keep them from falling into the Soviet sphere. This aid was to become the Marshall Plan, credited with saving Europe from communism and restoring its economy. When General Bradley considered retreating from Berlin, Clay objected, stating "If we mean that we are to hold Europe against Communism, we must not budge...the future of democracy requires us to stay here until forced out." On June 26, 1948, two days after the Soviets imposed the blockade, Clay gave the order for the Berlin Airlift. This was an act of defiance against the Soviets, an incredible feat of logistics (at one point planes landed at Tempelhof every three minutes, twenty-four hours a day), a defining moment of the Cold War, and a demonstration of American support for the citizens of Berlin. In saving Berlin, he saved Germany, Europe, and quite possibly the world, from a Russian takeover.

Colonel Gail Halvorsen—The "Candy Bomber"

A true "accidental" hero who also helped saved the world from Communism. Halvorsen flew cargo planes supplying Berlin with vital food and supplies. One day, he talked to some German children by the air-

Halvorsen assembling parachutes

field and promised to bring some candy the next day and drop it from his plane. When asked how they would know which plane was his, he said that he would wiggle his wings. Back at base, he rounded up candy and made parachutes from handkerchiefs. The next day over Berlin, he wiggled his wings and dropped his candy parachutes. "Uncle Wiggly Wings" had returned. For the next year, he and other pilots dropped 20 tons of candy to the grateful children of Berlin. He became the *"Candy Bomber."* U.S. companies donated tons of candy, school kids made handkerchief parachutes, and the drops were constantly in the news. Berliners finally knew the Americans would stay and support them, and they rebuked all Soviet advances, and formed a democratic government. The Soviets ended the blockade a year later, after British and American pilots had made 277,569 flights into West Berlin carrying 2 million tons of food, fuel, and supplies. Imagine how the Berlin citizens felt after years of hearing Allied planes dropping bombs of destruction, to suddenly welcome the sound of those planes bringing salvation. In half of their city, the Soviet occupiers had raped and pillaged, then purposely starved the civilians, all the while restricting their liberties. In the American half, their former enemies were risking and losing their lives flying in food and supplies to keep them alive, and giving their children candy. As a young German boy said, "It wasn't the chocolate that was most important. What it meant was that someone in America cared. That parachute was more important than candy. It represented hope. Hope that someday we would be free. Without hope the soul dies." The candy made the entire operation personal. Berliners who previously left restaurants if Americans walked in were now buying them drinks and inviting them to dinner. The 2002 German Olympic team honored Halvorsen by asking him to lead their team into the Olympic Stadium in Salt Lake City.

Bill Tunner

An Air Force officer and expert in airlifting material, Tunner had run the operations at "the Hump" in Asia during the war, bringing supplies to the troops fighting in China. He had increased the daily delivery from 2.6 million pounds to 10 million pounds. He  was finally called on to help the Berlin airlift when it became clear it was not meeting Berlin's requirements. He streamlined every step of the operation, devising an innovative plan that required a plane to take off or land every 90 seconds, 24 hours a day. As each plane passed over a pre-determined location, they would radio their position and the next plane in line would adjust their speed to ensure they kept the exact distance ensuring the proper separation. If a plane could not land, it would not circle overhead but would immediately return to its base. The plan worked like a charm and exceeded the needs of Berlin for the next year. His efforts helped save Europe, but he never received the honor that was due him.

Unnamed Heroes

Besides being often unknown or unappreciated, many heroes are often unnamed. They work in the shadows, or as members of larger groups tasked with carrying out impossible tasks. Or, they work diligently at their jobs for years, never fully realizing how important and heroic their work really is. These are just a few of those heroes.

100th Battalion/442nd Regiment: Formed by Japanese-Americans wanting to show their loyalty to their country during World War II, it became the most decorated outfit for its size in the history of our military, winning 9500 purple hearts and 21 Medals of Honor. They fought fiercely in Italy, France, and Germany.

Tuskegee Airmen: The military was effectively segregated during World War II. Under pressure from leaders and Congress, a base in Tuskegee, Alabama was opened to train blacks to fly and maintain airplanes. They received their baptism under fire in 1943 in Europe and North  Africa, and soon earned the respect of everyone. They rarely lost a bomber assigned to their protection, and earned many decorations, losing one-third of their pilots in the process.

Navajo code talkers: The government employed Navajo Indians  to transmit messages during World War II using their native language. Their code was never broken by the Japanese and saved countless American lives. They sent hundreds of messages during the battle for Iwo Jima to help win that battle.

MacArthur with native code talkers

Rosie the Riveter. During World War II, the huge increase in production of war material, combined with the absence of men who were fighting overseas, led to a huge labor shortage. Millions of American women left their homes and went to work doing everything from medical care to building ships. Their assembly lines turned out the thousands of tanks, weapons, ships, jeeps, and material needed to win the war.

American emigrant pioneers: These brave men, women, and children left their homes to travel in wagon trains across a hostile frontier with no guarantee they would ever complete the trip. It would take four to six months to reach California or Oregon.

Every soldier, sailor, airman, and Marine who has ever served their country: This includes the 3,471 winners of the Congressional Medal of Honor, the hundreds of thousands of recipients of Bronze Stars, Silver Stars, and Purple Hearts, and every other person in uniform since 1775.

Boy Scouts and Girl Scouts: Since their founding 100 years ago, these groups have helped over 120 million American boys and girls build character and learn to become responsible citizens. There are over 8 million boys and girls youth members now, with hundreds of thousands of adults supporting them. Five American presidents were Scouts, as were 90 U.S. astronauts, including 11 of the 12 that walked on the moon, and forty that attained the highest rank—Eagle Scout.

Neil Armstrong, Eagle Scout
The first man on the Moon

Mothers and fathers: Our country would not exist without the devotion, care, and hard work of every parent who sacrifices to raise the boys and girls who become the men and women that make this country great.

Other everyday heroes: This includes all those who work to protect us, educate us, and ensure our health and safety— teachers, police, firemen, doctors, and nurses.

Giving Back

Over the last 200 years, many have accumulated vast fortunes in areas as diverse as land, oil, computers, steel, and railroads. They were often accused of being "robber barons" but in reality, many used their wealth to help better mankind. Andrew Carnegie gave away $350 million dollars before his death, feeling that everyone should spend the last third of their lives giving money to worthwhile causes. John D. Rockefeller, Sr. founded the Rockefeller Institute, responsible for funding important contributions to mankind. They developed a Yellow Fever vaccine and helped fund Dr. Borlaug's efforts to develop better grain varieties, saving countless lives.

Chapter 8

SPEECHES

❧

GREAT ORATORS INSPIRE THEIR AUDIENCES to achieve noble goals, define their generation's place in history, and even change history. Their speeches don't have to be long—the greatest speech in our history was only two minutes long. The speeches are often neglected or ridiculed in their day, their importance seen only by future generations. Newspapers scoffed at the Gettysburg Address, and Reagan's historic challenge to Gorbachev was both cautioned against by his advisors and subsequently ignored by the press. Some speeches inspire the nation to achieve greatness, others mourn the loss of brave fellow Americans. Many are instantly identified by hearing only a few words.

Most of the speeches presented below do not contain the entire speech, but only the more important or significant sections. The most memorable lines have been bolded. The selections include a larger number of recent speeches as they are more relevant to the problems of today. Review the words that helped push the country into independence from Britain, and helped it survive during the bleak days of the Revolution. Read how President Kennedy pushed the country into space with a challenge to land a man on the moon by the end of the decade, or how President Reagan directly confronted the Soviet Union at the Berlin Wall, challenging them to "tear down this wall"—and they eventually did. And read the words of what is probably the greatest speech ever given, the Gettysburg Address, that honored the fallen soldiers at that deadly battle, and steeled the nation's resolve to complete the task at hand and reunite the country.

THE WAR INEVITABLE

PATRICK HENRY   MARCH 23, 1775

> This was the stirring speech delivered by the great patriot Patrick
> Henry in St. John's Church in Richmond, Virginia on March 23, 1775.
> The church still stands. These words were heard around the world and
> stood as a direct challenge to the English crown. These words were
> treasonous to the English crown, punishable by death, and Henry was
> putting his own life on the line when he said these magnificent words.
> He was willing to sacrifice his safety for his liberty. Henry was one of
> the first colonials to fully realize that war with Britain was inevitable.

They tell us, Sir, that we are weak—unable to cope with so
formidable an adversary. But when shall we be stronger? Will
it be the next week, or the next year? Will it be when we are
totally disarmed, and when a British guard shall be stationed in
every house? Shall we gather strength by irresolution and inac-
tion? Shall we acquire the means of effectual resistance by lying
supinely on our backs, and hugging the delusive phantom of hope,
until our enemies shall have bound us hand and foot? Sir, we are
not weak, if we make a proper use of those means which the God
of nature hath placed in our power.

Three millions of People, armed in the holy cause of liberty,
and in such a country as that which we possess, are invincible by
any force which our enemy can send against us. Beside, Sir, we
shall not fight our battles alone. There is a just God who presides
over the destinies of Nations, and who will raise up friends to
fight our battles for us. **The battle, Sir, is not to the strong alone;
it is to the vigilant, the active, the brave.** Besides, Sir, we have
no election. If we were base enough to desire it, it is now too late
to retire from the contest. There is no retreat but in submission
and slavery! Our chains are forged! Their clanking may be heard
on the plains of Boston! The war is inevitable; and let it come! I
repeat, Sir, let it come!

It is in vain, Sir, to extenuate the matter. Gentlemen may cry,
Peace, Peace!—but there is no peace. The war is actually begun!
**The next gale that sweeps from the North will bring to our
ears the clash of resounding arms!** Our brethren are already
in the field! Why stand we here idle? What is it that Gentlemen
wish? What would they have? **Is life so dear, or peace so sweet,
as to be purchased at the price of chains and slavery? Forbid
it, Almighty God! I know not what course others may take;
but as for me, give me liberty or give me death!**

THE AMERICAN CRISIS

THOMAS PAINE   DECEMBER, 1776

Paine released this pamphlet when things were looking bleak for the
Colonials. As Washington prepared to cross the Delaware River to at-
tack the British at Trenton, he ordered the pamphlet read to his troops.
This is an excerpt from that pamphlet.

**THESE are the times that try
men's souls. The summer soldier
and the sunshine patriot will, in this
crisis, shrink from the service of
their country; but he that stands it
now, deserves the love and thanks of
man and woman**. Tyranny, like hell,
is not easily conquered; yet we have
this consolation with us, that the hard-
er the conflict, the more glorious the
triumph. What we obtain too cheap,
we esteem too lightly: it is dearness
only that gives every thing its value.
Heaven knows how to put a proper
price upon its goods; and it would be
strange indeed if so celestial an article

First Page - Original Printing
by Thomas Paine

as FREEDOM should not be highly rated. Britain, with an army
to enforce her tyranny, has declared that she has a right (not only
to TAX) but "to BIND us in ALL CASES WHATSOEVER," and
if being bound in that manner is not slavery, then is there not such
a thing as slavery upon earth. Even the expression is impious; for
so unlimited a power can belong only to God.

WHETHER the independence of the continent was declared
too soon, or delayed too long, I will not now enter into as an ar-
gument; my own simple opinion is, that had it been eight months
earlier, it would have been much better. We did not make a proper
use of last winter, neither could we, while we were in a dependent state. However, the fault, if it were one, was all our own; we
have none to blame but ourselves. But no great deal is lost yet.
All that Howe has been doing for this month past, is rather a rav-
age than a conquest, which the spirit of the Jerseys, a year ago,
would have quickly repulsed, and which time and a little resolution will soon recover...

The Monroe Doctrine

James Monroe   1823

> John Quincy Adams proposed this doctrine that President James
> Monroe delivered in a message to Congress. He was concerned about
> Russian moves in Alaska and the Northwest, and about the Spanish
> colonies. It was a clear statement of our intent to keep European pow-
> ers out of America, but was not acted on until the administration of
> Teddy Roosevelt.

In the discussions to which this interest has given rise and
in the arrangements by which they may terminate the occasion
has been judged proper for asserting, as a principle in which the
rights and interests of the United States are involved, **that the
American continents, by the free and independent condition
which they have assumed and maintain, are henceforth not
to be considered as subjects for future colonization by any
European powers...**

In the wars of the European powers in matters relating to themselves we have never taken any part, nor does it comport with our
policy to do so. It is only when our rights are invaded or seriously
menaced that we resent injuries or make preparation for our defense. With the movements in this hemisphere we are of necessity more immediately connected, and by causes which must be
obvious to all enlightened and impartial observers. The political
system of the allied powers is essentially different in this respect
from that of America. This difference proceeds from that which
exists in their respective Governments; and to the defense of our
own, which has been achieved by the loss of so much blood and
treasure, and matured by the wisdom of their most enlightened
citizens, and under which we have enjoyed unexampled felicity,
this whole nation is devoted. We owe it, therefore, to candor and
to the amicable relations existing between the United States and
those powers to declare that **we should consider any attempt on
their part to extend their system to any portion of this hemisphere as dangerous to our peace and safety. With the existing colonies or dependencies of any European power we have
not interfered and shall not interfere.** But with the Governments who have declared their independence and maintain it, and
whose independence we have, on great consideration and on just
principles, acknowledged, we could not view any interposition
for the purpose of oppressing them, or controlling in any other

manner their destiny, by any European power in any other light than as the manifestation of an unfriendly disposition toward the United States...

Our policy in regard to Europe, which was adopted at an early stage of the wars which have so long agitated that quarter of the globe, nevertheless remains the same, which is, not to interfere in the internal concerns of any of its powers; to consider the government de facto as the legitimate government for us; to cultivate friendly relations with it, and to preserve those relations by a frank, firm, and manly policy, meeting in all instances the just claims of every power, submitting to injuries from none. But in regard to those continents circumstances are eminently and conspicuously different. It is impossible that the allied powers should extend their political system to any portion of either continent without endangering our peace and happiness; nor can anyone believe that our southern brethren, if left to themselves, would adopt it of their own accord. It is equally impossible, therefore, that we should behold such interposition in any form with indifference. If we look to the comparative strength and resources of Spain and those new Governments, and their distance from each other, it must be obvious that she can never subdue them. It is still the true policy of the United States to leave the parties to themselves, in hope that other powers will pursue the same course...

The Monroe Doctrine, 1823
by Allyn Cox

A HOUSE DIVIDED

ABRAHAM LINCOLN   JUNE 16, 1858

Lincoln accepted his nomination as the Republican Senatorial candidate with his famous *A House Divided* speech. He was clarifying his
stand against slavery and against his opponent, Stephen Douglas, who
favored allowing states to decide their own stance on slavery. Lincoln
felt strongly that the country had to end slavery for all states. The following contains the most famous excerpt from that speech.

If we could first know where we are, and whither we are tending, we could then better judge what to do, and how to do it. We
are now far into the fifth year, since a policy was initiated, with
the avowed object, and confident promise, of putting an end to
slavery agitation. Under the operation of that policy, that agitation
has not only, not ceased, but has constantly augmented. In my
opinion, it will not cease, until a crisis shall have been reached,
and passed.

**A house divided against itself cannot stand. I believe this
government cannot endure permanently half slave and half
free.** I do not expect the Union to be dissolved—I do not expect
the house to fall—but I do expect it will cease to be divided. It
will become all one thing, or all the other. Either the opponents of
slavery will arrest the further spread of it, and place it where the
public mind shall rest in the belief that it is in the course of ultimate extinction; or its advocates will push it forward, till it shall
become alike lawful in all the States, old as well as new—North
as well as South...

Abraham Lincoln - 1860
by Thomas Hicks

Lincoln-Douglas 4¢ Stamp - 1958

MESSAGE TO CONGRESS

ABRAHAM LINCOLN   DECEMBER 1, 1862

Shortly before signing the Emancipation Proclamation, Lincoln delivered his annual address to Congress. His speech concluded with the following lines:

The dogmas of the quiet past, are inadequate to the stormy present. The occasion is piled high with difficulty, and we must rise with the occasion. As our case is new, so we must think anew, and act anew. We must disenthrall ourselves, and then we shall save our country.

Fellow-citizens, we cannot escape history. We of this Congress and this administration, will be remembered in spite of ourselves. No personal significance, or insignificance, can spare one or another of us. The fiery trial through which we pass, will light us down, in honor or dishonor, to the latest generation. We say we are for the Union. The world will not forget that we say this. We know how to save the Union. The world knows we do know how to save it. We, even we here, hold the power, and bear the responsibility. In giving freedom to the slave, we assure freedom to the free—honorable alike in what we give, and what we preserve. **We shall nobly save, or meanly lose, the last best hope of earth.** Other means may succeed; this could not fail. The way is plain, peaceful, generous, just—a way which, if followed, the world will forever applaud, and God must forever bless...

First Reading of the Emancipation Proclamation
by Francis Carpenter

THE EMANCIPATION PROCLAMATION

ABRAHAM LINCOLN   SEPTEMBER 22, 1862

> Lincoln's main focus was always on keeping the Union together. Mid-
> way through the war, he felt it advantageous to formalize the govern-
> ment's position on slavery, and prepared a speech. He was advised to
> wait until the North achieved victory in battle. That victory finally
> came with the Battle of Antietam, and Lincoln released the proclama-
> tion officially freeing slaves only in the Confederate states in rebel-
> lion. He could not legally free the Northern slaves—that had to wait
> until future amendments to the Constitution. 200,000 blacks ended up
> fighting for the Union, while half a million fled the South to the North
> during the war. The proclamation went into effect on January 1, 1863.

Whereas, on the twenty-second day of September, in the year
of our Lord one thousand eight hundred and sixty-two, a proclamation was issued by the President of the United States, containing, among other things, the following, to wit:

"That on the first day of January, in the year of our Lord one
thousand eight hundred and sixty-three, **all persons held as slaves
within any State or designated part of a State, the people
whereof shall then be in rebellion against the United States,
shall be then, thenceforward, and forever free**; and the Executive Government of the United States, including the military and
naval authority thereof, will recognize and maintain the freedom of
such persons, and will do no act or acts to repress such persons, or
any of them, in any efforts they may make for their actual freedom.

"That the Executive will, on the first day of January aforesaid,
by proclamation, designate the States and parts of States, if any, in
which the people thereof, respectively, shall then be in rebellion
against the United States; and the fact that any State, or the people
thereof, shall on that day be, in good faith, represented in the Congress of the United States by members chosen thereto at elections
wherein a majority of the qualified voters of such State shall have
participated, shall, in the absence of strong countervailing testimony, be deemed conclusive evidence that such State, and the people
thereof, are not then in rebellion against the United States."

Now, therefore I, Abraham Lincoln, President of the United
States, by virtue of the power in me vested as Commander-in-
Chief, of the Army and Navy of the United States in time of actual
armed rebellion against the authority and government of the United States, and as a fit and necessary war measure for suppressing

said rebellion, do, on this first day of January, in the year of our Lord one thousand eight hundred and sixty-three, and in accordance with my purpose so to do publicly proclaimed for the full period of one hundred days, from the day first above mentioned, order and designate as the States and parts of States wherein the people thereof respectively, are this day in rebellion against the United States, the following, to wit:

Arkansas, Texas, Louisiana, (except the Parishes of St. Bernard, Plaquemines, Jefferson, St. John, St. Charles, St. James Ascension, Assumption, Terrebonne, Lafourche, St. Mary, St. Martin, and Orleans, including the City of New Orleans) Mississippi, Alabama, Florida, Georgia, South Carolina, North Carolina, and Virginia, (except the forty-eight counties designated as West Virginia, and also the counties of Berkley, Accomac, Northampton, Elizabeth City, York, Princess Ann, and Norfolk, including the cities of Norfolk and Portsmouth[)], and which excepted parts, are for the present, left precisely as if this proclamation were not issued.

And by virtue of the power, and for the purpose aforesaid, I do order and declare that all persons held as slaves within said designated States, and parts of States, are, and henceforward shall be free; and that the Executive government of the United States, including the military and naval authorities thereof, will recognize and maintain the freedom of said persons.

And I hereby enjoin upon the people so declared to be free to abstain from all violence, unless in necessary self-defence; and I recommend to them that, in all cases when allowed, they labor faithfully for reasonable wages.

And I further declare and make known, that such persons of suitable condition, will be received into the armed service of the United States to garrison forts, positions, stations, and other places, and to man vessels of all sorts in said service.

And upon this act, sincerely believed to be an act of justice, warranted by the Constitution, upon military necessity, I invoke the considerate judgment of mankind, and the gracious favor of Almighty God. In witness whereof, I have hereunto set my hand and caused the seal of the United States to be affixed. Done at the City of Washington, this first day of January, in the year of our Lord one thousand eight hundred and sixty three, and of the Independence of the United States of America the eighty-seventh.

THE GETTYSBURG ADDRESS

ABRAHAM LINCOLN   NOVEMBER 19, 1863

The president was initially not even invited to the dedication of the
National Cemetery at Gettysburg, Pennsylvania. That battle had involved 170,000 soldiers and resulted in 50,000 casualties. The fea-
tured speaker, Edward Everett, took 2 hours to deliver a speech no
one remembers. Abraham Lincoln took just 2 minutes to deliver his
speech. It is now known as one of the greatest speeches ever. It recast
the meaning of the Civil War as a struggle to ensure the Constitution
really means equality for all.

Fourscore and seven years ago our fathers brought forth upon
this continent a new nation, conceived in liberty, and dedicated
to the proposition that all men are created equal. Now we are engaged in a great civil war, testing whether that nation, or any nation so conceived and so dedicated, can long endure. We are met
on a great battlefield of that war. We have come to dedicate a portion of that field as a final resting-place for those who here gave
their lives that that nation might live. It is altogether fitting and
proper that we should do this. But in a larger sense we cannot dedicate, we cannot consecrate, we cannot hallow this ground. The
brave men, living and dead, who struggled here, have consecrated
it far above our poor power to add or detract. The world will little
note, nor long remember, what we say here; but it can never forget
what they did here. It is for us, the living, rather to be dedicated
here to the unfinished work which they who fought here have thus
far so nobly advanced. It is rather for us to be here dedicated to
the great task remaining before us, that from these honored dead
we take increased devotion to that cause for which they gave the
last full measure of devotion; that **we here highly resolve that
these dead shall not have died in vain; that this nation, under
God, shall have a new birth of freedom, and that government
of the people, by the people, and for the people, shall not perish from the earth.**

(It was) that sentiment in the Declaration of Independence which
gave liberty, not alone to the people of this country, but, I hope, to
the world, for all future time. It was that which gave promise that in
due time the weight would be lifted from the shoulders of all men.
This is a sentiment embodied in the Declaration of Independence...I
would rather be assassinated on this spot than surrender it.

—Abraham Lincoln, 1861

SECOND INAUGURAL ADDRESS

ABRAHAM LINCOLN   MARCH 4, 1865

His second inaugural address would be given just 5 weeks before his assassination. General Lee had not surrendered yet, but a Northern victory was assured and slavery was nearing an official end. He reminded the country of the scourge of war, and the need for the country to put their differences behind and "bind the nation's wounds." Unbeknownst, his future assassin, John Wilkes Booth, was in the audience listening to his speech. The following is a short excerpt.

On the occasion corresponding to this four years ago all thoughts were anxiously directed to an impending civil war. All dreaded it, all sought to avert it. While the inaugural address was being delivered from this place, devoted altogether to *saving* the Union without war, insurgent agents were in the city seeking to *destroy* it without war—seeking to dissolve the Union and divide effects by negotiation. Both parties deprecated war, but one of them would *make* war rather than let the nation survive, and the other would *accept* war rather than let it perish, and the war came....

Fondly do we hope, fervently do we pray, that this mighty scourge of war may speedily pass away. Yet, if God wills that it continue until all the wealth piled by the bondsman's two hundred and fifty years of unrequited toil shall be sunk, and until every drop of blood drawn with the lash shall be paid by another drawn with the sword, as was said three thousand years ago, so still it must be said, "The judgments of the Lord are true and righteous altogether."

With malice toward none, with charity for all, with firmness in the right as God gives us to see the right, let us strive on to finish the work we are in, to bind up the nation's wounds, to care for him who shall have borne the battle and for his widow and his orphan, to do all which may achieve and cherish a just and lasting peace among ourselves and with all nations.

The Assassination of President Lincoln
by Currier & Ives

WILSON WAR SPEECH

WOODROW WILSON   APRIL 2, 1917

President Wilson delivered this speech to a joint session of Congress. He outlined the reasons for declaring war on Germany. Germany had been at war in Europe since 1914, but the United States had remained neutral. However, support for the war had grown due to recent attacks on shipping, the resumption of unrestricted submarine warfare by the Germans, and the interception of the infamous Zimmerman Telegram which revealed a German attempt to enlist Mexico as an ally in the fight against America. Wilson still wanted to convince Americans that war was a necessity against a ruthless enemy. He also stated that the war was necessary to make the world "safe for democracy." Congress declared war on Germany four days later on April 6, 1917.

On the third of February last I officially laid before you the extraordinary announcement of the Imperial German Government that on and after the first day of February it was its purpose to put aside all restraints of law or of humanity and use its submarines to sink every vessel that sought to approach either the ports of Great Britain and Ireland or the western coasts of Europe or any of the ports controlled by the enemies of Germany within the Mediterranean.

That had seemed to be the object of the German submarine warfare earlier in the war, but since April of last year the Imperial Government had somewhat restrained the commanders of its undersea craft in conformity with its promise then given to us that passenger boats should not be sunk and that due warning would be given to all other vessels which its submarines might seek to destroy, when no resistance was offered or escape attempted, and care taken that their crews were given at least a fair chance to save their lives in their open boats.

The precautions taken were meager and haphazard enough, as was proved in distressing instance after instance in the progress of the cruel and unmanly business, but a certain degree of restraint was observed. The new policy has swept every restriction aside. Vessels of every kind, whatever their flag, their character, their cargo, their destination, their errand, have been ruthlessly sent to the bottom without warning and without thought of help or mercy for those on board, the vessels of friendly neutrals along with those of belligerents. Even hospital ships and ships carrying relief to the sorely bereaved and stricken people of Belgium, though the latter were provided with safe conduct through the proscribed areas by the German Government itself and were distinguished by unmistakable marks of identity, haven been sunk with the same reckless lack of compassion or of principle....

This minimum of right the German Government has swept aside under the plea of retaliation and necessity and because it had no weapons which it could use at sea except these which it is impossible to employ as it is employing them without throwing to the winds all scruples of humanity or of respect for the understandings that were supposed to underlie the intercourse of the world.

I am not now thinking of the loss of property involved, immense and serious as that is, but only of the wanton and wholesale destruction of the lives of non-combatants, men, women, and children, engaged in pursuits which have always, even in the darkest periods of modern history, been deemed innocent and legitimate. Property can be paid for; the lives of peaceful and innocent people cannot be.

The present German submarine warfare against commerce is a warfare against mankind. It is war against all nations.

American ships have been sunk, American lives taken, in ways which it has stirred us very deeply to learn of, but the ships and people of other neutral and friendly nations have been sunk and overwhelmed in the waters in the same way. There has been no discrimination. The challenge is to all mankind.

Each nation must decide for itself how it will meet it. The choice we make for ourselves must be made with a moderation of counsel and temperateness of judgment befitting our character and our motives as a nation. We must put excited feeling away. Our motive will not be revenge or the victorious assertion of the physical might of the nation, but only the vindication of right, of human right, of which we are only a single champion....

The German Government denies the right of neutrals to use arms at all within the areas of the sea which it has proscribed, even in the defense of rights which no modern publicist has ever before questioned their right to defend. The intimation is conveyed that the armed guards which we have placed on our merchant ships will be treated as beyond the pale of law and subject to be dealt with as pirates would be....

With a profound sense of the solemn and even tragical character of the step I am taking and of the grave responsibilities which it involves, but in unhesitating obedience to what I deem my constitutional duty, I advise that the Congress declare the recent course of the Imperial German Government to be in fact nothing less than war against the government and people of the United States; that it formally accept the status of belligerent which has thus been thrust upon it; and that it take immediate steps not only to put the country in a more thorough state of defense but also to exert all its power and employ all its resources to bring the Government of the German Empire to terms and end the war....

We have no quarrel with the German people. We have no feeling towards them but one of sympathy and friendship....

We are glad, now that we see the facts with no veil of false pretense about them, to fight thus for the ultimate peace of the world and for the liberation of its peoples, the German peoples included: for the rights of nations great and small and the privilege of men everywhere to choose their way of life and of obedience. **The world must be made safe for democracy.** Its peace must be planted upon the tested foundations of political liberty. We have no selfish ends to serve.

We desire no conquest, no dominion. We seek no indemnities for ourselves, no material compensation for the sacrifices we shall cheerfully make. We are but one of the champions of the rights of mankind. We shall be satisfied when those rights have been made as secure as the faith and the freedom of nations can make them.

We enter this war only where we are clearly forced into it because there are no other means of defending our rights....

But the right is more precious than peace, and we shall fight for the things which we have always carried nearest our hearts, for democracy, for the right of those who submit to authority to have a voice in their own governments, for the rights and liberties of small nations, for a universal dominion of right by such a concert of free peoples as shall bring peace and safety to all nations and make the world at last free.

To such a task we can dedicate our lives and our fortunes, everything that we are and everything that we have, with the pride of those who know that the day has come when America is privileged to spend her blood and her might for the principles that gave her birth and happiness and the peace which she has treasured. God helping her, she can do no other.

THE FOUR FREEDOMS

FRANKLIN D. ROOSEVELT   JANUARY 6, 1941

> The following are excerpts from Roosevelt's State of the Union ad-
> dress. The United States had not entered the war yet, though FDR
> was using the Lend-Lease program to help fight Germany. The iso-
> lationist movement was strong, with heroes like Charles Lindbergh
> forwarding their cause. Imagine what would have happened had the
> U.S. stayed out of the war...

I address you, the members of this new Congress, at a moment
unprecedented in the history of the union. I use the word "unprecedented" because at no previous time has American security been
as seriously threatened from without as it is today....

I suppose that every realist knows that the democratic way of
life is at this moment being directly assailed in every part of the
world—assailed either by arms or by secret spreading of poison-
ous propaganda by those who seek to destroy unity and promote
discord in nations that are still at peace.

During sixteen long months this assault has blotted out the
whole pattern of democratic life in an appalling number of independent nations, great and small. And the assailants are still on
the march, threatening other nations, great and small.

Therefore, as your President, performing my constitutional duty to "give to the Congress information of the state of the
union," I find it unhappily necessary to report that the future and
the safety of our country and of our democracy are overwhelm-
ingly involved in events far beyond our borders.

Armed defense of democratic existence is now being gallantly
waged in four continents. If that defense fails, all the population
and all the resources of Europe and Asia, Africa and Australia
will be dominated by conquerors. And let us remember that the
total of those populations in those four continents, the total of
those populations and their resources greatly exceeds the sum total of the population and the resources of the whole of the Western
Hemisphere—yes, many times over.

In times like these it is immature— and, incidentally, un-
true—for anybody to brag that an unprepared America, single-
handed and with one hand tied behind its back, can hold off the
whole world.

290 ❖ THE AMERICAN CHALLENGE

No realistic American can expect from a dictator's peace international generosity, or return of true independence, or world disarmament, or freedom of expression, or freedom of religion—or even good business. Such a peace would bring no security for us or for our neighbors. **Those who would give up essential liberty to purchase a little temporary safety deserve neither liberty nor safety...**

Let us say to the democracies: "We Americans are vitally concerned in your defense of freedom. We are putting forth our energies, our resources, and our organizing powers to give you the strength to regain and maintain a free world. We shall send you in ever-increasing numbers, ships, planes, tanks, guns. This is our purpose and our pledge."...

In the future days, which we seek to make secure, we look forward to a world founded upon four essential human freedoms.

The first is freedom of speech and expression—everywhere in the world.

The second is freedom of every person to worship God in his own way everywhere in the world.

The third is freedom from want, which, translated into world terms, means economic understandings which will secure to every nation a healthy peacetime life for its inhabitants—everywhere in the world.

The fourth is freedom from fear, which, translated into world terms, means a world-wide reduction of armaments to such a point and in such a thorough fashion that no nation will be in a position to commit an act of physical aggression against any neighbor—anywhere in the world.

That is no vision of a distant millennium. It is a definite basis for a kind of world attainable in our own time and generation. That kind of world is the very antithesis of the so-called "new order" of tyranny which the dictators seek to create with the crash of a bomb...

The American people will never knowingly adopt Socialism. But under the name of 'liberalism' they will adopt every fragment of the Socialist program, until one day America will be a Socialist nation, without knowing how it happened.

—*Norman Thomas, Socialist Party of America*

WHAT IS AN AMERICAN?

HAROLD ICKES, SECRETARY OF INTERIOR   MAY 18, 1941

> This speech was given during an "I am an American" day meeting
> in New York. It came at a time when Hitler's Nazis seemed headed
> toward victory over all of Europe, and perhaps the world. Many
> Americans, however, still objected to the U.S. getting involved in
> what they felt was Europe's war. Many even felt that Fascism could
> be the "wave of the future." Ickes defines what it means to be free
> and an American.

I say that it is time for the great American people to raise its
voice and cry out in mighty triumph what it is to be an American....What constitutes an American? Not color nor race nor religion. Not the pedigree of his family nor the place of his birth.
Not the coincidence of his citizenship. Not his social status nor
his bank account. Not his trade nor his profession. **An American is one who loves justice and believes in the dignity of
man. An American is one who will fight for his freedom and
that of his neighbor. An American is one who will sacrifice
property, ease and security in order that he and his children
may retain the rights of free men. An American is one in
whose heart is engraved the immortal second sentence of the
Declaration of Independence.**

Americans have always known how to fight for their rights and
their way of life. Americans are not afraid to fight. They fight joy-
ously in a just cause.

We Americans know that freedom, like peace, is indivisible.
We cannot retain our liberty if three-fourths of the world is enslaved. Brutality, injustice and slavery, if practiced as dictators
would have them, universally and systematically, in the long run
would destroy us as surely as a fire raging in our nearby neighbor's house would burn ours if we didn't help to put out his....
We should be clear on this point. What is convulsing the world
today is not merely another old-fashioned war. It is a counter
revolution against our ideas and ideals, against our sense of justice and our human values.... They have one common goal, the
destruction of democracy.

This is why this war is not an ordinary war. It is not a conflict
for markets or territories. It is a desperate struggle for the possession of the souls of men.... In this world war of ideas and of
loyalties we believers in democracy must do two things. We must

unite our forces to form one great democratic international. We must offer a clear program to freedom-loving peoples throughout the world. Freedom-loving men and women in every land must organize and tighten their ranks. The masses everywhere must be helped to fight their oppressors and conquerors.

We, free, democratic Americans are in a position to help. We know that the spirit of freedom never dies. We know that men have fought and bled for freedom since time immemorial…. No, liberty never dies. The Genghis Khans come and go. The Attilas come and go. The Hitlers flash and sputter out. But freedom endures.

These men and women, hundreds of millions of them, now in bondage or threatened with slavery, are our comrades and our allies. They are only waiting for our leadership and our encouragement, for the spark that we can supply…. Here in America we have something so worth living for that it is worth dying for! The so-called "wave of the future" is but the slimy backwash of the past. We have not heaved from our necks the tyrant's crushing heel, only to stretch our necks out again for its weight. Not only will we fight for democracy, we will make it more worth fighting for. We Americans know that when good will prevails among men there will be a world of plenty and a world of security.

———————— ❧ ————————

The thing they forget is that liberty and freedom and democracy are so very precious that you do not fight to win them once and stop. You do not do that. Liberty and freedom and democracy are prizes awarded only to those peoples who fight to win them and then keep fighting eternally to hold them!

—*Sergeant Alvin York*

There are those, I know, who will say that the liberation of humanity, the freedom of man and mind, is nothing but a dream. They are right. It is the American dream.

—*Archibald MacLeish*

We on this continent should never forget that men first crossed the Atlantic not to find soil for their ploughs but to secure liberty for their souls.

—*Robert J. McCracken*

DAY OF INFAMY SPEECH

FRANKLIN D. ROOSEVELT   DECEMBER 8, 1941

President Roosevelt addressed Congress the day after the Japanese attacked Pearl Harbor. The U.S. had lost more than 2,000 lives and a large number of ships in the surprise attack. Congress passed the Declaration of War against Japan the same day. Three days later, war was declared on Germany.

Yesterday, Dec. 7, 1941—a date which will live in infamy— the United States of America was suddenly and deliberately attacked by naval and air forces of the Empire of Japan.

The United States was at peace with that nation and, at the solicitation of Japan, was still in conversation with the government and its emperor looking toward the maintenance of peace in the Pacific.

Indeed, one hour after Japanese air squadrons had commenced bombing in Oahu, the Japanese ambassador to the United States and his colleagues delivered to the Secretary of State a formal reply to a recent American message. While this reply stated that it seemed useless to continue the existing diplomatic negotiations, it contained no threat or hint of war or armed attack.

It will be recorded that the distance of Hawaii from Japan makes it obvious that the attack was deliberately planned many days or even weeks ago. During the intervening time, the Japanese government has deliberately sought to deceive the United States by false statements and expressions of hope for continued peace.

The attack yesterday on the Hawaiian islands has caused severe damage to American naval and military forces. Very many American lives have been lost. In addition, American ships have been reported torpedoed on the high seas between San Francisco and Honolulu.

Yesterday, the Japanese government also launched an attack against Malaya. Last night, Japanese forces attacked Hong Kong. Last night, Japanese forces attacked Guam. Last night, Japanese forces attacked the Philippine Islands. Last night, the Japanese attacked Wake Island. This morning, the Japanese attacked Midway Island.

Japan has, therefore, undertaken a surprise offensive extending throughout the Pacific area. The facts of yesterday speak for themselves. The people of the United States have already formed their opinions and well understand the implications to the very life and safety of our nation.

As commander in chief of the Army and Navy, I have directed that all measures be taken for our defense. Always will we remember the character of the onslaught against us.

No matter how long it may take us to overcome this premeditated invasion, the American people in their righteous might will win through to absolute victory.

I believe I interpret the will of the Congress and of the people when I assert that we will not only defend ourselves to the uttermost, but will make very certain that this form of treachery shall never endanger us again.

Hostilities exist. There is no blinking at the fact that our people, our territory and our interests are in grave danger.

With confidence in our armed forces - with the unbounding determination of our people - we will gain the inevitable triumph - so help us God.

I ask that the Congress declare that since the unprovoked and dastardly attack by Japan on Sunday, Dec. 7, a state of war has existed between the United States and the Japanese empire.

USS Arizona Ablaze
December 7, 1941

*Roosevelt signs
Declaration of War
against Japan*
December 8, 1941

D-DAY ORDER

GENERAL DWIGHT EISENHOWER   JUNE 6, 1944

When Eisenhower finally gave approval to launch the invasion of France, he prepared the following message which was given to each of the 150,000 soldiers participating in the invasion. Although no one knew it at the time, Eisenhower had also written the following note to be released in case the mission failed. Fortunately, the note stayed stuffed in his pocket. Wouldn't it be refreshing today for politicians to similarly take direct blame for their actions?

> *Our landings in the Cherbourg-Havre area have failed to gain a satisfactory foothold and I have withdrawn the troops. My decision to attack at this time and place was based upon the best information available. The troops, the air and the Navy did all that bravery and devotion to duty could do. If any blame or fault attaches to the attempt it is mine alone.*

This is the real message that he delivered to the troops:

Soldiers, Sailors and Airmen of the Allied Expeditionary Force! You are about to embark upon the Great Crusade, toward which we have striven thee many months. **The eyes of the world are upon you. The hopes and prayers of liberty-loving people everywhere march with you.** In company with our brave Allies and brothers-in-arms on other Fronts, you will bring about the destruction of the German war machine, the elimination of Nazi tyranny over the oppressed peoples of Europe, and security for ourselves in a free world. Your task will not be an easy one. Your enemy is well trained, well equipped, and battle-hardened. He will fight savagely.

But this is the year 1944. Much has happened since the Nazi triumphs of 1940-41. The United Nations have inflicted upon the Germans great defeats, in open battle, man-to-man. Our air offensive has seriously reduced their strength in the air and their capacity to wage war on the ground. Our Home Fronts have given us an overwhelming superiority in weapons and munitions of war, and placed at our disposal great reserves of trained fighting men. The tide has turned! The free men of the world are marching together to Victory!

I have full confidence in your courage, devotion to duty and skill in battle. We will accept nothing less than full Victory. Good luck, and let us all beseech the blessings of Almighty God upon this great and noble undertaking.

Civil Rights Message

Harry S. Truman   February 2, 1948

Truman was shocked at the way black veterans were treated after World War II. The military had been segregated since President Wilson and World War I. Truman signed executive orders to abolish segregation laws, a move that might have cost him the election later that year. It is encouraging that Truman wanted equal "opportunities" for jobs, homes, health, and education, as opposed to FDR's earlier demand in his Second Bill of Rights that everyone has the "right" to a well-paying job, decent home, adequate health care, and good education.

In the State of the Union Message on January 7, 1948, I spoke of five great goals toward which we should strive in our constant effort to strengthen our democracy and improve the welfare of our people. The first of these is to secure fully our essential human rights. I am now presenting to the Congress my recommendations for legislation to carry us forward toward that goal.

This nation was founded by men and women who sought these shores that they might enjoy greater freedom and greater opportunity than they had known before. The founders of the United States proclaimed to the world the American belief that all men are created equal, and that governments are instituted to secure the inalienable rights with which all men are endowed. In the Declaration of Independence and the Constitution of the United States, they eloquently expressed the aspirations of…mankind for equality and freedom….

We believe that all men are created equal and that they have the right to equal justice under law.

We believe that all men have the right to freedom of thought and of expression and the right to worship as they please.

We believe that all men are entitled to equal opportunities for jobs, for homes, for good health and for education.

We believe that all men should have a voice in their government and that government should protect, not usurp, the rights of the people.

These are the basic civil rights, which are the source and the support of our democracy.

Today, the American people enjoy more freedom and opportunity than ever before. Never in our history has there been better reason to hope for the complete realization of the ideals of liberty and equality….

The Federal Government has a clear duty to see that Constitutional guarantees of individual liberties and of equal protection under the laws are not denied or abridged anywhere in our Union. That duty is shared by all three branches of the Government, but it can be fulfilled only if the Congress enacts modern, comprehensive civil rights laws, adequate to the needs of the day, and demonstrating out continuing faith in the free way of life. I recommend, therefore, that the Congress enact legislation at this session directed toward the following specific objectives:

1. Establishing a permanent Commission on Civil Rights, a Joint Congressional Committee on Civil Rights, and a Civil Rights Division in the Department of Justice.

2. Strengthening existing civil rights statues.

3. Providing Federal protection against lynching.

4. Protecting more adequately the right to vote.

5. Establishing a Fair Employment Practice Commission to prevent unfair discrimination in employment.

6. Prohibiting discrimination in interstate transportation facilities.

7. Providing home-rule and suffrage in Presidential elections for the residents of the District of Columbia.

8. Providing Statehood for Hawaii and Alaska and a greater measure of self-government for our island possessions.

9. Equalizing the opportunities for residents of the United States to become naturalized citizens.

10. Settling the evacuation claims of Japanese-Americans.

To sin by silence when they should protest makes cowards of men.
—*Abraham Lincoln*

All, too, will bear in mind this sacred principle, that though the will of the majority is in all cases to prevail, that will, to be rightful, must be reasonable; that the minority possess their equal rights, which equal laws must protect, and to violate would be oppression.
—*Thomas Jefferson*

Report to the American People on Korea

Harry S. Truman   April 11, 1951

> The Korean War had been going on for almost a year. The American and U.N. troops, under the command of General MacArthur, had made great progress before being pushed back below the 38th parallel by the entrance of the Chinese into the conflict. There were indications that a negotiated settlement was possible to end the war, but MacArthur continued to publicly advocate a more aggressive response on China itself. President Truman, as Commander-In-Chief, could not have MacArthur dictating our foreign policy, and, in this radio address, removed him from command. He also explains to the American people the reasons for our involvement in that war.

I want to talk to you plainly tonight about what we are doing in Korea and about our policy in the Far East. In the simplest terms, what we are doing in Korea is this: We are trying to prevent a third world war.

I think most people in this country recognized that fact last June. And they warmly supported the decision of the Government to help the Republic of Korea against the Communist aggressors. Now, many persons, even some who applauded our decision to defend Korea, have forgotten the basic reason for our action. It is right for us to be in Korea now. It was right last June. It is right today. I want to remind you why this is true.

The Communists in the Kremlin are engaged in a monstrous conspiracy to stamp out freedom all over the world. If they were to succeed, the United States would be numbered among their principal victims. It must be clear to everyone that the United States cannot—and will not—sit idly by and await foreign conquest. The only question is: What is the best time to meet the threat and how is the best way to meet it?

The best time to meet the threat is in the beginning. It is easier to put out a fire in the beginning when it is small than after it has become a roaring blaze. And the best way to meet the threat of aggression is for the peace-loving nations to act together. If they don't act together, they are likely to be picked off, one by one. If they had followed the right policies in the 1930s—if the free countries had acted together to crush the aggression of the dictators, and if they had acted in the beginning when the aggression was small—there probably would have been no World War II.

If history has taught us anything, it is that aggression anywhere in the world is a threat to the peace everywhere in the world. When that aggression is supported by the cruel and selfish rulers of a powerful nation who are bent on conquest, it becomes a dear and present danger to the security and independence of every free nation...

The aggression against Korea is the boldest and most dangerous move the Communists have yet made. The attack on Korea was part of a greater plan for conquering all of Asia...So far, we have prevented World War III. So far, by fighting a limited war in Korea, we have prevented aggression from succeeding, and bringing on a general war. And the ability of the whole free world to resist Communist aggression has been greatly improved...

We do not want to see the conflict in Korea extended. We are trying to prevent a world war—not to start one. And the best way to do that is to make it plain that we and the other free countries will continue to resist the attack...If the Communist authorities realize that they cannot defeat us in Korea, if they realize it would be foolhardy to widen the hostilities beyond Korea, then they may recognize the folly of continuing their aggression. A peaceful settlement may then be possible. The door is always open...

I believe that we must try to limit the war to Korea for these vital reasons: to make sure that the precious lives of our fighting men are not wasted; to see that the security of our country and the free world is not needlessly jeopardized; and to prevent a third world war. A number of events have made it evident that General MacArthur did not agree with that policy. **I have therefore considered it essential to relieve General MacArthur so that there would be no doubt or confusion as to the real purpose and aim of our policy.**

It was with the deepest personal regret that I found myself compelled to take this action. General MacArthur is one of our greatest military commanders. But the cause of world peace is much more important than any individual...

Free nations have united their strength in an effort to prevent a third world war. That war can come if the Communist rulers want it to come. But this Nation and its allies will not be responsible for its coming. We do not want to widen the conflict. We will use every effort to prevent that disaster. And in so doing, we know that we are following the great principles of peace, freedom, and justice.

EISENHOWER'S FAREWELL ADDRESS

DWIGHT D. EISENHOWER   **JANUARY 17, 1961**

> In his final address to the nation before turning over the government to the newly elected, and much younger, John F. Kennedy, Eisenhower expresses hope for the future. The speech is best known, however, for his warning about the growth of the "military-industrial complex." He also brings attention to the dangers of deficit spending. Here are some excerpts from his speech.

We now stand ten years past the midpoint of a century that has witnessed four major wars among great nations. Three of these involved our own country. Despite these holocausts, America is today the strongest, the most influential, and most productive nation in the world. Understandably proud of this pre-eminence, we yet realize that America's leadership and prestige depend, not merely upon our unmatched material progress, riches and military strength, but on how we use our power in the interests of world peace and human betterment.

Throughout America's adventure in free government, our basic purposes have been to keep the peace, to foster progress in human achievement, and to enhance liberty, dignity and integrity among peoples and among nations. To strive for less would be unworthy of a free and religious people. Any failure traceable to arrogance or our lack of comprehension or readiness to sacrifice would inflict upon us grievous hurt, both at home and abroad.

Progress toward these noble goals is persistently threatened by the conflict now engulfing the world. It commands our whole attention, absorbs our very beings. We face a hostile ideology global in scope, atheistic in character, ruthless in purpose, and insidious in method. Unhappily, the danger it poses promises to be of indefinite duration. To meet it successfully, there is called for, not so much the emotional and transitory sacrifices of crisis, but rather those which enable us to carry forward steadily, surely, and without complaint the burdens of a prolonged and complex struggle with liberty the stake. Only thus shall we remain, despite every provocation, on our charted course toward permanent peace and human betterment....

But threats, new in kind or degree, constantly arise. Of these, I mention two only.

A vital element in keeping the peace is our military establishment. Our arms must be mighty, ready for instant action, so that no potential aggressor may be tempted to risk his own destruction. Our military organization today bears little relation to that known by any of my predecessors in peacetime, or, indeed, by the fighting men of World War II or Korea.

Until the latest of our world conflicts, the United States had no armaments industry. American makers of plowshares could, with time and as required, make swords as well. But now we can no longer risk emergency improvisation of national defense. We have been compelled to create a permanent armaments industry of vast proportions. Added to this, three and a half million men and women are directly engaged in the defense establishment. We annually spend on military security alone more than the net income of all United States corporations.

Now this conjunction of an immense military establishment and a large arms industry is new in the American experience. The total influence -- economic, political, even spiritual --is felt in every city, every Statehouse, every office of the Federal government. We recognize the imperative need for this development. Yet we must not fail to comprehend its grave implications. Our toil, resources, and livelihood are all involved. So is the very structure of our society.

In the councils of government, we must guard against the acquisition of unwarranted influence, whether sought or unsought, by the military-industrial complex. The potential for the disastrous rise of misplaced power exists and will persist. We must never let the weight of this combination endanger our liberties or democratic processes. We should take nothing for granted. Only an alert and knowledgeable citizenry can compel the proper meshing of the huge industrial and military machinery of defense with our peaceful methods and goals, so that security and liberty may prosper together.

Akin to, and largely responsible for the sweeping changes in our industrial-military posture, has been the technological revolution during recent decades. In this revolution, research has become central, it also becomes more formalized, complex, and costly. A steadily increasing share is conducted for, by, or at the direction of, the Federal government.

Today, the solitary inventor, tinkering in his shop, has been overshadowed by task forces of scientists in laboratories and testing fields. In the same fashion, the free university, historically the fountainhead of free ideas and scientific discovery, has experienced a revolution in the conduct of research. Partly because of the huge costs involved, a government contract becomes virtually a substitute for intellectual curiosity. For every old blackboard there are now hundreds of new electronic computers. The prospect of domination of the nation's scholars by Federal employment, project allocations, and the power of money is ever present -- and is gravely to be regarded.

Yet, in holding scientific research and discovery in respect, as we should, we must also be alert to the equal and opposite danger that public policy could itself become the captive of a scientific-technological elite.

It is the task of statesmanship to mold, to balance, and to integrate these and other forces, new and old, within the principles of our democratic system – ever aiming toward the supreme goals of our free society.

Another factor in maintaining balance involves the element of time. **As we peer into society's future, we--you and I, and our government--must avoid the impulse to live only for today, plundering for our own ease and convenience the precious resources of tomorrow. We cannot mortgage the material assets of our grandchildren without risking the loss also of their political and spiritual heritage.** We want democracy to survive for all generations to come, not to become the insolvent phantom of tomorrow....

To all the peoples of the world, I once more give expression to America's prayerful and continuing aspiration: We pray that peoples of all faiths, all races, all nations, may have their great human needs satisfied; that those now denied opportunity shall come to enjoy it to the full; that all who yearn for freedom may experience its spiritual blessings. Those who have freedom will understand, also, its heavy responsibilities; that all who are insensitive to the needs of others will learn charity; and that the scourges of poverty, disease and ignorance will be made to disappear from the earth; and that, in the goodness of time, all peoples will come to live together in a peace guaranteed by the binding force of mutual respect and love.

Now, on Friday noon, I am to become a private citizen. I am proud to do so. I look forward to it.

Thank you, and good night.

Inauguration Speech

JOHN F. KENNEDY   JANUARY 20, 1961

> This speech epitomized the new generation that was assuming the responsibilities of running a great nation. He was the first president born in the 20th century. His speech was an appeal to the citizens of America, and a promise to the world that we would support freedom everywhere. The following is taken from his speech.

We dare not forget today that we are the heirs of that first revolution. **Let the word go forth from this time and place, to friend and foe alike, that the torch has been passed to a new generation of Americans**—born in this century, tempered by war, disciplined by a hard and bitter peace, proud of our ancient heritage—and unwilling to witness or permit the slow undoing of those human rights to which this nation has always been committed, and to which we are committed today at home and around the world.

Let every nation know, whether it wishes us well or ill, that we shall pay any price, bear any burden, meet any hardship, support any friend, oppose any foe to assure the survival and the success of liberty. This much we pledge—and more.

To those old allies whose cultural and spiritual origins we share, we pledge the loyalty of faithful friends. United, there is little we cannot do in a host of cooperative ventures. Divided, there is little we can do—for we dare not meet a powerful challenge at odds and split asunder....

Let us never negotiate out of fear. But let us never fear to negotiate...In the long history of the world, only a few generations have been granted the role of defending freedom in its hour of maximum danger. I do not shrink from this responsibility—I welcome it. I do not believe that any of us would exchange places with any other people or any other generation. The energy, the faith, the devotion which we bring to this endeavor will light our country and all who serve it—and the glow from that fire can truly light the world.

And so, my fellow Americans: ask not what your country can do for you—ask what you can do for your country.

My fellow citizens of the world: ask not what America will do for you, but what together we can do for the freedom of man...

Challenge to Land on the Moon

John F. Kennedy   **May 25, 1961**

Excerpts from Kennedy's speech to Congress challenging the United States to put a man on the moon by the end of the decade. His challenge was fulfilled on July 20, 1969 when Neil Armstrong stepped on the Moon.

Recognizing the head start obtained by the Soviets with their large rocket engines, which gives them many months of lead-time, and recognizing the likelihood that they will exploit this lead for some time to come in still more impressive successes, we nevertheless are required to make new efforts on our own. For while we cannot guarantee that we shall one day be first, we can guarantee that any failure to make this effort will make us last. We take an additional risk by making it in full view of the world, but as shown by the feat of astronaut Shepard, this very risk enhances our stature when we are successful. But this is not merely a race. Space is open to us now; and our eagerness to share its meaning is not governed by the efforts of others. We go into space because whatever mankind must undertake, free men must fully share.

I therefore ask the Congress, above and beyond the increases I have earlier requested for space activities, to provide the funds which are needed to meet the following national goals:

First, I believe that this nation should commit itself to achieving the goal, before this decade is out, of landing a man on the moon and returning him safely to the earth. No single space project in this period will be more impressive to mankind, or more important for the long-range exploration of space; and none will be so difficult or expensive to accomplish. We propose to accelerate the development of the appropriate lunar space craft. We propose to develop alternate liquid and solid fuel boosters, much larger than any now being developed, until certain which is superior....

It is a most important decision that we make as a nation. But all of you have lived through the last four years and have seen the significance of space and the adventures in space, and no one can predict with certainty what the ultimate meaning will be of mastery of space.

Duty, Honor, Country

General Douglas MacArthur   May 12, 1962

General MacArthur accepted the Sylvanus Thayer Award and delivered this memorable speech to the cadets at West Point, regarded as one of the greatest speeches ever given. MacArthur had been in the Army his entire life and was instrumental in defeating the Japanese in World War II and guiding them back to prosperity after the war. He led our forces in the Korean War until a dispute with President Truman ended his career. When he gave this speech in 1962, he was 82 years old and spoke without notes. Following are excerpts from that speech.

Duty, honor, country: Those three hallowed words reverently dictate what you ought to be, what you can be, what you will be. They are your rallying point to build courage when courage seems to fail, to regain faith when there seems to be little cause for faith, to create hope when hope becomes forlorn…. They build your basic character. They mold you for your future roles as the custodians of the Nation's defense. They make you strong enough to know when you are weak, and brave enough to face yourself when you are afraid…. And what sort of soldiers are those you are to lead? Are they reliable? Are they brave? Are they capable of victory?

Their story is known to all of you. **It is the story of the American man-at-arms. My estimate of him was formed on the battlefield many, many years ago, and has never changed. I regarded him then, as I regard him now, as one of the world's noblest figures; not only as one of the finest military characters, but also as one of the most stainless.**

His name and fame are the birthright of every American citizen. In his youth and strength, his love and loyalty, he gave all that mortality can give. He needs no eulogy from me; or from any other man. He has written his own history and written it in red on his enemy's breast.

But when I think of his patience in adversity of his courage under fire and of his modesty in victory, I am filled with an emotion of admiration I cannot put into words. He belongs to history as furnishing one of the greatest examples of successful patriotism. He belongs to posterity as the instructor of future generations in the principles of liberty and freedom. He belongs to the present, to us, by his virtues and by his achievements.

In 20 campaigns, on a hundred battlefields, around a thousand camp fires, I have witnessed that enduring fortitude, that patriotic self-abnegation, and that invincible determination which have carved his statue in the hearts of his people...

I do not know the dignity of their birth, but I do know the glory of their death. They died, unquestioning, uncomplaining, with faith in their hearts, and on their lips the hope that we would go on to victory. Always for them: Duty, Honor, Country. Always their blood, and sweat, and tears, as they saw the way and the light...

The long gray line has never failed us. Were you to do so, a million ghosts in olive drab, in brown khaki, in blue and gray, would rise from their white crosses, thundering those magic words: Duty, Honor, Country.

This does not mean that you are warmongers. On the contrary, the soldier above all other people prays for peace, for he must suffer and bear the deepest wounds and scars of war.

The shadows are lengthening for me. The twilight is here. My days of old have vanished—tone and tint. They have gone glimmering through the dreams of things that were. Their memory is one of wondrous beauty, watered by tears and coaxed and caressed by the smiles of yesterday. I listen vainly, but with thirsty ear, for the witching melody of faint bugles blowing reveille, of far drums beating the long roll.

In my dreams I hear again the crash of guns, the rattle of musketry, the strange, mournful mutter of the battlefield. But in the evening of my memory always I come back to West Point. Always there echoes and re-echoes: Duty, honor, country. Today marks my final roll call with you. **But I want you to know that when I cross the river, my last conscious thoughts will be of the corps, and the corps, and the corps.**

I bid you farewell.

———————————— ❦ ————————————

The world has turned over many times since I took the oath on the plain at West Point, and the hopes and dreams have long since vanished, but I still remember the refrain of one of the most popular barrack ballads of that day which proclaimed most proudly that "old soldiers never die; they just fade away." And like the old soldier of that ballad, I now close my military career and just fade away, an old soldier who tried to do his duty as God gave him the light to see that duty.

—*General Douglas MacArthur, 1951 Farewell Address*

I Have a Dream

Dr. Martin Luther King   **August 28, 1963**

Dr. King delivered this speech on the steps of the Lincoln Memorial during the height of the Civil Rights Movement. Over 200,000 supporters had gathered to hear the speech. He called for an end to racial discrimination. This speech has been ranked by many as the top American speech of the century. No discussion on civil rights in America is complete without this speech.

I am happy to join with you today in what will go down in history as the greatest demonstration for freedom in the history of our nation.

Five score years ago, a great American, in whose symbolic shadow we stand today, signed the Emancipation Proclamation. This momentous decree came as a great beacon light of hope to millions of Negro slaves who had been seared in the flames of withering injustice. It came as a joyous daybreak to end the long night of their captivity.

But one hundred years later, the Negro still is not free. One hundred years later, the life of the Negro is still sadly crippled by the manacles of segregation and the chains of discrimination. One hundred years later, the Negro lives on a lonely island of poverty in the midst of a vast ocean of material prosperity. One hundred years later, the Negro is still languished in the corners of American society and finds himself an exile in his own land. And so we've come here today to dramatize a shameful condition.

In a sense we've come to our nation's capital to cash a check. When the architects of our republic wrote the magnificent words of the Constitution and the Declaration of Independence, they were signing a promissory note to which every American was to fall heir. This note was a promise that all men, yes, black men as well as white men, would be guaranteed the "unalienable Rights" of "Life, Liberty and the pursuit of Happiness." It is obvious today that America has defaulted on this promissory note, insofar as her citizens of color are concerned. Instead of honoring this sacred obligation, America has given the Negro people a bad check, a check which has come back marked "insufficient funds."

But we refuse to believe that the bank of justice is bankrupt. We refuse to believe that there are insufficient funds in the great vaults of opportunity of this nation. And so, we've come to cash this check, a check that will give us upon demand the riches of freedom and the security of justice.

We have also come to this hallowed spot to remind America of the fierce urgency of Now. This is no time to engage in the luxury of cooling off or to take the tranquilizing drug of gradualism. Now is the time to make real the promises of democracy. Now is the time to rise from the dark and desolate valley of segregation to the sunlit path of racial justice. Now is the time to lift our nation from the quicksands of racial injustice to the solid rock of brotherhood. Now is the time to make justice a reality for all of God's children.

It would be fatal for the nation to overlook the urgency of the moment. This sweltering summer of the Negro's legitimate discontent will not pass until there is an invigorating autumn of freedom and equality. Nineteen sixty-three is not an end, but a beginning. And those who hope that the Negro needed to blow off steam and will now be content will have a rude awakening if the nation returns to business as usual. And there will be neither rest nor tranquility in America until the Negro is granted his citizenship rights. The whirlwinds of revolt will continue to shake the foundations of our nation until the bright day of justice emerges.

But there is something that I must say to my people, who stand on the warm threshold which leads into the palace of justice: In the process of gaining our rightful place, we must not be guilty of wrongful deeds. Let us not seek to satisfy our thirst for freedom by drinking from the cup of bitterness and hatred. We must forever conduct our struggle on the high plane of dignity and discipline. We must not allow our creative protest to degenerate into physical violence. Again and again, we must rise to the majestic heights of meeting physical force with soul force.

The marvelous new militancy which has engulfed the Negro community must not lead us to a distrust of all white people, for many of our white brothers, as evidenced by their presence here today, have come to realize that their destiny is tied up with our destiny. And they have come to realize that their freedom is inextricably bound to our freedom.

We cannot walk alone. And as we walk, we must make the pledge that we shall always march ahead. We cannot turn back.

There are those who are asking the devotees of civil rights, "When will you be satisfied?" We can never be satisfied as long as the Negro is the victim of the unspeakable horrors of police brutality. We can never be satisfied as long as our bodies, heavy with the fatigue of travel, cannot gain lodging in the motels of the highways and the hotels of the cities. We cannot be satisfied as long as the Negro's basic mobility is from a smaller ghetto to a larger one. We can never be satisfied as long as our children are stripped of their self-hood and robbed of their dignity by a sign stating: "For Whites Only." We cannot be satisfied as long as a Negro in Mississippi cannot vote and a Negro in New York believes he has nothing for which to vote. No, no, we are not satisfied, and we will not be satisfied until "justice rolls down like waters, and righteousness like a mighty stream."

I am not unmindful that some of you have come here out of great trials and tribulations. Some of you have come fresh from narrow jail cells. And some of you have come from areas where your quest—quest for freedom left you battered by the storms of persecution and staggered by the winds of police brutality. You have been the veterans of creative suffering. Continue to work with the faith that unearned suffering is redemptive. Go back to Mississippi, go back to Alabama, go back to South Carolina, go back to Georgia, go back to Louisiana, go back to the slums and ghettos of our northern cities, knowing that somehow this situation can and will be changed.

Let us not wallow in the valley of despair, I say to you today, my friends. And so even though we face the difficulties of today and tomorrow, I still have a dream. It is a dream deeply rooted in the American dream.

I have a dream that one day this nation will rise up and live out the true meaning of its creed: "We hold these truths to be self-evident, that all men are created equal."

I have a dream that one day on the red hills of Georgia, the sons of former slaves and the sons of former slave owners will be able to sit down together at the table of brotherhood.

I have a dream that one day even the state of Mississippi, a state sweltering with the heat of injustice, sweltering with the heat of oppression, will be transformed into an oasis of freedom and justice.

I have a dream that my four little children will one day live in a nation where they will not be judged by the color of their skin but by the content of their character.

I have a dream today! I have a dream that one day, down in Alabama, with its vicious racists, with its governor having his lips dripping with the words of "interposition" and "nullification"—one day right there in Alabama little black boys and black girls will be able to join hands with little white boys and white girls as sisters and brothers.

I have a dream today! I have a dream that one day every valley shall be exalted, and every hill and mountain shall be made low, the rough places will be made plain, and the crooked places will be made straight; "and the glory of the Lord shall be revealed and all flesh shall see it together."

This is our hope, and this is the faith that I go back to the South with. With this faith, we will be able to hew out of the mountain of despair a stone of hope. With this faith, we will be able to transform the jangling discords of our nation into a beautiful symphony of brotherhood. With this faith, we will be able to work together, to pray together, to struggle together, to go to jail together, to stand up for freedom together, knowing that we will be free one day.

And this will be the day – this will be the day when all of God's children will be able to sing with new meaning: My country 'tis of thee, sweet land of liberty, of thee I sing. Land where my fathers died, land of the Pilgrim's pride, From every mountainside, let freedom ring!

And if America is to be a great nation, this must become true.

And so let freedom ring from the prodigious hilltops of New Hampshire. Let freedom ring from the mighty mountains of New York. Let freedom ring from the heightening Alleghenies of Pennsylvania. Let freedom ring from the snow-capped Rockies of Colorado. Let freedom ring from the curvaceous slopes of California.

But not only that: Let freedom ring from Stone Mountain of Georgia. Let freedom ring from Lookout Mountain of Tennessee. Let freedom ring from every hill and molehill of Mississippi. From every mountainside, let freedom ring.

And when this happens, when we allow freedom ring, when we let it ring from every village and every hamlet, from every state and every city, we will be able to speed up that day when all of God's children, black men and white men, Jews and Gentiles, Protestants and Catholics, will be able to join hands and sing in the words of the old Negro spiritual:

Free at last! Free at last!

Thank God Almighty, we are free at last!

MESSAGE TO CONGRESS

LYNDON JOHNSON   MARCH 15, 1965

> The Civil Rights Act had been passed the year before, but just a few
> days before this speech, police had beaten civil rights protestors in
> Selma, Alabama. Johnson wanted to address the nation about those
> actions, and also push for the passage of the Voting Rights Act to
> protect the voting rights of all Americans. That act was passed later in
> 1965. Excerpts from his speech follow.

At times history and fate meet at a single time in a single place
to shape a turning point in man's unending search for freedom. So
it was at Lexington and Concord. So it was a century ago at Appomattox. So it was last week in Selma, Alabama.

There, long-suffering men and women peacefully protested the
denial of their rights as Americans. Many were brutally assaulted.
One good man, a man of God, was killed.

There is no cause for pride in what has happened in Selma.
There is no cause for self-satisfaction in the long denial of equal
rights of millions of Americans. But there is cause for hope and
for faith in our democracy in what is happening here tonight....

Rarely are we met with a challenge, not to our growth or abundance, our welfare or our security, but rather to the values and the
purposes and the meaning of our beloved Nation.

The issue of equal rights for American Negroes is such an issue. **And should we defeat every enemy, should we double our
wealth and conquer the stars, and still be unequal to this issue, then we will have failed as a people and as a nation.**

For with a country as with a person, "What is a man profited, if
he shall gain the whole world, and lose his own soul?"

**There is no Negro problem. There is no Southern prob-
lem. There is no Northern problem. There is only an American problem**. And we are met here tonight as Americans—not
as Democrats or Republicans—we are met here as Americans to
solve that problem.

This was the first nation in the history of the world to be founded with a purpose. The great phrases of that purpose still sound
in every American heart, North and South: "All men are created
equal" - "government by consent of the governed"-"give me liberty or give me death." Well, those are not just clever words, or
those are not just empty theories. In their name Americans have

fought and died for two centuries, and tonight around the world they stand there as guardians of our liberty, risking their lives.

Those words are a promise to every citizen that he shall share in the dignity of man. This dignity cannot be found in a man's possessions; it cannot be found in his power, or in his position. It really rests on his right to be treated as a man equal in opportunity to all others. It says that he shall share in freedom, he shall choose his leaders, educate his children, and provide for his family according to his ability and his merits as a human being.

To apply any other test—to deny a man his hopes because of his color or race, his religion or the place of his birth—is not only to do injustice, it is to deny America and to dishonor the dead who gave their lives for American freedom.…

Yet the harsh Act is that in many places in this country men and women are kept from voting simply because they are Negroes.

Every device of which human ingenuity is capable has been used to deny this right. The Negro citizen may go to register only to be told that the day is wrong, or the hour is late, or the official in charge is absent And if he persists, and if he manages to present himself to the registrar, he may be disqualified because he did not spell out his middle name or because he abbreviated a word on the application. And if he manages to fill out an application he is given a test. The registrar is the sole judge of whether he passes this test. He may be asked to recite the entire Constitution, or explain the most complex provisions of State law. And even a college degree cannot be used to prove that he can read and write.

For the fact is that the only way to pass these barriers is to show a white skin. Experience has clearly shown that the existing process of law cannot overcome systematic and ingenious discrimination. No law that we now have on the books—and I have helped to put three of them there—can ensure the right to vote when local officials are determined to deny it.

In such a case our duty must be clear to all of us. The Constitution says that no person shall be kept from voting because of his race or his color. We have all sworn an oath before God to support and to defend that Constitution. We must now act in obedience to that oath.

Wednesday I will send to Congress a law designed to eliminate illegal barriers to the right to vote...

This bill will strike down restrictions to voting in all elections —Federal, State, and local—which have been used to deny Negroes the right to vote.

This bill will establish a simple, uniform standard which cannot be used, however ingenious the effort, to flout our Constitution.

It will provide for citizens to be registered by officials of the United States Government if the State officials refuse to register them....

There is no moral issue. It is wrong—deadly wrong—to deny any of your fellow Americans the right to vote in this country. **There is no issue of States rights or national rights. There is only the struggle for human rights.**

I have not the slightest doubt what will be your answer....

But even if we pass this bill, the battle will not be over. What happened in Selma is part of a far larger movement which reaches into every section and State of America. It is the effort of American Negroes to secure for themselves the full blessings of American life.

Their cause must be our cause too. Because it is not just Negroes, but really it is all of us, who must overcome the crippling legacy of bigotry and injustice. And we shall overcome.

As a man whose roots go deeply into Southern soil I know how agonizing racial feelings are. I know how difficult it is to reshape the attitudes and the structure of our society.

But a century has passed, more than a hundred years, since the Negro was freed. And he is not fully free tonight.

It was more than a hundred years ago that Abraham Lincoln, a great President of another party, signed the Emancipation Proclamation, but emancipation is a proclamation and not a fact.

A century has passed, more than a hundred years, since equality was promised. And yet the Negro is not equal...

In giving rights to others which belong to them, we give rights to ourselves and to our country.

—*John F. Kennedy*

THE AMERICANS

GORDON SINCLAIR   JUNE 5, 1973

A Canadian radio commentator had finally heard enough bash-
ing of Americans and made the following broadcast. Another
foreigner gets it right.

The United States dollar took another pounding on German,
French and British exchanges this morning, hitting the lowest
point ever known in West Germany. It has declined there by 41%
since 1971 and **this Canadian thinks it is time to speak up for
the Americans as the most generous and possibly the least-
appreciated people in all the world.**

As long as sixty years ago, when I first started to read newspapers, I read of floods on the Yellow River and the Yangtze. Well,
Who rushed in with men and money to help? The Americans did,
that's who.

They have helped control floods on the Nile, the Amazon, the
Ganges and the Niger. Today, the rich bottom land of the Mississippi is under water and no foreign land has sent a dollar to help.
Germany, Japan and, to a lesser extent, Britain and Italy, were
lifted out of the debris of war by the Americans who poured in billions of dollars and forgave other billions in debts. None of those
countries is today paying even the interest on its remaining debts
to the United States.

When the franc was in danger of collapsing in 1956, it was the
Americans who propped it up and their reward was to be insulted
and swindled on the streets of Paris. And I was there. I saw that.

When distant cities are hit by earthquakes, it is the United
States that hurries into help...Managua Nicaragua is one of the
most recent examples. So far this spring, 59 American communities have been flattened by tornadoes. Nobody has helped.

The Marshall Plan...the Truman Policy...all pumped billions
upon billions of dollars into discouraged countries. And now,
newspapers in those countries are writing about the decadent war-
mongering Americans.

I'd like to see one of those countries that is gloating over the
erosion of the United States dollar build its own airplanes.

Come on...let's hear it! Does any other country in the world
have a plane to equal the Boeing Jumbo Jet, the Lockheed Tristar
or the Douglas 10? If so, why don't they fly them? Why do all

international lines except Russia fly American planes? Why does no other land on earth even consider putting a man or a women on the moon?

You talk about Japanese technocracy and you get radios. You talk about German technocracy and you get automobiles. You talk about American technocracy and you find men on the moon, not once, but several times…and safely home again. You talk about scandals and the Americans put theirs right in the store window for everybody to look at. Even the draft dodgers are not pursued and hounded. They are right here on our streets in Toronto, most of them…unless they are breaking Canadian laws…are getting American dollars from Ma and Pa at home to spend here.

When the Americans get out of this bind…as they will…who could blame them if they said 'the hell with the rest of the world'. Let someone else buy the bonds, let someone else build or repair foreign dams or design foreign buildings that won't shake apart in earthquakes.

When the railways of France, Germany and India were breaking down through age, it was the Americans who rebuilt them. When the Pennsylvania Railroad and the New York Central went broke, nobody loaned them an old caboose. Both of them are still broke. I can name to you 5,000 times when the Americans raced to the help of other people in trouble.

Can you name to me even one time when someone else raced to the Americans in trouble? I don't think there was outside help even during the San Francisco earthquake.

Our neighbors have faced it alone and I am one Canadian who is damned tired of hearing them kicked around. They will come out of this thing with their flag high. And when they do, they are entitled to thumb their noses at the lands that are gloating over their present troubles.

I hope Canada is not one of these. But there are many smug, self-righteous Canadians. And finally, the American Red Cross was told at its 48th Annual meeting in New Orleans this morning that it was broke.

This year's disasters…with the year less than half-over…has taken it all and nobody…but nobody…has helped.

FIRST INAUGURAL ADDRESS

RONALD REAGAN   JANUARY 20, 1981

> The inauguration was held on the west terrace of the Capitol for the
> first time. On the same day, Iran released our hostages that had been
> held for a year. Reagan warns of the dangers of too much government,
> and bluntly states that "government is not the solution."

To a few of us here today, this is a solemn and most momentous
occasion; and yet, in the history of our Nation, it is a common-
place occurrence. The orderly transfer of authority as called for
in the Constitution routinely takes place as it has for almost two
centuries and few of us stop to think how unique we really are.
In the eyes of many in the world, this every-4-year ceremony we
accept as normal is nothing less than a miracle....

**In this present crisis, government is not the solution to our
problem.** From time to time, we have been tempted to believe
that society has become too complex to be managed by self-rule,
that government by an elite group is superior to government for,
by, and of the people. But if no one among us is capable of governing himself, then who among us has the capacity to govern
someone else? All of us together, in and out of government, must
bear the burden. The solutions we seek must be equitable, with no
one group singled out to pay a higher price...

So, as we begin, let us take inventory. **We are a nation that
has a government—not the other way around. And this makes
us special among the nations of the Earth. Our Government
has no power except that granted it by the people. It is time
to check and reverse the growth of government which shows
signs of having grown beyond the consent of the governed.**

It is my intention to curb the size and influence of the Federal
establishment and to demand recognition of the distinction between the powers granted to the Federal Government and those
reserved to the States or to the people. All of us need to be reminded that **the Federal Government did not create the States;
the States created the Federal Government.**

Now, so there will be no misunderstanding, it is not my intention to do away with government. It is, rather, to make it work—
work with us, not over us; to stand by our side, not ride on our
back. Government can and must provide opportunity, not smother
it; foster productivity, not stifle it.

If we look to the answer as to why, for so many years, we achieved so much, prospered as no other people on Earth, it was because here, in this land, we unleashed the energy and individual genius of man to a greater extent than has ever been done before. Freedom and the dignity of the individual have been more available and assured here than in any other place on Earth. The price for this freedom at times has been high, but we have never been unwilling to pay that price.

It is no coincidence that our present troubles parallel and are proportionate to the intervention and intrusion in our lives that result from unnecessary and excessive growth of government. It is time for us to realize that we are too great a nation to limit ourselves to small dreams. We are not, as some would have us believe, doomed to an inevitable decline. I do not believe in a fate that will fall on us no matter what we do. I do believe in a fate that will fall on us if we do nothing. So, with all the creative energy at our command, let us begin an era of national renewal. Let us renew our determination, our courage, and our strength. And let us renew our faith and our hope…

To those neighbors and allies who share our freedom, we will strengthen our historic ties and assure them of our support and firm commitment. We will match loyalty with loyalty. We will strive for mutually beneficial relations. We will not use our friendship to impose on their sovereignty, for our own sovereignty is not for sale.

As for the enemies of freedom, those who are potential adversaries, they will be reminded that peace is the highest aspiration of the American people. We will negotiate for it, sacrifice for it; we will not surrender for it—now or ever.

Our forbearance should never be misunderstood. Our reluctance for conflict should not be misjudged as a failure of will. When action is required to preserve our national security, we will act. **We will maintain sufficient strength to prevail if need be, knowing that if we do so we have the best chance of never having to use that strength.**

Above all, we must realize that no arsenal, or no weapon in the arsenals of the world, is so formidable as the will and moral courage of free men and women. It is a weapon our adversaries in today's world do not have. It is a weapon that we as Americans do have. Let that be understood by those who practice terrorism and prey upon their neighbors…

EVIL EMPIRE SPEECH

RONALD REAGAN   MARCH 8, 1983

President Reagan delivered this speech to a meeting of the National Association of Evangelicals in Orlando, Florida. It referred to communism as an evil empire and focus of evil, and became known as his "Evil Empire Speech." Congress was debating a resolution in support of a "nuclear freeze" that would have prevented the deployment of U.S. missiles in Europe. The president had added the stronger wording to the speech the day before, and those words turned it into a history-making and regime-changing speech. The press and many politicians at the time were appalled at his boldness, but history has proven that Reagan was right on the mark. Following are excerpts from that speech.

Well, I think the refusal of many influential people to accept this elementary fact of Soviet doctrine illustrates an historical reluctance to see totalitarian powers for what they are. We saw this phenomenon in the 1930s. We see it too often today.

This doesn't mean we should isolate ourselves and refuse to seek an understanding with them. I intend to do everything I can to persuade them of our peaceful intent, to remind them that it was **the West that refused to use its nuclear monopoly in the forties and fifties for territorial gain** and which now proposes 50-percent cut in strategic ballistic missiles and the elimination of an entire class of land-based, intermediate-range nuclear missiles.

At the same time, however, they must be made to understand we will never compromise our principles and standards. We will never give away our freedom. We will never abandon our belief in God. And we will never stop searching for a genuine peace. But we can assure none of these things America stands for through the so-called nuclear freeze solutions proposed by some.

The truth is that a freeze now would be a very dangerous fraud, for that is merely the illusion of peace. The reality is that we must find peace through strength.

I would agree to a freeze if only we could freeze the Soviets' global desires. A freeze at current levels of weapons would remove any incentive for the Soviets to negotiate seriously in Geneva and virtually end our chances to achieve the major arms reductions which we have proposed. Instead, they would achieve their objectives through the freeze.

A freeze would reward the Soviet Union for its enormous and unparalleled military buildup. It would prevent the essential and long overdue modernization of United States and allied defenses and would leave our aging forces increasingly vulnerable. And an honest freeze would require extensive prior negotiations on the systems and numbers to be limited and on the measures to ensure effective verification and compliance. And the kind of a freeze that has been suggested would be virtually impossible to verify. Such a major effort would divert us completely from our current negotiations on achieving substantial reductions....

But if history teaches anything, it teaches that simple-minded appeasement or wishful thinking about our adversaries is folly. It means the betrayal of our past, the squandering of our freedom.

So, I urge you to speak out against those who would place the United States in a position of military and moral inferiority....So, in your discussions of the nuclear freeze proposals, I urge you to beware the temptation of pride—the temptation of blithely declaring yourselves above it all and label both sides equally at fault, to ignore the facts of history and the aggressive impulses of an **evil empire**, to simply call the arms race a giant misunderstanding and thereby remove yourself from the struggle between right and wrong and good and evil.

I ask you to resist the attempts of those who would have you withhold your support for our efforts, this administration's efforts, to keep America strong and free, **while we negotiate real and verifiable reductions in the world's nuclear arsenals and one day, with God's help, their total elimination.**

While America's military strength is important, let me add here that I've always maintained that the struggle now going on for the world will never be decided by bombs or rockets, by armies or military might. The real crisis we face today is a spiritual one; at root, it is a test of moral will and faith....

I believe we shall rise to the challenge. I believe that communism is another sad, bizarre chapter in human history whose last pages even now are being written. I believe this because the source of our strength in the quest for human freedom is not material, but spiritual. And because it knows no limitation, it must terrify and ultimately triumph over those who would enslave their fellow man....

POINTE DU HOC SPEECH

RONALD REAGAN   JUNE 6, 1984

At the ceremony to honor the 50th anniversary of the D-Day invasion at Normandy, President Reagan delivered a stirring speech honoring the Rangers that scaled the cliffs of Pointe du Hoc in the face of relentless German fire. They suffered 60% casualties in two days of fighting. This speech is an example of Reagan's carrot-and-stick approach to the Soviets; as he praised their actions and welcomed their friendship, he was also strengthening the American military.

We're here to mark that day in history when the Allied armies joined in battle to reclaim this continent to liberty. For four long years, much of Europe had been under a terrible shadow. Free nations had fallen, Jews cried out in the camps, millions cried out for liberation. Europe was enslaved, and the world prayed for its rescue. Here in Normandy the rescue began. Here the Allies stood and fought against tyranny in a giant undertaking unparalleled in human history.

We stand on a lonely, windswept point on the northern shore of France. The air is soft, but forty years ago at this moment, the air was dense with smoke and the cries of men, and the air was filled with the crack of rifle fire and the roar of cannon. At dawn, on the morning of the 6th of June, 1944, 225 Rangers jumped off the British landing craft and ran to the bottom of these cliffs. Their mission was one of the most difficult and daring of the invasion: to climb these sheer and desolate cliffs and take out the enemy guns. The Allies had been told that some of the mightiest of these guns were here and they would be trained on the beaches to stop the Allied advance.

The Rangers looked up and saw the enemy soldiers - at the edge of the cliffs shooting down at them with machine guns and throwing grenades. And the American Rangers began to climb. They shot rope ladders over the face of these cliffs and began to pull themselves up. When one Ranger fell, another would take his place. When one rope was cut, a Ranger would grab another and begin his climb again. They climbed, shot back, and held their footing. **Soon, one by one, the Rangers pulled themselves over the top, and in seizing the firm land at the top of these cliffs, they began to seize back the continent of Europe.** Two hundred and twenty-five came here. After two days of fighting, only ninety could still bear arms.

Behind me is a memorial that symbolizes the Ranger daggers that were thrust into the top of these cliffs. And before me are the men who put them there. **These are the boys of Pointe du Hoc. These are the men who took the cliffs. These are the champions who helped free a continent. These are the heroes who helped end a war.**

Gentlemen, I look at you and I think of the words of Stephen Spender's poem. You are men who in your "lives fought for life... and left the vivid air singed with your honor."...

Forty summers have passed since the battle that you fought here. You were young the day you took these cliffs; some of you were hardly more than boys, with the deepest joys of life before you. Yet, you risked everything here. Why? Why did you do it? What impelled you to put aside the instinct for self-preservation and risk your lives to take these cliffs? What inspired all the men of the armies that met here? We look at you, and somehow we know the answer. It was faith and belief; it was loyalty and love.

The men of Normandy had faith that what they were doing was right, faith that they fought for all humanity, faith that a just God would grant them mercy on this beachhead or on the next. It was the deep knowledge—and pray God we have not lost it—**that there is a profound moral difference between the use of force for liberation and the use of force for conquest. You were here to liberate, not to conquer, and so you and those others did not doubt your cause. And you were right not to doubt.**

You all knew that some things are worth dying for. One's country is worth dying for, and democracy is worth dying for, because it's the most deeply honorable form of government ever devised by man. All of you loved liberty. All of you were willing to fight tyranny, and you knew the people of your countries were behind you....

In spite of our great efforts and successes, not all that followed the end of the war was happy or planned. Some liberated countries were lost. The great sadness of this loss echoes down to our own time in the streets of Warsaw, Prague, and East Berlin. **Soviet troops that come to the center of this continent did not leave when peace came. They're still there, uninvited, unwanted, unyielding, almost forty years after the war. Because of this, allied forces still stand on this continent. Today, as forty years ago, our armies are here for only one purpose—to protect and defend democracy. The only territories we hold are memorials like this one and graveyards where our heroes rest....**

We in America have learned bitter lessons from two world wars: It is better to be here ready to protect the peace, than to take blind shelter across the sea, rushing to respond only after freedom is lost. We've learned that isolationism never was and never will be an acceptable response to tyrannical governments with an expansionist intent.

But we try always to be prepared for peace; prepared to deter aggression; prepared to negotiate the reduction of arms; and yes, prepared to reach out again in the spirit of reconciliation. **In truth, there is no reconciliation we would welcome more than a reconciliation with the Soviet Union, so, together we can lessen the risks of war, now and forever.**

It's fitting to remember here the great losses also suffered by the Russian people during World War II: 20 million perished, a terrible price that testifies to all the world the necessity of ending war. **I tell you from my heart that we in the United States do not want war. We want to wipe from the face of the earth the terrible weapons that man now has in his hands.** And I tell you, we are ready to seize that beachhead. We look for some sign from the Soviet Union that they are willing to move forward, that they share our desire and love for peace, and that they will give up the ways of conquest. There must be a changing there that will allow us to turn our hope into action.

We will pray forever that someday that changing will come. But for now, particularly today, it is good and fitting to renew our commitment to each other, to our freedom, and to the alliance that protects it.

We are bound today by what bound us forty years ago, the same loyalties, traditions, and beliefs. We're bound by reality. The strength of America's allies is vital to the United States, and the American security guarantee is essential to the continued freedom of Europe's democracies. We were with you then; we are with you now. Your hopes are our hopes, and your destiny is our destiny.

Here, in this place where the West held together, let us make a vow to our dead. Let us show them by our actions that we understand what they died for. Let our actions say to them the words for which Matthew Ridgway listened: "I will not fail thee nor forsake thee."

Strengthened by their courage, heartened by their valor and borne by their memory, let us continue to stand for the ideals for which they lived and died.

Thank you very much, and God bless you all.

CHALLENGER DISASTER

RONALD REAGAN   JANUARY 28, 1986

The Space Shuttle Challenger took off from Florida this day on a mission into orbit with seven people onboard, including teacher Christa McAuliffe, the first non-astronaut into space. A little more than one minute into its flight, the rocket blew up, destroying the shuttle and killing all on board. President Reagan addressed the nation that night.

Ladies and Gentlemen, I'd planned to speak to you tonight to report on the state of the Union, but the events of earlier today have led me to change those plans. Today is a day for mourning and remembering. Nancy and I are pained to the core by the tragedy of the shuttle Challenger. We know we share this pain with all of the people of our country. This is truly a national loss.

Nineteen years ago, almost to the day, we lost three astronauts in a terrible accident on the ground. But, we've never lost an astronaut in flight; we've never had a tragedy like this. And perhaps we've forgotten the courage it took for the crew of the shuttle; but they, the Challenger Seven, were aware of the dangers, but overcame them and did their jobs brilliantly. We mourn seven heroes: Michael Smith, Dick Scobee, Judith Resnik, Ronald McNair, Ellison Onizuka, Gregory Jarvis, and Christa McAuliffe. We mourn their loss as a nation together.

For the families of the seven, we cannot bear, as you do, the full impact of this tragedy. But we feel the loss, and we're thinking about you so very much. Your loved ones were daring and brave, and they had that special grace, that special spirit that says, 'Give me a challenge and I'll meet it with joy.' They had a hunger to explore the universe and discover its truths. They wished to serve, and they did. They served all of us.

We've grown used to wonders in this century. It's hard to dazzle us. But for twenty-five years the United States space program has been doing just that. We've grown used to the idea of space, and perhaps we forget that we've only just begun. We're still pioneers. They, the members of the Challenger crew, were pioneers.

And I want to say something to the schoolchildren of America who were watching the live coverage of the shuttle's takeoff. I know it is hard to understand, but sometimes painful things like this happen. It's all part of the process of exploration and discovery. It's all part of taking a chance and expanding man's horizons.

The future doesn't belong to the fainthearted; it belongs to the brave. The Challenger crew was pulling us into the future, and we'll continue to follow them.

I've always had great faith in and respect for our space program, and what happened today does nothing to diminish it. We don't hide our space program. We don't keep secrets and cover things up. We do it all up front and in public. That's the way freedom is, and we wouldn't change it for a minute. We'll continue our quest in space. There will be more shuttle flights and more shuttle crews and, yes, more volunteers, more civilians, more teachers in space. Nothing ends here; our hopes and our journeys continue. I want to add that I wish I could talk to every man and woman who works for NASA or who worked on this mission and tell them: "Your dedication and professionalism have moved and impressed us for decades. And we know of your anguish. We share it."

There's a coincidence today. On this day 390 years ago, the great explorer Sir Francis Drake died aboard ship off the coast of Panama. In his lifetime the great frontiers were the oceans, and a historian later said, 'He lived by the sea, died on it, and was buried in it.' Well, today we can say of the Challenger crew: Their dedication was, like Drake's, complete.

The crew of the space shuttle Challenger honoured us by the manner in which they lived their lives. **We will never forget them, nor the last time we saw them, this morning, as they prepared for the journey and waved goodbye and 'slipped the surly bonds of earth' to 'touch the face of God.'** Thank you.

(front) Michael J. Smith, Dick Scobee, Ronald McNair (back) Ellison Onizuka, Christa McAuliffe, Gregory Jarvis, Judith Resnik.

Tear Down This Wall

RONALD REAGAN   JUNE 12, 1987

At the end of World War II in 1945, Berlin was divided into 4 sectors:
American, British, French in the West, and Soviet in the East. Three
years later, the Soviets blockaded Berlin, and the West answered with
the year-long Berlin Airlift. In 1952, the Soviets finally closed the
border between East and West Germany, but more than 2.6 million
East Germans escaped to the West from 1949 to 1961. In 1961, the
Soviets erected the Berlin Wall to seal the border between East and
West Berlin. Over the next 28 years, 171 people will die attempting
to escape over or under the Berlin Wall. Following are excerpts from
Reagan's prophetic speech. His advisers had strongly urged him not to
include confrontational language. Fortunately, he ignored that advice.

Behind me stands a wall that encircles the free sectors of this
city, part of a vast system of barriers that divides the entire continent of Europe. From the Baltic, south, those barriers cut across
Germany in a gash of barbed wire, concrete, dog runs, and guard
towers. Farther south, there may be no visible, no obvious wall.
But there remain armed guards and checkpoints all the same—
still a restriction on the right to travel, still an instrument to impose upon ordinary men and women the will of a totalitarian state.
Yet it is here in Berlin where the wall emerges most clearly; here,
cutting across your city, where the news photo and the television
screen have imprinted this brutal division of a continent upon the
mind of the world. Standing before the Brandenburg Gate, every
man is a German, separated from his fellow men. Every man is a
Berliner, forced to look upon a scar....

Where four decades ago there was rubble, today in West Berlin
there is the greatest industrial output of any city in Germany—
busy office blocks, fine homes and apartments, proud avenues,
and the spreading lawns of park land. Where a city's culture
seemed to have been destroyed, today there are two great univer-
sities, orchestras and an opera, countless theatres, and museums.
Where there was want, today there's abundance—food, clothing,
automobiles—the wonderful goods of the Ku'damm. From devastation, from utter ruin, you Berliners have, in freedom, rebuilt
a city that once again ranks as one of the greatest on Earth. The
Soviets may have had other plans. But, my friends, there were a
few things the Soviets didn't count on—berliner Herz, berliner
Humor, ja, und berliner Schnauze. [Berliner heart, Berliner hu-
mour, yes, and a Berliner schnauze.]

In the 1950s, Khrushchev predicted: "We will bury you." But in the West today, we see a free world that has achieved a level of prosperity and well-being unprecedented in all human history. In the Communist world, we see failure, technological backwardness, declining standards of health, even want of the most basic kind—too little food. Even today, the Soviet Union still cannot feed itself. After these four decades, then, there stands before the entire world one great and inescapable conclusion: **Freedom leads to prosperity. Freedom replaces the ancient hatreds among the nations with comity and peace. Freedom is the victor.**

And now the Soviets themselves may, in a limited way, be coming to understand the importance of freedom. We hear much from Moscow about a new policy of reform and openness. Some political prisoners have been released. Certain foreign news broadcasts are no longer being jammed. Some economic enterprises have been permitted to operate with greater freedom from state control. Are these the beginnings of profound changes in the Soviet state? Or are they token gestures, intended to raise false hopes in the West, or to strengthen the Soviet system without changing it? We welcome change and openness; for we believe that freedom and security go together, that the advance of human liberty can only strengthen the cause of world peace.

There is one sign the Soviets can make that would be unmistakable, that would advance dramatically the cause of freedom and peace. General Secretary Gorbachev, if you seek peace, if you seek prosperity for the Soviet Union and Eastern Europe, if you seek liberalization: Come here to this gate! Mr. Gorbachev, open this gate! **Mr. Gorbachev, tear down this wall!...**

The Berlin Wall came down two years later on Nov. 9, 1989.

Ronald Reagan's "Tear down this wall!" speech
June 12, 1987

Berliners start to tear down the wall
November 10, 1989

FAREWELL ADDRESS

RONALD REAGAN   JANUARY 11, 1989

> President Reagan had served two terms and this was his last address
> to the Nation. He used the speech to re-emphasize the qualities of
> America and remind the citizens that the government works for them.
> His entreaty for everyone to learn their history was, in part, an inspi-
> ration for this book.

Well, back in 1980, when I was running for President, it was
all so different. Some pundits said our programs would result in
catastrophe. Our views on foreign affairs would cause war. Our
plans for the economy would cause inflation to soar and bring
about economic collapse. I even remember one highly respected
economist saying, back in 1982, that "The engines of economic
growth have shut down here, and they're likely to stay that way
for years to come." Well, he and the other opinion leaders were
wrong. The fact is what they call "radical" was really "right."
What they called "dangerous" was just "desperately needed."

And in all of that time I won a nickname, "The Great Communicator." But I never thought it was my style or the words I used
that made a difference: it was the content. **I wasn't a great communicator, but I communicated great things, and they didn't
spring full bloom from my brow, they came from the heart of
a great nation—from our experience, our wisdom, and our
belief in the principles that have guided us for two centuries**.
They called it the Reagan revolution. Well, I'll accept that, but for
me it always seemed more like the great rediscovery, a rediscovery of our values and our common sense.

**Common sense told us that when you put a big tax on some-
thing, the people will produce less of it.** So, we cut the people's
tax rates, and the people produced more than ever before. The
economy bloomed like a plant that had been cut back and could
now grow quicker and stronger. Our economic program brought
about the longest peacetime expansion in our history: real family income up, the poverty rate down, entrepreneurship booming, and an explosion in research and new technology. We're exporting more than ever because American industry became more
competitive and at the same time, we summoned the national
will to knock down protectionist walls abroad instead of erecting
them at home.

Common sense also told us that to preserve the peace,
we'd have to become strong again after years of weakness

and confusion. So, we rebuilt our defenses, and this New Year we toasted the new peacefulness around the globe...

Ours was the first revolution in the history of mankind that truly reversed the course of government, and with three little words: *We the People.* *We the People* **tell the government what to do; it doesn't tell us.** *We the People* **are the driver; the government is the car. And we decide where it should go, and by what route, and how fast. Almost all the world's constitutions are documents in which governments tell the people what their privileges are. Our Constitution is a document in which** *We the People* **tell the government what it is allowed to do.** *We the People* **are free. This belief has been the underlying basis for everything I've tried to do these past 8 years....**

Finally, there is a great tradition of warnings in Presidential farewells, and I've got one that's been on my mind for some time. But oddly enough it starts with one of the things I'm proudest of in the past 8 years: the resurgence of national pride that I called the new patriotism. This national feeling is good, but it won't count for much, and it won't last unless it's grounded in thoughtfulness and knowledge.

An informed patriotism is what we want. And are we doing a good enough job teaching our children what America is and what she represents in the long history of the world? Those of us who are over 35 or so years of age grew up in a different America. We were taught, very directly, what it means to be an American. And we absorbed, almost in the air, a love of country and an appreciation of its institutions. If you didn't get these things from your family you got them from the neighborhood, from the father down the street who fought in Korea or the family who lost someone at Anzio. Or you could get a sense of patriotism from school. And if all else failed you could get a sense of patriotism from the popular culture. The movies celebrated democratic values and implicitly reinforced the idea that America was special. TV was like that, too, through the mid-sixties.

But now, we're about to enter the nineties, and some things have changed. Younger parents aren't sure that an unambivalent appreciation of America is the right thing to teach modern children. And as for those who create the popular culture, wellgrounded patriotism is no longer the style. Our spirit is back, but we haven't reinstitutionalized it. We've got to do a better job of getting across that America is freedom—freedom of speech, freedom of religion, freedom of enterprise. And freedom is special and rare. It's fragile; it needs protection.

So, we've got to teach history based not on what's in fashion but what's important—why the Pilgrims came here, who Jimmy Doolittle was, and what those 30 seconds over Tokyo meant…And let me offer lesson number one about America: All great change in America begins at the dinner table. So, tomorrow night in the kitchen I hope the talking begins. And children, if your parents haven't been teaching you what it means to be an American, let 'em know and nail 'em on it. That would be a very American thing to do.

And that's about all I have to say tonight, except for one thing. The past few days when I've been at that window upstairs, I've thought a bit of the 'shining city upon a hill.' The phrase comes from John Winthrop, who wrote it to describe the America he imagined. What he imagined was important because he was an early Pilgrim, an early freedom man. He journeyed here on what today we'd call a little wooden boat; and like the other Pilgrims, he was looking for a home that would be free. I've spoken of the shining city all my political life, but I don't know if I ever quite communicated what I saw when I said it. But in my mind it was a tall, proud city built on rocks stronger than oceans, windswept, God-blessed, and teeming with people of all kinds living in harmony and peace; a city with free ports that hummed with commerce and creativity. And if there had to be city walls, the walls had doors and the doors were open to anyone with the will and the heart to get here. That's how I saw it, and see it still.

And how stands the city on this winter night? More prosperous, more secure, and happier than it was 8 years ago. But more than that: After 200 years, two centuries, she still stands strong and true on the granite ridge, and her glow has held steady no matter what storm. And she's still a beacon, still a magnet for all who must have freedom, for all the pilgrims from all the lost places who are hurtling through the darkness, toward home.

We've done our part. And as I walk off into the city streets, a final word to the men and women of the Reagan revolution, the men and women across America who for 8 years did the work that brought America back. My friends: We did it. We weren't just marking time. We made a difference. We made the city stronger, we made the city freer, and we left her in good hands. All in all, not bad, not bad at all. And so, goodbye, God bless you, and God bless the United States of America.

TERRORIST ATTACK SPEECH

GEORGE W. BUSH   SEPTEMBER 11, 2001

> Bush delivered this speech to the American people after the terrible
> and deadly attacks on the World Trade Center Towers and the Penta-
> gon. More than 3000 people had been killed, and the conflict between
> militant Islam and the West had been redefined. Terrorism had finally
> struck the American continent with a vengeance.

**Today, our fellow citizens, our way of life, our very freedom
came under attack in a series of deliberate and deadly terrorist acts.** The victims were in airplanes or in their offices: secre-
taries, business men and women, military and federal workers,
moms and dads, friends and neighbors. Thousands of lives were
suddenly ended by evil, despicable acts of terror. The pictures of
airplanes flying into buildings, fires burning, huge—huge structures collapsing have filled us with disbelief, terrible sadness,
and a quiet, unyielding anger. These acts of mass murder were
intended to frighten our nation into chaos and retreat. But they
have failed. Our country is strong.

**A great people has been moved to defend a great nation. Ter-
rorist attacks can shake the foundations of our biggest buildings, but they cannot touch the foundation of America.** These
acts shatter steel, but they cannot dent the steel of American resolve.
America was targeted for attack because we're the brightest beacon
for freedom and opportunity in the world. And no one will keep that
light from shining. Today, our nation saw evil—the very worst of
human nature—and we responded with the best of America. With
the daring of our rescue workers, with the caring for strangers and
neighbors who came to give blood and help in any way they could.

Immediately following the first attack, I implemented our government's emergency response plans. Our military is powerful,
and it's prepared. Our emergency teams are working in New York
City and Washington D.C. to help with local rescue efforts. Our
first priority is to get help to those who have been injured, and to
take every precaution to protect our citizens at home and around
the world from further attacks. The functions of our government
continue without interruption. Federal agencies in Washington
which had to be evacuated today are reopening for essential personnel tonight and will be open for business tomorrow. Our financial institutions remain strong, and the American economy will be
open for business as well.

The search is underway for those who were behind these evil acts. I have directed the full resources of our intelligence and law enforcement communities to find those responsible and to bring them to justice. We will make no distinction between the terrorists who committed these acts and those who harbor them.

I appreciate so very much the members of Congress who have joined me in strongly condemning these attacks. And on behalf of the American people, I thank the many world leaders who have called to offer their condolences and assistance. America and our friends and allies join with all those who want peace and security in the world, and we stand together to win the war against terrorism.

Tonight, I ask for your prayers for all those who grieve, for the children whose worlds have been shattered, for all whose sense of safety and security has been threatened. And I pray they will be comforted by a Power greater than any of us, spoken through the ages in Psalm 23:

Even though I walk through the valley of the shadow of death, I fear no evil for you are with me.

This is a day when all Americans from every walk of life unite in our resolve for justice and peace. America has stood down enemies before, and we will do so this time. None of us will ever forget this day, yet we go forward to defend freedom and all that is good and just in our world.

Thank you. Good night. And God bless America.

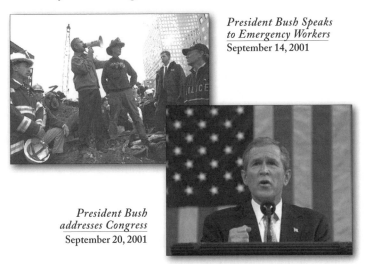

*President Bush Speaks
to Emergency Workers*
September 14, 2001

*President Bush
addresses Congress*
September 20, 2001

Yankee Stadium Prayer Service

| Mayor Rudolph Giuliani | September 23, 2001 |

The Mayor gave this speech at a service held at Yankee Stadium, shortly after the 9/11 bombing and destruction of the World Trade Centers, and the attack on the Pentagon.

On September 11th, New York City suffered the darkest day in our history. It is now up to us to make this our finest hour. Today we come together in the Capital of the World, as a united City. We're accompanied by religious leaders of every faith, to offer a prayer for the families of those who have been lost…to offer a prayer for our City…and to offer a prayer for America.

The proud Twin Towers that once crowned our famous skyline—no longer stand. But our skyline will rise again. In the words of President George W. Bush, "we will rebuild New York City." **To those who say that our City will never be the same, I say you are right. It will be better.**

Now we understand much more clearly why people from all over the globe want to come to New York, and to America…why they always have, and why they always will.

It's called freedom, equal protection under law, respect for human life, and the promise of opportunity. All of the victims of this tragedy were innocent. All of them were heroes.

The Bible says [John 15:13] "Greater love hath no man than this, that a man lay down his life for his friends." Our brave New York City Firefighters…New York City Police Officers…Port Authority Police Officers…EMS workers…health care workers…court officers…and uniformed service members…

They laid down their lives for strangers. They were inspired by their sense of duty and their love for humanity. As they raced into the Twin Towers and the other buildings to save lives, they didn't stop to ask how rich or poor the person was, they didn't stop to ask what religion, what race, what nationality. They just raced in to save their fellow human beings.

They are the best example of love that we have in our society. The people they were trying to rescue—the people who worked in the World Trade Center and the buildings around it—were each engaged in the quiet heroism of supporting their families, pursuing their dreams and playing their own meaningful part in a diverse, dynamic and free society. They represented more than 60 different nations. They will also occupy a permanent and sacred place in our history and in our hearts.

Even in the midst of the darkest tragedy there are miracles that help our faith to go on. I would like to share one miracle of September 11th with you.

St. Paul's Chapel is one of the oldest and most historic buildings in the City of New York. It was built in 1766, when the surrounding area was still countryside. The Chapel survived our war of independence—including seven years of wartime occupation.

After George Washington was inaugurated the first President of the United States, in New York City on April 30th, 1789, he walked to St. Paul's, and he kneeled down to pray. The pew where he worshipped is still there. Framed on the wall beside it is the oldest known representation of the Great Seal of the United States of America—it's a majestic eagle, holding in one talon an olive branch, proclaiming our abiding desire for peace…and in the other, a cluster of arrows, a forewarning of our determination to defend our liberty. On a banner above the Eagle is written E Pluribus Unum, "Out of Many, One."

For the past 25 years, the chapel stood directly in the shadow of the World Trade Center Towers. When the Towers fell, more than a dozen modern buildings were destroyed and damaged. Yet somehow, amid all the destruction and devastation, St. Paul's Chapel still stands…without so much as a broken window.

It's a small miracle in some ways, but the presence of that chapel standing defiant and serene amid the ruins of war sends an eloquent message about the strength and resilience of the people of New York City, and the people of America.

We unite under the banner of E Pluribus Unum. We find strength in our diversity. We're a city where people look different, talk different, think different. But we're a City at one with all of the people at the World Trade Center, and with all of America. We love our diversity, and we love our freedom.

Like our founding fathers who fought and died for freedom… like our ancestors who fought and died to preserve our union and to end the sin of slavery…like our fathers and grandfathers who fought and died to liberate the world from Nazism, and Fascism, and Communism…the cluster of arrows to defend our freedom, and the olive branch of peace have now been handed to us.

We will hold them firmly in our hands, honor their memory, and lift them up toward heaven to light the world.

In the days since this attack, we have met the worst of humanity with the best of humanity.

We pray for our President, George W. Bush…and for our Governor George Pataki…who have provided us with such inspiring leadership during these very, very difficult times. We pray for all of those whose loved ones are lost or missing…we pray for our children, and we say to them: "Do not be afraid. It's safe to live your life." Finally, we pray for America…and for all of those who join us in defending freedom, law, and humanity.

We humbly bow our heads and we ask God to bless the City of New York, and we ask God to bless the United States of America. Thank you.

U.S. FACTS   **Washington Monument** Work was started in 1848 but stopped repeatedly, including delays for the Civil War. It was finally finished in 1884 and, at 555 feet, was the tallest man-made structure in the world until the Eiffel Tower was built in 1889. It is made of marble blocks and both the color of the marble and the skill of assembling the tower changed abruptly halfway through the building process, result-ing in half the tower looking quite different from the other half—a two-tone tower.

Freedom is never more than one generation away from extinction. We didn't pass it to our children in the bloodstream. It must be fought for, protected, and handed on for them to do the same, or one day we will spend our sunset years telling our children and our children's children what it was once like in the United States where men were free.

—*Ronald Reagan*

Address to the Economic Forum

> Colin Powell was addressing the World Economic Forum in Swit-
> zerland shortly before the U.S. would attack Iraq. He was defending
> the American position on the use of military force against Saddam
> Hussein. He was questioned afterwards by the former Archbishop of
> Canterbury, George Carey, who felt that the U.S. should use more
> "soft power" to disarm Saddam, such as pushing moral and demo-
> cratic values without the use of force. Here is part of Powell's answer:

There is nothing in American experience or in American political
life or in our culture that suggests we want to use hard power. But
what we have found over the decades is that unless you do have
hard power, and here I think you're referring to military power, then
sometimes you are faced with situations that you can't deal with.

**I mean, it was not soft power that freed Europe. It was hard
power.** And what followed immediately after hard power? Did the
United States ask for dominion over a single nation in Europe? No.
Soft power came in the Marshall Plan. Soft power came with American GIs who put their weapons down once the war was over and
helped all those nations rebuild. We did the same thing in Japan.

So our record of living our values and letting our values be
an inspiration to others I think is clear. And I don't think I have
anything to be ashamed of or apologize for with respect to what
America has done for the world.

**We have gone forth from our shores repeatedly over the last
hundred years and we've done this as recently as the last year
in Afghanistan and put wonderful young men and women at
risk, many of whom have lost their lives, and we have asked for
nothing except enough ground to bury them in, and otherwise
we have returned home to seek our own, you know, to seek
our own lives in peace, to live our own lives in peace.** But there
comes a time when soft power or talking with evil will not work
where, unfortunately, hard power is the only thing that works.

It is worth saying once again that no nation has ever come into
the possession of such powers for good or ill, for freedom or tyranny, for friendship or enmity among the peoples of the world, and
that no nation in history has used those powers, by and large, with
greater vision, restraint, responsibility and courage.

—*London Times, 1954*

Address to the U.S. Congress

Iraq Prime Minister Ayad Allawi   September 23, 2004

> More than a year into the Iraq conflict, the new Prime Minister of Iraq
> came to the United States and spoke to our Congress about a number
> of issues. The initial fighting had been completed fairly quickly, but
> the violence continued, causing many to question whether the United
> States should even be in Iraq. The Prime Minister's words helped re-
> mind America of the reasons we were there.

Before I turn to my government's plan for Iraq, I have three important messages for you today.

First, we are succeeding in Iraq. It's a tough struggle with set-
backs, but we are succeeding. I have seen some of the images that
are being shown here on television. They are disturbing. They focus on the tragedies, such as the brutal and barbaric murder of two
American hostages this week.

We Iraqis are grateful to you, America, for your leadership and
your sacrifice for our liberation and our opportunity to start anew.

Third, I stand here today as the prime minister of a country
emerging finally from dark ages of violence, aggression, corruption
and greed. Like almost every Iraqi, I have many friends who were
murdered, tortured or raped by the regime of Saddam Hussein.

Well over a million Iraqis were murdered or are missing. We
estimate at least 300,000 in mass graves, which stands as monuments to the inhumanity of Saddam's regime. Thousands of my
Kurdish brothers and sisters were gassed to death by Saddam's
chemical weapons.

Millions more like me were driven into exile. Even in exile, as I
myself can vouch, we were not safe from Saddam.

And as we lived under tyranny at home, so our neighbors lived
in fear of Iraq's aggression and brutality. Reckless wars, use of
weapons of mass destruction, the needless loss of hundreds of
thousands of lives and the financing and exporting of terrorism,
these were Saddam's legacy to the world.

My friends, today we are better off, you are better off and the
world is better off without Saddam Hussein. Your decision to go
to war in Iraq was not an easy one but it was the right one.

**There are no words that can express the debt of gratitude that
future generations of Iraqis will owe to Americans. It would have
been easy to have turned your back on our plight, but this is not
the tradition of this great country, nor for the first time in history you stood up with your allies for freedom and democracy.**

Speech to the U.S. Congress

French President Nicolas Sarkozy November 7, 2007

The French President delivered this inspiring speech to the American Congress. It is a wonderful tribute from our French ally that helped this country win its independence. It's too bad that it took a foreigner to deliver such an eloquent praise of America. The following contains excerpts from his speech. It neatly summarizes what makes this country great and praises her contributions to the world.

The state of our friendship and our alliance is strong.

Friendship, first and foremost, means being true to one's friends. Since the United States first appeared on the world scene, the loyalty between the French and American people has never failed. And far from being weakened by the vicissitudes of History, it has never ceased growing stronger.

Friends may have differences; they may have disagreements; they may have disputes. But in times of difficulty, in times of hardship, friends stand together, side by side; they support each other; and help one another.

In times of difficulty, in times of hardship, America and France have always stood side by side, supported one another, helped one another, fought for each other's freedom....

From the very beginning, the American dream meant putting into practice the dreams of the Old World.

From the very beginning, the American dream meant proving to all mankind that freedom, justice, human rights and democracy were no utopia but were rather the most realistic policy there is and the most likely to improve the fate of each and every person.

America did not tell the millions of men and women who came from every country in the world and who—with their hands, their intelligence and their heart—built the greatest nation in the world: "Come, and everything will be given to you." She said: "Come, and the only limits to what you'll be able to achieve will be your own courage and your own talent." America embodies this extraordinary ability to grant each and every person a second chance.

Here, both the humblest and most illustrious citizens alike know that nothing is owed to them and that everything has to be earned. That's what constitutes the moral value of America. America did not teach men the idea of freedom; she taught them how to practice it. And she fought for this freedom whenever she felt it to be threatened somewhere in the world. It was by watching America grow that men and women understood that freedom was possible.

What made America great was her ability to transform her own dream into hope for all mankind.

The men and women of my generation heard their grandparents talk about how in 1917, America saved France at a time when it had reached the final limits of its strength, which it had exhausted in the most absurd and bloodiest of wars.

The men and women of my generation heard their parents talk about how in 1944, America returned to free Europe from the horrifying tyranny that threatened to enslave it.

Fathers took their sons to see the vast cemeteries where, under thousands of white crosses so far from home, thousands of young American soldiers lay who had fallen not to defend their own freedom but the freedom of all others, not to defend their own families, their own homeland, but to defend humanity as a whole.

Fathers took their sons to the beaches where the young men of America had so heroically landed. They read them the admirable letters of farewell that those 20-year-old soldiers had written to their families before the battle to tell them: "We don't consider ourselves heroes. We want this war to be over. But however much dread we may feel, you can count on us." Before they landed, Eisenhower told them: "The eyes of the world are upon you. The hopes and prayers of liberty-loving people everywhere march with you."

And as they listened to their fathers, watched movies, read history books and the letters of soldiers who died on the beaches of Normandy and Provence, as they visited the cemeteries where the star-spangled banner flies, the children of my generation understood that these young Americans, 20 years old, were true heroes to whom they owed the fact that they were free people and not slaves. France will never forget the sacrifice of your children.

To those 20-year-old heroes who gave us everything, to the families of those who never returned, to the children who mourned fathers they barely got a chance to know, I want to express France's eternal gratitude.

On behalf of my generation, which did not experience war but knows how much it owes to their courage and their sacrifice; on behalf of our children, who must never forget; to all the veterans who are here today and, notably the seven I had the honor to decorate yesterday evening, one of whom, Senator Inouye, belongs to your Congress, I want to express the deep, sincere gratitude of the French people. I want to tell you that whenever an American soldier falls somewhere in the world, I think of what the American army did for France. I think of them and I am sad, as one is sad to lose a member of one's family.

The men and women of my generation remember the Marshall Plan that allowed their fathers to rebuild a devastated Europe. They remember the Cold War, during which America again stood as the bulwark of the Free World against the threat of new tyranny.

I remember the Berlin crisis and Kennedy who unhesitatingly risked engaging the United States in the most destructive of wars so that Europe could preserve the freedom for which the American people had already sacrificed so much. No one has the right to forget. Forgetting, for a person of my generation, would be tantamount to self-denial.

But my generation did not love America only because she had defended freedom. We also loved her because for us, she embodied what was most audacious about the human adventure; for us, she embodied the spirit of conquest. We loved America because for us, America was a new frontier that was continuously pushed back—a constantly renewed challenge to the inventiveness of the human spirit.

My generation shared all the American dreams. Our imaginations were fueled by the winning of the West and Hollywood. By Elvis Presley, Duke Ellington, Hemingway. By John Wayne, Charlton Heston, Marilyn Monroe, Rita Hayworth. And by Armstrong, Aldrin and Collins, fulfilling mankind's oldest dream.

What was so extraordinary for us was that through her literature, her cinema and her music, America always seemed to emerge from adversity even greater and stronger; that instead of causing America to doubt herself, such ordeals only strengthened her belief in her values.

What makes America strong is the strength of this ideal that is shared by all Americans and by all those who love her because they love freedom.

America's strength is not only a material strength, it is first and foremost a spiritual and moral strength. No one expressed this better than a black pastor who asked just one thing of America: that she be true to the ideal in whose name he—the grandson of a slave—felt so deeply American. His name was Martin Luther King. He made America a universal role model.

The world still remembers his words—words of love, dignity and justice. America heard those words and America changed. And the men and women who had doubted America because they no longer recognized her began loving her again.

Fundamentally, what are those who love America asking of her, if not to remain forever true to her founding values?

Today as in the past, as we stand at the beginning of the 21st century, it is together that we must fight to defend and promote the values and ideals of freedom and democracy that men such as Washington and Lafayette invented together.

Together we must fight against terrorism. On September 11, 2001, all of France—petrified with horror—rallied to the side of the American people. The front-page headline of one of our major dailies read: "We are all American." And on that day, when you were mourning for so many dead, never had America appeared to us as so great, so dignified, so strong. The terrorists had thought they would weaken you. They made you greater. The entire world felt admiration for the courage of the American people. And from day one, France decided to participate shoulder to shoulder with you in the war in Afghanistan. Let me tell you solemnly today: France will remain engaged in Afghanistan as long as it takes, because what's at stake in that country is the future of our values and that of the Atlantic Alliance. For me, failure is not an option. **Terrorism will not win because democracies are not weak, because we are not afraid of this barbarism. America can count on France.**...

Long live the United States of America! Vive la France! Long live French-American friendship!

Washington and Lafayette at Mount Vernon - 1784
by Thomas Rossiter and Louis Mignot

Meuse-Argonne Cemetery - France
Graves of 14,246 American soldiers

Chapter 9

POEMS AND SONGS

❦

THIS IS A COMPILATION OF POEMS AND SONGS that are part of the American psyche. They tell stories about this country's history; they reflect on the mood of the country; they represent the most well-known works of American writers; they celebrate the military that protects the country; and they help spread the message of freedom and patriotism. They were important expressions about our country in the days before radio, movies, and television, and gave the entire country the means to share in the feelings expressed in these verses.

SURRENDER OF LORD CORNWALLIS ❦ BY JOHN TRUMBULL

The British had used the song "Yankee Doodle" to mock the unsophisticated colonials before the war. However, it soon became a popular patriotic song for the Americans. At the surrender of Cornwallis at Yorktown in 1781, the British band played "The World Turned Upside Down." As the British soldiers laid down their arms, the Americans played "Yankee Doodle."

YANKEE DOODLE

The British troops would sing this song to make fun of the Colonial troops during the French and Indian Wars. A 'doodle' was a dimwit; 'macaroni' referred to a fancy Italian style of dressing. There were hundreds of different versions that have appeared over the years. The Americans played it when the British surrendered at Yorktown.

Yankee Doodle went to town,
    A-Riding on a pony;
He stuck a feather in his hat,
    And called it macaroni.

Chorus:
    Yankee Doodle, keep it up,
    Yankee Doodle dandy;
    Mind the music and the step,
    And with the girls be handy!

Father and I went down to camp,
    Along with Captain Gooding,
And there we saw the men and boys
    As thick as hasty pudding.
    Chorus

THE SPIRIT OF '76
BY ARCHIBALD MACNEAL

And there we saw a thousand men
    As rich as Squire David,
And what they wasted every day,
    I wish it could be saved.
    Chorus

And every time they shoot it off,
    It takes a horn of powder;
It makes a noise like father's gun,
    Only a nation louder.
    Chorus

I saw a little barrel too,
    The heads were made of leather.
They knocked on it with little clubs
    And called the folks together.
    Chorus

And there was Captain Washington,
    and gentlefolks about him.
They say he's grown so tarnal proud,
    He will not ride without them.
    Chorus

THE STAR-SPANGLED BANNER

SIR FRANCIS SCOTT KEY   **SEPTEMBER 16, 1814**

During the War of 1812, Key went aboard a British warship in an effort
to secure the release of a friend who had been captured. He was still
aboard when the British fleet shelled Fort McHenry, one of the many
defenses of Baltimore. Key watched the flag flying during the night,
and when it was still there in the morning, put together these lines as
a tribute to the Star Spangled Banner. Congress waited until 1931 to
officially make this our National Anthem.

O! say, can you see, by the dawn's early light,
What so proudly we hailed at the twilight's last gleaming—
Whose broad stripes and bright stars, through the perilous fight,
O'er the ramparts we watched were so gallantly streaming!
And the rocket's red glare, the bombs bursting in air,
Gave proof through the night that our flag was still there:
O! say, does that star-spangled banner yet wave
O'er the land of the free, and the home of the brave

On that shore dimly seen through the mists of the deep,
Where the foe's haughty host in dread silence reposes,
What is that which the breeze, o'er the towering steep,
As it fitfully blows, now conceals, now discloses?
Now it catches the gleam of the morning's first beam,
In full glory reflected now shines on the stream;
'Tis the star-spangled banner; O long may it wave
O'er the land of the free, and the home of the brave!

And where is that band who so vauntingly swore
That the havoc of war and the battle's confusion
A home and a country should leave us no more?
Their blood has washed out their foul footsteps' pollution.
No refuge could save the hireling and slave
From the terror of or the gloom of the grave;
And the star-spangled banner in triumph doth wave
O'er the land of the free, and the home of the brave.

O! thus be it ever, when freemen shall stand
Between their loved homes and the war's desolation!
Blest with victory and peace, may the heav'n-rescued land
Praise the power that hath made and preserved us a nation.
Then conquer we must, for our cause it is just,
And this be our motto—"In God is our trust";
And the star-spangled banner in triumph shall wave
O'er the land of the free, and the home of the brave.

HOME, SWEET HOME

JOHN HOWARD PAYNE   1823

Originally presented in a 1823 opera, the words were set to a melody by the English Sir Henry Bishop. The phrase "there's no place like home" has become part of our culture. It was a favorite of Abraham Lincoln, and appeared in movies from *The Wizard of Oz* to *Meet Me in St. Louis.* Payne spent the last twenty years of his life abroad in Africa as American consul in Tunis, and he missed his home country.

'Mid pleasures and palaces though we may roam,
Be it ever so humble, there's no place like home;
A charm from the sky seems to hallow us there,
Which, seek through the world, is ne'er met with elsewhere.
    Home! Home! sweet, sweet Home!
There's no place like Home! there's no place like Home!

An exile from Home, Splendour dazzles in vain;
O, give me my lowly thatched cottage again!
The birds singing gaily, that came at my call,—
Give me them,—and the peace of mind, dearer than all!
    Home! Home! sweet, sweet Home!
There's no place like Home! there's no place like Home!

How sweet 'tis to sit 'neath a fond father's smile,
And the cares of a mother to soothe and beguile!
Let others delight 'mid new pleasures to roam,
But give me, oh, give me, the pleasures of Home!
    Home! Home! sweet, sweet Home!
There's no place like Home! there's no place like Home!

To thee I'll return, overburdened with care;
The heart's dearest solace will smile on me there;
No more from that cottage again will I roam;
Be it ever so humble, there's no place like Home.
    Home! Home! sweet, sweet Home!
There's no place like Home! there's no place like Home!

11. Home, Sweet Home

John Howard Payne, an American who spent most of his life as a wanderer over Europe, with no settled home, became famous as the author of this best known and loveliest home-song the world has ever sung. He was at various times, and actor, translator of plays, and finally U.S. Consul at Tunis, where he died in 1852. The music was probably composed by Henry R. Bishop, although he himself designated it as a "Sicilian air."

John Howard Payne
Henry R. Bishop

Woodman, Spare That Tree

George Pope Morris   1830

Written in 1830 as an early environmental protest piece, it was later set to music
in 1837 by Henry Russell.

Woodman! Spare that Tree!
Sheet music - 1837

Woodman, spare that tree!
 Touch not a single bough!
In youth it sheltered me,
 And I'll protect it now.
'Twas my forefather's hand
 That placed it near his cot;
There, woodman, let it stand,
 Thy axe shall harm it not!

That old familiar tree,
 Whose glory and renown
Are spread o'er land and sea,
 And wouldst thou hew it down?
Woodman, forbear thy stroke!
 Cut not its earth bound ties;
O, spare that aged oak,
 Now towering to the skies!

When but an idle boy
 I sought its grateful shade;
In all their gushing joy
 Here too my sisters played.
My mother kissed me here;
 My father pressed my hand—
Forgive this foolish tear,
 But let that old oak stand!

My heart strings round thee cling,
 Close as thy bark, old friend!
Here shall the wild bird sing,
 And still thy branches bend.
Old tree! the storm still brave!
 And, woodman, leave the spot;
While I've a hand to save,
 Thy axe shall hurt it not.

OLD IRONSIDES

OLIVER WENDELL HOLMES   1830

The USS *Constitution* was launched in 1797, and saw action in the Barbary War. It became famous in the War of 1812 due to its string of victories, and the defeat of the HMS *Guerièrre*. In that battle, shot from the British ship bounced harmlessly off the stout sides of the *Constitution*, earning her the name *Old Ironsides*. In 1830, the U.S. Navy announced plans to dismantle the ship which had become a famous symbol for Americans and represented the importance of the command of the seas. Holmes read of the impending destruction, and wrote this poem to both honor the ship and save her from this fate. It worked and the ship floats today in Boston harbor as the oldest commissioned ship in the U.S. Navy.

Ay, tear her tattered ensign down!
    Long has it waved on high,
And many an eye has danced to see
    That banner in the sky;
Beneath it rung the battle shout,
    And burst the cannon's roar;
The meteor of the ocean air
    Shall sweep the clouds no more.

Her deck, once red with heroes' blood,
    Where knelt the vanquished foe,
When winds were hurrying o'er the flood,
    And waves were white below,
No more shall feel the victor's tread,
    Or know the conquered knee;
The harpies of the shore shall pluck
    The eagle of the sea!

Oh, better that her shattered bulk
    Should sink beneath the wave;
Her thunders shook the mighty deep,
    And there should be her grave;
Nail to the mast her holy flag,
    Set every threadbare sail,
And give her to the god of storms,
    The lightning and the gale!

AMERICA

SAMUEL FRANCIS SMITH   1831

> Smith wrote this when he was studying to be a minister in 1831. It
> was set to the same music as the British song "God Save the King."

My country 'tis of thee
Sweet land of liberty:
Of thee I sing.
Land where my fathers died
Land of the Pilgrims' pride
From every mountainside
Let freedom ring.

My native country—thee
Land of the noble free
Thy name I love:
I love thy rocks and rills
Thy woods and templed hills
My heart with rapture thrills
Like that above.

Let music swell the breeze
And ring from all the trees
Sweet freedom's song.
Let all that breathe partake
Let mortal tongues awake
Let rocks their silence break
The sound prolong.

Our fathers' God to thee
Author of liberty
To thee we sing.
Long may our land be bright
With freedom's holy light
Protect us by thy might
Great God, our King.

The cause of America is in great measure the cause of all mankind.
—*Thomas Paine*

CONCORD HYMN

RALPH WALDO EMERSON   1837

> Emerson wrote this short but stirring tribute to the men who fought
> and died at the Battle of Lexington and Concord in 1775. It was
> sung on July 4, 1837 at the ceremony celebrating the completion of
> the Concord Monument erected in those men's honor. It contains the
> well-known line: "And fired the shot heard round the world."

By the rude bridge that arched the flood,
    Their flag to April's breeze unfurled,
Here once the embattled farmers stood,
    And fired the shot heard round the world.

The foe long since in silence slept;
    Alike the conqueror silent sleeps;
And Time the ruined bridge has swept
    Down the dark stream which seaward creeps.

On this green bank, by this soft stream,
    We set today a votive stone;
That memory may their deed redeem,
    When, like our sires, our sons are gone.

Spirit, that made those spirits dare
    To die, and leave their children free,
Bid Time and Nature gently spare
    The shaft we raise to them and thee.

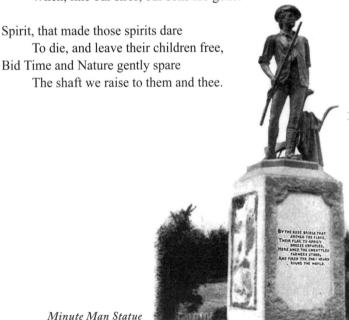

Minute Man Statue
First verse is carved on statue

THANKSGIVING DAY

LYDIA MARIA CHILD   1844

Lydia Child was an abolitionist, activist, and nov-
elist who wrote in the earlier part of the 19th century. She is best remembered for this poem and the
instant recognition of the first two lines of verse.

Over the river and through the wood,
    To grandfather's house we go;
        The horse knows the way
        To carry the sleigh
    Through the white and drifted snow.

Over the river and through the wood—
    Oh, how the wind does blow!
        It stings the toes
        And bites the nose,
    As over the ground we go.

Over the river and through the wood,
    To have a first-rate play.
        Hear the bells ring,
        "Ting-a-ting-ding!"
    Hurrah for Thanksgiving Day!

Over the river and through the wood
    Trot fast, my dapple-gray!
        Spring over the ground,
        Like a hunting-hound!
    For this is Thanksgiving Day.

Over the river and through the wood,
    And straight through the barn-yard gate,
        We seem to go
        Extremely slow,—
    It is so hard to wait!

Over the river and through the wood—
    Now grandmother's cap I spy!
        Hurrah for the fun!
        Is the pudding done!
    Hurrah for the pumpkin-pie!

THE RAVEN

EDGAR ALLAN POE   1845

Many regard this as one of the most famous poems ever produced. Its
supernatural and mysterious style is seen in many of Poe's other stories
and poems. He was to die four years later.

Once upon a midnight dreary, while I pondered, weak and weary,
Over many a quaint and curious volume of forgotten lore,
While I nodded, nearly napping, suddenly there came a tapping,
As of someone gently rapping, rapping at my chamber door.
"'Tis some visitor," I muttered, "tapping at my chamber door;
    Only this, and nothing more."

Ah, distinctly I remember, it was in the bleak December,
And each separate dying ember wrought its ghost upon the floor.
Eagerly I wished the morrow; vainly I had sought to borrow
From my books surcease of sorrow, sorrow for the lost Lenore,
For the rare and radiant maiden whom the angels name Lenore,
    Nameless here forevermore.

And the silken sad uncertain rustling of each purple curtain
Thrilled me—filled me with fantastic terrors never felt before;
So that now, to still the beating of my heart, I stood repeating,
"'Tis some visitor entreating entrance at my chamber door,
Some late visitor entreating entrance at my chamber door
    This it is, and nothing more."

Presently my soul grew stronger; hesitating then no longer,
"Sir," said I, "or madam, truly your forgiveness I implore;
But the fact is, I was napping, and so gently you came rapping,
And so faintly you came tapping, tapping at my chamber door,
That I scarce was sure I heard you." Here I opened wide the door;
    Darkness there, and nothing more.

Deep into the darkness peering, long I stood there, wondering, fearing,
Doubting, dreaming dreams no mortals ever dared to dream before;
But the silence was unbroken, and the stillness gave no token,
And the only word there spoken was the whispered word, "Lenore?"
This I whispered, and an echo murmured back the word, "Lenore!"
    Merely this, and nothing more.

Back into the chamber turning, all my soul within me burning,
Soon again I heard a tapping, something louder than before,
"Surely," said I, "surely, that is something at my window lattice
Let me see, then, what thereat is, and this mystery explore;
Let my heart be still a moment, and this mystery explore;
    'Tis the wind, and nothing more."

Open-here I flung the shutter, when, with many a flirt and flutter,
In there stepped a stately raven, of the saintly day of yore.
Not the least obeisance made he; not a minute stopped or stayed he;
But with mien of lord or lady, perched above my chalice door;
Perched upon a bust of Pallas, just above my chamber door,
   Perched, and sat, and nothing more.

Then this ebony bird beguiling my sad fancy into smiling,
By the grave and stern decorum of the countenance it wore,
"Though thy crest be shorn and shaven, thou," I said, "art sure no craven,
Ghastly, grim, and ancient raven, wandering from the nightly shore.
Tell me what thy lordly name is on the Night's Plutonian shore."
   Quoth the raven, "Nevermore."

Much I marvelled this ungainly fowl to hear discourse so plainly,
Though its answer little meaning, little relevancy bore;
For we cannot help agreeing that no living human being
Ever yet was blessed with seeing bird above his chamber door,
Bird or beast upon the sculptured bust above his chamber door,
   With such name as "Nevermore."

But the raven, sitting lonely on that placid bust, spoke only
That one word, as if his soul in that one word he did outpour.
Nothing further then he uttered; not a feather then he fluttered;
Till I scarcely more than muttered, "Other friends have flown before;
On the morrow he will leave me, as my hopes have flown before."
   Then the bird said, "Nevermore."

Startled at the stillness broken by reply so aptly spoken,
"Doubtless," said I, "what it utters is its only stock and store,
Caught from some unhappy master, from unmerciful disaster
Followed fast and followed faster, till his songs one burden bore,—
Till the dirges of his hope that melancholy burden bore
   Of Never-nevermore."

But the raven still beguiling all my fancy into smiling,
Straight I wheeled a cushioned seat in front of bird and bust and door;
Then, upon the velvet sinking, I betook myself to linking
Fancy unto fancy, thinking what this ominous bird of yore,
What this grim, ungainly, ghastly, gaunt, and ominous bird of yore
   Meant in croaking, "Nevermore."

Thus I sat engaged in guessing, but no syllable expressing
To the fowl, whose fiery eyes now burned into my bosom's core
This and more I sat divining with my head at ease reclining
On the cushion's velvet lining that the lamplight gloated o'er
But whose velvet violet lining with the lamplight gloat'ing o'er
  She shall press, ah, nevermore.

Then, methought, the air grew denser, perfumed from an unseen censer
Swung by seraphim whose footfalls tinkled on the tufted floor.
"Wretch," I cried, "thy God hath lent thee—by these angels he
  hath sent thee
Respite—respite and nepenthe from thy memories of Lenore!
Quaff, O quaff this kind nepenthe, and forget this lost Lenore!"
  Quoth the raven, "Nevermore!"

"Prophet!" said I, "thing of evil!—prophet still, if bird or devil!
Whether Tempter sent, or whether tempest tossed thee here ashore,
Desolate, yet all undaunted, on this desert land enchanted
On this home by horror haunted—tell me truly, I implore:
Is there—is there balm in Gilead?—tell me—tell me I implore!"
  Quoth the raven, "Nevermore."

"Prophet!" said I, "thing of evil-prophet still, if bird or devil!
By that heaven that bends above us,—by that God we both adore—
Tell this soul with sorrow laden, if, within the distant Aidenn,
It shall clasp a sainted maiden, whom the angels name Lenore—
Clasp a rare and radiant maiden, whom the angels name Lenore?"
  Quoth the raven, "Nevermore."

"Be that word our sign of parting, bird or fiend!" I shrieked,
  upstarting—
"Get thee back into the tempest and the Night's Plutonian shore!
Leave no black plume as a token of that lie thy soul hath spoken!
Leave my loneliness unbroken!—quit the bust above my door!
Take thy beak from out my heart, and take thy form from off my
  door!"
  Quoth the raven, "Nevermore."

And the raven, never flitting, still is sitting, still is sitting
On the pallid bust of Pallas just above my chamber door;
And his eyes have all the seeming of a demon's that is dreaming;
And the lamplight o'er him streaming throws the shadow on the floor;
And my soul from out that shadow that lies floating on the floor
  Shall be lifted—nevermore!

O Ship of State!

Henry Wadsworth Longfellow   **1849**

Longfellow released a new volume of his poetry in 1849 which show-cased the lengthy poem, *The Building of the Ship*. The following well-known lines are at the end of this poem.

Thou, too, sail on, O Ship of State!
Sail on, O UNION, strong and great!
Humanity with all its fears,
With all the hopes of future years,
Is hanging breathless on thy fate!
We know what Master laid thy keel,
What Workmen wrought thy ribs of steel,
Who made each mast, and sail, and rope,
What anvils rang, what hammers beat,
In what a forge and what a heat
Were shaped the anchors of thy hope!
Fear not each sudden sound and shock,
'Tis of the wave and not the rock;
'Tis but the flapping of the sail,
And not a rent made by the gale!
In spite of rock and tempest's roar,
In spite of false lights on the shore,
Sail on, nor fear to breast the sea!
Our hearts, our hopes, are all with thee.
Our hearts, our hopes, our prayers, our tears,
Our faith triumphant o'er our fears,
Are all with thee, -are all with thee!

Henry Wadsworth Longfellow
1850

I HEAR AMERICA SINGING

WALT WHITMAN   **1855**

Walt Whitman loved writing about all the varied aspects of his country. This is one of his most favorite poems that portrays America at its best. Now we just have to live up to his expectations.

I hear America singing, the varied carols I hear,

Those of mechanics, each one singing his as it should be blithe and strong,

The carpenter singing his as he measures his plank or beam,

The mason singing his as he makes ready for work, or leaves off work,

The boatman singing what belongs to him in his boat, the deck–hand singing on the steamboat deck,

The shoemaker singing as he sits on his bench, the hatter sing-ing as he stands,

The woodcutter's song, the ploughboy's on his way in the morn-ing, or at noon intermission or at sundown,

The delicious singing of the mother, or of the young wife at work, or of the girl sewing or washing,

Each singing what belongs to him or her and to none else,

The day what belongs to the day—at night the party of young fel-lows, robust, friendly,

Singing with open mouths their strong melodious songs.

Walt Whitman - 1854
by Samuel Hollyer

Paul Revere's Ride

Henry Wadsworth Longfellow   **1860**

Longfellow wrote this epic poem in 1860 after climbing the tower
in the Old North Church in Boston. The country was on the verge
of the Civil War, and the poem served as a warning to the North
about the perils of the upcoming conflict, much as Paul Revere had
warned the colonists. Though not entirely accurate, the poem depicts the general events that happened in 1775. It does omit, however, the similar actions of William Dawes and Samuel Prescott
who also rode to warn the militia.

Listen, my children, and you shall hear
Of the midnight ride of Paul Revere,
On the eighteenth of April, in Seventy-five;
Hardly a man is now alive
Who remembers that famous day and year.

He said to his friend, "If the British march
By land or sea from the town to-night,
Hang a lantern aloft in the belfry arch
Of the North Church tower as a signal light,—
One if by land, and two if by sea;
And I on the opposite shore will be,
Ready to ride and spread the alarm
Through every Middlesex village and farm,
For the country folk to be up and to arm."

Then he said "Good-night!" and with muffled oar
Silently rowed to the Charlestown shore,
Just as the moon rose over the bay,
Where swinging wide at her moorings lay
The Somerset, British man-of-war;
A phantom ship, with each mast and spar
Across the moon like a prison bar,
And a huge black hulk, that was magnified
By its own reflection in the tide.

Meanwhile, his friend through alley and street
Wanders and watches, with eager ears,
Till in the silence around him he hears
The muster of men at the barrack door,
The sound of arms, and the tramp of feet,
And the measured tread of the grenadiers,
Marching down to their boats on the shore.

Then he climbed the tower of the Old North Church,
By the wooden stairs, with stealthy tread,
To the belfry chamber overhead,
And startled the pigeons from their perch
On the sombre rafters, that round him made
Masses and moving shapes of shade,—
By the trembling ladder, steep and tall,
To the highest window in the wall,
Where he paused to listen and look down
A moment on the roofs of the town
And the moonlight flowing over all.

Beneath, in the churchyard, lay the dead,
In their night encampment on the hill,
Wrapped in silence so deep and still
That he could hear, like a sentinel's tread,
The watchful night-wind, as it went
Creeping along from tent to tent,
And seeming to whisper, "All is well!"
A moment only he feels the spell,
Of the place and the hour, and the secret dread
Of the lonely belfry and the dead;
For suddenly all his thoughts are bent
On a shadowy something far away,
Where the river widens to meet the bay,—
A line of black that bends and floats
On the rising tide like a bridge of boats.

Meanwhile, impatient to mount and ride,
Booted and spurred, with a heavy stride
On the opposite shore walked Paul Revere.
Now he patted his horse's side,
Now he gazed at the landscape far and near,
Then, impetuous, stamped the earth,
And turned and tightened his saddle girth;
But mostly he watched with eager search—
The belfry tower of the Old North Church,
As it rose above the graves on the hill,
Lonely and spectral and sombre and still.
And lo! as be looks, on the belfry's height
A glimmer, and then a gleam of light!
He springs to the saddle, the bridle he turns,
But lingers and gazes, till full on his sight
A second lamp in the belfry burns.

A hurry of hoofs in a village street,
A shape in the moonlight, a bulk in the dark,
And beneath, from the pebbles, in passing, a spark
Struck out by a steed flying fearless and fleet;
That was all! And yet, through the gloom and the light,
The fate of a nation was riding that night;
And the spark struck out by that steed, in his flight,
Kindled the land into flame with its heat.

He has left the village and mounted the steep,
And beneath him, tranquil and broad and deep,
Is the Mystic, meeting the ocean tides;
And under the alders that skirt its edge,
Now soft on the sand, now loud on the ledge,
Is heard the tramp of his steed as he rides.
It was twelve by the village clock
When he crossed the bridge into Medford town.
He heard the crowing of the cock,
And the barking of the farmer's dog,
And felt the damp of the river fog,
That rises after the sun goes down.
It was one by the village clock,
When he galloped into Lexington.
He saw the gilded weathercock
Swim in the moonlight as he passed,
And the meeting-house windows, black and bare,
Gaze at him with a spectral glare,
As if they already stood aghast
At the bloody work they would look upon.

It was two by the village clock,
When he came to the bridge in Concord town.
He heard the bleating of the flock,
And the twitter of birds among the trees,
And felt the breath of the morning breeze
Blowing over the meadow brown.
And one was safe and asleep in his bed
Who at the bridge would be first to fall,
Who that day would be lying dead,
Pierced by a British musket ball.

You know the rest. In the books you have read
How the British Regulars fired and fled,—
How the farmers gave them ball for ball,
From behind each fence and farmyard wall,
Chasing the redcoats down the lane,

Then crossing the fields to emerge again
Under the trees at the turn of the road,
And only pausing to fire and load.

So through the night rode Paul Revere;
And so through the night went his cry of alarm
To every Middlesex village and farm,—
A cry of defiance, and not of fear,
A voice in the darkness, a knock at the door,
And a word that shall echo for evermore!
For, borne on the night-wind of the Past,
Through all our history, to the last,
In the hour of darkness and peril and need,
The people will waken and listen to hear
The hurrying hoof-beats of that steed,
And the midnight message of Paul Revere.

Old North Church
Boston

BATTLE HYMN OF THE REPUBLIC

JULIA WARD HOWE 1862

> First published in 1862, the song was based on music from the abolitionist song "John Brown's Body." It became a popular song in the North during the Civil War and has remained a classic ever since. The version below is the more commonly sung version, omitting original verses three and six. It is still a very stirring hymn.

Mine eyes have seen the glory of the coming of the Lord:
He is trampling out the vintage where the grapes of wrath are stored;
He hath loosed the fateful lightning of his terrible swift sword:
    His truth is marching on.

I have seen him in the watch fires of a hundred circling camps;
They have builded him an altar in the evening dews and damps;
I can read his righteous sentence by the dim and flaring lamps:
    His day is marching on.

He has sounded forth the trumpet that shall never call retreat;
He is sifting out the hearts of men before his judgment seat:
O, be swift, my soul, to answer him! be jubilant, my feet!
    Our God is marching on.

In the beauty of the lilies Christ was born across the sea,
With a glory in his bosom that transfigures you and me;
As he died to make men holy, let us die to make men free,
    While God is marching on.

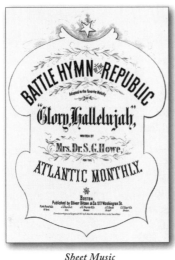

Sheet Music
Published 1862

First Published Copy
Atlantic Monthly - 1862

BARBARA FRIETCHIE

JOHN GREENLEAF WHITTIER   1863

During the Civil War, Robert E. Lee and Stonewall Jackson were able
to invade the North on only a very few occasions. On one of these
trips, this episode was said to have occurred in Frederick, Maryland.

Up from the meadow rich with corn,
Clear in the cool September morn,
The clustered spires of Frederick stand
Green walled by the hills of Maryland.
Round about them orchards sweep,
Apple and peach tree fruited deep,
Fair as the garden of the Lord
To the eyes of the famished rebel horde,
On that pleasant morn of the early fall
When Lee marched over the mountain wall;
Over the mountains winding down,
Horse and foot, into Frederick town.

Forty flags with their silver stars,
Forty flags with their crimson bars,
Flapped in the morning wind: the sun
Of noon looked down, and saw not one.
Up rose old Barbara Frietchie then,
Bowed with her fourscore years and ten;
Bravest of all in Frederick town,
She took up the flag the men hauled down;
In her attic window the staff she set,
To show that one heart was loyal yet.

Up the street came the rebel tread,
Stonewall Jackson riding ahead.
Under his slouched hat left and right
He glanced; the old flag met his sight.
"Halt"—the dust brown ranks stood fast.
"Fire"—out blazed the rifle blast.
It shivered the window, pane and sash;
It rent the banner with seam and gash.
Quick, as it fell, from the broken staff
Dame Barbara snatched the silken scarf.
She leaned far out on the windowsill,
And shook it forth with a royal will.
"Shoot, if you must, this old gray head,
But spare your country's flag," she said.
A shade of sadness, a blush of shame,

Over the face of the leader came;
The nobler nature within him stirred
To life at that woman's deed and word;
"Who touches a hair on yon gray head
Dies like a dog! March on!" he said.
All day long through Frederick street
Sounded the tread of marching feet:
All day long that free flag tossed
Over the heads of the rebel host.
Ever its torn folds rose and fell
On the loyal winds that loved it well;
And through the hill gaps sunset light
Shone over it with a warm good night.

Barbara Frietchie's work is o'er,
And the Rebel rides on his raids no more.
Honor to her! and let a tear
Fall, for her sake, on Stonewall's bier.
Over Barbara Frietchie's grave
Flag of Freedom and Union, wave!
Peace and order and beauty draw
Round thy symbol of light and law;
And ever the stars above look down
On thy stars below in Frederick town!

Barbara Frietchie

When Johnny Comes Marching Home

Patrick S. Gilmore   1863

> Written by the Irish immigrant Patrick Gilmore, this was first pub-
> lished in 1863. It was sung by both sides during the Civil War, and
> is often played to celebrate returning troops.

When Johnny comes marching home again
    Hurrah! Hurrah!
We'll give him a hearty welcome then
    Hurrah! Hurrah!
The men will cheer and the boys will shout
The ladies they will all turn out
And we'll all feel gay
When Johnny comes marching home.

The old church bell will peal with joy
    Hurrah! Hurrah!
To welcome home our darling boy,
    Hurrah! Hurrah!
The village lads and lassies say
With roses they will strew the way,
And we'll all feel gay
When Johnny comes marching home.

Get ready for the Jubilee,
    Hurrah! Hurrah!
We'll give the hero three times three,
    Hurrah! Hurrah!
The laurel wreath is ready now
To place upon his loyal brow
And we'll all feel gay
When Johnny comes marching home.

Let love and friendship on that day,
    Hurrah, hurrah!
Their choicest pleasures then display,
    Hurrah, hurrah!
And let each one perform some part,
To fill with joy the warrior's heart,
And we'll all feel gay
When Johnny comes marching home.

O Captain! My Captain!

Walt Whitman   1865

> The tragic assassination of President Abraham Lincoln, "My Captain",
> inspired Walt Whitman to write this poem. The Captain refers to Lin-
> coln; the fearful trip is the Civil War; and the ship is America.

O Captain! my Captain! our fearful trip is done;
The ship has weather'd every rack, the prize we sought is won;
The port is near, the bells I hear, the people all exulting,
While follow eyes the steady keel, the vessel grim and daring:

> But O heart! heart! heart!
> > O the bleeding drops of red,
> > > Where on the deck my Captain lies,
> > > > Fallen cold and dead.

O Captain! my Captain! rise up and hear the bells;
Rise up—for you the flag is flung—for you the bugle trills;
For you bouquets and ribbon'd wreaths for you the shores a-crowding;
For you they call, the swaying mass, their eager faces turning:

> Here Captain! dear father!
> > This arm beneath your head;
> > > It is some dream that on the deck
> > > > You've fallen cold and dead.

My Captain does not answer, his lips are pale and still;
My father does not feel my arm, he has no pulse or will;
The ship is anchor'd safe and sound, its voyage closed and done;
From fearful trip the victor ship comes in with object won:

> Exult, O shores, and ring, O bells!
> > But I, with mournful tread,
> > > Walk the deck my Captain lies,
> > > > Fallen cold and dead.

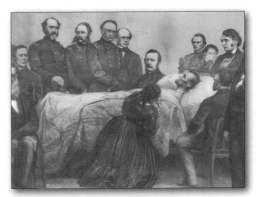

*Death Bed of
Lincoln*
by A. Brett & Co.

MARINES' HYMN

UNKNOWN   1800s

The exact origin of this hymn is unknown, but the war with the
Barbary Pirates in 1805 is referenced by the words "shores of
Tripoli." The Marines then captured and occupied Mexico City
during the Mexican War, adding the "Halls of Montezuma." At
the end of that war, the first verse was most likely written by a
Marine on duty in Mexico.

From the halls of Montezuma, to the shores of Tripoli,
  We fight our country's battles in the air, on land and sea.
First to fight for right and freedom, and to keep our honor clean;
  We are proud to claim the title of United States Marine.

Our flag's unfurled to every breeze from dawn to setting sun.
  We have fought in every clime and place, where we could take
  a gun.
In the snow of far off northern lands and in sunny tropic scenes,
  You will find us always on the job, The United States Marines.

Here's health to you and to our Corps which we are proud to serve.
  In many a strife we've fought for life and never lost our nerve.
If the Army and the Navy ever look on heaven's scenes,
  They will find the streets are guarded by United States Marines.

Raising the Flag on Iwo Jima - February 23, 1945
by Joe Rosenthal

THE NEW COLOSSUS

EMMA LAZARUS   1883

> The Statue of Liberty was given as a gift of friendship from the people of France to mark the two nations' commitment to liberty. The American poet Emma Lazarus wrote this poem to help raise money for the pedestal and this poem is carved on that pedestal. It captures what the statue has meant to millions of immigrants who came here seeking freedom. The statue was dedicated on October 28, 1886 by President Cleveland to the cheers of thousands. The first two lines refer to the Ancient Colossus of Rhodes, while "twin cities" refers to New York City and Brooklyn which were separate cities then.

Not like the brazen giant of Greek fame,
With conquering limbs astride from land to land;
Here at our sea-washed, sunset gates shall stand
A mighty woman with a torch, whose flame
Is the imprisoned lightning, and her name
Mother of Exiles. From her beacon-hand
Glows world-wide welcome; her mild eyes command
The air-bridged harbor that twin cities frame.
"Keep, ancient lands, your storied pomp!" cries she
With silent lips. "Give me your tired, your poor,
Your huddled masses yearning to breathe free,
The wretched refuse of your teeming shore.
Send these, the homeless, tempest-tost to me,
I lift my lamp beside the golden door!"

Statue of Liberty
being built in Paris

Head of Statue of Liberty in
Paris park - 1883

CASEY AT THE BAT

ERNEST LAWRENCE THAYER   1888

> Published in the San Francisco Examiner in 1888, this classic poem about baseball highlights those traits that make the game so American. The poem affected popular culture, spawning parodies, movies, songs, and even towns claiming to be the original "Mudville."

The outlook wasn't brilliant for the Mudville nine that day;
The score stood two to four, with but an inning left to play.
So, when Cooney died at second, and Burrows did the same,
A pallor wreathed the features of the patrons of the game.

A straggling few got up to go, leaving there the rest,
With that hope which springs eternal within the human breast.
For they thought: "If only Casey could get a whack at that,"
They'd put even money now, with Casey at the bat.

But Flynn preceded Casey, as did also Jimmy Blake,
And the former was a pudd'n, and the latter was a fake.
So on that stricken multitude a deathlike silence sat;
For there seemed but little chance of Casey's getting to the bat.

But Flynn let drive a "single," to the wonderment of all.
And the much despised Blakey "tore the cover off the ball."
And when the dust had lifted, and they saw what had occurred,
There was Blakey safe at second, and Flynn a huggin' third.

Then from the gladdened multitude went up a joyous yell—
It rumbled in the mountaintops, it rattled in the dell;
It struck upon the hillside and rebounded on the flat;
For Casey, mighty Casey, was advancing to the bat.

There was ease in Casey's manner as he stepped into his place,
There was pride in Casey's bearing and a smile on Casey's face;
And when responding to the cheers he lightly doffed his hat,
No stranger in the crowd could doubt 'twas Casey at the bat.

Ten thousand eyes were on him as he rubbed his hands with dirt,
Five thousand tongues applauded when he wiped them on his
    shirt;
Then when the writhing pitcher ground the ball into his hip,
Defiance glanced in Casey's eye, a sneer curled Casey's lip.

And now the leather covered sphere came hurtling through the air,
And Casey stood a watching it in haughty grandeur there.
Close by the sturdy batsman the ball unheeded sped;
"That ain't my style," said Casey. "Strike one," the umpire said.

From the benches, black with people, there went up a muffled roar,
Like the beating of the storm waves on the stern and distant shore.
"Kill him! kill the umpire!" shouted someone on the stand;
And it's likely they'd have killed him had not Casey raised his
    hand.

With a smile of Christian charity great Casey's visage shone;
He stilled the rising tumult, he bade the game go on.
He signaled to the pitcher, and once more the spheroid flew;
But Casey still ignored it, and the umpire said, "Strike two."

"Fraud!" cried the maddened thousands, and the echo answered
    "Fraud!"
But one scornful look from Casey and the audience was awed;
They saw his face grow stern and cold, they saw his muscles
    strain,
And they knew that Casey wouldn't let the ball go by again.

The sneer is gone from Casey's lips, his teeth are clenched in hate,
He pounds with cruel vengeance his bat upon the plate;
And now the pitcher holds the ball, and now he lets it go,
And now the air is shattered by the force of Casey's blow.

Oh, somewhere in this favored land the sun is shining bright,
The band is playing somewhere, and somewhere hearts are light;
And somewhere men are laughing, and somewhere children shout,
But there is no joy in Mudville: Mighty Casey has struck out.

COLUMBUS

JOAQUIN MILLER   1892

> Known as the "Poet of the Sierras," Miller was once referred to as
> "Whitman without the coarseness." This tribute to Christopher Colum-
> bus was widely known and recited after it was published on the 400th
> anniversary of Columbus' voyage.

Behind him lay the gray Azores,
Behind the Gates of Hercules,
Before him not the ghost of shores,
Before him only shoreless seas.
The good mate said: "Now must we pray,
For lo! the very stars are gone.
Brave Adm'r'l, speak; what shall I say?"
"Why, say: 'Sail on! sail on! and on!'"

"My men grow mutinous day by day;
My men grow ghastly wan and weak."
The stout mate thought of home; a spray
Of salt wave washed his swarthy cheek.
"What shall I say, brave Adm'r'l, say,
If we sight naught but seas at dawn?"
"Why, you shall say, at break of day:
'Sail on! sail on! sail on! and on!'"

They sailed and sailed, as winds might blow,
Until at last the blanched mate said:
"Why, now not even God would know
Should I and all my men fall dead.
These very winds forget their way,
For God from these dread seas is gone.
Now speak, brave Adm'r'l; speak and say"—
He said: "Sail on! sail on! and on!"

They sailed. They sailed. Then spake the mate:
"This mad sea shows his teeth to-night;
He curls his lips, he lies in wait,
With lifted teeth, as if to bite:
Brave Adm'r'l, say but one good word;
What shall we do when hope is gone?"
The words leapt like a leaping sword:
"Sail on! sail on! sail on! and on!"

Then, pale and worn, he kept his deck,
And peered through darkness. Ah, that night
Of all dark nights! And then a speck—
A light! a light! a light! a light!
It grew, a starlit flag unfurled!
It grew to be Time's burst of dawn.
He gained a world; he gave that world
Its grandest lesson: "On! sail on!"

THE COMING AMERICAN

SAM WALTER FOSS 1894

Foss was a librarian who sometimes produced a poem each day for the local newspaper. He released this tribute to America on July 4, 1894.

Bring me men to match my mountains;
Bring me men to match my plains, —
Men with empires in their purpose,
And new eras in their brains.
Bring me men to match my prairies,
Men to match my inland seas,
Men whose thought shall pave a highway
Up to ampler destinies;
Pioneers to clear Thought's marshlands,
And to cleanse old Error's fen;
Bring me men to match my mountains —
Bring me men!

Bring me men to match my forests,
Strong to fight the storm and blast,
Branching toward the skyey future,
Rooted in the fertile past.
Bring me men to match my valleys,
Tolerant of sun and snow,
Men within whose fruitful purpose
Time's consummate blooms shall grow.
Men to tame the tigerish instincts
Of the lair and cave and den,
Cleans the dragon slime of Nature —
Bring me men!

Bring me men to match my rivers,
Continent cleavers, flowing free,
Drawn by the eternal madness
To be mingled with the sea;
Men of oceanic impulse,
Men whose moral currents sweep
Toward the wide-enfolding ocean
Of an undiscovered deep;
Men who feel the strong pulsation
Of the Central Sea, and then
Time their currents to its earth throb —
Bring me men!

AMERICA, THE BEAUTIFUL

KATHARINE LEE BATES   1895

Bates, a school teacher, was inspired by a trip to the top of Pike's
Peak in Colorado, and wrote the words to this song when she returned home that night. It was published in 1895, and the music was
later composed by Samuel A. Ward.

O beautiful for spacious skies,
        For amber waves of grain,
For purple mountain majesties
        Above the fruited plain!
America! America!
        God shed His grace on thee
And crown thy good with brotherhood
        From sea to shining sea!

O beautiful for pilgrim feet,
        Whose stern, impassioned stress
A thoroughfare for freedom beat
        Across the wilderness!
America! America!
        God mend thine every flaw,
Confirm thy soul in self control,
        Thy liberty in law!

O beautiful for heroes proved
        In liberating strife,
Who more than self their country loved,
        And mercy more than life!
America! America!
        May God thy gold refine,
Till all success be nobleness
        And every gain divine!

O beautiful for patriot dream
        That sees beyond the years
Thine alabaster cities gleam
        Undimmed by human tears!
America! America!
        God shed His grace on thee,
And crown thy good with brotherhood
        From sea to shining sea!

THE FLAG GOES BY

HENRY HOLCOMB BENNETT   1900

Bennett wrote this poem during the patriotic fever that swept the country during the Spanish-American War of 1898. It stayed popular into the next century.

Flag Day Poster
June 14, 1917

Hats off
Along the street there comes
A blare of bugles, a ruffle of drums,
A flash of color beneath the sky:
    Hats off!
The flag is passing by!

Blue and crimson and white it shines,
Over the steel-tipped, ordered lines.
    Hats off!
The colors before us fly;
But more than the flag is passing by.

Sea-fights and land-fights, grim and great,
Fought to make and to save the State:
Weary marches and sinking ships;
Cheers of victory on dying lips;

Days of plenty and years of peace;
March of a strong land's swift increase;
Equal justice, right and law,
Stately honor and reverend awe;

Sign of a nation, great and strong
To ward her people from foreign wrong:
Pride and glory and honor,—all
Live in the colors to stand or fall.

    Hats off!
Along the street there comes
A blare of bugles, a ruffle of drums;
And loyal hearts are beating high:
    Hats off!
The flag is passing by!

I'M A YANKEE DOODLE DANDY

GEORGE M. COHAN 1904

This song was written for the Broadway musical *Little Johnny Jones* in 1904. James Cagney performed this in the 1942 movie *Yankee Doodle Dandy*.

I'm a Yankee Doodle Dandy,
    A Yankee Doodle, do or die;
A real live nephew of my Uncle Sam's,
    Born on the Fourth of July.

I've got a Yankee Doodle sweetheart,
    She's my Yankee Doodle joy.
Yankee Doodle came to London, just to ride the ponies;
    I am the Yankee Doodle Boy.

George M. Cohan
1908

YOU'RE A GRAND OLD FLAG

GEORGE M. COHAN 1906

Written in 1906 for the musical *George Washington, Jr.*, this pays obvious tribute to our country's flag. George Cohan himself was born on the 4th of July in 1878.

There's a feeling comes a-stealing,
And it sets my brain a-reeling,
When I'm listening to the music of a military band.
Any tune like "Yankee Doodle"
Simply sets me off my noodle,
It's that patriotic something that no one can understand.

You're a grand old flag,
You're a high flying flag
And forever in peace may you wave.
You're the emblem of
The land I love.
The home of the free and the brave.

Ev'ry heart beats true
'neath the Red, White and Blue,
Where there's never a boast or brag.
But should auld acquaintance be forgot,
Keep your eye on the grand old flag.

The Unknown Soldier

Billy Rose

A stirring tribute to the Tomb of the Unknown Soldier at Arlington Cemetery across from Washington, D.C. The northern government confiscated the home of Robert E. Lee after the start of the Civil War and turned it into a national cemetery. An unidentified body from each war is buried at this site. The Tomb has been guarded continuously, 24 hours a day, since 1937. Everyone should see the changing of the guard ceremony.

Tomb of the Unknown Soldier
Arlington Cemetery

There's a Graveyard near the White House
    Where the Unknown Soldier lies,
And the flowers there are sprinkled
    With the tears from mother's eyes.

I stood there not so long ago
    With roses for the brave,
And suddenly I heard a voice
    Speak from out the grave:

"I am the Unknown Soldier,"
    The spirit voice began,
"And I think I have the right
    To ask some questions man to man.

"Are my buddies taken care of?
    Was their victory so sweet?
Is that big reward you offered
    Selling pencils on the street?

"Did they really win the freedom
    They battled to achieve?
Do you still respect that Croix de Guerre
    Above that empty sleeve?

"Does a gold star in the window
    Now mean anything at all?
I wonder how my old girl feels
    When she hears a bugle call.

"And that baby who sang
   'Hello, Central, give me no man's land—'
Can they replace her daddy
   With a military band?

"I wonder if the profiteers
   Have satisfied their greed?
I wonder if a soldier's mother
   Ever is in need?

"I wonder if the kings, who planned it all
   Are really satisfied?
They played their game of checkers
   And eleven million died.

"I am the Unknown Soldier
   And maybe I died in vain,
But if I were alive and my country called,
   I'd do it all over again."

MUSIC USUALLY PLAYED WITHOUT LYRICS

VARIOUS

These instantly recognizable tunes are usually played at special occasions without any accompanying lyrics.

Hail to the Chief

This has become the official anthem for the President of the United States, usually used to announce the President's arrival. It is almost always played without any words.

Taps

Taps is a bugle call that was created during the Civil War by a Union general. It is used today, primarily in the military, to announce "lights out" at the end of the day, and at funerals and memorial services.

Stars and Stripes Forever

The stirring patriotic march was written by John Philip Sousa in 1896. Although there are words to the song, it is almost always played without lyrics. It was made the National March of the United States of America by an act of Congress.

ANCHORS AWEIGH
(U.S. NAVY ANTHEM)

ALFRED MILES AND CHARLES ZIMMERMAN   1906

> Originally written as a college football fight song in 1906, the words have been changed over the last 100 years and it is now the anthem of the U.S. Navy, although there are still several versions being sung.

Stand, Navy, out to sea, Fight our battle cry;
We'll never change our course, So vicious foe steer shy-y-y-y.
Roll out the TNT, Anchors Aweigh. Sail on to victory
And sink their bones to Davy Jones, hooray!

Anchors Aweigh, my boys, Anchors Aweigh.
Farewell to college joys, we sail at break of day-ay-ay-ay.
Through our last night on shore, drink to the foam,
Until we meet once more. Here's wishing you a happy voyage
    home.

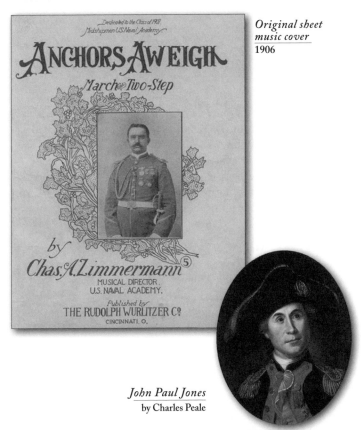

Original sheet music cover
1906

John Paul Jones
by Charles Peale

THE ARMY GOES ROLLING ALONG

MAJOR EDMUND L. GRUBER 1908

The original song was "The Caissons go Rolling Along" written in 1908. John Philip Sousa made it into a marching song and the lyrics were changed to remove direct references to the outdated horse-drawn field artillery. It is now the official song of the Army.

March along, sing our song, with the Army of the free
Count the brave, count the true, who have fought to victory
We're the Army and proud of our name
We're the Army and proudly proclaim

First to fight for the right,
And to build the Nation's might,
    And The Army Goes Rolling Along
Proud of all we have done,
Fighting till the battle's won,
    And the Army Goes Rolling Along.

Refrain
    Then it's Hi! Hi! Hey!
    The Army's on its way.
        Count off the cadence loud and strong (Two! Three!)
    For where e'er we go,
    You will always know
        That The Army Goes Rolling Along.

Valley Forge, Custer's ranks,
San Juan Hill and Patton's tanks,
    And the Army went rolling along
Minute men, from the start,
Always fighting from the heart,
    And the Army keeps rolling along.

    Refrain

Men in rags, men who froze,
Still that Army met its foes,
    And the Army went rolling along.
Faith in God, then we're right,
And we'll fight with all our might,
    As the Army keeps rolling along.

    Refrain

An older verse from the original
Over hill, over dale, As we hit the dusty trail,
    And the Caissons go rolling along.
In and out, hear them shout, Counter march and right about,
    And the Caissons go rolling along.

TAKE ME OUT TO THE BALLGAME

JACK NORWORTH AND ALBERT VON TILZER   1908

Jack Norworth was riding a train in 1908 and saw a sign advertising a baseball game at Polo Grounds. He penned the words to this song and Albert Von Tilzer set them to music. They did not see their first Major League Baseball game until 20 years later. It is now sung at every ballpark, but usually just the chorus.

Katie Casey was baseball mad,
  Had the fever and had it bad.
Just to root for the home town crew,
  Ev'ry sou, Katie blew.
On a Saturday her young beau
  Called to see if she'd like to go
To see a show, but Miss Kate said "No,
  I'll tell you what you can do:"

Chorus:
  Take me out to the ball game,
    Take me out with the crowd;
  Buy me some peanuts and Cracker Jack,
    I don't care if I never get back.
  Let me root, root, root for the home team,
    If they don't win, it's a shame.
  For it's one, two, three strikes, you're out,
    At the old ball game.

Katie Casey saw all the games,
  Knew the players by their first names.
Told the umpire he was wrong,
  All along, Good and strong.
When the score was just two to two,
  Katie Casey knew what to do,
Just to cheer up the boys she knew,
  She made the gang sing this song:

  Chorus

The Constitution only gives people the right to pursue happiness, you have to catch it yourself.

—*Benjamin Franklin*

AMERICA FOR ME

HENRY VAN DYKE   1909

Henry van Dyke was an educator, clergyman, and author who was born in 1852. He was an English professor at Princeton for 24 years and is perhaps best known for his hymn, "Joyful, Joyful, We Adore Thee," sung to the tune of Beethoven's *Ode to Joy*. His *America for Me* must have been written after an extended stay abroad as he longed to be home in America again.

'TIS fine to see the Old World, and travel up and down
    Among the famous palaces and cities of renown,
To admire the crumbly castles and the statues of the kings,—
    But now I think I've had enough of antiquated things.

    So it's home again, and home again, America for me!
      My heart is turning home again, and there I long to be,
    In the land of youth and freedom beyond the ocean bars,
      Where the air is full of sunlight and the flag is full of stars!

Oh, London is a man's town, there's power in the air;
    And Paris is a woman's town, with flowers in her hair;
And it's sweet to dream in Venice, and it's great to study Rome;
    But when it comes to living, there is no place like home.

I like the German fir-woods, in green battalions drilled;
    I like the gardens of Versailles with flashing fountains filled;
But, oh, to take your hand, my dear, and ramble for a day
    In the friendly western woodland where Nature has her way!

I know that Europe's wonderful, yet something seems to lack:
    The Past is too much with her, and the people looking back.
But the glory of the Present is to make the Future free,
    We love our land for what she is and what she is to be.

    Oh, it's home again, and home again, America for me!
      I want a ship that's westward bound to plough the rolling sea,
    To the blessed Land of Room Enough beyond the ocean bars,
      Where the air is full of sunlight and the flag is full of stars.

THE ROAD NOT TAKEN

ROBERT FROST   1916

This popular poem was published in 1916. It is usually seen as expressing individualism and the benefits of following one's own path through life. Others interpret the poem as a reflection on how one's life could have turned out if different decisions had been made.

Two roads diverged in a yellow wood,
And sorry I could not travel both
And be one traveler, long I stood
And looked down one as far as I could
To where it bent in the undergrowth;

Then took the other, as just as fair,
And having perhaps the better claim,
Because it was grassy and wanted wear;
Though as for that the passing there
Had worn them really about the same,

And both that morning equally lay
In leaves no step had trodden black.
Oh, I kept the first for another day!
Yet knowing how way leads on to way,
I doubted if I should ever come back.

I shall be telling this with a sigh
Somewhere ages and ages hence:
Two roads diverged in a wood, and I—
I took the one less traveled by,
And that has made all the difference.

Robert Frost – circa 1915
New York World-Telegram & Sun

Over There

George M. Cohan   1917

Written in 1917, this was popular in both world wars. He supposedly came up with the words and music on a train in New York after the war started. Cohan received the Congressional Gold Medal for the song.

Johnny, get your gun, get your gun, get your gun.
Take it on the run, on the run, on the run.
Hear them calling you and me,
Every Son of Liberty.
Hurry right away, no delay, go today.
Make your Daddy glad to have had such a lad.
Tell your sweetheart not to pine,
To be proud her boy's in line.

Sheet Music - 1917
William Jerome Publishing

Over there, over there,
Send the word, send the word over there
That the Yanks are coming, the Yanks are coming
The drums rum-tumming everywhere.
So prepare, say a prayer,
Send the word, send the word to beware -
We'll be over, we're coming over,
And we won't come back till it's over, over there.

God Bless America

Irving Berlin   1918

The Russian immigrant Irvin Berlin wrote this song while in the Army in 1918. Kate Smith introduced the song in 1938 on Armistice Day after Berlin made some changes.

While the storm clouds gather
Far across the sea,
Let us swear allegiance
To a land that's free;
Let us all be grateful
For a land so fair,
As we raise our voices
In a solemn prayer.

God bless America,
Land that I love,
Stand beside her and guide her
Through the night with the light from above.
From the mountains, to the prairies,
To the oceans white with foam,
God bless America,
My home sweet home.

OFF WE GO INTO THE WILD BLUE YONDER
(U.S. AIR FORCE ANTHEM)

ROBERT MACARTHUR CRAWFORD   1939

This was written in 1939 and was originally titled "The Army Air Corps." In 1947, when the Army Air Corps was essentially transformed into the U.S. Air Force, the title and any references to the Army Air Corps were changed to reflect the new name. It was adopted as the official U.S. Air Force song in 1979.

Off we go into the wild blue yonder
  Climbing high into the sun;
Here they come zooming to meet our thunder, At'em boys, giv'er
  the gun!
Down we dive spouting our flames from under,
  Off with one hell-uv-a roar!
We live in fame or go down in flame,
  Nothing'll stop the US Air Force!

Minds of men fashioned a crate of thunder
  Sent it high into the blue
Hands of men blasted the world asunder,
  How they lived God only knew!
Souls of men dreaming of skies to conquer
  Gave us wings ever to soar,
With scouts before and bombers galore,
  Nothing can stop the US Air Force!

Here's a toast to the host of those
  Who love the vastness of the sky,
To a friend we send the message
  Of his brother men who fly.
We drink to those who gave their all of old,
  Then down we roar
To score the rainbow's pot of gold.
  A toast to the host of men we boast the US Air Force.

Off we go into the wild sky yonder,
  Keep the wings level and true!
If you'd live to be a gray-haired wonder,
  Keep your nose out of the blue!
Flying men guarding our nation's borders,
  We'll be there followed by more,
In echelon we carry on!
  Nothing'll stop the US Air Force!

Unveiling the Statue of Liberty - 1886
by Edward Moran

Stand your ground; don't fire unless fired upon, but if they mean to have a war, let it begin here.

—*Captain Parker, Battle of Lexington, 1775*

Our country is not the only thing to which we owe our allegiance. It is also owed to justice and to humanity. Patriotism consists not in waving the flag, but in striving that our country shall be righteous as well as strong.

—*James Bryce*

I believe in America because we have great dreams - and because we have the opportunity to make those dreams come true.

—*Wendell Wilkie*

Chapter 10

U.S. CITIZENSHIP TEST

———— ✦ ————

THE FOLLOWING QUESTIONS are used for the U.S. Citizenship Test given by our government. New citizens only have to answer 6 out of 10 of these questions. Natural-born citizens should be able to answer all of them. Can you? You can use the page numbers below to find the answers, or go to our website at www.miravista.com/AmericanChallenge. It is more important to understand the principles than to memorize an answer.

Principles of Democracy

1. What is the supreme law of the land? *(p. 144)*
2. What does the Constitution do? *(p. 168)*
3. The idea of self-government is in the first three words of the Constitution. What are these words? *(p. 144)*
4. What is an amendment? *(p. 155)*
5. What do we call the first 10 amendments to the Constitution? *(p. 155)*
6. What is 1 right or freedom from the First Amendment? *(p. 155)*
7. How many amendments does the Constitution have? *(p. 163)*
8. What did the Declaration of Independence do? *(p. 138)*
9. What are two rights in the Declaration of Independence? *(p. 138)*
10. What is freedom of religion? *(p. 17)*
11. What is the economic system in the United States? *(p. 207)*
12. What is the "rule of law"? *(p. 172)*

System of Government

13. Name one branch or part of the government. *(p. 170)*
14. What stops one branch of government from becoming too powerful? *(p. 172)*
15. Who is in charge of the executive branch? *(p. 170)*
16. Who makes federal laws? *(p. 171)*
17. What are the two parts of the U.S. Congress? *(p. 171)*

18. How many U.S. Senators are there? *(p. 171)*

19. We elect a U.S. Senator for how many years? *(p. 171)*

20. Who is one of your state's U.S. Senators? *(www.senate.gov)*

21. The House of Representatives has how many voting members? *(p. 171)*

22. We elect a U.S. Representative for how many years? *(p. 171)*

23. Name your U.S. Representative. *(www.house.gov)*

24. Who does a U.S. Senator represent? *(p. 171)*

25. Why do some states have more Representatives than other states? *(p. 171)*

26. We elect a President for how many years? *(p. 170)*

27. In what month do we vote for President? *(p. 178)*

28. What is the name of the President of the United States now? *(www.whitehouse.gov)*

29. What is the name of the Vice President of the United States now? *(www.whitehouse.gov)*

30. If the President can no longer serve, who becomes President? *(p. 175)*

31. If both the President and the Vice President can no longer serve, who becomes President? *(p. 175)*

32. Who is the Commander in Chief of the military? *(p. 170)*

33. Who signs bills to become laws? *(p. 170)*

34. Who vetoes bills? *(p. 170)*

35. What does the President's Cabinet do? *(p. 173)*

36. What are two Cabinet-level positions? *(p. 174)*

37. What does the judicial branch do? *(p. 172)*

38. What is the highest court in the United States? *(p. 172)*

39. How many justices are on the Supreme Court? *(p. 172)*

40. Who is the Chief Justice of the United States? *(www.supremecourt.gov)*

41. Under our Constitution, some powers belong to the federal government. What is one power of the federal government? *(p. 177)*

42. Under our Constitution, some powers belong to the states. What is one power of the states? *(p. 177)*

43. Who is the Governor of your state? *(www.nga.org)*

44. What is the capital of your state? *(p. 130)*

45. What are the two major political parties in the United States? *(p. 181)*

46. What is the political party of the President now? *(www.whitehouse.gov)*

47. What is the name of the Speaker of the House of Representatives now? *(www.house.gov)*

Rights and Responsibilities

48. There are four amendments to the Constitution about who can vote. Describe one of them. *(p. 159) (p. 160) (p. 162) (p. 163)*

49. What is one responsibility that is only for United States citizens? *(p. 183)*

50. What are two rights only for United States citizens? *(p. 183)*

51. What are two rights of everyone living in the United States? *(p. 155)*

52. What do we show loyalty to when we say the Pledge of Allegiance? *(p. 188)*

53. What is one promise you make when you become a United States citizen? *(p. 183)*

54. How old do citizens have to be to vote for President? *(p. 163)*

55. What are two ways that Americans can participate in their democracy? *(p. 183) (inside back cover)*

56. When is the last day you can send in federal income tax forms? *(p. 176)*

57. When must all men register for the Selective Service? *(p. 179)*

American History

58. What is one reason colonists came to America? *(p. 3)*

59. Who lived in America before the Europeans arrived? *(p. 125)*

60. What group of people was taken to America and sold as slaves? *(p. 7)*

61. Why did the colonists fight the British? *(p. 11)*

62. Who wrote the Declaration of Independence? *(p. 138)*

63. When was the Declaration of Independence adopted? *(p. 138)*

64. There were 13 original states. Name three. *(p. 125)*

65. What happened at the Constitutional Convention? *(p. 144)*

66. When was the Constitution written? *(p. 144)*

67. The Federalist Papers supported the passage of the U.S. Constitution. Name one of the writers. *(p. 16)*

68. What is one thing Benjamin Franklin is famous for? *(p. 256)*

69. Who is the "Father of Our Country"? *(p. 104)*

70. Who was the first President? *(p. 105)*

71. What territory did the U.S. buy from France in 1803? *(p. 20)*

72. Name one war fought by the United States in the 1800s. *(p. 22) (p. 30) (p. 34) (p. 48)*

73. Name the U.S. war between the North and the South. *(p. 35)*

74. Name one problem that led to the Civil War. *(p. 34)*

75. What was 1 important thing that Abraham Lincoln did? *(p. 111)*

76. What did the Emancipation Proclamation do? *(p. 282)*

77. What did Susan B. Anthony do? *(p. 259)*

78. Name one war fought by the United States in the 1900s. *(p. 54)* *(p. 65)* *(p. 72)* *(p. 80)* *(p. 91)*

79. Who was President during World War I? *(p. 53)*

80. Who was President during the Great Depression and World War II? *(p. 116)*

81. Who did the United States fight in World War II? *(p. 65)*

82. Before he was President, Eisenhower was a general. What war was he in? *(p. 117)*

83. During the Cold War, what was the main concern of the United States? *(p. 71)*

84. What movement tried to end racial discrimination? *(p. 74)*

85. What did Martin Luther King, Jr. do? *(p. 264)*

86. What major event happened on September 11, 2001 in the United States? *(p. 96)*

87. Name one American Indian tribe in the United States. *(p. 125)*

Geography

88. Name one of the two longest rivers in the United States. *(p. 129)*

89. What ocean is on the West Coast of the United States? *(p. 129)*

90. What ocean is on the East Coast of the United States? *(p. 129)*

91. Name one U.S. territory. *(p. 131)*

92. Name one state that borders Canada. *(p. 132)*

93. Name one state that borders Mexico. *(p. 132)*

94. What is the capital of the United States? *(p. 19)*

95. Where is the Statue of Liberty? *(p. 45)*

Symbols

96. Why does the flag have 13 stripes? *(p. 187)*

97. Why does the flag have 50 stars? *(p. 187)*

98. What is the name of the national anthem? *(p. 343)*

Holidays

99. When do we celebrate Independence Day? *(p. 184)*

100. Name two national U.S. holidays. *(p. 184)*

How did you do?

———————————— ❧ ————————————

Some Americans need hyphens in their names, because only part of them has come over; but when the whole man has come over, heart and thought and all, the hyphen drops of its own weight out of his name.

—*Woodrow Wilson*

Chapter 11

CONCLUSION

———— ❧ ————

O UR COUNTRY NEEDS AN INFORMED and active citizenry as never before. And that means understanding our history, knowing how the government works, and being familiar with the documents that guide our country. This should be a goal of all Americans, whether native-born or naturalized. New citizens are the building blocks of America's future, and everyone benefits when they become participating and informed members of our society. Native-born citizens have an equal responsibility to stay informed about their country—a recent poll of American citizens showed that more than one-third of them would fail the U.S. Citizenship Test given to immigrants.

THE AMERICAN OPPORTUNITY

America provides the opportunities for every citizen to pursue their hopes and aspirations. People are free to do virtually whatever they want, as long as they do not infringe upon the rights of someone else. Move to another state to take a job, start working in a different profession, start your own small business...you can do whatever you set your mind to. You have the same freedoms and rights as everyone else in this country. You are free to fail... but you are also free to make unlimited profits.

America doesn't guarantee you riches, a decent home, or a meaningful job—instead, it has a Constitution and a Bill of Rights that protect your rights, your property, and your freedom to achieve your dreams. That unique American opportunity was described by French President Sarkozy in a recent speech to our Congress:

America did not tell the millions of men and women who came from every country in the world and who—with their hands, their intelligence and their heart—built the greatest na-

tion in the world: "Come, and everything will be given to you."
She said: "Come, and the only limits to what you'll be able to
achieve will be your own courage and your own talent."

The American experience is full of rags-to-riches stories.
Countless immigrants, penniless and often uneducated, have
overcome adversity to become successful. This unique American
opportunity has also resulted in the sons of blacksmiths, tobacco
planters, tavern keepers, farmers, tanners, storekeepers, wrestlers,
ministers, gas station owners, and salesmen, becoming presidents.
It has created the highest standard of living in the world while
helping to raise the living standards of much of the world. It has
provided the economic and political climate that has encouraged
millions of entrepreneurs and small businesses to flourish. And
it created a country with the moral courage and strength to defeat
tyranny in two world wars.

The Importance of a Common Heritage

This is a map of Europe and a large portion of Russia. This
area is the cradle of western civilization, and is a unique collection
of diverse societies, hard-working people, and local histories. The
distinct cultures of these countries all make positive contributions
to the world. The map outlines 38 countries, though the borders

and country names are still changing. Until recently, almost every
border was either fortified or fenced to restrict free flow between
countries, or, in some cases, to forcibly prevent citizens from leaving their own country. Hundreds of languages and dialects have
existed here, and the new European Union still has 23 official languages and many more dialects. Until recently, each country had
their own unique currency. They have different driving laws, and

even electrical outlets vary from location to location. Each country has their own unique culture, educational system, and government. Moving from one country to the next, crossing borders for a new job, or marrying someone from another country, all involve distinct cultural changes, new languages, different food, and working with people that have very different backgrounds and beliefs. In addition to these cross-cultural problems is the recent emphasis on multi-culturalism within each country. Many are now realizing these policies are endangering the fabric of their societies.

Now, let's compare this to America.

A map of the United States drawn to the same scale closely matches Europe, but that is where the similarity ends, even though America sprang mainly from European immigration. Everyone is equal and free to live their lives as they see fit. The state borders have always been completely open...you rarely know when you have crossed one. Our national borders are there to keep people out, never to force people to remain, and our border with Canada is the longest peaceful border in the world. There are 48 states depicted in this map, as compared to the 38 countries in Europe. Each state has its own government, boundaries, and laws. But all the states have much in common--an educational system, politics, holidays, magazines, TV, sports, entertainment...and a common language—English. Moving to another state, marrying someone from another part of the country, taking a job across the country--there are essentially no adjustments that need to be made. Our common heritage ensures that. There are regional differences that we celebrate and enjoy--but not regional differences that lead to animosity and war. We all drive on the same side of the road, and you can plug in your hair dryer anywhere in the country.

America works. Our shared national identity works. It has worked for over 200 years. Mistakes have been made, most notably slavery and the treatment of Native Americans and women, but the system has always been better than anything else in the world, and it has continually evolved to correct its shortcomings. Remember why it works and resist any changes that threaten to undermine the common heritage that makes it work. Our system is tampered with at great peril. There have been hundreds of other countries with every kind of political and economic system imaginable...but not one system has produced a country like America.

THE ROAD AHEAD

A metaphor about travel illustrates a basic difference in American attitudes and beliefs. In Europe, a lot of travel tends to be directed. You ride a train, along with hundreds of other passengers, from one city to another. Or you drive and follow the highway signs that almost always direct you from point to point, city to city. In America, we treasure the freedom of the open road. With a driver's license and a car, the entire country opens up to you. You can go wherever you feel like going, and do whatever you want. Find a desert with no one else around for miles, or plop yourself down in the middle of a city of 7 million people. Our road signs don't point to a single destination, they point to the horizon—it is Route 66 West, or Interstate 80 East—you decide upon your final destination. Some criticize the inefficient use of gasoline and attempt to curtail your travel. But this touches an American nerve. We don't like having our rights and liberties restricted, and our choices narrowed. We see this as a challenge. We will solve the problem, and keep our freedom to follow our own desires.

America has plenty of serious challenges ahead, but Americans always rise to the challenge. That is when they are at their best. America will always have a frontier. Her optimism demands it. Our challenge is to preserve this country's greatness and ensure she will always be able to follow that frontier.

———————— ❦ ————————

The true meaning of America, you ask? It's in a Texas rodeo, in a policeman's badge, in the sound of laughing children, in a political rally, in a newspaper... In all these things, and many more, you'll find America. In all these things, you'll find freedom. And freedom is what America means to the world. And to me.

—Audie Murphy

INDEX

❧

ACKNOWLEDGMENTS

Some special acknowledgements are listed below for material used in this book. A complete bibliography and list of credits can be found on our website at: http://www.miravista.com/AmericanChallenge

- Presidential Vote Tallies (p.16-99): en.wikipedia.org
- Picture of Nikita Khruschev (p. 73): Bundesarchiv, Bild 183-B0628-0015-035 / Junge, Peter Heinz
- Map of former Yugoslavia (p. 94): ser:Hoshie at en.wikipedia
- Map of Indonesian Tsunami (p. 98): Cantus en.wikipedia
- Map of New Orleans (p. 98): Alexdi en.wikipedia
- Picture of Chrysler Building (p. 225): David Shankbone, w:User:Overand
- Picture of SR-71 (p. 227): www.compilots.com
- Picture of Saturn rocket (p. 249): Flominator en.wikipedia
- Samuel Adams quote (p. 258): "The Sharpened Quill" by Jill LePore, October 16, 2006
- Picture of collapse of Berlin Wall (p. 326): Lear 21 at en.wikipedia
- "I Have A Dream" Copyright 1963 Dr. Martin Luther King Jr; copyright renewed 1991 Coretta Scott King

Know Your Government

One of the most important duties of being an American citizen is staying involved in your government. You can join a political party, run for office, help a campaign, write letters to your newspaper...or just stay informed and vote in every election. Enter the names of your elected officials on this page, and hold them accountable for their actions. If you don't agree with their stances, vote them out at the next election. That is the purpose and the power of the ballot.

National Government

President: _____

Vice-President: _____

Secretary of State: _____

Secretary of Defense: _____

Speaker of the House: _____

Leader of the Senate: _____

Chief Justice: _____

State Government

State Name: _____

State Capital: _____

Governor: _____

Local Government

City Name: _____

Mayor: _____

Who Represents You?

U.S. Senator #1: _____

U.S. Senator #2: _____

U.S. Representative: _____

State Senator: _____

State Representative: _____